"Not only a fascinating pi~~...~~ ~~..~~ ~~............~~ sketches of a changing city and world and the ways in which black Americans in Paris were influenced by these forces. It is a commitment to African Americans as simultaneously distinct and yet part of a broader context that makes *Paris Noir* such a wonderful and important book . . . Beautifully written, rich with detail, insight, humor and great pictures, *Paris Noir* is a book to be read, enjoyed, and read again."

—Jill Nelson, *The Nation*

"Revelatory . . . Engrossing."

—*Publishers Weekly* (starred review)

"A wealth of anecdotal information as well as an intriguing analysis of the complex relationship between this expatriate community and the burgeoning civil rights movement in America."

—*San Francisco Chronicle*

"In this fascinating, richly detailed study, Tyler Stovall assesses the influence of Paris—tolerant and often joyous place of exile—on African American music, literature, and culture, and the contributions of African Americans to Parisian life. With skill and passion, Stovall brings this community to life."

—John Merriman, author of *A History of Modern Europe from the Renaissance to the Present* and *The Margins of City Life*

"An engaging chronicle of African American life in Paris since the dawn of the Jazz Age."

—*Kirkus Reviews*

"Stovall's prose draws a century's worth of black Parisian life and art in well-researched detail."

—*Vibe*

"A most welcome and rewarding volume. *Paris Noir* offers the first comprehensive chronicle of the changing yet steady presence of African American creators of culture in France during our century. Tyler Stovall explores with great honesty the impact of their experiences and the complexities of racial prejudice. While providing a wealth of well-researched information, *Paris Noir* makes very pleasurable reading for anyone interested in the exchange between the European cultural scene and American sensibilities."

—Michael Fabre, author of *From Harlem to Paris* and *The Unfinished Quest of Richard Wright*

PARIS NOIR

African Americans in the City of Light

TYLER STOVALL

A MARINER BOOK

Houghton Mifflin Company

BOSTON   NEW YORK

For information about permission to reproduce selections from this book, write to Permissions, Houghton Mifflin Company, 215 Park Avenue South, New York, New York 10003.

LIBRARY OF CONGRESS CATALOGING-IN-PUBLICATION DATA

Stovall, Tyler Edward.
Paris noir: African Americans in the City of Light/Tyler Stovall.
p. cm.
Includes bibliographical references and index.
ISBN 0-395-68399-8   ISBN 0-395-90140-5 (pbk.)
1. Afro-Americans—France—Paris—History—20th century. 2. Paris (France)—Intellectual life—20th century.   3. Paris (France)—Race relations—History—20th century.   4. Toleration—France—Paris—History—20th century. 5. Liberty. I. Title.
DC718.A36S76 1996   944'.3600496073—dc20   96-24566·   CIP

Text design by Anne Chalmers; Text type Linotype-Hell Electra

Printed in the United States of America

MP 10 9 8 7 6 5 4 3 2 1

The author gratefully acknowledges permission to quote from:
Bricktop by Bricktop with James Haskins, copyright © 1983, by permission of James Haskins.
   The Quality of Hurt and *My Life of Absurdity* by Chester Himes. Reprinted by permission of Roslyn Targ Literary Agency, Inc. *The Quality of Hurt*, copyright © 1971, 1972, by Chester Himes; *My Life of Absurdity*, copyright © 1976 by Chester Himes.
   Gwendolyn Bennett's diary, 1925. Gwendolyn Bennett Papers; Manuscripts, Archives and Rare Books Division; Schomburg Center for Research in Black Culture; The New York Public Library; Lenox, Astor, and Tilden Foundations.
   Letter from S. Emery Delaney to Beauford Delaney, December 1963. Beauford Delaney Papers; Manuscripts, Archives and Rare Books Division; Schomburg Center for Research in Black Culture; The New York Public Library; Lenox, Astor, and Tilden Foundations.
   "I Choose Exile" by Richard Wright. Reprinted by permission of Ellen Wright.
   Photographs credited to the New York Public Library are reprinted by permission of the Photographs and Prints Division; Schomburg Center for Research in Black Culture; The New York Public Library; Lenox, Astor, and Tilden Foundations.

FOR DENISE A. HERD,

Beloved Friend, Partner, Wife

And for the Memory of

OTHA FULLER,

My Grandfather, and a Soldier in France

during the Great War

CONTENTS

LIST OF ILLUSTRATIONS

African American soldiers attacking German lines with hand grenades, France, World
   War I
Officers of the 367th Infantry Regiment with a French friend
A black infantry band returning from service in France
Harlem's "Hell Fighters" parade up Fifth Avenue upon their return to New York.

INTRODUCTION

ALTHOUGH MADISON, WISCONSIN, has many charms, February is certainly not the best time to appreciate them. The lakes freeze, grimy snow piles up on the sidewalks, and arctic winds bite through even the warmest clothing. I nonetheless remember it fondly, for it was during that month in 1981 that I learned I had won a Fulbright fellowship to study in France for a year. At the time, I was enrolled as a graduate student at the University of Wisconsin and had applied for funding to spend time researching my dissertation in French history. Receiving the Fulbright was a dream come true, and enabled me to spend the next twelve months living in Paris while pursuing knowledge about an appropriately obscure topic in the history of twentieth-century France.

I begin this book with an account of my own life in Paris, not because it was so extraordinary, but because it touches upon some important aspects of the broader black American experience there in recent years. For some African Americans, the idea of exile in Paris no longer appears as remarkable as it once did, thanks to changes in both France and America. I had visited the city as a tourist years before I arrived in the fall of 1981 to begin my studies, so its beauty and culture were not a revelation to me. And instead of declaring myself an expatriate who was searching for an alternative to life in America, I was simply a student with a specific professional agenda. Moreover, far from falling in love with the city, I often found life there stressful, alienating, and in general more difficult than back home. I still remember my shock at learning, for example, that a forwarding address cost a substantial sum of money and required notarized proof of residency! At the time, Fulbright fellowships paid more in prestige than in cash, and though living in a sixth-floor walk-up apartment had some advantages (including strengthening my legs), bourgeois dreams of elevators, my own telephone, and dining out haunted my imagination. In addition, the city never impressed me as a paradise of racial good feelings. I noticed the Arabs and Africans sweeping its streets, and I remember being searched in Barbès-Rochechouart (a neighborhood French friends

called the "Harlem of Paris") by police who were convinced that I fit the profile of an international terrorist. When my fellowship ended, I chose not to
stay in Paris, in spite of an offer to teach history at a local high school. I was
drawn more by the prospect of returning to America, finishing my dissertation,
and getting on with my life.

Yet at the same time the allure of the City of Light proved undeniable and
irresistible, even for an impecunious and somewhat skeptical foreign graduate
student. I had to admit that the police who frisked me were more polite than
their American counterparts would have been, at one point complimenting
me on my French. Although small and by no means luxurious, my apartment
lay in the heart of Montmartre, whose picturesque appeal was not the fabrication of postcard manufacturers. Walking around the city, by day and by night,
offered an unending spectacle of beautiful sights and unexpected discoveries.
Surprisingly, I found Paris an easy place to meet people, individuals of all
descriptions who fully lived up to the city's reputation for cosmopolitan,
unusual characters. I met expatriate Americans, both black and white, native
Parisians, people from France's former colonies, and others from the four corners of the globe. Like many other African Americans in Paris, I did not associate solely or even primarily with other blacks from the United States, nor did I
come to France conscious of being the latest in a long line of African Americans who were there to study. Yet the presence of a black American community in the city helped shape my life. I can remember meeting Leroy Haynes
while eating at his restaurant, listening to a black jazz singer in a stylish *cave*,
and hearing James Baldwin discuss his views on politics and literature at a
scholarly forum on the Left Bank. Like many other African Americans, life in
Paris gave me a new level of self-confidence and success. I began to think of
myself as a *chercheur* (researcher), not just a student. Even after returning to
America the prestige of having studied in France opened many doors, ultimately enabling me to secure a professorship in a tremendously competitive
job market. I still remain close to friends in Paris, and find myself in the pleasant position of having to return frequently for the sake of my work.

In short, Paris possesses a magic that is hard to resist. The city today retains
all its glamour, combining the dynamism of a world capital with the rich
charms of tradition and a storied past. The tourist and resident alike can still
stroll along elegant boulevards or wander through tiny ancient streets, admiring some of the most beautiful architecture in the world. Or one can seek out
the many spectacular monuments, from Notre-Dame to the Arc de Triomphe
to the Eiffel Tower, that combine history and majesty in an impressive visual
display. The city offers a tremendous variety of urban amenities — bookstores,

museums, art galleries, shops, restaurants, nightclubs, theaters — providing something for every conceivable taste. Above all, life in Paris gives one the sense of being in a unique place, among the best that humanity has to offer. It is both the capital of France and a city of unparalleled cosmopolitanism, and those who spend time there can easily feel themselves to be at the center of the world.

This book tells the tale of those blacks who have found their way from the United States to experience life in Paris. Their story is a fascinating one, full of the romance for which the French capital is justly celebrated. African Americans have lived in garrets and whiled away days at cafés writing or debating politics and literature with many different kinds of people. They have admired the masterpieces in the Louvre, strolled along the Champs-Elysées, and explored the byways of Montmartre and the Latin Quarter. They have danced the night away in cabarets and nightclubs, going to bed only as the rest of the city awoke. And they have fallen in love there, enjoying promenades along the Seine and the flowering chestnut trees of April through the eyes of their heart's desire. Yet this book is not simply the black version of A Moveable Feast. The experience of African Americans in Paris has been a special one, thanks to both their status as blacks and as Americans, and reveals much about France and the United States in the modern era. An explanation of the unique nature of this experience, and its implications for African American life in general, constitute the core of the chapters that follow.

Unlike the white American presence in Paris, the presence of black Americans there has usually been seen, by both themselves and others, as a commentary on race. Some blacks left the United States expressly to escape the burdens of discrimination and came to Paris as self-conscious refugees from racism. Others, more typically, journeyed to France for a variety of different reasons, including job opportunities, the hazards of war, or the spirit of adventure. Once there, however, most African Americans shared the surprising realization that whites could treat them with affection and respect, that a color-blind society just might be possible after all. As this book will take pains to show, the myth of color-blind France is complex and flawed. Nonetheless, it has exercised a powerful attraction upon both black Americans and the French themselves. The perceived difference between racial attitudes in France and the United States has given a singular political dimension to the history of African Americans in Paris that distinguishes it sharply from the experience of white expatriates.

Contacts between France and black Americans go back to the beginnings of the history of the United States. Sally Hemings, slave and reputedly mistress of

Thomas Jefferson, accompanied her famous master to Paris in the 1780s along with her brother James. Many of the elite "free people of color" in antebellum New Orleans sent their sons to Paris for the education that prejudice denied them at home. One of these students, Victor Séjour, established a successful career in Paris as a playwright during the 1850s and 1860s. Many distinguished African Americans visited France during the nineteenth century, as tourists or unofficial ambassadors of the black people of the United States. The distinguished actor Ira Aldridge toured the country in 1866 and 1867, receiving favorable reviews in the French press for his starring role in *Othello*. Frederick Douglass traveled to Paris as a tourist in 1886, as did Booker T. Washington in 1899. Other black American visitors of note to France during these years included Mary Church Terrell, William Wells Brown, and W.E.B. Du Bois.

These contacts are important, but I have chosen to focus on African Americans in Paris during the twentieth century, from World War I to the present. The years since 1914 have witnessed the growth of nonwhite populations, and race as a social issue, on both sides of the Atlantic. The Great War brought large populations of color to France for the first time in that nation's history, starting a process of non-European immigration that has reached crisis proportions for many French today. At the same time, the war helped spur the migration of blacks to the ghettos of Northern cities in the United States, so that African Americans, heretofore seen as a Southern "problem," played an increasingly central role in the nation's consciousness. Black Americans in modern Paris have ties both to the blacks of America's urban ghettos and to other nonwhites in France, so that their experience exemplifies international perspectives on race today.

This sui generis experience sheds light on the histories of both the United States and France in recent years. African Americans have decided to come to Paris because of their views of American life: the idea of France as a refuge from American racism had far more to do with conditions in the United States than conditions in Paris. Moreover, with few exceptions black Americans in France not only kept their U.S. nationality, but remained in close contact with events back home. African American life in Paris, by providing an alternate model of the black experience, underscores the centrality of race in American history: blacks in the French capital were able to achieve a level of success usually unavailable to their brothers and sisters in the States. At the same time, their history also reveals much about their French hosts. The intense French interest in African American culture during much of the twentieth century derived from contradictory perspectives on both blackness and America. From primitivism in the 1920s to anti-Americanism after World War II, African

Americans served as a powerful barometer of how the French viewed the world, and, by extension, themselves.

The African Americans of Paris have always been an extremely diverse group, making any generalizations about them a risky enterprise. Every good story needs a guiding theme, however, and in writing this history I have decided that the concept of black community has been central to the life of blacks in the French capital. It distinguishes the twentieth century from earlier eras, and Paris from most other places in the world where African Americans have settled in exile. Although small, the black community in Paris has generally achieved enough of a critical mass to generate its own institutions, traditions, and presence within the larger city, constituting a crucial innovation in life overseas: the rise of a collective black American life in the French capital enabled blacks to leave American racism behind without therefore also forsaking African American culture. The concept of black community casts in bold relief both the similarities and differences of African American life in Paris and in the United States. It is in many ways a paradoxical concept: more than a few blacks in Paris have denied its very existence, while at the same time demonstrating a variety of interconnections with other African Americans there. Far from invalidating the concept of a black community in Paris, such contradictions reaffirm its roots in the African American experience as a whole. African Americans in France pioneered a new type of black community, one based on positive affinities and experiences rather than the negative limitations of segregation, one that included a wide variety of individuals yet at the same time celebrated black culture. This vision of community was an important collective achievement, one with much to offer to all Americans.

Finally, I've written this book as a success story, without illusions or apologies. Certainly not all African Americans in Paris found the fame or fortune of a Josephine Baker. Some found themselves lost in the cracks of French society, scrounging for room and board, adrift on silent boulevards or in cold cafés. Others, especially in more recent years, felt they could have achieved greater financial or professional success in America but valued the release from racism that Paris provided. It is not my intention to embrace a certain kind of triumphalism that only considers the positive aspects of black life. Yet the fact remains that in different ways most African Americans in Paris have not only enjoyed life there, but derived something of value from the experience. Many did achieve success, often significantly greater than they could realistically have expected in the United States. Without necessarily being wealthy, the black American community in Paris has been an exceptionally accomplished one, so much so that it can be seen as a metaphor for the experience of America's black middle class. It is perhaps no accident that the classic text on this group, E. Franklin Frazier's *Black Bourgeoisie*, was written and first published in the French capital. More generally, most blacks have felt Paris offered a degree of freedom not available at home. The African American community in Paris symbolizes the potential of African American life in general once it is fully liberated from the shackles of racism.

Success stories are, of course, a quintessentially American genre. As a consequence, African American achievements in Paris both exemplify the American-ness of this group and differentiate it from more typical perceptions of the black experience. In particular, *Paris Noir* integrates blacks into one of our cherished national myths, that of immigrant upward mobility, by turning that myth upside down. It tells the traditional story of a group of people who crossed the ocean to find freedom and financial reward. However, in this case those people were *leaving* the United States, not seeking it; America loomed as the obstacle to freedom, not its attainment. This group of African Americans thus found that leaving their homeland made them feel more American. In this respect as in so many others, the history of blacks in Paris underscores the antithetical nature of the African American experience. Given the tendency of American discussions of race to present blacks as failures or as a "problem," writing a book about black success represents a political statement. Ultimately *Paris Noir* is a tale of romance and freedom, of the things that make life worthwhile and the ability to enjoy them to the fullest. A small group of African Americans discovered this quality in the French capital, and perhaps their greatest accomplishment of all is the vision of complete human liberation that their experience has bequeathed to their brothers and sisters across the sea.

PARIS
NOIR

FREEDOM OVERSEAS:
AFRICAN AMERICAN SOLDIERS
FIGHT THE GREAT WAR

THE SUMMER of 1914 was one of the most beautiful that Europeans had experienced in many years. Henry Ossawa Tanner, an African American artist living in Paris, spent that summer working at his rural retreat in the small Picard village of Trepied, glorying in the pure light and air of eastern France and painting scenes of biblical life full of luminous mysticism. On August 1, however, Tanner's peaceful idyll shattered as Europe plunged into the First World War. The approach of German armies forced Tanner and his family to evacuate Trepied, taking refuge in England for two weeks. The outbreak of war made a major impact on Tanner, as he revealed in a letter to a friend: "What right have I to do, what right to be comfortable? In London I saw some of the Canadian contingent and many volunteers, fine, handsome, intelligent men going out to fight, to suffer and to die for principles which I believe in as strongly as they and sit down to paint a little picture, and thus make myself happy — No it cannot be done." During the war years Tanner painted very little. By the end of 1917 he had begun a project with the American Red Cross working with wounded U.S. soldiers in France to raise vegetables.

The world of Henry Ossawa Tanner, of Parisian ateliers and cafés, of conversations with artists from around the world and favorable reviews in the French and international press, was light years removed from that of virtually all African Americans in the early twentieth century. War brought these two worlds together. For Tanner this interlude would be brief; after the war he returned to his artistic endeavors, remaining in Paris until his death in 1937. But for the black soldier the glimpse of a world where a man or woman of color could rise to the heights of renown achieved by Henry Ossawa Tanner came as a revelation. African Americans had visited and lived in Paris throughout the nineteenth century, but usually as individuals isolated from one another. The experiences of black American soldiers in war-torn France brought a new type of African American expatriate to Paris, one who both interacted with the French and formed his own community in exile as well. Where Tanner had led, many would now follow, leaving their mark on the City of Light.

BLACK AMERICA ON THE EVE OF WAR

In 1914 life in France could not have been further from the thoughts of most African Americans. Little more than two generations removed from slavery, black America as a whole remained trapped by virulent white racism and grinding poverty at the bottom of American society. The gap between the races was especially striking in the South, home to the overwhelming majority of African Americans. Southern blacks lived a life that in many ways resembled the bondage they had so recently escaped. Most worked as sharecroppers, owning little or no land of their own. They were the first to suffer hard times and economic ruin in case of crop failure or recession. The South in 1914 was the poorest region of the country, and much of the white population lived in conditions of dire poverty. However, racist policies ensured that blacks always got the smallest slice of the pie. In the early years of the century, Southerners spent over $10 for the education of each white child, but less than $3 for the education of each black child. This discrepancy resulted in shockingly high illiteracy rates among blacks; one in three Southern blacks could not read in 1910, as opposed to one in thirty Southern whites.

In 1914 Southern blacks lived in a world determined to suppress their slightest efforts to achieve equality with, or even respect from, their white neighbors. They learned at an early age that failure to observe the expected deferential posture in public could and would be met with savage reprisals. Although in theory full citizens of the United States, African Americans in the South dared not exercise their Constitutional right to vote, so that the Southern states remained a racial oligarchy in the midst of a supposedly democratic nation. In 1916 fifty-four blacks (including one woman) were lynched in the South, their silenced bodies eloquently testifying to the dank climate of racist terror enshrouding the former Confederacy.

Although Southern blacks remained de facto slaves in many ways, they did have one advantage over their ancestors: they could leave the South if they so chose. What had been a steady stream of African Americans heading north toward freedom in the opening years of the century turned into a torrent after 1914. War in Europe both caused an economic boom in the industrial North and abruptly cut off the supply of white immigrant labor that staffed the great American factories, so that employers scrambled to recruit black Southerners. Some 400,000 Southern blacks elected to follow the North Star from 1910 to 1920; the black population of Chicago more than doubled during those years. In the North, African Americans generally found better jobs and a somewhat improved racial climate. But while white Northerners eschewed the vicious racial terrorism that prevailed below the Mason-Dixon Line, they used other means to keep blacks subordinate. African Americans were relegated to the worst jobs, the worst schools, and the worst neighborhoods. Flight to the North certainly brought some changes for the better, but it could not erase the fact that, from Mississippi to Manhattan, blacks remained a victimized, oppressed caste excluded from the mainstream of American life.

Given their desperate conditions, it is not surprising that at first few African Americans paid much attention to the outbreak of war in Europe; for most, France might as well have been on a different planet. Certainly the majority of those who considered the question at all favored the cause of the Allies. France already enjoyed a reputation for decent treatment of peoples of color, based on the enthusiastic reports of distinguished nineteenth-century visitors like Ira Aldridge, Bishop Daniel Payne, Booker T. Washington, and Frederick Douglass. In particular, the NAACP journal *The Crisis*, headed by the Francophile W.E.B. Du Bois, embraced the cause of France as that of enlightened civilization under assault from Teutonic racism.

There were even cases of African Americans who felt strongly enough about France's plight to join her fighting forces before America's entry into the conflict. Eugene Jacques Bullard was born the grandson of slaves in 1894 in Columbus, Georgia. His father, Octave Bullard, came from Martinique and had often told his young son glowing tales about France. As Bullard noted many years later in his journal, "My father had told me in France there are not different white churches and black churches, or white schools and black schools, or white graveyards and black graveyards. People, colored and white, just live together and treat each other the same and that was where I wanted to go." Gene Bullard left home at the tender age of seven, shortly after a lynch mob forced his family to flee Columbus. He roamed around the South for a few years, and then, at the age of ten, stowed away on a ship bound for Germany, hoping eventually to reach France. A strongly built man with a volcanic temper, Bullard spent the next several years in Britain working as a boxer before finally reaching Paris in 1913, having just turned nineteen:

"When I got off the boat train in Paris I was as excited as a kid on Christmas morning. Here I was in the place I had wanted to be in and to see all my life. And it was wonderful."

Eugene Bullard returned to France the following year as a member of a traveling dance troupe, Freedman's Pickaninnies. He stayed in Paris after the troupe left, and when the war broke out he joined the French foreign legion along with Bob Scanlon, another African American boxer he'd known in London. Transferring to a French unit in 1915, Bullard took part in the great battle at Verdun, suffering shrapnel wounds and receiving the croix de guerre for his wartime service. After his recovery he trained as a flyer, transferring again to the French Air Service in October 1916. Bullard became an ace pilot with the Lafayette Flying Corps, a group of American pilots who fought for France before their own nation joined the war, and he earned the sobriquet the Black Swallow of Death for his daring in battle.

As the war continued and the United States drew closer to intervention on the side of the Allies, African American public opinion increasingly favored the war effort. Those black leaders who spoke up for the Allied cause portrayed the war as a worldwide struggle for democracy, in which victory could not fail to improve the conditions of their people. Such arguments generally fell on receptive ears, and when the U.S. government declared war on Germany in April 1917 most blacks eagerly proclaimed their willingness to do their part. In the pages of The Crisis, W.E.B. Du Bois and other prominent spokesmen called upon African Americans to join the fight for freedom and equality by assisting the war effort.

Not surprisingly, some blacks refused to join this chorus of support, believing that a nation which had treated them so poorly had no right to demand sacrifices. The labor leader A. Philip Randolph stated that rather than volunteer to make the world safe for democracy, he would fight to make Georgia safe for the Negro. Yet most African Americans ignored such protests. They argued that blacks had a moral responsibility to take part in such a struggle for freedom. More concretely, many believed that once black Americans had willingly borne their share of the wartime burden, their white fellow citizens would be more likely to grant them the respect and equality they had so clearly earned.

Events in 1917 did not support such fond hopes. The number of blacks lynched in that year rose to seventy. The increase in racist violence was especially noteworthy in the North, often sparked by white workers resentful of the ever increasing black population. Race riots, which usually involved attacks upon African Americans by white mobs, took place in New York; Newark; New Jersey; Chicago; and most tragically in East Saint Louis, Illinois. There whites killed or wounded more than a hundred black men, women, and children. For the eleven-year-old Josephine Baker, across the river in Saint Louis, it was a racial baptism of fire she would never forget.

In many other, less violent ways white Americans demonstrated that black support of the war effort would not bring them better treatment. Many whites, especially Southerners, strongly opposed drafting African American soldiers. The very thought of furnishing black men with rifles and sending them overseas to shoot white people gave many pause. More significantly, most whites considered military service in the uniform of the United States a signal honor requiring intelligence and courage, qualities they found lacking in most African American men. Most of the many blacks who volunteered for war duty before the institution of selective service in May 1917 were turned away as unsuitable. Once it became clear that the exigencies of war mandated the use of blacks, Southern draft boards signed them up in massive numbers; five Southern states drafted more blacks than whites. However, the army was very reluctant to commission black officers. It forced a top African American soldier, Colonel Charles Young, to retire because of high blood pressure, even after Young had demonstrated his physical stamina by riding from Ohio to Washington, D.C., on horseback. It soon became clear that the army intended to use African American soldiers as unskilled physical labor, and had no intention of sending trained black soldiers to fight in France. If, for blacks, participation in the war effort meant earning glory on foreign battlefields, whites more often conceived of their lot as a militarized version of the chain gang.

More than 400,000 African Americans served in the United States armed forces during World War I, and about half of those saw duty in France. Almost all of these enrolled in the army, because the marines barred blacks altogether, while the navy permitted them to serve only in a few menial positions. Black army recruits performed a wide variety of combat and noncombat functions. However, from the outset the army leadership made it clear that blacks would be used only in segregated units, to appease white Southern concerns.

The black soldier of World War I usually experienced a long wait from the moment of his enlistment to the time when he set foot on French soil. All soldiers must first be trained, and the training of black recruits remained controversial throughout the war. White Southerners strongly opposed sending "uppity" Northern blacks to be trained in Southern camps, and white civilians living next to these camps consistently treated the new black soldiers with hostility and contempt. Incidents abounded; the most serious took place in Houston in September 1917. There repeated provocations led to a clash between black soldiers and armed white civilians, in which seventeen of the latter perished. After a summary court-martial the army hanged thirteen of the soldiers, sentencing forty-one others to life imprisonment.

As this incident reveals, African American recruits could expect little or no assistance from the army leadership in case of conflicts with white civilians. Moreover, white officers and soldiers engaged at times in discriminatory practices. The YMCA buildings in Camp Greene, North Carolina, were reserved for white soldiers, and no equivalent facilities were provided for the ten thousand black recruits stationed there. White officers frequently referred to blacks with derogatory terms like *nigger* and *coon*. Those who dared protest such indignities often ended up in a military prison as their reward. In addition to such insults, blacks suffered from more endemic forms of discrimination in the training camps. Conditions for African American recruits were consistently inferior to those of whites. Many worked long hours outside, wearing only summer clothing in wintry weather. In a camp near Baltimore two barracks of equal size were used for blacks and whites; the black building housed three hundred soldiers; the white one, thirty-five. More than a few black recruits never lived to see combat, perishing from a combination of poor hygiene, inadequate and spoiled food, and overwork.

The road that led to combat on the fields of France was thus a hard one. Its rigors ensured that those African Americans sent to work and fight overseas had already been severely tested, preparing them to withstand the trials they would soon face. In France they would continue to face racist discrimination by their white superiors. Yet in spite of the numerous roadblocks in their paths, in spite of the harsh treatment and countless petty indignities visited upon them by racist whites, African Americans made a major contribution to America's effort in the First World War, forging a record of distinction and at times brilliance on French battlefields.

And they were the first black Americans to go to France in large numbers, introducing the French to the distinctive culture of their people. Many would discover in their dealings with the French people that discrimination and oppression did not have to characterize relations across the color line. Black GIs came to France to fight the Germans, but in the process they also laid the foundations for the vibrant African American community that would settle in Paris after the war.

OVER THERE!

Right from the beginning, black Americans were present in the military forces sent by the United States overseas. The first American troop convoy to sail for

France, in June 1917, included more than four hundred African American stevedores, or longshoremen, who worked to unload the ships upon arrival. Many others soon followed, so that by the end of the war fifty thousand blacks were working in French ports for the American army. In December the first black American soldiers arrived in France, and tens of thousands of black troops were engaged on French battlefields by the summer of 1918.

Although wartime accounts usually give pride of place to the fighting man, it is appropriate and only just that we begin with the story of those African Americans who worked as laborers for the U.S. Army in France. Most black Americans in France served as workers, not soldiers. Roughly 80 percent, or 160,000, of those who crossed the seas during World War I shouldered the shovel rather than the rifle, and one third of all army laborers were black. This division came as no coincidence: army policy consistently favored using blacks to do the dirtiest, least glamorous work of the war. A May 1918 report on the status of African American draftees commented: "The poorer class of backwoods negro has not the mental stamina and moral sturdiness to put him in the line against opposing German troops who consist of men of high average education and thoroughly trained. . . . It is recommended that these colored drafted men be organized in reserve labor battalions, put to work at useful constructive labor that furthers the prosecution of the war." The army reasoned that employing blacks as laborers would not only suit their inferior capabilities, but also free up white draftees for use as soldiers.

African American laborers worked in a variety of organizations, generally known as labor battalions, during World War I. In 1918 the army gave these battalions a new name, the Services of Supply, which it hoped would remove their associations with chain gang labor. However, they soon received the nickname S.O.S., the radio code for help, symbolizing their oppression. Black workers in France performed many different types of jobs, including loading and unloading ships, building roads and military camps, hauling building materials, laying railroad tracks, digging ditches, caring for livestock, removing garbage, and burying the dead. As a rule they performed the least skilled, most physically exhausting tasks. Unlike many white laborers, they rarely received any military training, usually being rushed overseas as quickly as possible to fill the army's critical need for support work.

In contrast to the poor opinions the army leadership expressed about their abilities, black laborers in France often performed impressive physical feats, especially black longshoremen. To an important extent port workers formed the linchpin of the entire American military effort in France. The United States Army had never before fought such an extensive campaign so far away from home. Unloading and deploying both soldiers and war material in

French ports had to be done as quickly and efficiently as possible in order to ensure an Allied victory. By the middle of 1918, large numbers of black long-shoremen were busy unloading American ships in French harbors like Brest, Saint-Nazaire, and Bordeaux. Many of these workers had never even seen a ship before coming to France, much less worked on one, and yet their accomplishments frequently astonished French and white American observers alike. One compared their speed to that of Noah loading the Ark, and another commented, "They are the finest workers you ever saw. One Negro can do four times as much work as any other man, and have fun doing it. The French stevedores stand by and watch with amazement at my hustling gangs. The way they handle a 100-pound crate makes the Frenchman's eyes bulge." In one instance, African American longshoremen unloaded five thousand tons of material in one day, when French officials had estimated that six thousand could only be moved over an entire month. During the month of September 1918, black stevedores set a record by unloading an incredible twenty-five thousand tons of cargo *per day* for several weeks.

Such performances seem all the more impressive when one considers the conditions under which they were achieved. Black dockworkers often worked in twenty-four-hour shifts, taking only brief breaks for food and rest. As in the training camps at home, black workers in France usually got the worst clothing, food, and housing the army had to offer. In addition to these physical hardships, African Americans in the S.O.S. had to put up with the indignities of racial discrimination. They rarely received the opportunities for leisure and entertainment that meant so much to their white fellow workers. Addie Hunton and Kathryn Johnson, two black American women working as YMCA volunteers in France, testified to the prevalence of this discrimination: "While white American soldiers were permitted to go freely about the towns, the great mass of colored American soldiers saw them for the most part, as they marched in line to and from the docks. Passes for them were oftener than otherwise as hard to secure as American gold."

In addition to loading and unloading ships, black laborers performed many other kinds of tasks. Construction crews built warehouses, barracks, and supply dumps, as well as modernizing crumbling port facilities in old French harbors like that of Marseilles. Some lucky recruits, usually those with prewar job experience, were able to obtain lighter assignments. Several Pullman car waiters found themselves performing the same duties on military trains in wartime France. Others, however, worked right at the front, in conditions every bit as dangerous as those experienced by any soldier. In several instances black labor battalions worked to repair roads and railroads on the front lines, unarmed and fully exposed to enemy shellfire. Other African Americans worked as motorcycle couriers, delivering vital information despite the most hazardous conditions. Ralph W. Tyler, a black American newspaper correspondent in wartime France, praised their skill and courage:

It is really marvelous how these colored motorcyclists ride pell-mell, in the darkest nights, without headlights, along these strange, devious, forking, and merging roads of France . . . I rode several miles with one last night, from one front to another, at a 65-mile-per-hour clip. He was indifferent to the bursting of American anti-aircraft shells, aimed at the Boche airplane in the sky above us; he was oblivious to the thunder of the German cannon, and their shrieking shells to our right; he merely had his mind, as he kept his eyes to the front, on getting me back to the point which we had left a few hours before, a distance of five miles, in ten minutes. And he made it without slip or hit.

These laudatory descriptions, by both black and white American observers, of the Herculean tasks that African American workers acquitted in France, highlight a central contradiction of the black experience during the Great War. Blacks were expected and required by military discipline to perform a tremendous amount of work under terrible conditions. Praiseworthy accounts of black physical prowess on the job, complete with references to the beauty of their singing, not only underline a view of African Americans as beasts of burden, but also run very close to traditional plantation imagery. In effect, for most blacks called to the colors the war simply transferred slave labor from the cotton fields of the South to the harbors of France. At the same time, many blacks saw service in the American army, even in the labor battalions, as a chance for African Americans to prove themselves worthy of acceptance and equal treatment by their white fellow citizens. This explains the enthusiastic portraits of black labor achievements left by African American writers like Emmett J. Scott and W. Allison Sweeney who argued enthusiastically that in spite of their degrading treatment black workers in France accomplished super-human feats because of their love of their country and their determination to prove themselves worthy of her. African Americans' desire to win the respect of a nation that had always treated them shabbily was paradoxical and deeply tragic, yet its importance to those who served in France cannot be denied.

The strength of this desire tends to obscure instances of resistance by black workers. Complaints about overwork, poor housing and food, or segregated conditions were considered military insubordination and treated accordingly. Given the harsh conditions that greeted blacks in France, organized protest was extremely difficult if not impossible. Attempts to feign illness or work at an

easier pace were held up as proof of black laziness and inferiority. Consequently, African American reporters and commentators tended to minimize
examples of resistance, fearful of confirming white stereotypes, and showed
little sympathy for those who committed them. As Charles Williams commented in his 1923 book, *Sidelights on Negro Soldiers,* after praising black
workers in France: "On the other hand, the Negro soldiers themselves were
not without faults. Some of their difficulties were due to their own ignorance
and to customs that they brought into the army from civil life. On plantations
and public works some had been used to 'ducking the boss' and slipping away,
and attempts to continue this practice in the army sometimes resulted in their
being placed in the guardhouse."

Though instances of resistance did occur (one general noted with dismay
examples of blacks refusing to work, even after being fined and imprisoned),
this kind of defiance resulted not from the harsh nature of the work itself, but
rather from the racist treatment meted out to black workers by white officers.
At one large camp in France, for example, three hundred black workers were
imprisoned, largely for violating orders preventing them (but not their white
colleagues) from going off base and associating with French civilians. When a
new commanding officer reformed such discriminatory practices, the number
of blacks in the guardhouse was reduced to fifty.

So the army intentionally consigned most African American recruits to
positions in which they would not only be forced to perform the most demanding and ignoble tasks, but also receive as little attention and praise as
possible, justifying the stereotype of blacks as inferiors. Aside from Ralph
Tyler, few reporters commented on the achievements of black laborers. Yet
when one examines the record, it becomes clear that these workers transformed lowly assignments into opportunities to prove their skill and value to
the American war effort.

This determination also characterized the black American soldiers who
fought in France. At one point, several African Americans stationed in Ohio
while waiting to be sent overseas were asked if they were going to France. "No,
sir, I am not going to France," replied one of them. "I am going to Berlin and
I may stop in France for a short time on the way." Like the laborers, black
soldiers in World War I fought a war on two fronts. In addition to combating
German troops, they also had to struggle against the racist attitudes and
practices of both the army leadership and many white soldiers. Against great
odds African American soldiers made a valuable contribution to the Allied
war effort, even though that contribution rarely received the recognition it
deserved.

Black Americans served in two army units, the Ninety-second and Ninety-third divisions. The former was the only all-black division of World War I, whereas the latter, which was never brought up to full strength, had a heavy majority of African Americans. The Ninety-third Division was the first to be organized and deployed in France. It consisted primarily of black National Guard units plus some draftees. The latter formed the 371st Infantry Regiment, while the guardsmen constituted three other infantry regiments: the 369th, of New York; the 370th, of Illinois; and the 371st, of Maryland, Massachusetts, Ohio, and Washington, D.C. The Ninety-second Division was formed somewhat later and consisted almost entirely of African American draftees. It contained four infantry regiments: the 365th, of Texas and Oklahoma; the 366th, of Alabama; the 367th, of New York; and the 368th, of Tennessee, Pennsylvania, and Maryland. The Ninety-second also included several smaller regiments, such as three devoted to field artillery. More than thirty thousand black combat troops, from the North, South, and all over America, saw duty in France.

First to go was the 369th Infantry Regiment of New York, perhaps the most celebrated group of black soldiers in World War I. This unit, popularly known as the Harlem Hellfighters, had been organized in the fall of 1916 as part of the National Guard, and consisted mostly of men from Harlem and other black neighborhoods of New York City. These soldiers received their first lessons in warfare in the city's streets before moving to a South Carolina training camp in October 1917. The local white population lost no time in making sure that these big-city Northern blacks knew their place in the South, subjecting them to a number of humiliating racist outrages. Faced with the angry reactions of the black recruits, the War Department decided to ship them to France as quickly as possible, in order to avoid further incidents. Therefore, after a few more weeks of training at camps in New Jersey and Long Island, the unit set sail in December 1917, landing at the port of Brest two days after Christmas.

Eager to go into action, the men of the 369th soon learned that waiting often formed a central part of the soldier's experience, and they spent their first several weeks in France engaged in noncombat duties. Like many African American regiments in France, the 369th was formally assigned to the French high command for more training, and ended up fighting under its leadership. Working well with the French, the regiment received orders in April to move to the front lines. By May it was fighting a German offensive along the Champagne front in eastern France. The 369th remained in this sector through July, earning the respect of all observers and helping to break the last German offensive of the war. In September the soldiers of the 369th took part in the first American offensive, fighting on the front lines until they were relieved in mid-October.

While in France the 369th Infantry Regiment earned a record of distinction equaled by few other bodies of American troops during World War I. In the words of Emmett J. Scott, who was secretary to Booker T. Washington and adviser to the War Department on Negro affairs, "The regiment never lost a man captured, a trench, or a foot of ground . . . and . . . it had less training than any American unit before going into action." In October 1918 the French army awarded this regiment the croix de guerre for its bravery and successes in battle on the Champagne front. In addition, many individual soldiers won military decorations. Sergeant Henry Johnson, a railroad porter from Albany, New York, became the first American soldier in France to win the individual croix de guerre with palm. On the night of May 12, 1918, Johnson and Private Needham Roberts alone stood off the attack of a much larger German force, in the process killing four and wounding thirty-two enemy soldiers. In August Sergeant William Butler won the American army's Distinguished Service Cross for single-handedly putting a German raiding party to flight. In November the regiment achieved a signal honor when it became the first Allied unit to advance to the Rhine River, thus symbolizing Germany's defeat.

Although the 369th reaped the lion's share of press and public attention, other African American fighting units won glory on French battlefields. The 370th Infantry Regiment fought in northern France and Belgium, and came to be called the "Black Bastards" by the Germans for their daring in combat. These soldiers from Chicago and other parts of Illinois fought the last battle of World War I, capturing a German train minutes after the Armistice was declared. The 371st Regiment also fought bravely, winning a collective decoration from the French government as well as numerous individual citations. One of its white officers, in commenting on its achievements, noted:

> In the engagements around Verdun the fighting qualities and courage of our boys won the admiration and most profuse praise of the French. Citations were showered upon the valorous boys for their unflinching conduct in the face of withering machine-gun fire, which they overcame and silenced at the point of the bayonet. We broke the Hindenburg line at Monthois, and so rapidly did our boys move that a halt was called to enable the right and left flanks of our line to catch up. An excellent opportunity was furnished by comparisons as to just how good our colored soldiers were.

The Ninety-second Division, which landed in France in June 1918, did not achieve the same distinction as its fellow black division. The white American officers who criticized the Ninety-second generally pointed to the failure of its 368th Regiment to withstand German attacks in the Argonne forest at the end of September 1918. Such criticisms usually ignored the fact that white regiments had performed just as poorly in that battle. Instead, they used the defeat as an excuse to condemn the entire division, even though its other three infantry regiments had not taken part. Colonel Allen Greer said that these black soldiers "failed in all their missions, laid down and sneaked to the rear," while Major B. F. Norris, who later admitted that he hid in a ditch during the German attack, condemned them as cowards.

The soldiers of the Ninety-second Division were not above reproach, but such slanders were patently unfair and obscured their very real achievements. In fact, members of the 368th Infantry Regiment received numerous decorations from both the French and American governments. The 367th Infantry Regiment in particular established a reputation as a fine combat force. Christened the Buffaloes, in memory of the blacks who fought on the American frontier under the name Buffalo Soldiers, this regiment's first battalion won the croix de guerre. Often poorly trained and fighting under the worst conditions, the African American soldiers of the Ninety-second Division proved their mettle under fire.

If the American army failed to appreciate their worth, the same could not be said of the enemy. The Germans on the other side of the trenches soon learned they were fighting black soldiers and began to address propaganda to them in particular. On September 3, a German airplane dropped leaflets over a section of the Vosges front where the 367th regiment was stationed:

TO THE COLORED SOLDIERS OF THE UNITED STATES ARMY

Hello, boys, what are you doing over here? Fighting the Germans? Why? Have they ever done you any harm? Of course some white folks and the lying English-American papers told you that the Germans ought to be wiped out for the sake of humanity and Democracy. What is Democracy? Personal freedom; all citizens enjoying the same rights socially and before the law. Do you enjoy the same rights as the white people do in America, the land of freedom and Democracy, or are you not rather treated over there as second class citizens?

Can you get into a restaurant where white people dine? Can you get a seat in a theatre where white people sit? Can you get a seat or a berth in a railroad car, or can you even ride in the South in the same street car with the white people?

And how about the law? Is lynching and the most horrible crimes connected therewith a lawful proceeding in a Democratic country? Now all this is entirely different in Germany, where they do like colored people. . . . To carry a gun in this service is not an honor but a shame. Throw it away and come over to the German lines. You will find friends who will help you.

In spite of such appeals, however, African American soldiers in France remained overwhelmingly loyal to the American cause.

Such loyalty is all the more remarkable given the treatment black soldiers in France received at the hands of the American army. The army leadership as a whole took a dim view of the combat potential of black troops, consistently undervaluing their skill and courage. This prejudice led General John Pershing, commander in chief of the American Expeditionary Force in France, to transfer the four infantry regiments of the Ninety-third Division to the French army. The move both helped satisfy the French demand for American troops and keep the American army as white as possible. Those African American soldiers, chiefly of the Ninety-second Division, who did remain under the direct control of the American army rarely received treatment equal to that given white soldiers. A study comparing the Ninety-second Division with the white Thirty-fifth Division concluded that the latter had received much more extensive training before coming to France. In general, black troops experienced worse conditions, less leave time, and more harassment by military police. Yet white officers ascribed any failings on their part to innate racial inadequacies. As General Robert Bullard, commander of the American Second Army that included the Ninety-second Division, noted in his diary, "Poor negroes! they are hopelessly inferior."

The use of black officers posed a particular problem for the army brass. Most white officers believed that African Americans had little capability for leadership, and that only whites could effectively command fighting men. One memo from August 1918 argued, "With a few exceptions there is a characteristic tendency among the colored officers to neglect the welfare of their men and to perform their duties in a perfunctory manner. They are lacking in initiative also." The army was reluctant to commission black officers, and many highly educated African Americans with previous military experience found themselves employed as foot soldiers or common laborers during the war. Those appointed as officers generally received less training than whites, and once in France were forced to use segregated and inferior facilities. White officers often treated them with contempt, frequently requesting their transfer to other units.

Most of all, the American army tried to restrict contacts between black soldiers and the French population, as far as possible. Like blacks, many white Americans believed that the French were relatively color-blind, and feared that African Americans in France would grow accustomed to being treated as equals, and would then want the same treatment when they returned home. To prevent this expectation, in August 1918 the army drew up guidelines to explain to the French how they should treat black soldiers. Called "Secret Information Concerning Black American Troops," this document instructed

French military and civilian officials in the finer points of American race relations. It noted that whereas many French were inclined to be friendly toward blacks, in America it was imperative to maintain strict separation of the races in order to prevent "mongrelization," and that white Americans saw such friendliness as offensive. Implicit was the threat that American aid might be withheld if the French did not learn the proper way of dealing with blacks. In particular, the document warned against intimacies between blacks and Frenchwomen.

Although American authorities could only advise the French on this matter, it could and did take sterner measures to compel "appropriate" behavior from blacks in the U.S. Army. Members of the 367th Regiment were informed that the penalty for visiting a French home was twenty-four hours on bread and water, followed by an eighteen-mile hike with a full pack. In at least one city black soldiers were confined to certain streets in order to limit their contact with the French. Army concerns increased after the Armistice, as black soldiers waited to be sent home. One black regiment received an order that stated, "Enlisted men of this organization will not talk to or be in company with any white women, regardless of whether the women solicit their company or not." Several black soldiers were shot by military police, often for having consorted with Frenchwomen. In April 1919 a riot broke out in the Breton port of Saint-Nazaire between white American soldiers and French civilians, after the former insulted a Frenchwoman for going into a restaurant with a Frenchman of color. A number of violent incidents took place between white American military personnel and their French hosts over the latter's friendly relations with nonwhite soldiers in the year after the war. Paris, Bordeaux, and other cities witnessed clashes, usually provoked by drunken Americans. In his novel of the war, 1919, John Dos Passos depicted the death of one of his characters, the American sailor Joe Williams, in just such a situation on the night of the Armistice.

> Joe went cruising looking for Jeanette, who was a girl he'd kinder taken up with whenever he was in St. Nazaire. . . . He went in back where there was a cabaret all red plush with mirrors and the music was playing *The Star-Spangled Banner* and everybody cried Vive L'Amérique and pushed in his face as he came in and then . . . he'd seen Jeanette. . . . She was dancing with big sixfoot black Senegalese. Joe saw red. He pulled her away from the nigger who was a frog officer all full of gold braid and she said, "Wazamatta chérie" and Joe hauled off and hit the damn nigger as hard as he could right on the button, but the nigger didn't budge. . . . A waiter and a coupla frog soldiers came up and tried to pull Joe away . . . Joe laid out a couple of frogs and was backing off

towards the door, when he saw in the mirror that a big guy in a blouse was bringing down a bottle on his head held with both hands. He tried to swing around, but he didn't have time. The bottle crashed his skull and he was out.

The case of Captain Boutte of the Ninety-second Division typified the paranoia with which many white Americans viewed contact between African Americans and the French. Matthew Virgil Boutte was a Creole from Louisiana, with degrees from Fisk University and the University of Illinois. Fluent in French as a result of his background, he became one of the very few blacks to achieve a high position in the American Expeditionary Force in France. Arriving in France in June 1918, Captain Boutte found that his language abilities enabled him to procure rooms for black officers and facilitated many friendly contacts with the French. Jealous, his white commander charged him with twenty-three violations of military law and had him arrested. Fortunately, the case against Boutte was so clearly discriminatory that an army disciplinary hearing dismissed all the charges and released him.

In spite of the best efforts of the American army, however, black American soldiers and the people of France did get to know one another during World War I. These contacts were not always easy, but for the most part African Americans felt that the French treated them with far more decency and respect than they had ever received from whites before. The memories of such pleasant encounters endured long after the war, motivating many of the blacks who chose to settle in Paris during the 1920s.

ENCOUNTERS WITH THE FRENCH

Although blacks have lived in France for several hundred years, most French people during the early twentieth century had never seen one face to face. This isolation was especially true of those living in the small villages through which detachments of African American soldiers passed en route to battle. Yet from the early nineteenth century on, many had read popular novels, travelers' accounts, and children's stories set in Africa. Writers like Marius-Ary Leblond, Eugène Fromentin, and above all Pierre Loti had painted a lurid portrait of life in the Dark Continent, emphasizing savagery and cannibalism under the hot tropical sun. For the average French man and woman, blacks meant Africa, where sensuous dark-skinned natives danced in the jungle or labored under the benevolent tutelage of the French Empire. Imagine the surprise, therefore, that these people experienced upon meeting blacks who spoke English and marched beneath the Stars and Stripes!

The Americans! For months they had been discussed; they had been expected, and there was great curiosity; groups of people go down to the public square of the town, where they see upon our white streets the first ranks of the Allied troops. But what a surprise! They are black soldiers! Black soldiers? There is great astonishment, a little fear. The rural population, not well informed, knows well the Negro of Africa, but those from America's soil, the country of the classical type, characterized by the cold, smooth white face; that from America could come this dark troupe — none could believe his own eyes.

They dispute among themselves; they are a little irritated; some of the women become afraid; one of them confides to me that she feels the symptoms of an attack of indigestion. Smiling, reassurably, "lady with all too emotional stomach, quiet yourself! They do not eat human flesh; two or three days from now you will be perfectly used to them." I said two or three days, but from that very evening the ice is broken. Natives and foreigners smile at each other, and try to understand each other. The next day we see the little children in the arms of the huge Negroes, confidently pressing their rosy cheeks to the cheeks of ebony, while their mothers look on with approbation.

A deep sympathy is in store for these men, which, yesterday, was not surmised. Very quickly it is seen they have nothing of the savage in them, but, on the other hand, one could not find a soldier more faultless in his bearing, and in his manners more affable, or more delicate than these children of the sun. . . . Now one honors himself to have them at his table. He spends hours in long talks with them; with a great supply of dictionaries and manuals of conversation. . . . Late at night the workers of the field forget their fatigue as they hear arise, in the peaceful night, the melancholy voices which call up to the memory of the exile his distant country, America. In the lanes along the flowery hedges, more than one group of colored American soldiers fraternize with our people, while the setting sun makes blue the neighboring hills, and gently the song of night is awakened.

This rather florid letter, written by a Frenchwoman to a local newspaper and republished in *The Crisis*, sets forth many of the themes that characterized French reactions to black American soldiers during the war. There is the initial apprehension, followed by the realization that black Americans are indeed civilized, not fierce cannibals but benign, gentle giants. The writer notes the attraction of black music, and subtly hints at romantic liaisons between the soldiers and young Frenchwomen. Far from being color-blind, the French looked at African American soldiers through a haze of stereotypes.

All accounts agree that both French officials and ordinary citizens welcomed their black American guests cordially; after all, they had come to fight for France! The men of the Ninety-third Division fought under French command, and many received praise and citations of valor from the French government. One American officer noted that "the French soldiers have not the slightest prejudice or feeling. The poilus and my boys are great chums, eat, dance, sing, march and fight together in absolute accord." French civilians voiced few complaints about African American soldiers billeted in their villages, usually praising their polite, dignified conduct. They frequently used the expression *"soldat noir, très gentil, très poli"* (black soldier very nice, very polite) to describe them. The French welcomed American blacks into their homes and cheered them when they marched through on parade. As a result of such treatment, one soldier of the Ninety-third Division wrote his mother, "These French people don't bother with no color line business. They treat us so good that the only time I ever know I'm colored is when I look in the glass."

Both French officials and ordinary citizens often reacted with surprise and dismay to the bigoted attitudes of white Americans. Many simply could not understand why Americans would treat their fellow countrymen so poorly. French parliamentarians sharply criticized the American army's "Secret Information" memo, passing a resolution in the national assembly reaffirming their commitment to the equality of man. The French government eventually ordered destroyed all U.S. Army leaflets advocating discriminatory treatment of black soldiers. One French village had the experience of hosting detachments of first black, then white, American troops. While relations with the first proceeded smoothly, the white Americans behaved arrogantly and thoroughly alienated the local population. The village mayor responded by protesting, "Take back these soldiers and send us some real Americans, black Americans." A letter written by a Frenchwoman to an African American soldier provides another example of these sentiments:

> Thank you for your friendship, I am happy to give mine in exchange, because I know now what is your hard condition. I have spoken to white men, and always I have seen the same flash (lightning) in their angry eyes, when I have spoken them of colored men. But I do not fear them for myself; I am afraid of them for you, because they have said me the horrible punishment of colored men in America. As I am a French girl I have answered, "It is not Christian." . . . When a colored man goes in the house of a white girl, the policeman wait for him and kill him when he goes away! I have thought this way to do is savage, and it is why I was pitiful for the colored man . . . I should like to express you how much I am revolted of that I have learned of your condition, and how amused I am to have heard many injurious opinions of white men upon ourselves, French women!

Such reactions did not necessarily prove that the French had no biases of their own, however. African Americans were not the only people of color to come to France during the Great War, and other nonwhites had a very different experience there. For years before 1914, French military authorities, masters of the second largest colonial empire on earth, had debated the possibility of using black Africans as soldiers. Mindful of France's relatively small population and low birthrate vis-à-vis rival Germany, some officers argued that only imperial manpower could compensate for the lack of young Frenchmen, whereas others asserted that Africans were not disciplined or civilized enough to make good soldiers. In 1910 this debate came to a head when an ambitious young French officer named Charles Mangin published *La Force Noire*, a spirited argument in favor of the use of colonial troops. Mangin not only reemphasized the demographic importance of Africa's contribution to the French army, but also provided an exhaustive account of black military prowess throughout human history! Mangin's arguments carried the day, and in 1912 the French government decreed the systematic recruitment of men for military service in its African colonies.

Right from the beginning of the war, black African troops took part in the conflict, and the total number of soldiers furnished by French West Africa alone reached 135,000 by the end of 1918. Like African American soldiers, these recruits fought mostly in segregated units under the command of white officers. The officers, and the French population as a whole, often held prejudiced views of their charges. Many worried that Africans would not possess the technical skill necessary to handle a rifle, or would simply flee after their first encounters with artillery shelling and trench warfare. Once African troops had proved themselves in 1914, however, the French image of them shifted to one of ferocious, bloodthirsty maniacs on the field. In particular, the theme of African soldiers chopping off the heads of their opponents with bayonets recurred frequently in wartime France. One detachment of African riflemen found itself warmly greeted upon its arrival by French crowds shouting, "Bravo riflemen! Cut off the heads of the Germans!"

Yet in general French African soldiers did not encounter anything like the racism visited upon black American troops by white Americans on both sides of the Atlantic. Although African casualties were often extremely heavy, so were those of white French units. Recent scholarship has largely demolished the belief that France systematically used African soldiers as "cannon fodder" during the war. Moreover, the Africans seem to have been received hospitably wherever they went in France. In his interviews with twenty French African war veterans, the historian Charles John Balesi found that all rejected any suggestions of French racism. As one noted, "Blacks were highly esteemed there; there was no question of race."

If one considers the treatment of colonial workers in wartime France, a very different picture emerges. The French government brought more than half a million immigrant workers into France during the war to work in its war industries and on its farms; the majority of these were Europeans, but more than 200,000 came from the empire, principally Indochina, North Africa, and Madagascar, as well as China. Almost without exception, like their African American brothers, these nonwhite laborers performed the worst jobs and received the lowest pay of anyone in France during the war. There are also numerous instances of conflicts between colonial and French workers, especially toward the end of the war, ranging from fistfights to a few full-scale race riots, which had numerous causes. Fears that colonial workers were being used to lower wages or break strikes certainly played a role, as did outrage at sexual relationships between nonwhite men and Frenchwomen. In February 1918, one French labor union complained about the presence in France of "promiscuous peoples of manifestly inferior levels of civilization."

Few African American soldiers in France were aware of these problems. From the start of the war in Europe, America's black press had publicized the use of black troops by both France and Britain, highlighting their successes to support demands for the inclusion of African Americans in the United States Army. During the interwar years, movements like Pan-Africanism and negritude would bring blacks from America, Africa, and the Caribbean together in Paris to explore common experiences with racism. Yet such internationalism remained distant for most black Americans in France during World War I. All most knew was that the French treated them far better than white people ever had before, and they responded accordingly.

If they pitied the racist oppression of black Americans, in contrast the French immediately fell in love with that central product of African American culture, jazz. The classical music of black America, jazz has played a key role in the life of Paris's black community during the twentieth century, and it was the African American GIs of World War I who first introduced it to the French people. Right from the beginning of its history in New York, the 369th Infantry Regiment included an excellent forty-four-piece jazz band, led by two of Harlem's finest musicians, the bandmaster James Reese Europe and the drum major Noble Sissle. The people of France first heard Europe's band when the 369th Regiment landed at Brest. As an American reporter noted, "The first thing that Jim Europe's outfit did when it got ashore wasn't to eat. It wanted

France to know that it was present, so it blew some plain ordinary jazz over the town. Twenty minutes before the 369th disembarked, Brest wasn't at all la-la, so to speak; but as soon as Europe had got to work, that part of France could see that hope wasn't entirely dead."

During the early months of 1918 Europe's band toured France, playing concerts in Nantes, Angers, Tours, and Aix-les-Bains. Everywhere the musicians met with an enthusiastic reception. The city of Aix presented the band with a beautiful silver vase in formal appreciation of its visit. Adept at many musical styles, Europe's ensemble would play both the French and American national anthems, Sousa marches, and other selections: in one city Noble Sissle moved his listeners to tears by singing "Joan of Arc" in both English and French. However, the band's jazz tunes always received the most attention. Sissle later described the impact of one of their concerts:

> the whole audience began to sway, dignified French officers began to pat their feet along with the American general, who, temporarily, had lost his style and grace. Lieutenant Europe was no longer the Lieutenant Europe of a moment ago, but once more Jim Europe, who a few months ago rocked New York with his syncopated baton. His body swayed in willowy motions and his head was bobbing as it did in days when terpsichorean festivities reigned supreme. He turned to the trombone players, who sat impatiently waiting for their cue to have a "Jazz spasm," and they drew their slides out to the extremity and jerked them back with that characteristic crack.
>
> The audience could stand it no longer; the "Jazz germ" hit them, and it seemed to find the vital spot, loosening all muscles and causing what is known in America as an "Eagle Rocking Fit."

In August 1918 Europe's jazz orchestra won further acclaim when it played a concert at the Theatre des Champs-Elysées in Paris attended by the French president Raymond Poincaré.

The 369th Regiment's band was the most famous example of African American music in France during World War I, but many other musicians helped bring the sounds of jazz to the French people. Most of the other black regiments had their own bands and played frequently before French audiences. The musicians of the 370th, led by George Dulf, made a very successful tour of northern and eastern France with the coloratura soprano Anita Brown of Chicago. Other African Americans came to France to perform; some, like Opal Cooper, would return to live in Paris after the war. Most important of all, the love of music displayed by the average black GI deeply impressed the French. Whether at work, on leave, or even at times in battle, black soldiers sang and played constantly. Those French men and women who listened to their songs experienced not only a new form of music, but also the deeper mysteries of the soul of a people. When one searches for the roots of the Jazz Age in 1920s Paris, one must consider the impact of energetic rhythms and haunting melodies overheard on the dusty plains of war-torn France.

Black American soldiers responded gratefully to the warm reception they received in France, frequently contrasting French decency with white American racism. As a token of their esteem for their hosts, African American GIs contributed 300,000 francs to a fund for French war orphans. Most significantly for the future, in letters to friends and relatives back home they commented enthusiastically on the generosity and fairness of the French people, praising France as a land where a man could be a man. Although the myth of French color blindness already existed among black Americans, the experiences of their soldiers in France during World War I powerfully reinforced it. In March 1919, W.E.B. Du Bois published a landmark article, "The Black Man in the Revolution of 1914–1918," in *The Crisis*. Arguing that "the black soldier saved civilization" during the war years, Du Bois emphasized the kind treatment these men had received from the French. Even after their return to a hostile America, Du Bois noted, "They will ever love France."

The affection that many African American doughboys felt for France resulted not just from the warmth of its people, but even more so from the contrast between this warmth and the studied hostility of white America. The proud record of black American soldiers in the Great War did nothing to diminish this hostility; on the contrary, whites seemed more determined than ever to keep "the darker brother" in his place. African Americans received ample evidence of this attitude while waiting to return home after the Armistice. The U.S. Army banned black American troops from participating in the great victory parade staged by Allied soldiers in Paris on Bastille Day, 1919, even though black French and British troops took part. Several black GIs were executed without trial that year, prompting a congressional investigation. When soldiers of the 367th Regiment prepared to sail for home on the USS *Virginia*, the captain had them removed on the grounds that no blacks had ever traveled on an American battleship.

Not surprisingly, such incidents sharpened the contrast between French tolerance and white American racism. This division certainly existed, but it was also a product of circumstances. Black soldiers of all nationalities were welcome in France during the war because they were fighting France's enemies. Unlike the United States, France had been invaded by the enemy (10 percent of her national territory lay under German occupation for most of the war), which on more than one occasion had come within striking distance of Paris itself. One million French soldiers had been killed in battle by the end of 1917. These conditions help explain the often rapturous welcome African American troops received in French villages; many would no doubt have welcomed the devil himself had he come prepared to fight the Germans. Also, both black and white American soldiers frequently won over French civilians by their unconscious willingness to pay local inhabitants ridiculously inflated prices for goods and services. In contrast, the French viewed colonial workers as competitors for jobs and women, and some argued that they only freed up more Frenchmen for slaughter in the trenches of the western front. Colonials often encountered a hostility that, while not usually as vicious as white American treatment of blacks, certainly called the idea of color-blind France into question. Black laborers, working separately from the French, did not pose the same kind of competitive threat. As a result, both African American workers and soldiers were viewed as honored guests who did not threaten to overstay their welcome.

After the Armistice, black soldiers had more opportunity to explore the country they had fought to protect. During 1919, soldiers briefly became tourists, visiting great French sights like the Reims cathedral, Mont-Saint-Michel, and, significantly, black madonnas in Myans and Puy. But the attraction of all these sights paled before that of Paris, the sophisticated heart of France. In 1919 the city shook off the privations and dreariness of wartime, resuming its glory as the City of Light. African American GIs visiting Paris marveled at its physical and historical beauty.

But when the French had finally won, life and light once again filled Paris, and with it the urge and joy of long days of sight-seeing for the Americans. Soldiers "on three days' leave" wanted to see luxurious Versailles whatever else was omitted. Others preferred Fontainebleau with its stately palace, or St. Denis with its hundreds of royal tombs. All wanted to go to the tombs of Lafayette and Napoleon. One would find the Chapel of the Invalides crowded with soldiers looking down upon the great sarcophagus, while a Y man related the history . . . one liked to go out to Pere la Chaise with a group of men and show them its wonderful beauty, even though a cemetery — show them the graves of great scholars and artists of France, even those of its great lovers like Heloise and Abelard. Often the day would be closed with a restful ride on the Seine, where, somehow, one came into more intimate touch with historical Paris and a keener understanding of it than from any other point.

Most black American soldiers who visited Paris in 1919 experienced it as a welcome diversion from the hard work and boredom of army life while waiting to go home, but little more than that. Others, however, saw it as a vision of a new life that beckoned, an exciting life full of art and literature, of peaceful afternoons in charming cafés and wild nights in music clubs. Above all, it offered a life free from the heavy burden of white racism so omnipresent in the United States. Some of those who glimpsed this vision acted to make it a reality, returning to Paris a few years later. They, and those African American men and women who followed them, finding inspiration in their tales of France, formed the vital black community that arose in Paris during the 1920s. World War I may not have brought freedom to America, but at least it showed the nation's black citizens one place where racial equality already seemed to exist, making the concept of color-blind France a rallying cry for a new day across the Atlantic.

2

BRINGING
THE JAZZ AGE
TO PARIS

EVER SINCE Ernest Hemingway labeled Paris a moveable feast, Americans have been fascinated by the brilliance and daring of life in the French capital between World War I and the Depression. Paris in those years held its arms wide open to the adventurous and young at heart, welcoming people of talent and imagination from throughout the world. The American writer Samuel Putnam once called Paris the literary capital of America during the 1920s, describing it as the spiritual mistress of the Lost Generation. The French capital had attracted refugees and expatriates for centuries, offering them political asylum and intellectual stimulation. But during the 1920s the restless, desperate gaiety of the city seemed to sum up all the anxieties of a world shattered by the Great War. Paris became the creative center of the planet in those years, and artists, writers, and thinkers flocked to it like moths to a flame.

The list of accomplished and renowned foreigners who lived or spent time in Paris during the 1920s seems almost endless. The Irish novelist James Joyce first published his path-breaking modernist novel, *Ulysses*, there in 1922. The Russian exiles Igor Stravinsky and Sergei Diaghilev produced avant-garde musical works and ballet. The Prince of Wales spent many evenings in Parisian cafés and cabarets. Artists like the Spaniard Pablo Picasso and the Japanese Tsuguharu Foujita pioneered new forms of visual expression. And of course no account of expatriates in Paris would be complete without mention of great American writers like Gertrude Stein, F. Scott Fitzgerald, and Ernest Hemingway.

However, few of the tens of thousands of illustrious exiles in Paris during the 1920s had a greater impact on the city than the hundreds of African Americans who chose to call it home in those years. At the center of that storm the French called *les anneés folles*, the crazy years, stood black jazz musicians and performers. Parisians danced frenetically to their music and eagerly followed their gyrations on the stages of the capital. Unlike many expatriates who came to Paris to learn from the French, African American musicians journeyed to Paris as teachers, and found many willing pupils.

Yet not all the black Americans who lived in Paris during the 1920s were performers. Black creativity assumed many different forms during the Jazz Age, and representatives from a wide variety of experiences and walks of life journeyed across the ocean. Numerous writers, including some of the great names of the Harlem Renaissance, visited the French capital to gain experience and literary skill. Painters and sculptors, drawn by the reputation of Paris as the world's center of the arts, spent time in the city's ateliers. Even the world of black sports, one of the very few avenues to success open to black men at the time, had its representatives in the City of Light.

Two common experiences united African Americans in Paris during the 1920s. First and foremost, the city offered them a life free from the debilitating limitations imposed by American racism. Many came to Paris accidentally, not as self-conscious refugees from Yankee discrimination. Yet all learned that in France a black man or woman could live among whites as an equal, fully accepted human being. Second, for the most part black Americans in Paris chose not to remake themselves as black Frenchmen or Frenchwomen, but instead established an expatriate African American community. Writers, musicians, artists, and others ate at the same restaurants, danced at the same clubs, and in general shared their discoveries, hopes, and dreams. During the 1920s blacks in Paris opened a new chapter in the life of that city and America. To Parisians they gave the gift of a dynamic, innovative black culture. To Americans they gave the vision of black community life liberated from the negative burden of racial oppression, a vision that they hoped someday African Americans would not have to cross the ocean to find.

A WORLD SAFE FOR THE NEGRO?

Black American soldiers and laborers who served with the U.S. Army in France during World War I had witnessed the strange spectacle of whites willing to treat them with dignity and respect. However, they had also learned through bitter experience that, in spite of their contributions to the Allied cause, white Americans insisted on maintaining the color line. Nonetheless, many African Americans continued to hope that the end of the war would bring about a brighter day for race relations in the United States. Unfortunately, the harsh realities of postwar America soon crushed this fond illusion.

Black veterans returning from France encountered mixed reactions. Those who came home to cities in the North were often well treated. New York, where the 369th Infantry Regiment landed in triumph on February 12, 1919, rolled out the red carpet for the returning veterans. Hundreds of thousands of whites and blacks cheered as the soldiers, led by Jim Europe's band, marched in formation up Fifth Avenue to Harlem five days later. When they crossed 110th Street, the band struck up a lively jazz tune and Harlemites rushed out to embrace their loved ones, safely home from the battlefield. Later that day the veterans attended a celebratory dinner in their honor hosted by the city of New York.

Things were very different in the South, however. Many white Southerners feared that glimpses of racial tolerance in France had spoiled black soldiers, and that these returning veterans would refuse to accept their subordinate position in society and incite other blacks to resist discrimination. As always, the fear of miscegenation was paramount. Justifying the lynching of a black man accused of rape, Senator James Vardaman of Mississippi declared that "every community in Mississippi ought to organize and the organization should be led by the bravest and best white men in the community. And they should pick out these suspicious characters — those military, French-women-ruined negro soldiers and let them understand that they are under surveillance and that when crimes similar to this are committed, take care of the individual who commits the crime."

This attitude resulted in a sharp increase in the number of lynchings after the war. Whereas fifty-eight African Americans had been murdered by white mobs in 1918, seventy-seven were lynched in 1919. Ten of these were black veterans. In Sylvester, Georgia, Daniel Mack was beaten to death by a white mob while in uniform, after having allegedly said that he had fought in France and therefore would not accept racist treatment. Officials in the South refused to take any effective actions to stop the wave of lynchings, often implying that the black victims deserved their fates. In 1919 white Southerners insisted that the best the black veteran could expect was a return to subordinate status, and they underlined this argument in blood.

Racists bent on making sure that blacks remembered their place in postwar America did not stop at individual lynchings. The summer of 1919 witnessed the largest wave of race riots in American history, a period so violent that blacks called it the Red Summer in memory of the blood shed during those months. Unlike the lynchings, many of the riots took place in the North, as white working-class resentment of blacks who had come to work in the war plants intensified with the return of black veterans and fears of postwar unemployment. The worst violence took place in Washington, D.C., and Chicago, with other riots breaking out in Omaha, Nebraska; Charleston, South Carolina; Elaine, Arkansas; Bisbee, Arizona; and New York City.

In contrast to the disturbances of the 1960s, race riots in 1919 involved large-scale battles between whites and blacks. They usually began with invasions of African American neighborhoods by young white men who would indiscriminately beat or kill any black person unlucky enough to fall into their hands. Violence spread as blacks organized and defended themselves, often with firearms. In Washington, white soldiers attacked a black neighborhood on a hot weekend in July, and were soon joined by white civilians. Blacks armed with guns resisted, and the fighting lasted four days. A week later similar white aggression in Chicago produced an even more deadly conflict that lasted nearly two weeks and claimed the lives of fifteen whites and twenty-three blacks.

The riots proved that, North or South, few white Americans would accept greater racial equality at home as a consequence of the victorious war for liberty abroad. However, they also indicated that black Americans were more ready than ever to resist racist and discriminatory treatment, violently if necessary. The taste of freedom many had experienced in France made African Americans reluctant to swallow the bitter wine of bigotry after the Armistice. As *The Crisis* editorialized in May 1919, "We *return. We return from fighting. We return fighting.* Make way for Democracy! We saved it in France, and by the Great Jehovah, we will save it in the U.S.A., or know the reason why." Blacks fought not just to defend their homes and neighborhoods from violent attacks, but to secure for themselves the fundamental human rights that the Constitution supposedly guaranteed to all Americans.

While failing to make Mississippi safe for democracy, the world war did, however, produce the New Negro, a term used to indicate the increased racial pride and resistance to discrimination expressed by American blacks in the 1920s. The New Negro movement took many different forms. Black organizations, especially the National Association for the Advancement of Colored People, stepped up the fight against lynchings and racism in general. Led by Dr. W.E.B. Du Bois, the NAACP sponsored protest meetings against "Judge Lynch" and sued Southern states over laws denying blacks their right to vote. While the NAACP and most other African American organizations demanded full equality, Marcus Garvey argued that whites would never grant it, and therefore the only hope for blacks lay in the liberation of Africa, the mother continent. While harshly condemned by most other black leaders, Garvey's United Negro Improvement Association attracted hundreds of thousands of members and many more followers. Confronted by the continued virulence of white racism, many ordinary African Americans agreed that life in America held little appeal.

The racial pride that lay behind the activism of both Du Bois and Garvey also fueled new departures in African American culture. The spirit of the New Negro shone most brightly in the literary, artistic, and musical movement known as the Harlem Renaissance. During the 1920s Manhattan's African American neighborhood played host to a vibrant and colorful collection of young men and women of talent who crafted new expressions of blackness, making Harlem the spiritual capital of black America. Literature in particular came to symbolize the creative enterprise of the Harlem Renaissance. In 1922 the Jamaican-born writer Claude McKay published a volume of poetry entitled *Harlem Shadows*. McKay's proud lyrics, castigating white racism and clearly proclaiming the dignity of the black race, spoke for a new generation of African Americans. Other poets, novelists, and essayists, most notably Langston Hughes, James Weldon Johnson, Jessie Fauset, Countee Cullen, Walter White, and Zora Neale Hurston, expressed impassioned protests against the continued subjugation of black Americans in elegant, sophisticated literary styles.

Yet for all the renown achieved by Harlem's writers, musicians came even closer to revealing the heart and soul of the community. Jazz in particular symbolized the new black city within a city. At the turn of the century, Harlem was a quiet, peaceful neighborhood made up of solidly built brownstones inhabited almost exclusively by middle-class whites. Over the next two decades blacks began moving into the area, so that by 1920 most whites had left and Harlem had emerged as the African American heart of New York. At the same time jazz invaded the city, replacing ragtime as the most popular form of black musical expression. These two developments made Harlem the center of both musical innovation and nightclub life in the Roaring Twenties. During those years it became the custom for wealthy and prominent white New Yorkers to finish up an evening on the town listening to jazz in one of Harlem's many speakeasies. At clubs like the Bamboo Inn, Tillie's Chicken Shack, the Lenox Club, Connie's Inn, Small's Paradise, and above all the Cotton Club, white debutantes, socialites, politicians, performers, and gangsters lived it up until the wee hours, indulging themselves in the hottest dancing and music in town.

Harlem's black jazz musicians did more than just provide the tunes for white nightlife, however. The area attracted many of the best African American musicians in the country. Duke Ellington, Louis Armstrong, Ethel Waters, Noble Sissle, Lester Young, Fats Waller, Count Basie, and Eubie Blake were only some of the jazz greats who cut their musical teeth in Harlem during the 1920s. They and other musicians experimented with different forms of black popular music, ragtime, blues, stride piano, and Dixieland to come up with a new form of jazz. This music, produced in a climate of constant innovation and friendly but spirited competition, took the nation and ultimately the world by storm in the decade after the war. Relatively few of the white Harlem night owls realized, as they cradled their illicit martinis, that they were witnessing America's most unique art form.

For all its creative splendor, however, the Harlem Renaissance could not and did not alter the tragic realities of life in black America. Glamorous and seductive by night, Harlem wore an entirely different face by day, one that most whites chose not to see. For it was a desperately poor community, full of families crammed into tiny rooms and apartments, of malnourished children suffering from rickets, of women who got up at the crack of dawn every day to go downtown and scrub the grimy floors of white families, of men shut out of decent jobs by white employers and unions. Even in the heart of Harlem, the fanciest nightclubs featured black entertainers but did not admit black clients. The hope of equality for African Americans had once again proved false, and while the Harlem Renaissance celebrated black creativity, its leading lights always portrayed racism as the central theme of the black experience in America. Ultimately, pride in blackness meant a forthright resistance to white racism. Few poems better expressed this mood than Claude McKay's "If We Must Die," published in 1919 at the height of the Red Summer:

> If we must die, let it not be like hogs
> Hunted and penned in an inglorious spot . . .
> Like men we'll face the murderous, cowardly pack,
> Pressed to the wall, dying, but fighting back!

Yet between death and submission to racism lay another choice, exile abroad. During the 1920s and 1930s Claude McKay became one of the most important African American expatriates in Europe.

How different was Paris! The early 1920s in the French capital had all the vigor and freshness of the first weeks of spring coming after the long, grim winter of wartime. Restrictions on food and wine were quickly abandoned, and restaurants, cafés, and nightclubs soon filled to overflowing. France had won its great trial of arms, and now it was time for Parisians to enjoy the victory and the prosperity that it had brought, forgetting the past and rushing head-long into the new. The popularity of technological innovations like the auto-mobile, the radio, and the movies was unprecedented. Young women embraced the scandalous designs pioneered by Coco Chanel, strolling down boulevards in short dresses and bobbed hair. Paris seemed bent on having a good time; the war was over, and young people now had the freedom to experience life to the fullest.

Yet one could not forget the war so easily. More than one and a half million young Frenchmen had died in the conflict, and many more had returned from the trenches crippled or maimed, so that few French families were unaffected. Everywhere in Paris one saw young men on crutches, missing an arm or a leg. It seemed that the best and brightest men of an entire generation had been lost. But more than young soldiers had died. Prewar France, and Europe, had been supremely confident of their success and position at the center of the world. Before 1914 French men and women believed that the future would always bring ever greater material and moral progress, that science, technology, and rationalism would ensure a better world for future generations. Instead, the glories of European civilization had managed to produce the most destructive, bloody war in human history, a war that, as far as many were concerned, had resolved nothing and was essentially a pointless slaughter of innocents. This lost self-confidence lay at the heart of the Roaring Twenties in Paris, leading many thoughtful Parisians to look toward other traditions as a way of restoring their shattered faith.

One result was a new interest in Africa and blacks as a whole. Before the war many Parisian artists and intellectuals had displayed a fascination with "primitivism," and especially with African painting and sculpture. The obvi-ous borrowings of Pablo Picasso represented only the best-known example. But the dreadful, mechanical slaughter of the war sharply increased this fascination, for African culture seemed to embody a lush, naive sensuality and spirituality that cold, rational Europeans had lost. Consequently, blackness became the rage in Paris during the 1920s. The distinguished art collector Paul Guillaume became a champion of primitivism, at one point asserting that "the intelligence of modern man (or woman) must be Negro." The radical group of Parisian writers and artists who took the name *surrealists* championed black art for its subjectivity and directness of expression. In Paris black was not just beautiful, but creative, mysterious, seductive, and soulful.

Such a view of African culture owed more than a little to some hoary stereotypes, in particular that of the "noble savage." Far from maintaining that blacks were the equals of whites, it asserted or at least implied that their lack of intelligence and civilization were virtues, not vices. Similar preconceptions of black exoticism motivated white American intellectuals who frequented Harlem nightspots. But there were important differences. Parisian intellectuals took black culture seriously, considering it to represent the spirit of the age. Indeed, in 1921 the Goncourt Academy, by no means a stronghold of the avant-garde, gave the Prix Goncourt for literature to the novel *Batouala*, by the black author René Maran. The Goncourt prize was the most prestigious literary award in France, and its presentation to Maran signaled a new level of respect for black literature and culture in general.

The case of *Batouala* provides an excellent example of the complex, contradictory French attraction to primitivism and black culture. Far from being an African noble savage, René Maran was a black Frenchman of the most assimilated kind. Born in Martinique, Maran attended school in Bordeaux. After finishing his education he worked for ten years as a French colonial administrator in central Africa. His disenchantment with local French rule formed the raw material out of which he crafted his novel. In particular, the preface to *Batouala* shocked many French readers with its sharp attack on French colonialism and praise of African culture. In it, Maran stated, "Civilization, civilization, pride of the Europeans, and charnel house of innocents . . . You build your kingdom on corpses." In the light of World War I, this view of civilization as ultimately murderous seemed self-evident to many avant-garde Parisians, and became a leading theme of postwar French life. *Batouala* and primitivism in general were by no means universally popular in France: Maran's critique of French imperialism prompted a press campaign against him, and the overwhelming majority of educated French men and women clung to a belief in the superiority of European culture during the 1920s. Yet the fascination with Africa and blackness emerged as a central concern of the most advanced Parisian intellectuals in the years after the Great War.

Primitivism constituted one response to the crisis of values and search for the new so evident in interwar Paris, but there were others. If some Parisian intellectuals looked to Africa for new sources of inspiration, many ordinary Parisians found American mass culture more attractive. Most of all, Paris fell in love with Hollywood during the 1920s. Before the war the French cinematic industry had been one of the strongest in the world, and had dominated the French market. Moreover, Paris had many popular theaters that attracted large working-class audiences with their standard fare of comedies and melodramas. But by 1920 both French movies and theaters were rapidly losing their clientele to American films. Entrepreneurs built enormous movie theaters capable of seating several thousand spectators at a time. In these ornate fantasy palaces Parisians from all walks of life sat enraptured as the magic of Hollywood drew them into visions of a glamorous new world. Everyone talked about stars like Rudolph Valentino, Gloria Swanson, Mae West, and Charlie Chaplin ("Charlot"), and young people carefully imitated their hair and clothing styles.

The techniques of American mass culture also transformed the musical life of the capital in the 1920s. Prewar Paris had a lively tradition of cabarets and music halls where ordinary people went to listen and dance to French per-formers. The advent of the radio changed this tradition dramatically. The first radio broadcasts in France were transmitted from the Eiffel Tower in 1921, and by the end of the decade French households collectively owned several hun-dred thousand sets. The radio exposed Parisian listeners to a much broader range of music, especially music from America. Jazz in particular soon tri-umphed in the cabarets, nightclubs, and dance halls of the city.

Both the interest in primitivism and the attraction to American mass cul-ture help explain the warm reception African Americans received in Paris during the 1920s. When the French looked at black Americans, they saw a new version of the sensuous, spontaneous African. In particular this image shaped their perception of African American music and dance, as the career of Josephine Baker made clear. Yet the fascination of Parisians with black Americans cannot be separated from the general impact of American culture. Many regarded African American forms of expression as the most dynamic and original examples of that culture. Jazz attracted both the Parisian intellec-tual interested in black subjectivity and the Parisian shopgirl bent on dancing the night away. As a result, the dual nature of African American culture ensured that its representatives would be twice as welcome in the City of Light.

In the spring of 1919, as America's postwar upsurge of white racism cres-cendoed to a summertime catharsis of violence and blood, France by contrast played genial host to some of the world's most important black leaders. At the beginning of the year, W.E.B. Du Bois sent out letters to prominent blacks throughout the world proposing a new Pan-African Congress. The last such meeting had taken place in London in 1900, but Du Bois suggested that this congress should convene in Paris. Because the victorious Allied powers would soon assemble there to draw up a formal peace treaty and redraw the map of the world, he thought African peoples of all nations should come together "to obtain authoritative statements of policy toward the Negro race from the Great Powers." Thanks to the influence of Blaise Diagne, a Senegalese official and former French cabinet minister, the government of Georges Clemenceau extended a cordial welcome to the congress.

The Pan-African Congress took place in Paris on February 19, 20, and 21, with the participation of fifty-seven delegates from fifteen nations and colonial territories. Du Bois and fifteen other African Americans attended. Although it was an important symbolic gathering of the world's black people, the congress did not accomplish much of substance. Most notably, the delegates failed to draft a forthright condemnation of European colonial rule of Africa. In fact, Blaise Diagne opened the congress with a speech that praised the civilizing mission of French imperialism, and the final resolutions passed by the delegates merely asked that Africans be allowed "to participate in the government as fast as their development permits." Although representatives from several European governments attended the congress, its deliberations had little impact on the peace treaty signed in Versailles that summer.

Yet for politically aware black Americans, the Pan-African Congress represented one more example of French racial tolerance. Several delegates, including two black members of the French chamber of deputies, sharply condemned white American racism, noting the contributions of black American soldiers to the war effort. Given the current racial climate in the United States, these denunciations were music to the ears of many African Americans. W.E.B. Du Bois described the work of the Congress in the pages of *The Crisis*, strongly praising its stand in favor of racial equality. While acknowledging that the French were not perfect and that their rule in Africa still represented colonialism, Du Bois thanked them for hosting the Congress, noting that the American State Department had opposed it. Added to the contrast between racial attitudes in France and the United States, experienced so sharply by returning African American soldiers, the Paris Pan-African Congress furnished one more motivation for some to consider life overseas.

BLACK MONTMARTRE: THE BIRTH OF A COMMUNITY

By the early 1920s a tiny black American community had taken root in Paris. It was a diverse assemblage of people, who had come to the French capital by many different roads and for many different reasons. Some had been attracted by the legends of intimate cafés and the bright lights of the Champs-Elysées, whereas others came there as self-conscious refugees from American racism.

Still others ended up in the city by chance, drawn by the serendipity of their careers or personal relations. But African Americans living in Paris after the war shared a common feeling of liberation from the harsh limitations of life in the United States.

Former black soldiers who had chosen to stay on in France after the Armistice formed the core of this new community. Although most African American GI's eagerly anticipated returning home after the end of the war, some had no desire to give up the freedoms they had experienced and opted not to go back to the United States. This decision was of course not so easily carried out because the French government had no desire to play host to demobilized foreign soldiers of any color. Study at a French university offered one possibility of remaining in France. The French and American governments had made arrangements to permit American ex-soldiers to attend schools in France, and many whites took advantage of this opportunity. Army officials showed less enthusiasm for the prospect of black veterans enrolling in the program, at times trying to speed up the demobilization of black officers before they had time to apply. Nonetheless, thirteen African American soldiers did succeed in attending French universities after the war, including seven who enrolled in different branches of the University of Paris.

Other ex-soldiers stayed on in France as tourists or got involved in various business ventures. Rayford Logan, who later became a professor of history at Howard University, served as an officer in France during the war, where he encountered numerous examples of white American racism in the army. Afterward, he "decided to remain in France, where I would not . . . run the risk of humiliating experiences." Taking advantage of the postwar strength of the dollar, Logan traveled widely in Europe for the next few years. Light-skinned and speaking fluent French and German, Logan frequently found himself in situations where people mistook him for white, and he gained some unusual insights into racial preconceptions. At one point in 1919, shortly after a clash between American soldiers and French people in Brest, Logan was attacked by four French sailors as he walked through the city at night.

> The effectiveness of their blows and the repetition of their oaths finally reminded me that I was not an American, but only a Negro. I told them so. I appealed to their friendship for Negroes. A punch on the nose and a jab to the ribs punctuated my statement and my appeal. Then, as one fist sought an unbruised spot on my face, I grabbed it and rubbed it over my hair.
> "*Tiens,* he *is* colored. His hair is *frisés* . . . *Mille pardons, mon ami.* . . . We thought you were white."
> Their apologies were profuse; their dismay touching.

After his travels, Logan settled down in Paris, where he lived for much of the 1920s.

Albert Curtis was another African American soldier who opted to stay on in France after the war. Originally from Chicago, where he had sold issues of the black newspaper the *Chicago Defender,* by the early 1920s Curtis had settled in Bordeaux. In 1922 he wrote two letters to the *Defender* declaring his love of France, where he had encountered no color prejudice, and his intention to stay. Curtis noted that he had become involved in an alcohol distillery with several partners and argued that France offered plenty of eco-nomic opportunity for blacks because of its need to rebuild after the war. Curtis's letters confirmed for *Defender* readers the observations of Dr. A. Wilberforce Williams, who in December 1921 described meeting several Afri-can Americans living in Paris. These businessmen, students, and veterans all professed a great love for their adopted city, where they seemed to be doing very well.

One of the most fascinating black American veterans, Eugene Bullard, like many foreigners in Paris had to scramble to make ends meet, earning money by giving massages and teaching physical culture. Bullard soon learned that jazz musicians were in great demand in the city, so he taught himself to play the drums and got a job with the house band at one of the first jazz clubs in Paris. When the club was bought out by an entrepreneur from London named Joe Zelli, Bullard used the connections he had made while fighting with the French air force to obtain the necessary government permits, and Zelli's quickly became the toast of the city. As Bullard noted later in his journal, "Well, you never saw or heard of such a successful nightclub. Zelli, who was an Italian, knew all there was to know about the cabaret business. I had many important friends and they said I had some pull — and I used it — but I had no idea how to run a business. People felt they had to come to Zelli's. It was the only place in Paris that was open all night and everybody who was anybody went there." Bullard soon became the manager in his own right of a series of nightclubs and remained a central figure of the African American community in Paris during the 1920s and 1930s.

Eugene Bullard's experience in Paris after the war underscored the impor-tance of jazz both to Parisians and to black Americans in the city. Most African Americans during the 1920s either came there as jazz performers or else quickly established some kind of connection to the world of nightclubs and cabarets as a way of keeping body and soul together. Because Parisians were ready to pay for what they had to offer, black jazz musicians could earn a living, and in a few notable cases a fortune. Whereas in America both the white concert hall and the black church shunned this form of musical expression, abroad it gave African Americans the key to the world's most glamorous city.

Although no one knows for certain who first played jazz in Paris, at least one account awards the credit to the drummer Louis Mitchell. Born in Philadelphia, Mitchell had moved to New York in 1912, then first toured Europe with the band of the famous Broadway dancers Vernon and Irene Castle in the summer of 1914. In 1917 he returned to Europe with his own band, the Seven Spades, playing a series of jazz concerts in Paris that November. The French reaction to this strange new music was mixed at first, and some in the audience booed Mitchell's band. The musicians soon won over the crowd, however, and after a brief but successful appearance in the capital the Seven Spades departed for a triumphant tour of the Riviera in 1918. That year also witnessed the landing of James Europe's jazz orchestra in France. Europe's musicians and several other regimental bands of black American soldiers toured the country in 1918, spreading the new music to every corner of France.

A few of these musicians gravitated to Paris after the war. Opal Cooper, a singer, originally came to France during the war with the band of the 807th Pioneer Infantry, a labor battalion. After the war, he returned to France with a group named the Red Devils and became one of the leading African American jazz musicians in Paris, not going back to the United States until the end of the 1930s. Others soon followed in his path. In 1919 several black jazz bands, most notably Palmer Jones's International Five, played concerts in the city while on tour in Europe. The same year Will Marion Cook's Southern Syncopated Orchestra toured in Europe, bringing many of its jazz artists across the Atlantic for the first time. The group settled in London, where it won great acclaim, even performing for the Prince of Wales. Eventually some of its members crossed the English Channel to Paris. The most important, Sidney Bechet, took an immediate liking to the French capital, beginning an association that would last almost forty years.

Conditions in both Paris and New York spurred this postwar jazz migration across the Atlantic. By 1919 musical opportunities were drying up in the United States for black jazz musicians, in part the result of increasing competition and the end of the wartime industrial boom that had drawn so many blacks to the North. In May 1919, James Europe was murdered by one of his own musicians during a Boston concert, symbolizing the end of an era of innocence and hope for America's lovers of jazz. At the same time, musicians who had served in France spread fantastic stories about the popularity (and profitability) of jazz among the French, and soon solid job offers to play in Paris seemed to lend credence to these tales of wonder. Elliot Carpenter, a pianist and leader of the Red Devils, later recalled how he was offered a chance to perform in France.

> Two of the boys, Opal Cooper and Sammy Richardson, had just come back from the war. So I went to them and said, "Do you guys want to go to France?" And they said, "My God, yes!" And they started to tell me about the beauties of Paris — what they did and didn't do. They raved, "Yeah, man. Let's go back there!" So I said, "Hey, wait a minute. I haven't said anything about money." And they said, "The hell with that! Let's just get back to Paris." My wife tells me I must be crazy. I said, "Listen, these boys want to go so bad! And from what they tell me, we're going to be millionaires twenty-four hours after we get there."

As it turned out, this prediction was not so far from the truth. The band agreed to go for fifty dollars per musician per week, a very good salary at the time in New York. As soon as they arrived in Paris they met other black musicians who said they should be getting at least triple that. One of these, the cornet player Cricket Smith, was earning $250 to $300 a week at the Casino de Paris. Within two weeks of their arrival in Paris, Carpenter and his musicians had been hired away to perform in London, at a salary of $350 a week.

As Carpenter, Cooper, and others soon discovered, Parisians did not just love jazz, but they loved *black* jazz in particular — or at least jazz played by black musicians. Although white performers were common enough in the musical circles of the United States, and frequently traveled to Europe, many French fans considered jazz black music and did not especially want to see it played by whites, neither Americans nor French. As the French drummer Alain Romans noted, "At that time there was no racism between musicians. If there was any racism it was our people that used to give preference to the colored musicians. It was quite difficult to get a job as a white musician because they used to prefer to give it to blacks." Gene Bullard was hired as a drummer even though he had never really played before and admitted in his journal that he had no talent for it. Romans himself played at least one gig in blackface, the only white member of a black band, something that proved quite embarrassing one evening when a little girl touched him and the paint came off on her fingers. (When the girl screamed, her father rushed over and, to demonstrate that black skin doesn't rub off, wiped the faces of all the musicians *except* Romans with a cloth. He thereupon spanked his daughter for lying!) This example of blackface in France, a staple of vaudeville theater in the United States, illustrates an important difference between the two nations. Whereas in America blackface enabled theaters to present the black aesthetic without blacks, thus freezing them out of the white entertainment world, in Paris a white musician's use of blackface reflected the dominant position of blacks as jazz performers.

By 1924 the number of black Americans in Paris remained very small, probably no more than twenty-five or thirty individuals, virtually all musicians. But this tiny group already had established the beginnings of a viable urban community, with its own institutions and its own neighborhood. Most African Americans who came to Paris between the wars lived in Montmartre, a picturesque and storied area on top of a hill in the northern part of the city's Right Bank. Then as now, Montmartre (or "Mo-mart," as black Americans called it) was one of the most interesting parts of the French capital. Primarily a working-class neighborhood, in the late nineteenth century it had been the capital of Bohemian Paris. The impressionist painters in particular made it their headquarters, and artists like Monet, Picasso, and Van Gogh all worked there in ateliers. The Butte, as Parisians called the top of the hill, was a peaceful area full of small torturous streets meandering lazily up to the glistening white basilica of Sacré-Coeur, one of the city's great landmarks.

Yet Montmartre had two faces. In contrast to the pacific, chaste atmosphere surrounding Sacré-Coeur, the main boulevards of the area offered the liveliest nightlife in Paris, perhaps the world. The Place Pigalle, a tawdry square at the foot of the hill, functioned as the city's center of prostitution, drugs, and various other kinds of vice. Foreign tourists seeking to be shocked and thrilled by the decadence of Gay Paree usually ended up there. Not far from Pigalle stood the venerable Moulin Rouge, the impressionists' favorite dance hall, and the nighttime air of the boulevards throbbed with the beat of lively music emanating from clubs of all descriptions. The celebrated jazz singer Bricktop captured the charm and complexity of the area in her description of what she first saw upon arrival:

> A rickety, open-air Paris taxi took us to Montmartre, atop a hill above the rest of the city. It was a tumbledown little place, with red and yellow one-story buildings lining its narrow, twisting streets, and as many cafes and dance halls and bordellos as on State Street in Chicago . . . After the sun went down, Paris did become the City of Light, and Montmartre changed from a sleepy little village to a jumpin' hot town.
>
> The Moulin Rouge was tops among the big places. . . . There were dozens of other clubs in Montmartre. Most of them featured jazz. Even the smallest clubs were classy. The hostesses were beautifully dressed — no bummy girls hanging around. The patrons dressed to the hilt and wore their chic clothes with the ease of people accustomed to finery.

Home to a diverse and very lively population, both French and international, Montmartre was a natural place for African Americans to gather during the 1920s. For many decades, the area's cabarets and nightclubs had welcomed wealthy tourists from the four corners of the world. Russian nobles, American millionaires, and South American night owls danced, sang, and drank overpriced champagne at crowded tables until the stars faded with the coming of the dawn. After the Armistice, American tourists flooded into Paris, drawn by wartime rumors and cheap francs, soon turning the neighborhood into a Yankee colony. As one cynical newspaper reporter noted, "Two more shiploads of savages arrived at Cherbourg yesterday. Look out, Montmartre!"

But tourists were not the only foreigners in Montmartre. An audacious band of Polish gangsters operated there in 1924 and 1925, scandalizing the Paris press by committing seventeen muggings and sixty-eight robberies. Montmartre was home to the city's large community of White Russians. These unfortunate individuals, named for their opposition to the victorious "red" Communist revolution in Russia, streamed into Paris by the thousands after 1917. During the 1920s, they set up a number of Russian restaurants and cabarets in the neighborhood, picturesque places with doormen in full Cossack uniform, gypsy orchestras and dancers, and waiters who all claimed to be at least distantly related to the martyred tsar. The French novelist and adventurer Joseph Kessel left a vivid description of the area in his 1927 novel, *Princes of the Night*:

> Those who in the years 1924–1925 dragged out their idle hours, or desire for debauch, beguiled their melancholy, or simply their nocturnal tastes in the artificial daylight of Montmartre, those who love the inimitable landscape formed by the rues Pigalle, Fontaine, and Douai, landscape peopled by drunken americans, saxophone-playing negroes, tango-dancing Argentines, gaunt-faced prostitutes, pimps in dinner jackets, flower-girls, chauffeurs and beggars — a landscape smelling of petrol, perfumes, make-up, and, stealthily, of drugs, those who . . . mixed with the strange folk whose work begins when the rest of the world goes to bed . . . hysterical people, perverted and simple, outside humanity, pleasure-fodder — they will remember the abnormal number of Russian restaurants crowded together within a few square yards of this infested zone . . .
>
> *Pigal*, a corner cut off from the world, port without a harbor for ruined bodies and derelict souls, a sterile, neurotic retreat, of use only to those degraded by alcohol, enfeebled by cocaine; the hallucination of an unnatural enjoyment that flies before the first rays of the sun.

Although Kessel may have overdramatized the situation, alcohol and drug abuse certainly characterized the Montmartre music scene. Clubs made their money from poor quality champagne, and musicians were often encouraged to drink their fill. A variety of stupefacients, including marijuana, opium, and cocaine, were available for those in search of more unconventional highs. *The Black Light*, a novel by Francis Carco, the unofficial poet laureate of Montmartre in the early twentieth century, used lurid tones to describe opium abuse in the neighborhood. Most African American musicians in Paris could tell tales of colleagues whose music and lives had been ruined by overindulgence. Elliot Carpenter, who chose not to stay in France, later described the underside of the Paris jazz colony.

> The Negroes would go into them cafes up in Montmartre and they'd throw their money away as soon as they got it. Drinking wine and spending it on those whores they had up there. . . . They had a freedom you didn't get here. Over there you didn't have to hide away. So they were just out for fun. In a way they wasted themselves. They didn't pick out the best women. They all had wives back in the States so they just went for the whores. And the whores took 'em for everything they could get when they saw they were in demand. One of my best friends, Usher Watts, he was working with the International Five. It killed him. He just died from dissipation. He had a brain tumor. That's what brought me back to America. I didn't want to kill myself like Usher.

A small population of blacks lived in Montmartre well before the arrival of African American musicians after 1918. A late-nineteenth-century painting by Théophile-Alexandre Steinlen, *Le Bal du 14 Juillet (The Bastille Day Dance)*, prominently features a black man drinking at a table with several white companions, both male and female. At the turn of the century, French observers noted blacks strolling through the area's streets or dancing at nightspots like the Moulin Rouge. Immediately after the war, a number of violent incidents took place in the clubs of Montmartre between black French soldiers and white American sailors. Drunk on both victory and cheap wine, these sailors caused a number of disturbances in the neighborhood. As one Frenchwoman noted, "In 1919 it was impossible to cross the Place Pigalle after midnight without hearing the gunshots of drunk Americans." The sailors would fly into a rage at the sight of white Frenchwomen (usually prostitutes) dancing with black men, and would attack. Not only did the blacks resist energetically, but the French prostitutes and pimps usually came to their aid. In one such incident a Frenchwoman shouted, "This is disgusting! This is France, not Chicago!" while another exclaimed, "After all, the Senegalese fought for us!"

This was the neighborhood that welcomed African Americans in the 1920s. Although Montmartre certainly had its charming and picturesque side, it did not cater to the faint of heart. But for musicians used to the rough streets of Harlem or Chicago's South Side, life there posed no great obstacles. Above all, it offered some of the world's best nightlife and a tolerant atmosphere that gladly accepted outsiders. When Sidney Bechet arrived there from London, he liked it immediately, commenting that he could hardly walk down the street without running into other entertainers he knew. Montmartre soon became the closest thing to home that a black American could find in Europe.

Any tour of black Montmartre must begin with the area's jazz clubs. Zelli's was the first in the area to feature jazz after the war, and it became one of the most luxurious places in Paris. Joe Zelli featured two dance bands, one of black American jazz musicians and the other an Argentine tango band, which alternated playing music in twenty-minute sets. To increase business, Joe Zelli paid young women to dance with unaccompanied male guests. Shortly after Zelli's opened, both Louis Mitchell and Palmer Jones set up their own Montmartre nightclubs. Jones quickly achieved success by featuring his wife, the singer Florence Embry Jones. "Her grace, charm and personality, to say nothing of her artistic ability, made her a sensation. Wealthy and prominent Americans and titled and distinguished Europeans that patronized their place showered Florence with all the respect humanly possible and bowed to kiss her hands." In 1924 the Joneses opened a new club, appropriately named Chez Florence, which was an immediate hit. The same year Eugene Bullard moved over from Zelli's to start his own club, Le Grand Duc.

Clustered together around the intersection of the rues Fontaine and Pigalle, just south of the Place Pigalle, these clubs did not open for business until late in the evening. Ranging from tiny holes-in-the-wall to grand, sumptuous dance palaces, they usually consisted of a stage for the band with a dance floor in front, tables and chairs for the guests, and a bar for solitary drinkers. Although by the mid-1920s many nightclubs in Paris featured jazz bands, the ones in Montmartre, especially those owned or managed by African Americans, usually offered the best music, played by black Americans. And although some Parisian intellectuals would rhapsodize at length about the aesthetic and innovative qualities of jazz, the crowds in the Montmartre clubs saw this new music as something to dance to. The popularity of new steps from across the Atlantic, notably the Charleston, reinforced the appeal of jazz. For young Parisians intent on asserting their modernity, dancing to the music of jazz bands was as much a part of their self-image as slicked-back hair and short dresses. Nowhere in the city could one "shake that thing" better than in Montmartre.

Florence's in the Rue Blanche, a late night resort which occupies the site of an old and charming garden, is crowded from midnight to dawn with revellers who have begun the night at other places. This is the headquarters of the Charleston, which visitors willing or unwilling are sometimes made to dance . . . participation in the dance is one of the rules laid down by Florence, the half-caste who gives her name to the place. Such compulsory dancing, of course, produces ludicrous effects, the sight of an old gentleman in spectacles or a fat old South American lady covered with jewellery executing the Charleston, sending everyone into fits of laughter, the sound of which even the strident notes of the jazz band are powerless to drown.

Not all was laughter and song in the black nightclubs of Montmartre. Although less violent than New York or Chicago, the area still had its share of gangsters and mayhem. Corsican protection rackets infested the neighborhood, demanding and usually getting money from club owners who wanted to stay open. Eugene Bullard got into a vicious battle with one such gangster named Justin Pereti, who ended up shooting him, putting him in the hospital. Too much champagne or whiskey frequently led to bloody clashes. Langston Hughes once observed a fight in Le Grand Duc between two women "who shattered champagne glasses on the edge of the table, then slashed at each other with the jagged stems."

For self-protection and out of habits learned in America, African American musicians in Paris often carried firearms. One musician recalled getting paid only when his friend Louis Mitchell pulled a gun on the club owner. In 1928 Sidney Bechet, a man known for his fierce temper, got into a gunfight with another musician, Mike McKendrick. This particular battle, which one witness described as "straight out of a cowboy movie," took place late at night outside a Montmartre club and ended up with several wounded people, including a young Australian dancer and a Frenchwoman walking by on her way to work. Bechet was arrested, imprisoned for a year, and then deported from France, not to return until 1949.

Life in Montmartre during the 1920s was passionate, joyous, outrageous, dangerous, and at times tragic, but never dull. Lewis Erenberg, a historian of New York nightlife, has argued that after the war Harlem came to resemble Montmartre. Yet given the crucial impact of African American musicians on this celebrated Parisian neighborhood, the reverse also seems true. Like Harlem, Montmartre was an area with a seedy reputation located north of the places inhabited by the wealthy and genteel, who came to visit it in the dead of night to finish up an evening on the town. Both areas were the centers of the local black population, and places where whites intent on exotic slumming could come to experience black culture. Many of the black Americans who played the Montmartre clubs came there directly from New York, like many of their white expatriate fellow citizens. If the latter sought out a receptive area, Montparnasse, in which to re-create Greenwich Village, the former established a reflection of the Harlem Renaissance uptown, on the other side of the Seine.

At the center of this lively, cosmopolitan whirlwind stood a small, light-skinned and red-haired black woman from a small town in West Virginia. Born in 1894, Ada Louise Smith, later nicknamed Bricktop, grew up in Chicago, where she had the opportunity to see many of the leading black entertainers at theaters downtown. At the age of sixteen Smith got her first job in show business working for a vaudeville troupe. She spent the next several years as a singer and entertainer, both in Chicago and on tour throughout the United States. In 1922 Bricktop moved to New York to perform at the Exclusive Club. This nightclub, owned by Barron Wilkins, was one of the showplaces of the Harlem music scene, and it introduced Bricktop to the kind of international celebrities she would later cultivate so skillfully in Paris. Soon moving on to Connie's Inn, Bricktop met many of the great black musicians in New York and became one of Harlem's leading entertainers.

In 1924 Bricktop received the thrilling call to perform in Paris. At the time Florence Jones was the only black American woman working as an entertainer in the city. When she and her husband established their own club, Gene Bullard decided he needed a similar entertainer to work at his Grand Duc. Palmer Jones had heard of Bricktop and suggested she would do very well, so Bullard had a New York friend contact her to offer her a job, which she accepted with equanimity.

Success in Paris did not come instantly for Bricktop. She broke into tears at her first sight of Le Grand Duc, horrified by its small size. Night after night, the club stood empty as the crowds flocked to Chez Florence down the street. And to cap it off, Bricktop came down with appendicitis and needed an operation shortly after her arrival. All this changed, however, after a fortuitous meeting with Fannie Ward, the white American movie star. She and her numerous friends began stopping by the little club late in the evening, and the crowds grew larger and the profits fatter from night to night. By the spring of 1925 Bricktop had carved out a small but solid niche for herself in the unstable world of the Montmartre cabaret.

Nineteen twenty-five was a banner year for the young entertainer, as the "beautiful people" in Paris, both French and foreign, began flocking to Le Grand Duc. In the fall of that year the white American expatriates in

Montparnasse discovered Bricktop, adding her club to their wild nightly rounds. One night, F. Scott Fitzgerald and his wife, Zelda, came in with some friends, and quickly adopted Le Grand Duc as a regular hangout. Fitzgerald once said that "my greatest claim to fame is that I discovered Bricktop before Cole Porter," and he mentioned her in his fictional work. Charlie Wales, the older but wiser protagonist of the short story "Babylon Revisited," notes the role she played in his dissolute Parisian exile: "After an hour he left and strolled toward Montmartre, up the Rue Pigalle into the Place Blanche. The rain had stopped and there were a few people in evening clothes disembarking from taxis in front of cabarets, and *cocottes* prowling singly or in pairs, and many Negroes. He passed a lighted door from which issued music, and stopped with the sense of familiarity; it was Bricktop's, where he had parted with so many hours and so much money."

The great songwriter Cole Porter also first made Bricktop's acquaintance in the fall of 1925, becoming one of her biggest fans. After hearing her sing one of his songs at Le Grand Duc, Porter asked her if she could do the Charleston. Bricktop showed him she could, and soon Porter was organizing Charleston parties, featuring her as an entertainer and teacher, in his luxurious Left Bank mansion. Other wealthy expatriates also wanted to learn the Charleston, and Bricktop soon found herself in great demand at some of the fanciest houses in town. Even the Aga Khan requested lessons. This new career as an entertainer at private parties gave Bricktop the entrée she needed into the very exclusive, closed world of the cosmopolitan elite in Paris, ensuring her success, and that of any nightclub where she performed.

By the end of 1926, flush with her popularity as both a nightclub singer and a private entertainer, Bricktop decided it was time to open her own place. Florence and Palmer Jones had gone back to New York, so Bricktop took over the old Chez Florence and renamed it the Music Box. The place was a big hit, helped along by the Prince of Wales's decision to sponsor a private party there just before it opened to the public. However, licensing difficulties soon prompted French authorities to close the club, so Bricktop returned to Le Grand Duc for about a year. She then acquired a new nightclub right across the street, and this time named it Bricktop's, so that her fans would always know where to find her.

Bricktop's proved an even bigger success, soon making its star the queen of the Montmartre night. Like most of the Paris jazz clubs it was a small place, with about twelve to fourteen tables arranged on a glass floor lit from below, plus a bar and benches arranged along the walls. Bricktop's served champagne and whiskey, and provided simple breakfast food for hungry all-night revelers. Most important, Bricktop's served up the latest in African American jazz for the listening and dancing pleasure of its clientele. Bricktop made sure to keep in touch with the most recent sounds from New York, in effect bringing the Jazz Age to Paris. She employed many black American singers and musicians, as well as frequently taking center stage herself, to the delight of her customers.

In her club, Bricktop did more than just entertain. She created a fantasy world, a vision of America as it could and should be. While Bricktop's is now best known for the wealthy celebrities who made it such a success, the club welcomed all those who could afford a few drinks. Unlike Harlem's leading nightspots, at Bricktop's black customers enjoyed the same privileges as white ones, and black musicians mingled with white millionaires on a footing of complete equality. Bricktop's was at the same time a refuge from the burden of racism, for both black and white Americans, and a celebration of a uniquely African American art form. Like Paris itself, it offered the tourist or expatriate an escape from the downside of life in the United States, and yet no place could have been more American. When the gray light of dawn stole over Montmartre, the music would die down and the dream would fade, but at least in the 1920s one could always count on Bricktop to bring back the glory of the night.

African American life in Paris thus represented different things to different people. To Parisians, it provided a little bit of Africa in France, a living example of the black aesthetic. One could dance to the wild rhythms of black musicians or simply marvel at the exoticism of black faces. For white Americans, the clubs of Montmartre provided a space where one could kick up one's heels and experience the legendary decadence of Gay Paree, while at the same time enjoying an atmosphere reminiscent of home. In Montmartre one could transgress puritanical strictures against drink and interracial fellowship, secure in the knowledge that such boundaries would remain comfortably in place upon one's return home. For African Americans, the community in Paris provided good jobs for those who could play jazz (and even some who could only fake it), and a relief from Rayford Logan's "humiliating experiences." Moreover, even though blacks were still few and far between, Montmartre provided enough of a community to enable its African American members to escape white American racism without also abandoning black American culture.

By the time Bricktop opened her own nightclub, Paris could boast a small but energetic African American community. Several hundred strong, these people came from all parts of the United States and from all walks of life.

Following the advice of Albert Curtis, a few had gone into business in Paris, setting up their own small shops and restaurants. One of the central institutions of American life in Paris during the 1920s (and to the present day) was the American Express office, where expatriates and tourists could change money, receive mail from home, and get information about life in the French capital. A fixture at American Express was the shoeshine stand of John Kraton, originally from Roanoke, Virginia. The sight of a black shoeshine "boy" probably made white Americans feel more at home, especially because "Johnny" frequently proved to be a gold mine of valuable information about Paris.

Restaurants owned by black Americans also provided a taste of home. In addition to his entertainment ventures, Louis Mitchell ran a restaurant named Mitchell's in the heart of Montmartre, "where one may get sausages and hot cakes and other dishes which the American palate craves abroad." Margaret Brown from Philadelphia operated another restaurant in Montmartre, while William Morgan, who had left Galveston, Texas, to come to France during the war, served up American coffee and fried chicken at a restaurant near the Eiffel Tower. African Americans owned two women's clothing boutiques in Montmartre, and George Baker of Maine ran a successful home furnishings business in the neighborhood. In addition, blacks worked for both American and French concerns: Charles Baker worked as a messenger for the United States Lines, and W. Henry Lee was a chemist employed by a Parisian company.

One could find African Americans living in many different parts of the French capital. In 1929 one black reporter described a series of parties at the apartments of prominent black American expatriates in Montmartre, near the Eiffel Tower, and in the area around the Champs-Elysées. Mrs. Eva Lewis, the wife of a doctor studying in Switzerland, lived on the fashionable boulevard de Courcelles, while Henry Lee lived in the affluent suburb of Neuilly. Many blacks also resided on the Left Bank. The famed painter Henry Ossawa Tanner continued to live and work out of his studio in the boulevard Saint-Jacques, and students like Anna Julia Cooper and Gwendolyn Bennett resided amid the heady intellectual atmosphere of the Latin Quarter.

But throughout this period, Montmartre remained the undisputed center of black expatriate life in Paris. Even those who weren't musicians would often find a place to live there because friends or acquaintances had told them about the area. Black Americans who lived elsewhere in the city usually spent time in Montmartre visiting friends, eating at the restaurants, or passing lazy days at the cafés. One place, uninvitingly named the Flea Pit, typified these hangouts. The club supposedly owed its name to its popularity with the black musicians of Montmartre, who clustered there like fleas. A reporter for the *Chicago Defender* described the place at the end of 1926: "the headquarters for many of our well known artists, musicians, etc. in Paris . . . a combination of a pool room, public bar, cigar stand . . . located on the . . . corner of Rue Pigalle and Rue Bergère . . . if you happen to be in Montmartre you will in due time visit the Flea Pit."

Above all, for black Americans in Paris, Montmartre meant jazz. Like whites, African Americans flocked to the nightclubs gathered around the Place Pigalle and the neighborhood boulevards, but whereas for the former such excursions represented voyages of exploration into a strange, exotic culture, to black people the jazz clubs symbolized home and community, places where they unquestionably belonged in the midst of a great foreign city. These clubs came and went during the 1920s, some of the more famous ones being the Cosy Corner, the Palermo, Gerald's Bar, and the Royal Montmartre, as well as Bricktop's, Chez Florence, and Zelli's. In 1929 an American even opened a nightclub in Montmartre called the Cotton Club. Musicians would play for half the night at one club, then go to another club to visit friends, hear new musicians, play cards, or flirt with a new lover. Black students, writers, artists, and tourists would come to dance the Charleston, eat home cooking, and party the night away. In the short story "Wedding Day," Gwendolyn Bennett wrote, "Rue Pigalle in the early evening has a sombre beauty — gray as are most Paris streets and other-worldish. To those who know the district it is the Harlem of Paris and rue Pigalle is its dusty Seventh Avenue." The historian Joel Augustus Rogers, who lived in Paris during this time and wrote several columns for the African American press describing black life there, had this to say about Montmartre:

> The Boulevard de Clichy is the 42nd and Broadway of Paris. Most of the night life of Paris centers around it, and most of the colored folks from the States, too. If you hear that some friend from the States is in Paris, just circulate around this boulevard from the Moulin Rouge down Rue Pigalle as far as the Flea Pit, and it's a hundred to one shot you'll encounter him or her, at least twice during the night.
>
> Most of the colored folk live in this neighborhood. There is a surprising number of them, and it is increasing every year. Just now with the "Blackbirds" at the Moulin Rouge, this section of Montmartre reminds you more of Harlem than ever.

Black American musicians, singers, and dancers were very much in vogue in Paris during the 1920s, and many had settled there by the end of the decade.

Some of the better-known musicians included the bandleaders Leon Abbey and E. E. Thompson, the pianists Sammy Richardson, Charlie "Dixie" Lewis, Maisie Withers, and Palmer Jones, trumpet players Bobby Jones, Gut Bucket, and Arthur Briggs, and banjo players Al Hughes, Al Smith, and Greely Franklin. Besides performing in Paris, they often spent the summers working on the Riviera and in other resorts, and frequently toured other parts of Europe. In addition, many famous jazz artists came to Paris on tour, staying there for anywhere from a few days to several months. Noble Sissle returned to France in the late 1920s, giving several concerts in Paris. The great blues singer Alberta Hunter lived and sang there for about six months in 1927. The singer Florence Mills dazzled Parisians with her performance in the musical revue *Blackbirds*. This show, which toured France and England to great acclaim, also featured the comedian Johnny Hudgins. Hudgins stayed on in Paris, in 1928 starring at the Moulin Rouge in a lavish new production, *Paris aux Etoiles.*

African American dancers also found a warm reception in Paris. Embodying the complex rhythms of jazz, black dances attracted Parisians with their exoticism and eroticism. In 1927, Harry Fleming of Philadelphia was performing at the Moulin Rouge, while a boy nicknamed Snowball danced for audiences at the Casino de Paris. At the Jardin d'Acclimatation nightclub in the Bois de Boulogne, a large park on the west side of the city, a black dance troupe performed. "All are in a Negro village, which is supposed to represent a plantation scene in the South. They sing and dance, especially the Charleston, which is still a favorite in the Paris dance halls."

Representatives of the black American aesthetic thus scored many triumphs in the City of Light. Stars like Florence Mills were big hits in the city's music halls, and Parisians danced the night away to the sounds of black jazz musicians in the nightclubs of Montmartre. The greatest of them all, Josephine Baker, combined both dance and song. She took Paris by storm when she arrived there in 1925, and remained one of its brightest stars for fifty years. More than anyone else, Josephine Baker symbolized *les années folles* in Paris.

JOSEPHINE BAKER CONQUERS PARIS

The woman who would dazzle Paris and all of Europe in the 1920s was born Freda J. McDonald in Saint Louis, Missouri, on June 3, 1906. She inherited her theatrical talent and ambition from her mother, Carrie McDonald, who had done some singing in bars and restaurants. Although Baker believed her father was a white man, his actual identity has remained a mystery to this day. Freda, who everyone called Josephine, grew up in conditions of the most terrible poverty. Her family lived in a one-room shack infested with bugs and rats, and the young girl soon learned to look for food in trash cans. When she was eleven years old, the fearsome East Saint Louis race riots broke out, and she witnessed blacks streaming across the bridge to Saint Louis, forced to run for their lives to escape the bands of rampaging whites. To young Josephine, the riots seemed like a vision of the Apocalypse: "I never forget my people screaming, pushing to get to the bridge, a friend of my father's face shot off, a pregnant woman cut open. I see them running to get to the bridge. I have been running ever since."

This kind of life was all too common for black children in the early twentieth century. Yet in spite of the heavy burdens of poverty and racism, Josephine's childhood had its measure of laughter, joy, and hope. Singing and dancing in particular appealed to the young girl as a way of escaping the grim realities of life in Saint Louis. Love of music helped Josephine survive the harsh conditions of her childhood. For many poor black children it created a beautiful fantasy world into which they could escape for a time. But for Josephine Baker it did more, enabling her to escape Saint Louis permanently and make the fantasy world a glittering reality.

Childhood ended early for the young Josephine. At the age of thirteen she left her mother's house, married a boy named Willie Wells, and worked as a waitress in a nightspot named the Old Chauffeur's Club. There she met a couple and their daughter who performed as the Jones Family Band. Josephine soon joined them as they played for money outside dance halls and theaters. At one point they were performing outside the Booker T. Washington Theater, which featured black vaudeville acts, during a run by a group named the Dixie Steppers. Thanks to her own daring as well as the Steppers' need for more dancers, Josephine managed to get herself hired. She made the first stage appearance of her life dressed as Cupid in wings and baggy pink tights. Right from the start, Josephine demonstrated the genius for comic performance that was to make her career. Her funny faces and frantic wrigglings literally stole the show, getting the biggest laughs of the evening. Josephine continued to play the Booker T. Washington, and when the Dixie Steppers asked her to go on tour with them in 1920 she agreed. She had found her calling.

Although the Dixie Steppers were definitely a show business act, they remained light years away from the glories of the Paris stage. After her first accidental success, Josephine worked for the troupe as a dresser and assistant to its leading lady, Clara Smith. The school of Southern vaudeville was rough;

the Steppers traveled from one small town to another, playing before all-black audiences in theaters lit by candles and heated by charcoal fires. By watching these performances, and listening to the advice Clara Smith gave her, Josephine learned what audiences wanted and how to give it to them. When she got the chance to replace a sick dancer, she proved that these lessons had not been wasted.

After several weeks of travel, the tour ended in Philadelphia, where the Dixie Steppers disbanded. On her own, Josephine once again demonstrated the skills for survival that would take her so far. She remarried, this time to a Pullman porter named William Baker. More importantly, by dint of luck and determination, she managed to land a job in the chorus line of Broadway's hit black musical, *Shuffle Along*. Ever since Josephine left Saint Louis, she had wanted to dance in a major New York production, but the theater was rigidly segregated for both audiences and performers, and no blacks had worked on Broadway for years. In 1921, however, Noble Sissle teamed up with songwriter Eubie Blake to create the landmark black musical. Featuring songs like "I'm Just Wild about Harry," *Shuffle Along* played to enthusiastic audiences on its tour, reaching the Sixty-third Street Theater in New York on May 23, 1921. The show soon became a big hit, running for more than five hundred performances and conclusively proving that a black musical could attract white mainstream audiences. It scored a historic blow against segregation in the American entertainment world, opening the way to success for many black productions and performers.

Working in *Shuffle Along* was Josephine Baker's big chance, and she took full advantage of it. She soon began making a name for herself as audiences warmed to the skinny dancer with the long legs and goofy expressions:

> She was the little girl on the end. You couldn't forget her once you'd noticed her, and you couldn't escape noticing her. She was beautiful but it was never her beauty that attracted your eyes. In those days her brown body was disguised by an ordinary chorus costume. She had a trick of letting her knees fold under her, eccentric wise. And her eyes, just at the crucial moment when the music reached the climactic "he's just wild about, cannot live without, he's just wild about me," her eyes crossed.
>
> Nothing very beautiful about a cross-eyed coloured girl. Nothing very appealing. But it was the folding knees and the cross-eyes that helped bring back the choruses for those unforgettable encores.

For two years, Josephine Baker danced in the chorus line of *Shuffle Along*. The company toured all over the East and Midwest; it even played in Saint Louis, giving Baker the signal pleasure of revisiting her family and hometown in style. During her time with *Shuffle Along*, she began to mature from a gawky adolescent into a seasoned performer, but she never lost her originality and her ability to make people laugh. Recognizing her talent, Sissle and Blake gave her valuable suggestions and promoted her career. Her work in their new show, *Chocolate Dandies*, won praise from the New York critics, and the poet e. e. cummings described her by saying that "she resembled some tall, vital, incomparably fluid nightmare which crossed its eyes and warped its limbs in a purely unearthly manner." At the age of eighteen, Josephine Baker was already a star on Broadway.

After *Chocolate Dandies* closed, Baker went to work as a dancer in the Plantation Club on Broadway and Fiftieth Street, a midtown Manhattan version of the Harlem clubs that catered to a white clientele. The Plantation Club created a complete antebellum Southern fantasy for its customers, with a log-cabin decor, black mammies, and even an actress playing Aunt Jemima making pancakes! Here Baker met Mrs. Caroline Dudley Reagan, a wealthy young socialite interested in black music and art. Mrs. Reagan typified the affluent white patrons of the 1920s who championed black art as a vital, primitive form of expression, and who supported many key figures of the Harlem Renaissance. Married to an attaché in the American embassy in Paris, Mrs. Reagan decided that the French would love the kind of black musical revue *Shuffle Along* had pioneered on Broadway, so she set about making the necessary arrangements and putting a cast together. She came to the Plantation Club to recruit its star, Ethel Waters, but when Waters declined she offered a role in the show to Josephine Baker instead. Baker accepted after Reagan agreed to pay her a salary of $250 a week, twice what Sissle and Blake had paid her. As she later noted in her memoirs: "France . . . I had dreamed of going there ever since Albert, one of the waiters at the Plantation, had shown me a photograph of the Eiffel Tower. It looked very different from the Statue of Liberty, but what did that matter? What was the good of having the statue without the liberty, the freedom to go where one chose if one was held back by one's color? No, I preferred the Eiffel Tower, which made no promises. I had sworn to myself that I would see it one day."

Caroline Dudley Reagan's troupe of twenty-five African American dancers, singers, and jazz musicians, which she christened La Revue Nègre, set sail from New York for Paris on September 16, 1925, aboard the SS *Berengaria*. During the crossing, Baker performed for the first-class passengers and struck up a friendship with Sidney Bechet, who was also traveling to France with the revue. When the ship landed in the French port of Cherbourg, a train whisked the players to Paris; there they were met by Andre Daven, the director of the Theatre des Champs-Elysées, where their show was scheduled to open on October 2. Daven took them straight from the train station to the theater and immediately began rehearsing them for their upcoming performance.

For the next ten days, the group worked frenetically to prepare for opening night. The French producer, Jacques Charles, made key changes in order to ensure the show's Parisian success, and most of these involved expanding Baker's role. Charles invented a new, more "African," dance routine, the Danse Sauvage, featuring a scantily clad Baker and a male partner, Joe Alex, gyrating to the rhythms of the jungle, bringing the show in line with French stereotypes of blacks. By opening night Baker had replaced the singer Maud de Forrest, the ostensible star, as its true main act. Publicity, especially posters by the soon-to-be-famous illustrator Paul Colin, focused on Baker as a symbol of torrid, exotic black sexuality.

On opening night, Josephine Baker more than lived up to these expectations. That night the Revue Nègre created perhaps the greatest theatrical sensation in Paris since the premiere of Stravinsky's *Rite of Spring*. Playing before a packed house featuring artistic luminaries like Darius Milhaud and Jean Cocteau, the performers sang and danced in a series of theatrical sketches. But the high point of the show was clearly Baker's performance in the Danse Sauvage. Dressed only in feathers, and nude from the waist up, she shimmied energetically and provocatively before a French audience stupefied by her overt sexuality. Many applauded, some booed, some even walked out, but no one present that night failed to take notice of the young American dancer. Janet Flanner later summed up the general reaction of those who witnessed Josephine Baker's Parisian debut:

> She made her entry entirely nude except for a pink flamingo feather between her limbs; she was being carried upside down and doing the split on the shoulder of a black giant. Midstage, he paused, and with his long fingers holding her basket-wise around the waist, swung her in a slow cartwheel to the stage floor, where she stood like his magnificent discarded burden, in an instant of complete silence. She was an unforgettable female ebony statue. A scream of salutation spread through the theater. Whatever happened next was unimportant. The two specific elements had been established and were unforgettable — her magnificent dark body, a new model that to the French proved for the first time that black was beautiful, and the acute response of the white masculine public in the capital of hedonism of all Europe — Paris. Within a half hour of the final curtain on opening night, the news and meaning of her arrival had spread by the grapevine up to the cafes on the Champs Elysees, where the witnesses of her triumph sat over their drinks excitedly repeating

their report of what they had just seen — themselves unsatiated in the retell-
ing, the listeners hungry for further fantastic truths. . . . She was the established
new American star for Europe.

October 2, 1925, was a stunning personal triumph for Josephine Baker. It
made her the toast of Paris, giving her a regal presence on the stages of the city
which would endure for half a century. But the significance of Baker's debut
extended far beyond her personal career. It also marked a new stage in the
history of the African American community in Paris. Other black Americans
had received acclaim in Paris before Josephine Baker; in 1867 the great actor
Ira Aldridge won rave reviews for his performances at the Odéon Theater. But
none had ever received the kind of attention from the French which Baker
won. Moreover, Josephine Baker scored her triumph not just as a talented
performer, but also as a representative of the black aesthetic. While the Danse
Sauvage owed far more to French exotic fantasies than to African culture,
Baker's performance was steeped in the traditions of African American jazz
and vaudeville. As a result, her success was a success for the black Americans
of Paris as a whole. The debut of the Revue Nègre symbolized the spirit of the
age in the French capital. The Jazz Age reigned in Paris, and the African
American performer served as its Pied Piper.

For Josephine Baker, the 1920s in Paris was truly a golden era. The Revue
Nègre played to enthusiastic Parisian audiences for two months, afterward
leaving for a tour of Europe. Baker particularly liked Berlin, which at the time
played decadent host to the wildest nightlife on the Continent, but was lured
back to Paris by a contract to perform at the Folies-Bergère. This venerable
music hall occupied a central place among the concert stages of the city, and
it gave her the chance to go beyond her temporary success and achieve a
lasting position as a Parisian star. In the summer of 1926, Baker debuted at the
Folies-Bergère in a show entitled La Folie du Jour, in which she again portrayed a genial, uninhibited savage. For the first time, she wore the skirt made
of bananas that became her trademark. A perfect symbol of both sexuality and
primitivism, the banana skirt accentuated rather than masked her splendid
nudity, bouncing wildly as she danced across the stage. Although the show in
general received mixed reviews, everyone loved her performance. The Revue
Nègre may have introduced her to France, but it was the Folies-Bergère that
made her a star. By the end of the year the little black girl from Saint Louis
had been transformed into a glamorous queen, draped in jewels and furs,
wearing opulent dresses created by the leading designer Paul Poiret. She
developed a flair for public presentation, by day strolling the boulevards with

her pet leopard, Chiquita, by night being chauffeured in a snakeskin-uphol-
stered limousine from one lavish party to the next. Frenchwomen bought her
trademark hair cream, Bakerfix, to help imitate Josephine Baker's slicked-
down coiffure. Tanned skin became fashionable in the English Channel
resort of Deauville for women envious of Baker's café-au-lait shading.

Josephine Baker soon established contacts with other black American performers in the city. She became friends with Bricktop, who remembered her
as enormously talented but very young and naive. In the fall of 1926, the
Imperial, a Montmartre nightclub on the other side of the rue Pigalle from Le
Grand Duc, hired Baker to perform, hoping to compete with Bricktop's
success. The two great *chanteuses* remained friends, however, as there was
more than enough business in Montmartre to support both of them, and
Baker frequently visited Le Grand Duc after her own performances. There
she met and fell in love with Giuseppe Abatino, an Italian gigolo and self-proclaimed count who she fondly called Pepito. Pepito had plenty of business
acumen and contacts, and he used both to promote Baker's career. In December 1926, she opened her own nightclub, Chez Josephine, in Montmartre. It
was an instant hit, welcoming members of both the African American community and the doyens of Parisian nightlife. The French journalist Pierre
Coiselet described it early in 1927: "Midnight. A sea of bare shoulders and
dinner jackets in a red, cream and gold décor. Pearls and ear-rings out of an
Arabian Night . . . drinking, eating. There is an air of despair: the flesh is
weak. Jazz music howls and wails. . . . All of a sudden something shimmers
through the room. Applause, shouts, commotion: Joséphine Baker has just
made her entrance."

Yet Pepito's ambitions for Baker went beyond the world of the Montmartre
nightclub. As her manager, he did everything possible to earn her publicity. In
1927 he secured leading roles for Josephine Baker in two French movies,
probably the first time in film history that an African American starred in a
white production. That year Baker also published her memoirs, at the age
of twenty-one. Most spectacularly, Pepito informed the press that he and
Josephine Baker had married, prompting a spate of stories in both France and
America dramatizing the union between an Italian count and the descendant
of black slaves. The fact that Pepito was no real count and the marriage never
actually took place did not detract from the value of the publicity stunt.

Josephine Baker's absence from Paris during much of 1928 and 1929, when
she toured Europe and South America, did nothing to reduce her popularity
in the French capital. Artists like Tsuguharu Foujita and Georges Rouault
painted her, while Alexander Calder's wire mobiles and sculptures brought

her dancing form to life. The famous Viennese architect Adolf Loos offered to build her a house in Paris after she taught him to do the Charleston at Chez Josephine. Gertrude Stein, leader of the white American expatriate community in Paris, also wrote about her, while Stein's celebrated lover, Alice B. Toklas, even invented a dessert named Custard Josephine Baker, featuring bananas.

Baker's return to Paris at the end of the decade brought her greater acclaim than ever before. She became the intimate of some of the leading lights of French society, including members of the titled nobility like the Countess de la Rochefoucauld, the Countess de Noailles, and the Baroness de Rothschild. The poet Jean Cocteau dedicated a verse to her. Josephine Baker was now a seasoned performer with a fluent command of the French language. During the 1930s she would continue to grow as a performer, winning even more praise and fame. In the 1920s she had burst into the French consciousness as a dancing symbol of exotic sexuality. In the new decade she would become known simply as a great star, the leading lady of the Paris music hall.

THE HARLEM RENAISSANCE OVERSEAS

For most observers of interwar Paris, French and American alike, Josephine Baker and other performers symbolized the African American experience in the French capital. Leading a glamorous and adventurous life, frequently lionized by their audiences, these black expatriates represented both the beauty of black culture and the ability of African Americans to transcend the narrow limits imposed by American racism. Never before had freedom seemed so elegant. Yet not all black Americans who came to Paris in the 1920s worked as performers. The community of black expatriates in the city included artists, writers, students, scholars, and athletes as well as jazz musicians and performers. Representing the many different sides of black life in America, these African Americans abroad carved out their own diverse spheres in Paris. Learning to adapt to a foreign land, and the exhilarating escape from racial oppression, gave all of their lives in the City of Light a common theme, however, forging many disparate experiences in a unified community.

Within this community, writers played an important role. Long before the 1920s, Paris had beckoned African American novelists, poets, and playwrights. During the early nineteenth century, a Paris-educated Creole, Armand Lanusse, had organized in New Orleans America's first black literary society, Les Cenelles. Many young Creoles with literary aspirations sailed to Paris to pursue studies forbidden people of color in Louisiana. Alexandre Dumas was well known among African Americans as a great black author adored by the people of France. Black writers who left America for France after World War I thus continued a long tradition. Like the white expatriates who colonized the Left Bank in the 1920s, they were drawn by the impressive literary heritage of the French. Unlike them, black American authors also came in search of the legendary color-blind France, a nation whose brilliance proved that racism was the enemy of culture. As with black music, Paris in the 1920s became a place where the best and the brightest African American writers came to improve their literary craft. Writers did not receive the fame, let alone the salaries, enjoyed by people like Josephine Baker in Paris. None settled permanently in the city, usually spending only a summer or a year away from home. Yet they became the main chroniclers of black life in Paris, shaping the perceptions both of members of this community and of the general black community in America.

For African American authors, the 1920s were above all the decade of the Harlem Renaissance, the literary movement that constituted a landmark in black letters. Many of these writers spent time in Paris during the 1920s. Langston Hughes and Claude McKay, two of the leading figures of the Harlem Renaissance, both lived there and wrote about the experience. In February 1924, Langston Hughes arrived in Paris at the age of twenty-two, having worked his way across the Atlantic from New York on a freighter. The young man, already a published poet, had been interested in French literature ever since reading de Maupassant in the original as a high school student. The adventurous spirit that would later carry Hughes around the world brought him to Paris on a cold winter's day. He was determined to stay even though he had only $7 in his pocket and no prospects for a job. His first reactions to the city were those of any first-time tourist:

I recognized the Champs Elysées, and the great Arc de Triomphe in the distance through the snow.

Boy, was I thrilled! I was torn between walking up the Champs Elysées or down along the Seine, past the Tuileries. Finally, I took the river, hoping to see the bookstalls and Notre Dame. But I ended up in the Louvre instead, looking at Venus.

It was warmer in the Louvre than in the street, and the Greek statues were calm and friendly. I said to the statues: "If you can stay in Paris as long as you've been here and still look O.K., I guess I can stay a while with seven dollars and make a go of it."

The glamour of the French capital could not long forestall the realities of cold, fatigue, and hunger, however, so Hughes soon began looking for a place to stay, as well as for someone to talk to. He soon found his way to Montmartre, spending the spring and summer of 1924 in the heart of the black American community in Paris. In his autobiography *The Big Sea*, Hughes gives one of the best descriptions available of black Montmartre in the 1920s. As he soon found out, while the community did not exactly embrace young poets with open arms, it did provide ways of staying in Paris.

When Hughes first arrived in Montmartre he met several black musicians who immediately threw cold water on his dreams of finding a job in the city. One told him, "'You must be crazy, boy. . . . There ain't no "any kind of a job" here. There're plenty of French people for ordinary work. 'Less you can play jazz or tap dance, you'd just as well go back home.'" After his initial job inquiries brought out the truth of these words, Hughes spent his next few days in Paris desperately trying to stretch his $7 as far as possible. A White Russian dancer named Sonya shared a tiny room with him for 50 francs a week, showed him how to live on bread and cheese once a day, and even helped support him after she'd found a job as a taxi dancer at Zelli's nightclub. After a month of this picturesque poverty, Langston Hughes managed to land a job as a doorman at a small nightclub in the rue Fontaine, which paid him 5 francs and dinner for a night's work.

The job introduced Hughes to the world of Montmartre nightlife at its seamiest. Not only was the salary derisory, but the proprietress expected him to break up the violent fights that frequently broke out between patrons. Fortunately he soon found a much better job, thanks to a tip from Rayford Logan, who told Hughes that Le Grand Duc needed a second cook. "Second cook" really meant busboy, but the job paid 15 francs a night plus breakfast, enough to live on.

More than his salary, Le Grand Duc gave the young writer a box seat at the spectacle of black expatriate life. He met Florence Jones, the first real African American diva in Paris, and helped dry Bricktop's tears after her first glimpse of the small nightclub. He saw his share of wealthy and famous white patrons as well as knock-down-drag-out bar fights. As with Hemingway, Paris in the 1920s offered Hughes a dazzling panorama of experiences. He got to see springtime in Paris, write poetry in a garret, and drink champagne for breakfast. He met other writers, notably Alain Locke, who visited Paris that summer, and fell in love with a young black woman from England, Anne Coussey. Hughes left Paris at the end of July, not to return for many years, but the city remained dear to his heart and inspired several of his future literary efforts.

The cream of the Negro musicians then in France, like Cricket Smith on the trumpet, Louis Jones on the violin, Palmer Jones at the piano, Frank Withers on the clarinet, and Buddy Gilmore at the drums, would weave out music that would almost make your heart stand still at dawn in a Paris night club in the rue Pigalle, when most of the guests were gone and you were washing the last pots and pans in a two-by-four kitchen, with the fire in the range dying and the one high window letting the soft dawn in.

Blues in the rue Pigalle. Black and laughing, heart-breaking blues in the Paris dawn, pounding like a pulse-beat, moving like the Mississippi!

Like Langston Hughes, Claude McKay lived in Paris during the mid-1920s, spending several years in France as a whole. Yet he experienced the city very differently from Hughes, developing a much more critical attitude. Born in Jamaica, McKay had immigrated to the United States in 1912, at the age of twenty-two, moving to New York two years later. During the war, he wrote poetry profusely, publishing important verses like "Harlem Shadows" (1917) and "If We Must Die" (1919). Key both to McKay's writings and his life as a whole was his political radicalism. His socialist convictions led him to write about the "proletarian" side of Harlem life, the masses of ordinary black people as opposed to the "talented tenth," the highly educated black elite whom W.E.B. Du Bois believed would lead the race to freedom. They also led him into alliances with white radicals in New York, most notably Max Eastman, whose journal *The Liberator* published some of his poetry. More than most black intellectuals in New York, therefore, Claude McKay served as a bridge between the Harlem Renaissance and the literary politics of Greenwich Village.

Claude McKay first came to Paris in the summer of 1923. The previous year he had left New York for a visit to the Soviet Union, eager to see the new symbol of world revolution. McKay spent a year there, impressed by the revolutionary ardor of Russian workers but disturbed by indications of intolerance and dogmatism. He arrived in Paris on his return from the USSR, and chose to spend most of the next ten years in France. Yet unlike Josephine Baker, Langston Hughes, or most of the African Americans who settled in Paris during the 1920s, McKay manifested no great enthusiasm for the city. A seasoned traveler who had spent the majority of his life outside America, Claude McKay did not find the relatively benign racial attitudes of the French so unusual; he had become accustomed to equal treatment in Russia. For him Paris was just one more place of exile; a very pleasant place in many ways, but by no means Paradise Found.

I never thought there was anything worth while for me in the bohemian glamor of Montparnasse. "The sidewalk cafés of Montmartre" held no special attraction for me. Attractive as Paris is, I have never stayed there for a considerable length of time . . . Montmartre I visited when I was invited by generous Americans who had money to treat themselves and their friends to a hectic time. The Montmartre of the cabarets and music halls never excited me. It is so obviously a place where the very formal French allow foreigners who can pay to cut up informally. It has no character of its own. . . . I appreciated, but was not specially enamored of Paris. . . . If I had to live in France, I would prefer life among the fisherfolk of Douarnenez, or in the city of Strassburg, or in sinister Marseilles.

Claude McKay spent much of his first visit to Paris in a hospital recovering from an illness he had contracted in Russia. Upon regaining his health, McKay began working as an artists' model, posing nude before painters in Left Bank studios. Since these rooms were usually poorly heated he soon came down with pneumonia. Friends discovered him shivering and penniless in a shabby hotel room, prompting Louise Bryant, a white radical journalist from Greenwich Village and the widow of John Reed, to send McKay to the south of France for three months to convalesce. More than other black Americans in Paris, Claude McKay got to experience life in the French provinces, and all in all he preferred the hinterland to Paris. He fell in love with the beautiful scenery and friendly inhabitants of Provence, and found the rough-and-tumble waterfront of Marseilles more to his taste than the sophisticated world of Parisian artists and intellectuals.

Yet for all the charm of regions like Provence and Brittany, the action was in Paris, so McKay returned at the end of 1923. Older and more established as a writer than Langston Hughes, Claude McKay was able to make contact with the American expatriate elite in the city. Whereas Hughes discovered a Parisian Harlem in Montmartre, McKay found Montparnasse to be very reminiscent of Greenwich Village. Yet he never felt completely at home in either Montmartre or Montparnasse, and soon left Paris for the sunny skies of the Riviera.

Langston Hughes and Claude McKay thus developed two starkly opposite images of Paris. McKay's viewpoint was the more exceptional of the two, for most black writers who came to Paris in the 1920s concurred with Hughes's glowing portrait of the city and the French people. So many visited Paris that at times it seemed that the entire Harlem Renaissance had transferred its seat of operations overseas. Countee Cullen, one of Harlem's most important young poets, first visited France for a few weeks in the summer of 1926. Traveling in the company of Alain Locke and several other companions, Cullen saw the sights of the city and tried, unsuccessfully, to meet René Maran. In 1928, Cullen returned to spend a year writing in Paris, having won a Guggenheim fellowship to support his studies. Settling into an apartment on the Left Bank, he wrote poetry, studied French, and occasionally traveled around Europe. Paris left a lasting impression on the young writer: he wrote poems about his love for France and returned frequently in the 1930s, at one point declaring, "Paris is where I would love to build my castles in Spain." Walter White visited Paris briefly in the summer of 1927, making contacts that resulted in the publication of a French translation of his novel, *Fire in the Flint*. He then moved on to the Riviera, where he spent time working on his study of lynchings in America, *Rope and Faggot*. Jean Toomer, the author of *Cane*, one of the major books of the Harlem Renaissance, went to France during the mid-1920s to study with the Russian mystic Gurdjieff at his institute in Fontainebleau, near Paris.

Women writers played a major role in the Harlem Renaissance, and many of them also spent time in the French capital. The novelist Jessie Fauset lived in Paris for several months during 1924 and 1925, and several of her novels, notably *Plum Bun, Comedy American Style*, and *There Is Confusion*, feature scenes of African American life in Paris. Nella Larsen traveled throughout Europe on a Guggenheim fellowship in the early 1930s. She visited Paris in the summer of 1931, seeing Josephine Baker perform and meeting many black expatriates. Gwendolyn Bennett, a young poet and professor of art at Howard University, learned perhaps the most from her sojourn in the French capital. In 1925, she received a $1,000 fellowship from the sorority Sigma Alpha Theta to study in Paris. Arriving there in June, Bennett stayed in the city for a year, recording her observations in a journal that provides an important glimpse of Parisian black expatriate life in the 1920s.

In some ways, Gwendolyn Bennett's Paris was worlds removed from the wealthy, glamorous existence of a Josephine Baker. Bennett had little money and she spent many of her days painting and writing poetry. She often felt homesick and isolated in a strange foreign city. On June 26, 1925, she wrote in her diary, "For two days now it has rained . . . A cold rain that eats into the very marrow of the bone . . . and I am alone and more homesick than I ever believed it possible to be." Yet her journal shows that she actually met many people in Paris, including Gertrude Stein, and carved out a place for herself in the African American community. Two days later she wrote, "There never was a more beautiful city than Paris . . . there couldn't be! On every hand are works of art and beautiful vistas . . . one has the impression of looking through at fairy-worlds as one sees gorgeous buildings, arches and towers rising from among mounds of trees from afar."

Bennett saw Josephine Baker perform in the Revue Nègre, met the actor and singer Paul Robeson and René Maran, and danced the night away at Bricktop's. She dated Louis Jones, a violinist working at Chez Florence who later became a professor of music at Howard University, and met many other black musicians in Montmartre. On August 8, 1925, Gwendolyn Bennett described a night on the town that summed up all the carefree joy of black Montmartre and Paris in the 1920s. The party began at a Chinese restaurant in the Latin Quarter, moving on to Montmartre at 1:45 in the morning.

> Thence to "Le Royal" in Montmartre. There much champaign [sic] and many cigarettes and much dancing. I get, in thinking back, a vivid impression of one or two very drunken women and hard, hard faces. . . . For one "charming" moment Louis [Jones] rushed up from "Florence's" to dance but one dance. Then at 4:15 A.M. to dear old "Bricktop's." The Grand Duc extremely crowded this night with our folk. . . . "Brick" singing as well as ever her hits — "Insufficient Sweetie" and "I'm In Love Again" . . . Louis dances with me one very lovely dance during . . . which "Brick" and everybody teases him about how happy he is to have his little brown skin in his arms . . . and he calling me "little lady" and grinning from ear to ear.
>
> And always the inevitable "Hot Cakes and Sausages" at "the Duc" — Home at 6:30 in the lovely grey morning light.
>
> I shall never quite forget the shock of beauty that I got when the door was opened at "Brick's" and as we stepped out into the early morning streets . . . looking up Rue Pigalle there stood Sacred Heart . . . beautiful, pearly Sacre-Coeur as though its silent loveliness were pointing a white finger at our night's debauchery. I wished then that so worthy an emotion as I felt might have been caught forever in a poem.

After her year in Paris, Gwendolyn Bennett returned to New York. She never lived in France again, but in short stories like "Wedding Day" and "Tokens," Bennett paid tribute to her Parisian idyll.

Paris thus definitely had an impact on the most important African American writers of the 1920s. Many of them drew inspiration from its historical monuments, its literary traditions, and its atmosphere of excitement, innovation, and racial tolerance. Yet none settled there permanently, and they did not create a literary expatriate community comparable to the white Americans of the Lost Generation. Not until the 1950s would such a group of African American writers take root in Paris. However, writers like Langston Hughes and Gwendolyn Bennett breathed new life into the idea that black writers should travel abroad to expand their literary horizons. The French capital became for them an extension of the Harlem Renaissance, a place where one could spend the summer or, if lucky enough to receive a fellowship, live for a year or two. There one could enjoy much of Harlem's literary camaraderie without encountering the racism that made it a ghetto. In both their fiction and prose these writers created an image of black Paris that would inspire other African Americans to make their own pilgrimages to the City of Light.

More than music, literature, or any other art form, painting and sculpture symbolized French creative genius in the interwar years. Paris reigned supreme as the center of modern art, and young artists from around the world flocked to the city. In the late nineteenth century, painters like Paul Cézanne, Vincent van Gogh, and Claude Monet had created a revolutionary new artistic movement, impressionism. By the 1920s, cubism and especially dadaism and surrealism dominated the avant-garde art world of Paris. The center of this world had migrated from Montmartre to the Left Bank, where Pablo Picasso, Salvador Dalí, Jean Arp, and Joan Miró lived and worked. The Ecole des Beaux Arts still brought students from all parts of the globe to learn the techniques of painting and sculpture in a city that was itself a work of art.

American artists had been coming to Paris to refine their craft since the early nineteenth century, and many young Americans continued this tradition in the 1920s. Man Ray, Alexander Calder, Jo Davidson, and Jules Pascin were only some of the better-known white artists to settle in Paris during these years. Yet Paris beckoned to African American artists as well, and the interwar years witnessed one of the high points of black expatriate artistic endeavor. Like the black American writers in Paris, they came both to learn at the feet of the French masters and to escape American racism. They also served as chroniclers of African American community life in Paris, in the process producing artistic works of enduring value.

During the 1920s Henry Ossawa Tanner remained by far the most important black American artist living in the French capital. He was now a very well established painter with a prestigious and growing reputation on both sides of the Atlantic. In 1922, blacks in Washington, D.C., set up a Tanner Art League, while a year later the French government granted him the Cross of the Legion of Honor, one of its top awards, in recognition of his artistic merit and numerous exhibits in France. Yet although Tanner continued to paint after the end of the First World War, he had clearly done his best work earlier. He still worked in his studio on the boulevard Saint-Jacques, but produced relatively little. Moreover, he failed to keep up with current artistic trends, and art critics began to comment on the conservatism of his style. Personal tragedies, including the deaths of his father and his wife, haunted Henry Tanner during these years, making it more and more difficult for him to pursue his art. Yet even in this period of decline, Henry Ossawa Tanner remained not only the preeminent black American artist in Paris, but one of the most important African Americans in the city. His fame in both Paris and New York, as well as the encouragement he gave to younger artists, was fundamental in attracting a new group of African American painters and sculptors to Paris during the 1920s.

Twelve black American artists of note, including Palmer Hayden, Augusta Savage, Aaron Douglas, William Johnson, and Hale Woodruff, crossed the Atlantic to study in France during these years. Unlike many of their white colleagues, few had much money to support their studies and thus had to obtain subsidies from charitable organizations and other groups. The Harmon Foundation, established in 1922 to aid black artists, helped pay for the travels of Hale Woodruff and Palmer Hayden in 1926, the Guggenheim Foundation gave the painter Archibald Motley a one-year fellowship, and the Carnegie Corporation subsidized both Augusta Savage and Nancy Elizabeth Prophet. Once in Paris, several of these artists chose to enroll in French art schools, such as the Julian Academy or the Académie de la Grande Chaumière, while others preferred to work on their own, visiting the capital's great museums or sketching scenes from its lively street life.

The African American artists who lived in Paris during the 1920s were a diverse group, and their paintings and sculptures testified to many different interests and influences. Several chose to paint Parisian landmarks, both out of interest and because such paintings sold well to Americans. Hale Woodruff's 1928 painting *Chartres* is a good example of this genre. Other painters, notably Palmer Hayden and Archibald Motley, chose to depict the life of Parisian jazz clubs. *Bal Jeunesse*, completed by Hayden in 1927, gives a vivid portrayal of black dancers and musicians swept up in the rhythms of the night.

More than just a source of new subject matter, however, Paris also exposed these artists to new styles, both European and African. Much of their work betrays a strong cubist influence, for example. Artists like Woodruff consciously looked to Picasso and Cézanne. Exposure to African art had an even greater impact on black American artists. African sculpture in particular was very popular in Paris during the 1920s, and its vital role in the development of cubism is well known. African American artists were very conscious of the African inspiration of cubism, and several used their time in France to become better acquainted with African art, integrating some of its themes into their own work. Life in Paris put African Americans in touch with the leaders of the art world as well as their own artistic heritage. The city also granted them the kind of recognition rarely granted to black artists in white America.

Works by Prophet, Savage, Woodruff, and Hayden were all exhibited by Parisian galleries during the 1920s. Prophet achieved the greatest success; her sculptures were featured in one of the city's top salons, the Salon d'Automne, from 1924 through 1927. Paradoxically but not atypically, their success in Paris paved the way for greater acknowledgment in the United States. At the end of the decade, several of these artists won prizes for their work in the annual exhibitions of black art sponsored by the Harmon Foundation in New York.

Painters and sculptors formed an integral part of the African American community in Paris during the 1920s. Henry Tanner met many black visitors to the city, taking a particular interest in the activities of younger expatriate artists. Palmer Hayden, Augusta Savage, and several others met the great painter, receiving advice and the benefit of his personal contacts. The black journalist and historian J. A. Rogers described a party given for Nancy Elizabeth Prophet by Countee Cullen, noting that "French artists and critics say that Elizabeth Phophit [*sic*] is the only artist of our group here doing great work." These artists did not exclusively associate with one another, and their many aesthetic differences prevented the emergence of any coherent Paris school of African American art. Yet they did know one another and help one another out on occasion. For example, Palmer Hayden helped Hale Woodruff find a place to live in Paris, and Augusta Savage took over Nancy Prophet's studio in the rue Broca on the Left Bank. Many, such as William Johnson, Aaron Douglas, Hayden, Woodruff, and Savage often visited each other and dined together. Moreover, they generally met most of the other African Americans living in or passing through the French capital. Hale Woodruff later noted, "During those years in Paris, I knew people like Eric Walrond, the writer, Claude McKay, the poet, Augusta Savage, the sculptor, Walter White of the NAACP, Alain Locke, philosopher and art critic. These and many others made up what was known as the 'Negro colony' in Paris which included the 'whirlwind' Josephine Baker, who had just come from the U.S. with a musical troupe called the Black Birds."

Throughout the twentieth century, many American artists, both black and white, have dreamed of making the pilgrimage to Paris, capital of the art world. Racism made it impossible for all but a handful of African Americans to realize this dream in the 1920s, but those fortunate enough to do so benefited enormously from the experience. Paris opened their eyes to many new artistic possibilities, giving them new confidence in the value of their work. In addition, the prestige of having studied in the world's art capital enabled them to play leading roles in America's black art world upon their return. Most of these artists studied in Parisian art schools and in general were more integrated into French life than most African Americans in Paris; their frequent choice of French landscapes and other subject matter reflects this primary interest in their host country. Similar to their literary colleagues, most black artists spent only a year or two in France, temporarily drawing upon the many resources offered by the French capital before returning home to renew contact with black America, their home and ultimate source of inspiration. Like African American writers, however, these painters and sculptors did find that even on the other side of the Atlantic, black culture had established a foothold.

Although most African Americans in Paris during the 1920s worked as musicians, writers, and artists, others came to the City of Light who did not fit into any of these categories but nonetheless participated in the life of the community. Businessmen, scholars, athletes, tourists, and adventurers all came to taste life in the French capital, and while for some the experience was a brief and pleasant interlude, others stayed for a more extended period of time. Not all became famous or even successful, but most learned to appreciate the freedom that came from escaping the constrained role imposed upon blacks by American society at the time.

The story of Anna Julia Cooper graphically illustrates the contrast between the United States and Paris for black Americans. Born in Raleigh, North Carolina, shortly before the end of slavery, Cooper was able to secure an education thanks to the greater opportunities open to blacks during the Reconstruction era. Excelling at her studies, she graduated from Oberlin College in 1884 and embarked upon a long and successful teaching career at both the high school and college levels. Anna Julia Cooper made her first trip to Europe in 1900, and returned to Paris to study several times in the years before World War I. Her work there enabled her to enroll as a doctoral student at Columbia University in 1914. In the early twenties, after several years of balancing education and teaching commitments, not to mention the care of her family of five children, Cooper decided to transfer her studies to the University of Paris. She moved to Paris and enrolled in the great institution in 1924, choosing as a dissertation subject "The Attitude of France on the Question of Slavery between 1789 and 1848." Cooper spent the next year researching her thesis in both France and the United States, and on March 23, 1925, after a three-hour formal defense, this woman who had been born in slavery became the first African American to win a doctorate from the Sorbonne. In fact, Anna Julia Cooper was only the fourth black woman in American history to receive a Ph.D. from any institution. When the diploma was formally presented to Cooper in a ceremony at Howard University that December, she responded by accepting it "not as a symbol of cold intellectual success in my achievement at the Sorbonne, but with the warm pulsing heart throbs of a people's satisfaction in my humble efforts to serve them."

"Panama" Al Brown provided an entirely different model of black culture and achievement in Paris during the 1920s. A native of Panama, Alfonso Brown had immigrated to the United States as a young man hoping to win fame and success as a boxer. Settling in Harlem in the early 1920s, Brown established a solid record of victories as a welterweight, but found that in the United States his options as a black boxer were limited because the leading white fighters would not agree to meet him in the ring. In particular, the rise and fall of the great black pugilist Jack Johnson convinced him to seek opportunities elsewhere. Thanks to his friendship with a French restaurant owner and ex-boxer in New York, Brown was invited to fight in Paris in 1926. He jumped at the chance, setting sail for France that fall, arriving in Le Havre after a sea voyage of six days. Brown later said, "In New York I had spent my first night in Harlem; in Paris I spent my first night in Montmartre. In all those nightclubs where now everyone is my friend I went from discovery to discovery. Everywhere I encountered the same warm, smiling welcome, the same excellent champagne . . . everywhere my checkered cap, my light beige suit, and my suede shoes made a sensation."

In France, Panama Al Brown fought under the sponsorship of a young white American from Mississippi, Jeff Dickson, who managed several boxers in Paris. He registered an auspicious debut in the city's Wagram Hall on November 10, 1926, when he knocked out a boxer from Marseilles in the third round. Although at first many French fans simply regarded Brown as another American curiosity, he soon won acclaim for his quick, dazzling boxing style. Within his first year in Paris, he had fought and won several fights, even scoring a draw against the welterweight champion of Europe, Henri Scillie of Belgium. As a result Brown found himself lionized as the new star of the Paris boxing world. His fights attracted huge crowds and earned record purses. The great French actor Maurice Chevalier insisted on posing with Brown for publicity photos. The young boxer had clearly come a long way from the streets of Harlem.

Panama Al Brown dazzled Parisians as much with his extravagant lifestyle as with his pugilistic skills. He dressed elegantly, frequenting the best tailors in London and at times changing clothes six times a day. In defiance of his training regimen, he stayed out all night at jazz clubs, often traveling to Deauville and the Riviera to gamble away thousands of francs. After winning one fight, Brown spent his earnings on a fancy new Bugatti racing car. When it blew up on its maiden drive in the Bois de Boulogne, Brown immediately went back to Bugatti and bought another one, pledging the winnings from his next fight as payment. This kind of devil-may-care extravagance perfectly fit the atmosphere of Jazz Age Paris; Brown once proclaimed that "all I need to live is 20,000 bottles of champagne." Moreover, Brown's grace and elegant demeanour, as well as his strength and speed inside the ring, corresponded to French primitivist images of the black man. A male Josephine Baker, Panama Al Brown charmed Parisians as a symbol of the power and beauty of black masculinity.

Anna Julia Cooper and Panama Al Brown represented two extremes of African American life in Paris during the 1920s. At first glance, one might find little in common between the cultivated historian and the flamboyant boxer. Yet both Cooper and Brown had experienced racism in the United States, and had discovered in Paris a warm, accepting, and color-blind milieu. In very different fields, both achieved the kind of success and recognition usually denied African Americans. Paris both facilitated and witnessed their triumphs, confirming in the minds of many African Americans its reputation for sophistication, tolerance, and generosity toward people of color.

IMAGES OF RACE IN JAZZ AGE PARIS

The African American community in Paris was tiny and cohesive, but not isolated. Blacks in France interacted with the wider white world to a much greater extent than in the United States. Therefore Parisians as a whole were fully aware of this explosion of black talent in the 1920s, labeling it *le tumulte noir*. What did the French think of these newcomers from a distant shore? The primitivist vogue so popular at the time shaped the reactions of many Parisians to the black Americans in their midst, making them objects of curiosity and fascination. Yet in general African Americans encountered a warm and tolerant reception in Paris, further confirming their beliefs about the lack of racial prejudice in France.

Although French interest in primitivism antedated 1914, the impact of the war, providing living images of black people, vastly increased its appeal. By 1917, the poet Guillaume Apollinaire was able to write that the prewar "melanophilia" had become a veritable "melanomania." Many of the nation's leading intellectuals echoed his own interest in blackness. Fellow author Blaise Cendrars would spend much of the interwar years traveling throughout the black world, from Senegal to Harlem to Bahia. Dadaism, the precursor of surrealism, led by the Rumanian writer Tristan Tzara, embraced black imagery from the outset. In Zurich in 1916, the young cultural revolutionaries staged several *soirées nègres*, public theatrical events that prominently displayed blacks as comic figures in a critique of European racism and Western civilization in general. When Tzara brought dadaism to Paris in 1920, he and others continued this practice there. In March 1920, for example, a play by Georges Ribemont-Dessaignes featured a black character posing as the famous French composer Gounod.

For most Parisians in the 1920s, black Americans meant entertainers. Few came into direct contact with the black artists, writers, or students who also lived in the city, and fewer still knew much about these aspects of African American life. Black Americans were those people who put the jazz into the Jazz Age, and this new music received a generally favorable reception. Not everyone in Paris liked jazz; many older Parisians in particular saw it as decadent, barbaric, even pornographic. The city still retained many traditional dance halls, where one could sway to French melodies played on the violin and accordion. And in 1927, one French doctor warned that dances like the Charleston and the Black Bottom could be dangerous to the health of young expectant mothers. Such a claim drew significance not so much from the prospect of hordes of pregnant Parisians dancing to jazz bands, but rather from the link it established between jazz and the nation's declining birthrate that so haunted conservative Frenchmen after World War I. In other words, jazz could imperil the condition of France as a whole.

Some Parisians, especially young people, ignored such warnings and embraced African American music. By the end of the 1920s, jazz had become the music of choice in many of the city's dance clubs. One French music critic even made the spurious claim that jazz was of French origin, deriving from ancient shepherd melodies taught to slaves in Louisiana by their French masters. Whatever the merits of such an idea, jazz did in return exercise a certain influence on contemporary French music. In 1923 the composer Darius Milhaud premiered a new ballet, *The Creation of the World*, which emphasized African legends and drew on jazz stylings. Maurice Ravel also found inspiration in the new sound; while a member of the Paris Symphony Orchestra, he took music lessons from the white American clarinetist Mezz Mezzrow. Many French intellectuals approached jazz with great respect, and have continued to do so to this day. The leading surrealist writer Louis Aragon claimed to be an intimate of Bricktop, and re-created scenes of Montmartre nightlife in his novel *Aurélien*.

Josephine Baker of course drew the strongest reactions from French observers. One correspondent for the newspaper *Paris-Midi* wrote an article on the Revue Nègre which summed up the feelings of many Parisians:

> everything we've ever read flashes across our enchanted minds: adventure novels, glimpses of enormous steamboats swallowing up clusters of Negroes . . . stories of missionaries and travelers, Stanley, the Tharaud brothers, Batouala, sacred dances . . . plantation landscapes, the melancholy songs of Creole nurses, the Negro soul with its animal energy, its childish joys, the sad bygone time of slavery, we had all that listening to the singer with the jungle voice, admiring Louis Douglas's hectic skill, the frenetic virtuosity of that dance with rubber legs, and the pretty coffee-colored ragamuffin who is the star of the troupe, Josephine Baker.

The music critic André Levinson, in general no fan of black art, praised Baker's "crazed body" and the "farouche and superb bestiality" of her dancing. Not all commentators approved of Baker's art, however, and her detractors expressed opinions every bit as violent as her supporters. In an article in *Le Figaro*, the eminent critic and playwright Robert de Flers called the Revue Nègre "the most direct assault ever perpetrated against French taste," adding for good measure that the show "makes us revert to the ape in less time than it took us to descend from it."

In general, the French strongly identified black Americans with Africa. Until World War I, Parisians knew much more about Africans than African Americans, thanks to their nation's colonial endeavors, so they simply tended to assimilate blacks from America into their preconceived ideas of blacks in general. The fact that Josephine Baker came from Saint Louis and had never set eyes on Africa did not prevent both her fans and foes in Paris from surrounding her with colonialist imagery. The assertion by many figures of the Harlem Renaissance that black Americans owed an aesthetic debt to Africa made perfect sense to both ordinary Parisians and avant-garde intellectuals, who often recognized no difference at all between the two peoples.

Paul Morand's *Magie Noire (Black Magic)* provides an excellent example of this phenomenon. The book, a popular exploration of black culture at the end of the 1920s, begins with a preface in which the author describes his travels in twenty-eight black lands over a thirty-year period. *Black Magic* itself consists of a series of short stories depicting black life all over the globe, from the Caribbean to Georgia to Upper Volta. In one story, a wealthy, young, light-skinned American woman named Pamela Freedman learns to rejoice in her black heritage after a cruise to the Ivory Coast: "She encountered in the heavy beat of the tom-tom the same torpor, the same ecstasy that she expected from jazz in Montmartre. . . . She had had enough of passing for white! Why should she take pride in progress borrowed from others? Her own progress consisted in embracing, in a surprising and harmonious union, her ancestral land." The story ends with Pamela throwing off her jewels, her clothes, and her westernized ideas to join in the savage dance of her people under moonlit African skies.

Paris appears frequently in Morand's chronicles of black life. In "Baton Rouge," he describes the Parisian adventures of an African American singer tellingly named Congo. A clear takeoff on Josephine Baker, Congo personifies black enthusiasm and sexuality. The story opens with a description of a ball staged by Congo in her sumptuous Left Bank mansion. Congo appears before crowds of her admirers in a rush of colors and gestures, leading them in a crazed dance all over the house: "this young witch pulverised the musical, sentimental, and political melodies of the whites, forcing them to return to the beginnings of the world, to the simplicity of the jungle. Under modern names like the fox-trot or the camel walk she imposed on them the old African totemic dances."

At the height of the festivities, however, Congo disappears, having fled the house in a panic after discovering a voodoo doll on her bed. Shortly thereafter she reappears at the apartment of an elderly black witch doctor, appealing for his aid in fighting off the voodoo curse. He leads her to the basement of a Montmartre jazz club, where, transformed into an African high priest, he leads a number of black worshippers in a ceremony to heal Congo by placing her in a trance.

"Baton Rouge" is an extraordinary juxtaposition of images from primitivist fantasies about black life. In Morand's fertile imagination a black dancer becomes a savage ultimately driven mad by civilization. A Montmartre nightclub is transformed into a temple where mystical African rituals, a veritable "Black Sabbath," take place. For French intellectuals in particular, African Americans became symbolic repositories of a wide range of stereotypes about black culture. Whereas the success of many black Americans in Paris during the 1920s ran counter to prejudices cherished by many white Americans, their achievements in music and dance served to confirm Parisian preconceptions. These stereotypes were not just the province of intellectuals, however. A 1919 music hall skit at the Casino de Montmartre demonstrated both French fascination with jazz and its basis in biased views of black life: jazz here is primitive music, deriving its seductive appeal from the rhythms of the jungle.

> In the most famous music halls
> They have been making unheard-of profits,
> Where one would expect to find funny comedians,

Beautiful music and young girls in tight skirts,
Instead, on the stage arrives, as the first act,
A dozen Negroes
These are musicians of whom one says
The poor guys have St. Vitus' dance
The public is stupefied,
In fact, brutalized (*abruti*)

To see this Negro
Who scrapes his banjo,
Or this one, who like a deaf man
Beats on his tom tom,
This sarabande that all demand
It is the jazz band
Oh yes, the jazz band
It's made me feel like dancing
Like the big Negro
The jazz band
Makes me want to let go

The point, however, is that these stereotypes were overwhelmingly positive. However demeaning they may seem from present-day perspectives, in the 1920s most black Americans in Paris welcomed and praised the racial attitudes of their French hosts. The French seemed to regard blackness as something of value, an attitude noticeably absent in the United States. One African American woman had the experience of going to a Parisian hair salon to get her hair straightened, only to have the *coiffeuse* curl it even more. The hairdresser simply didn't understand why black women wanted straight hair while all her white customers wanted to make theirs as curly as possible! Certainly by the end of the 1920s the public attitude of most Parisians toward black Americans took the form of friendly, if ignorant, curiosity, a vast improvement over the racial climate in the United States.

As proof of this difference, African Americans in Paris could point to French attitudes toward racist behavior exhibited by white Americans visiting the city. Josephine Baker tried to avoid her white countrymen in Paris, for fear of being insulted, and described an incident in a restaurant in which a white patron protested her presence, claiming that in the United States Baker would be in the kitchen. The proprietor responded by asking the white American woman to leave. On another occasion, a white American stormed out of her hotel after learning that a black woman was staying there, exclaiming, "I could never think of using the same bath as her." Responded the hotel owner, "What do you fear, madame, that the colored lady will stain the tub?" In 1923, several American tourists beat up a member of the royal family of Dahomey, Prince Kojo Touvalou Hovénou, in a Montmartre nightclub. The prince sued the club, and the courts ruled in his favor, shutting down the establishment and taking away its license. In response to this and other acts of violence perpetrated against blacks in Paris by American tourists, the French government banned showings of the racist American film *Birth of a Nation* later that year.

Parisian restaurants and nightclubs, especially those with a significant American clientele, sometimes collaborated with the color line. In 1929, the Coupole, famed Left Bank watering hole of the Lost Generation expatriates and familiar to many American tourists from the 1920s to the present, refused to admit Claude McKay because of his dark complexion. The café provoked a firestorm of indignation in the French press a few weeks later when it barred a Haitian diplomat and the wife of the crown prince of Egypt. At the initiative of a member of the French Parliament from Martinique, the government launched an inquiry, prompting the Coupole's owner to apologize for the incident. Gratien Candace, a black Frenchman and member of Parliament, commented on the increase of American-inspired racism in France:

> Recently I have received a very large number of complaints which seem to indicate that French justice is becoming tempered. The other day a negro who fought bravely for France during the war was thrown out of a dancing-place at Havre because this establishment was frequented by white Americans. I have called on the Minister of the Interior for an investigation.
>
> Several days before this incident a black man, who is a well-known doctor, and who fought during the war, went into a cafe in the Boulevard Montparnasse, which is frequented by Americans, and service was refused him. The proprietor told him that out of respect for his American clients he did not allow any black men in his place. The police had to inform the proprietor that on French soil blacks and whites were equal under French law, and the doctor got his drink.

Many have exaggerated the color blindness of the French, and it is quite possible that some restaurant and hotel owners used their white American customers to mask their own prejudices. Yet discrimination against African Americans in Paris did occur most often in areas of the city frequented by their white countrymen. Thousands of white American tourists came to Paris in the

1920s, bringing their racial biases with them. Given the importance of the dollars they spent to the city's tourist trade, Parisians involved in this industry were sorely tempted to conform to their desires. Yet many others condemned both the racism of white Americans and those French who allowed them to import discrimination. The Parisian columnist Georges de la Fouchardière satirically recommended ways of dealing with the problem:

> The Americans show themselves to be more savage than Robinson Crusoe, because Robinson had a negro in intimate companionship with him.
> Since the Americans are savages, it won't do to send them diplomatic notes that they don't understand. We must train them.
> At their debarkation in France we must put them under the subjection of negro customs officials, who will go through their baggage, and to negro conductors, who will punch their tickets on the train.
> In Paris we must form a brigade of negro cops, specially detailed to look out for Americans.

These reactions to white American racism vividly highlighted for many black Americans the absence of a color line in France. The African American press in the United States frequently commented on such incidents, further underscoring the belief in French tolerance among its readers. In the late 1920s, for example, the *Chicago Defender* ran a comic strip, "Bungleton Green," that praised France as a paradise of equal treatment for blacks. In one installment, a white Southerner finds himself condemned to fifty years in prison by a black French judge for the crime of insulting a black American. In another, Bungleton Green rejoices in his good fortune at being able to live in Paris, vowing to return to America only "when elephants live in bird nests, when snakes make love ta hummingbirds."

Of course the greatest contrast between French and American attitudes toward blacks had to do with sexual relations. African Americans living in Paris gradually formed personal relations with Parisians, and these relations often took on a physical dimension. As Bricktop noted in her autobiography, "Everybody was sleeping around. It was the thing to do . . . I slept with white men and black men." Josephine Baker took many French lovers, ranging from young men like Paul Colin and Georges Simenon, who were destined for stardom, to the obscure room service waiter in her first Parisian hotel. Black American men also crossed the traditional boundaries of race and sex, often finding willing partners among the young Parisian women who crowded into the jazz clubs. Few sights proved more shocking to the sensibilities of white American tourists than these couples openly displaying their affections. Paul Morand satirized these reactions in his short story "Charleston."

One thing stupefied me: to meet Frenchwomen, women like us, who dared show themselves in the street with men of color. . . . One day, if you can imagine, I saw in the middle of Paris a big negro chauffeur, very dark . . . with bloodshot eyes and lips that protruded beyond the edge of his cap, waiting for a model in the rue de la Paix. He welcomed her with a calm sweetness and assurance that shocked me. He had to have been four times her size. The pale, blonde Frenchwoman cuddled up against him in adoration. I looked around me; no one took any notice at all.

Many of the relationships between African Americans and white French-men and women were superficial, transitory dalliances based on mutual fantasies and a deliberate flouting of convention. Primitivist imagery included a strong emphasis on the sexuality of both black men and women, as the case of Josephine Baker made clear, and curiosity derived from such stereotypes undoubtedly precipitated many interracial relationships. For African American men, the chance to enjoy relations with white women was a key benefit of escaping America's racial puritanism. French prostitutes were all too willing to fulfill such fantasies. Some blacks, however, did build more meaningful attachments. During the war, Eugene Bullard had made the acquaintance of a young Parisian, Marcelle de Straumann, the daughter of a French countess. They continued to see each other after the Armistice, and on July 23, 1923, with the full approval of Marcelle's parents, they were married.

My father-in-law gave us a big wedding party . . . with the best of everything to eat and drink. The guests stayed all afternoon and in the evening moved up the hill to Montmartre. . . . When that party drove up to Montmartre with the private car leading the ten taxis following in a long stream, it looked like a parade.

The guests included nobles, artists, boxers, aviators, sportsmen of all kinds, and outstanding people in all walks of life and of all colors and religions. I felt as if I were back in the Foreign Legion where there is no prejudice and everybody appreciates everybody else just for himself as a human being.

Eugene Bullard's wedding was a fairy tale that never could have come true in America, and symbolized the joy of Paris in the 1920s for African Americans. The couple lived together happily for seven years, producing two daughters, until Bullard's workaholic tendencies led them to separate in 1930.

Bullard's marriage exemplified both the excitement and the difficulties that could arise in a close relationship between a Parisian and a black American expatriate. A much more graphic example was provided by the unfortunate fate of a twenty-four-year-old African American named Leon Crutcher. A successful nightclub pianist widely known as the "Don Juan of Montmartre," he married Marie Boyard, a young Frenchwoman working as a dancer in a nearby dance hall, on Christmas Day 1925. The couple moved into a hotel near the Gare Saint-Lazare, but evidently enjoyed little wedded bliss; neither seems to have cared much for monogamy, and neighbors reported frequent quarrels between the two. Events came to a tragic conclusion on February 26, 1926. *Le Figaro* reported:

> Leon Crutcher, musician in a nightclub, did not come home until a late hour, after having played several rounds of *belote* with his friends.
>
> Specifically, yesterday morning his wife went looking for him at the club's closing time. Crutcher refused to go back to the hotel, not returning until 3 P.M. When he got home he went to bed. A quarrel soon erupted. Suddenly, Madame Crutcher picked up a loaded revolver lying in a trunk, saying to her husband, "And if I killed you?"
>
> At that moment the shot was fired. Wounded on the left side, the musician collapsed, dying a few hours later.

At her trial Marie Crutcher pleaded innocent, calling her actions accidental and declaring her love for her husband. The trial received ample coverage in the Parisian press, attracted in part by the parade of witnesses testifying to the scandalous practices of Bohemian Montmartre. The jury, moved both by Madame Crutcher's testimony and also by her husband's failure to pay French taxes on his substantial income, acquitted her of murder, and Madame Crutcher immediately went free.

Gwendolyn Bennett's short story "Wedding Day" also gives a negative view of love across the color line in Paris. A fictional portrait of black Montmartre in the 1920s, the story features Paul Watson, a black boxer and jazz performer who strongly resembles Eugene Bullard. Unlike most of his friends, Paul seems immune to female attractions until the day he is propositioned by Mary, a white American prostitute down on her luck in Paris. The prospect of rescuing a white woman, a vulnerable member of the enemy race, softens his heart, and the two set a date to be married. Even the romance of Paris has its limits, however, and things do not turn out as planned.

> Mud on his nice gray suit that the English tailor had made for him. . . . The shrill whistle that is typical of the French subway pierced its way into his thoughts. . . . With one or two strides he reached the last coach as it began to move up the platform. A bit out of breath he stood inside the train and looking down at what he had in his hand he saw that it was a tiny pink ticket. A first class ticket in a second class coach. The idea set him to laughing. . . . First class ticket in a second class coach! — that was one on him. Wedding day today, and that damn letter from Mary. How'd she say it now, "just couldn't go through

with it," white women just don't marry colored men, and she was a street woman, too. Why couldn't she have told him flat that she was just getting back on her feet at his expense. Funny that first class ticket he bought, wish he could see Mary — him a-going there to wish her "happy wedding day," too. Wonder what that French woman was looking at him so hard for? Guess it was the mud.

The most famous interracial love affair in Paris during the 1920s did not involve a Frenchman or Frenchwoman. Henry Crowder was a black pianist from Georgia who had come to Europe in 1928 as part of a jazz band, Eddie South's Alabamians. While playing in Venice, he made the acquaintance of Nancy Cunard, the rebellious English heiress and descendant of the founder of the Cunard shipping line. Cunard had fled England at the end of the war to settle in the Left Bank of Paris, where she became an intimate of many of the leading French and foreign artists and intellectuals in Montparnasse, engaging in affairs with Louis Aragon and Aldous Huxley, among others. Surrealists like Aragon had awakened her interest in black culture, especially jazz and African art. She and Crowder soon fell in love, returning to Paris, where they lived together for the next three years.

The prospect of a black jazz musician openly living with a white woman of wealth and social position caused a major scandal. In England, Cunard's American-born mother reacted with fury to the news, especially after a friend taunted her at a party by asking, "Hello, Maud, what is it now — drink, drugs, or niggers?" Not only did Mrs. Cunard have the couple thrown out of a hotel in London, but she also stopped speaking to Nancy and cut her off financially. Nancy responded by publishing an essay, "Black Man and White Ladyship," in which she sharply criticized her mother's bigotry and white racism in general. Cunard's attacks on her mother included assertions that "she would not feel *chic* in Paris any longer as she had heard that all the chic Parisians nowadays consorted with Negroes," as well as the story that Mrs. Cunard had nearly fainted in a nightclub after glimpsing some black singers.

The reaction to Nancy Cunard's relationship with Henry Crowder was a case of the exception that proves the rule. In Paris, Crowder and Cunard escaped the racist reactions that greeted the couple in London and New York. Although Henry and Nancy experienced many problems with each other, their foreign hosts let them live their lives in peace. Paris in the 1920s sheltered refugees and exiles as well as expatriates, and its climate of racial tolerance gave the couple a haven in a harsh and unforgiving world.

Very few Parisians established personal ties with members of the small African American community in their midst; for most, black Americans were figures seen on stage or glimpsed in passing in the street. Even those enamored of primitivism and jazz rarely went beyond an abstract acquaintance with black culture. So it is not surprising that the "noble savage" stereotypes retained such force in the French imagination. Yet unlike in the United States, stereotypes did not translate into discrimination. In Paris, African Americans were free to live their lives as they chose, and could rely on equal treatment as a matter of course. However the French viewed black Americans, they treated them first and foremost simply as human beings, and that is what counted.

Finally, one must consider the relations between black and white American expatriates in describing the African American community in Paris during the 1920s. For American expatriates, both black and white, Paris represented an escape from the narrow prejudices of life in America, but the two groups defined the inadequacies of the American experience differently. Blacks sought above all to escape racial bias, whereas most whites fled from a broader constellation of attitudes that included a worship of Mammon, hostility to the arts, puritanical social mores, and Prohibition. Still, once in Paris both black and white Americans found themselves in a larger society that did not observe the racial segregation to which they had been accustomed at home. To what extent did they profit from this opportunity to cross the color line? African Americans in Paris learned to avoid white American tourists, finding that the Atlantic crossing often made no difference in their racial attitudes. Unlike the tourists, however, white expatriates in Paris consciously rejected many American customs and prejudices. Their interactions with their black fellow citizens in France displayed none of the overt bigotry and hostility commonly exhibited by so many whites in the United States. At the same time, however, no true equalization of relations between black and white Americans took place in Paris during the 1920s: while some occasionally crossed the color line, they never tore it down.

White American expatriates frequently visited Montmartre's nightclubs, where they enjoyed the majority of their contacts with African Americans. I have already noted the close relations established by both F. Scott Fitzgerald and Cole Porter with Bricktop. Ernest Hemingway, Man Ray, and other Left Bank habitués also often found their way to the rue Pigalle to dance and drink the night away. Josephine Baker attracted her share of white American admirers, although they did not count among her closest friends. Gertrude Stein, leader of the American expatriate colony in Paris, praised Baker in a section of her 1928 book, *Useful Knowledge*, entitled "Among Negroes," and other white Americans flocked to see her perform. Ernest Hemingway later boasted of his first encounter with Baker: "Tall, coffee skin, ebony eyes, legs of paradise, a smile to end all smiles. Very hot night but she was wearing a coat of black fur, her breasts handling the fur like it was silk. She turned her eyes on me — she was dancing with the big British gunner subaltern who had brought her — but I responded to the eyes like a hypnotic and cut in on them. . . . We danced nonstop for the rest of the night. She never took off her coat. Wasn't until the joint closed she told me she had nothing on underneath."

In general, however, the contacts between African American performers and white American expatriates did not lead to relations of true intimacy. The index to Baker's 1976 autobiography *Josephine* does not list a single one of the famous American expatriates of the 1920s, not even Hemingway. And although Bricktop may have admired Fitzgerald and Porter, she came to their homes as a hired musician, not as a friend and equal. The community established by African Americans in Paris during these years did not as a rule include their more famous white fellow citizens.

In part this separation arose not from differences of race but of interests and profession. Most of the white American expatriates were writers, whereas most blacks worked as musicians. African American writers in Paris did have more contact with their white peers. Gwendolyn Bennett bought a copy of *Ulysses* at Shakespeare and Company, and both she and Paul Robeson enjoyed Thanksgiving dinner in 1925 at the home of the bookstore's owner, Sylvia Beach. Claude McKay in particular got to know many of the Lost Generation writers during his stays in Paris. He frequented the cafés of Saint-Germain-des-Prés, read *Ulysses*, met Hemingway, Sinclair Lewis, and others, and was invited to the salon of Gertrude Stein. McKay enjoyed the cosmopolitan society created by the white American writers in Paris and approved of their desire to experience life by seeing the world, but nonetheless never truly felt that he was one of them.

> Frankly to say, I never considered myself identical with the white expatriates. . . . Color-consciousness was the fundamental of my restlessness. And it was something with which my white fellow-expatriates could sympathize but which they could not altogether understand. For they were not black like me. Not being black and unable to see deep into the profundity of blackness, some even thought that I might have preferred to be white like them . . . their education in their white world had trained them to see a person of color either as an inferior or as an exotic.

Even among fellow American writers in Paris, the color line still existed. If Claude McKay felt different from the writers of the Lost Generation, Langston Hughes was completely isolated from them. His descriptions of life in

Paris during the 1920s do not mention a single white American, writer or otherwise.

For white American expatriates, therefore, life in Jazz Age Paris did not necessarily bring liberation from all the social conventions prevalent in the United States. F. Scott Fitzgerald's love of Bricktop, for example, did not hinder him from writing notoriously racist passages about blacks in one of the great novels of American expatriate life, *Tender Is the Night*. Yet few demonstrated overt bigotry. Rather, as was true of so many Northern educated whites at the time, they were used to a world in which blacks and whites did not mix as equals, and their experiences in Paris did little to change that. For the most part, the interactions that occurred between white and black expatriates in Paris could have taken place (and did) in New York just as easily. Taxis took as many night owls from Greenwich Village to Harlem as they did from Montparnasse to Montmartre.

For black Americans in Paris, interracial contacts meant primarily contacts with the white people of France, not of their own country. In 1920s Paris, white Americans observed blacks with interest and sympathy but ultimately (in a way that characterized much of white expatriate life in the French capital) as outsiders. In *Paris Was Our Mistress*, the writer Samuel Putnam described an illustrative incident on his maiden voyage to France.

> On the *Rochambeau*, I made the acquaintance of two Negro artists to whom [H. L.] Mencken had given me a note of introduction: Taylor Gordon, the singer, and J. Rosamond Johnson, the composer. The jazz craze was on in Europe, blues and spirituals were popular, and Negro musicians were in demand. . . . On our last night at sea, just before coming into Le Havre early in the morning, Gordon and I and those members of the crew who were off duty gathered on deck around a small tub of *vin rouge* which the sailors had produced from somewhere; and without being asked, Taylor began singing. I can hear his voice rolling out over the waves, can see the look on the faces of those French seamen as they listened to "Water Boy" and "Swing Low, Sweet Chariot."

The 1920s introduced a new phase in the encounter of African Americans with the people of Paris. Many American blacks had come to the city before, but usually as isolated individuals and temporary visitors. During the years following the First World War, many more journeyed to the French capital and decided to stay. In doing so they created a small but genuine African American community in the heart of a vast foreign city. Life among the black expatriates in Paris differed in many ways from that of the urban ghettos or small Southern villages of the United States. Few elderly black Americans lived in Paris, relatively few women, and virtually no children. The bars and nightclubs of Harlem may have had their counterparts in Montmartre, but the churches did not. The Atlantic remained a very wide ocean in the 1920s, and Paris was a long way from Mississippi.

That of course constituted one of the city's main attractions. If one could not find the entire range of African American culture in Paris, on the other hand one did not have to worry about American racism. Few of the blacks who left the United States for Paris in the 1920s did so consciously to escape racial discrimination; job opportunities for musicians, or fellowships for artists and writers, provided a more immediate motivation. Yet once in the City of Light, most gloried in the strange and wonderful atmosphere of racial tolerance. In Paris, African Americans could walk down almost any street or go into any store or restaurant they chose to frequent without fearing rejection. The city attracted the best and brightest from black America, giving them the freedom to go as far as their talents would take them.

Judging from the impressive achievements of individuals like Henry Tanner, Bricktop, Josephine Baker, Anna Julia Cooper, Panama Al Brown, and many others, this was very far indeed. Yet, in a sense, their most significant accomplishment was a collective one, the re-creation of black American culture abroad. In Paris during the 1920s, one could escape white racism and still take part in the life of a community that retained much of the flavor of Harlem. There one could enjoy being black without facing discrimination and bigotry. This feeling of community enabled black expatriates to escape much of the desperate loneliness that traditionally haunted so many foreigners living in Paris. Instead, they found that Parisians praised the culture they had grown up in as an exotic and valuable contribution to the city's life. African Americans put the jazz in Paris's Jazz Age, and if the French capital was a moveable feast in the 1920s then for once they were able to take their rightful place at the table.

3

DEPRESSION AND WAR:
PARIS IN THE
1930s

IF THE 1920S represented the twentieth century at its most glamorous and carefree, the 1930s and early 1940s portrayed the horror and despair of modern life in equally extreme fashion. Rarely have two decades contrasted so sharply: the drunken gaiety of Saturday night succeeded by the hung-over misery of Sunday morning. Beginning with the great stock market crash in New York at the end of 1929, America and then Europe witnessed the end of the economic buoyancy of the 1920s as the Depression threw millions out of work around the world. The specter of poverty, an unwelcome and ignored presence at the "moveable feast" of the 1920s, now brutally seized center stage. Wall Street stockbrokers plummeted to their deaths, transforming their beloved skyscrapers from measures of confidence into symbols of dashed hopes. If the 1920s danced to the joyful tunes of jazz, in Europe the 1930s marched to the strident jackboot rhythms of military music, as fascism became the dominant note of the political era. If the 1920s celebrated the end of one war, the 1930s looked with dread and anticipation to the start of another. Ultimately World War II would shatter the last remnants of *les années folles*, leaving behind it a Europe in ruins. If the 1930s symbolized the bill for the pleasures of the 1920s, then it was an account that would be paid with the blood of tens of millions.

Paris lay at the heart of this transformation. While the contrast between the rollicking Age of Jazz and the Great Depression loomed even larger in that most tragic of European cities, Berlin, still the end of Gay Paree symbolized the passing of an era far beyond the borders of France. By the mid-1930s, little remained of the public high spirits that had captivated people from around the world. Although the Depression came relatively late to France, during most of the 1930s high unemployment rates were a central fact of life for Parisians. The city's cafés, centers of vibrant public life the decade before, became places of temporary refuge for those who no longer had homes, or homelands, awaiting their return. During the 1930s, the unemployed were joined by thousands of political refugees from an ever more fascist Europe. Whereas in the decade after World War I, Paris had been in the avant-garde of the general push for greater personal and creative freedom, during the Depression it seemed like an increasingly isolated and tenuous island in a continent dominated by the likes of Hitler and Mussolini. This island did not long endure: in June 1940, German troops occupied the City of Light, inflicting upon the French people one of the most cataclysmic disasters of their history. For the next four years, Paris was to live according to the Nazi agenda. By the summer of 1942, French police were rounding up thousands of Parisian Jews, forcing them onto a long road that ultimately ended at Auschwitz. For Paris, therefore, the 1930s and early 1940s were an era of tragic decline, from the glamorous heights of the Roaring Twenties to the depths of the Final Solution.

What did such a city offer the African American musicians, artists, and intellectuals who had settled in or visited Paris a decade earlier? A city hungry for work and fearing the outbreak of a new war would seem to have little room for black people leaving the United States in search of greater opportunities. The prototypical foreigner in Paris during the 1930s was the political refugee, a man or woman with few options; those who could go elsewhere generally did. By the middle of the decade, most of the white American writers and intellectuals who had colonized the French capital during the heyday of the Lost Generation had recognized the changing nature of the times and gone back to the States. Some left after the *Chicago Tribune* closed its Paris edition, a source of work for many writers, and others suffered financial losses from the Wall Street crash that suddenly rendered their pleasant European exile no longer affordable. Many simply felt that Paris wasn't fun anymore, that it was time to get serious and buckle down to responsibilities back home.

Some black Americans also chose to return across the Atlantic after the Depression, and relatively few came to replace them during that troubled decade. Yet in spite of the difficult times, the African American expatriate community endured during the 1930s. Having sunk deep roots in receptive Parisian soil during the years after World War I, many did not find it so easy to go back to a United States that they by now hardly knew. Even though the Jazz Age itself had faded into history, jazz continued to attract French listeners

and therefore provide a role for black musicians in the city's clubs and cabarets. Some felt that because the economic crisis was just as bad in America,
and the indignities of racism there were essentially unchanged, the idea of a
return home had little appeal. While few if any African American artists and
writers settled permanently in Paris during the 1930s, several traveled there on
fellowship or spent summers in the city. Virtually all of these exiles finally did
leave Paris at the beginning of World War II, as the possibility of a German
invasion became daily more menacing. Yet a very few, most notably Josephine
Baker, chose to stay with the people of France during their hour of trial,
enduring the Nazi occupation and ensuring the continuity of the African
American experience in Paris into the postwar years.

The African Americans who lived in Paris during the 1930s constituted a
community in transition, from the newcomers of the 1920s to a mature,
established part of the Parisian landscape. Fashions come and go quickly in
Paris, and by the 1930s blacks had ceased to be a novelty. Perhaps as a result,
members of the black community there seemed to gain a new sense of themselves, a new level of assurance. The early years of the decade in particular
were a period of prosperity and creativity, representing the coming to fruition
of the seeds sown in the 1920s. Jazz not only found a new level of acceptance
among the French musical establishment, but also began to attract some
skilled French musicians. African American painters and sculptors became
bolder in their acknowledgment and appropriation of African themes. Perhaps most notably, black American writers helped inspire the new literary
movement known as *nègritude*. The 1930s demonstrated that African Americans were no passing fancy, but a permanent part of the city, capable in even
the most adverse times of achievements that both delighted their French hosts
and did credit to the land that had produced them.

"AND WE ALL PLAYED ON"

In her autobiography, Bricktop used these terms to characterize her life in
Paris during the early 1930s. Her use of this phrase evokes the curious fact that
the first few years of the Depression witnessed one of the most brilliant (albeit
brief) episodes of African American life in Paris. Although the Depression
began later in France than in Britain, Germany, or the United States, by 1931
the crisis had made serious inroads into the French economy. Within a year,
the number of French men and women out of work had risen to 300,000, a
sharp and disturbing contrast to the full employment of the 1920s. Paris in
particular was hurt by the sudden collapse of the tourist trade, especially from

the United States. Businesses that catered to wealthy Americans, such as jewelry stores and symbols of luxury like the Café de la Paix and the Ritz Hotel, found themselves facing hard times. Complaints about the arrogance and ignorance of American tourists became passé, giving way to laments for the old days of prosperity and extravagance.

Yet as one historian has commented, "It takes more than political unrest and economic uncertainty to prevent Parisians from enjoying themselves." Nightlife continued to thrive in the French capital during the early years of the Depression, and even after the middle years of the decade maintained an important, if diminished, presence in the city's public life. Jazz was no longer new, but by the early 1930s it had carved out a permanent position for itself in the nightclubs of Paris, so there continued to be a market for black musicians from the United States. The two most prominent African Americans in Paris, Josephine Baker and Bricktop, experienced even greater successes during these years. Many French people continued to regard black music as beautiful, providing a few black musicians the possibility of earning a living even in the worst of times.

As a result, life for the African Americans of Montmartre remained sweet during the early years of the Depression decade. Playing jazz in Paris usually meant staying up all night, virtually every night, so that the nightclubs constituted the center of this subculture. One of the liveliest during these years was Frisco's, a club on the rue Fromentin. Run by Jocelyn "Frisco" Bingham, it featured a series of black jazz bands and catered to the same wealthy clientele that made Bricktop's fortune. Aristocrats like the Marquis de Polignac, the Count de la Rochefoucauld, and the Prince of Wales were regular guests, delighting not only in the booze and blues, but also in the expansive, outrageous personality of Frisco himself. "One may see Frisco suddenly leap into the orchestra, seize an instrument, utter some wild cries, and unloose a deafening hubbub. Then, as if possessed, he lances a kick in the big drum, sounds the clarinet, takes on the fly the cymbals, and sounds the charge." Another popular Montmartre nightspot was the Melody Bar, which achieved a certain notoriety (and greatly increased popularity) in September 1933, when Parisians learned that the musician Lucien François Pierre had been one of the many lovers of the young Violette Nozières. Nozières, who loved jazz clubs, drank cocktails, and in general symbolized everything wrong with France's younger generation, scandalized the nation when she poisoned her own parents, ostensibly for money to finance a dissolute lifestyle.

Yet Montmartre's musicians had a life outside the clubs as well. They participated actively in the street life of the neighborhood. Rarely rising before noon, they would often socialize at local cafés and restaurants like the Flea Pit. Edgar Wiggins worked in Paris during the 1930s as the French correspondent for several African American newspapers. Settling in the heart of Montmartre, at 36 rue Pigalle, he took the nom de plume "The Street Wolf of Paris" and became the leading commentator on black American life in the French capital during the 1930s.

> the Negroes of Montmartre . . . have a cafe which is reserved to them, rue Fontaine; certain of them are to [be] found at Boudon, where each afternoon may be seen the ex-boxer, Bob Scanlon, who covered himself with glory in the Foreign Legion, his face beaming with kindliness, smoking a big cigar, and displaying his white spats on the sidewalk.
>
> Each evening the Negroes of Montmartre put on their tuxedos and scatter themselves among the night clubs there where for the most part they are members of the orchestras.

Although the looming Depression would soon strip the area of its allure, in the early 1930s Montmartre still retained much of its disheveled charm. Its African American residents lived for the most part in the cheap hotels that abounded in the neighborhood, dimly lit establishments where conveniences like elevators and flush toilets represented unheard-of luxuries. The narrow streets that greeted musicians shaking off the hangovers of the previous evening were bordered by tall buildings whose peeling plaster façades were gray from the accumulation of soot and grime. The color of the buildings often matched that of the overcast and rainy skies, giving the neighborhood a dismal appearance even at noon. The streets were anything but elegant, and fastidious pedestrians had to avoid rotting produce and the leavings of man's best friend. The dampness and trash in the streets produced an odor of decay, further reinforcing the atmosphere of shabbiness that characterized Montmartre during the day. Yet at night the area would resume its fairy-like existence as the lights came on and the crowds gathered in the nightclubs, dance halls, and bars of ill repute. Prostitutes and pimps would solicit customers, money and cocaine would change hands, and *fêtards* (merrymakers) would frenetically dance the night away.

In addition to this daily pattern, by the early 1930s black American musicians in Montmartre had developed their own community rituals. Every Christmas, Bricktop would close her club to the public and invite all the black performers in Paris to a big holiday bash. Eugene Bullard instituted a traditional free concert given by black jazz musicians at the American Hospital in Paris every year at the nurses' graduation ceremony. At times, they would also give concerts for America's Gold Star mothers. Many young soldiers had lost their lives in wartime France and remained buried there, prompting the American government to send their mothers to France on special graveyard tours during the 1930s. Montmartre's jazz musicians would sometimes meet them at the boat trains in Paris and play for them. On at least one occasion, this practice provided an object lesson in American racism, when performers played for a group of almost one hundred black Gold Star mothers who had been segregated and sent to France on a separate ship.

During these years, Bricktop remained the reigning doyenne of Montmartre's jazz life. In fact, she did so well that she was able to move to a larger club in the rue Pigalle, also named Bricktop's, in November 1931, at a time when the magnitude of the economic disaster had already become clear. When she started her French career in the 1920s, Bricktop quickly became a successful nightclub owner, one of many in Montmartre who made a good living by peddling hot American jazz and abundant champagne. By 1932, Bricktop had become not just a Parisian institution, but the darling of the international elite. The pages of her autobiography dealing with this period read like a *Who's Who* of the leading wealthy, famous, and dissolute individuals of the Western world. These included spendthrift heirs to American fortunes like Jeff Crane and Ralph Beaver Strassburger, socialites like Barbara Hutton and Monty Woolley, and entertainers and film stars like Gloria Swanson, Sophie Tucker, and Edward G. Robinson. While Bricktop's catered in particular to wealthy Americans and other foreigners, French celebrities like Mistinguett, Maurice Chevalier, and the boxer Georges Carpentier could also be spotted enjoying an evening there.

Above all, the presence of members of the titled nobility in Bricktop's club symbolized her preeminent place in elite circles. Bricktop was no stranger to that peculiarly American fascination with the European aristocracy, monied or otherwise, and a small but constant stream of lords and ladies, barons and marquises, frequented Bricktop's in the early 1930s, kicking up their heels just like the common folk. Even the gangster who tried forcing Bricktop to buy protection in this period was known as the Baron, a title that was apparently legitimate. Most impressive of all was Britain's Prince of Wales, who first visited Bricktop's club in 1926. When Bricktop moved her club to Biarritz for the summer of 1933, the prince again became a regular, and she was able to follow his budding and controversial romance with the American socialite Wallis Simpson the following year. Their marriage shocked the world and scandalized the British upper classes, but the now Duke and Duchess of Windsor were as welcome as always at Bricktop's. Other aristocrats who frequented the Montmartre nightclub included the Russian baron Nicky de Gunzburg, the Aga Khan, and French nobility like the Marquis de la Falaise de la Coudraye.

For the contemporary reader, Bricktop's memoirs of this time bring to vivid life Paris in all its splendor: "Paris was as wild and gay as ever. There was an *awful* lot of money. . . . There was an attitude of total abandon." However, they also provide a disturbing example of the limits to interracial tolerance in the interwar years. During the 1920s, Bricktop's was the leading example of a Parisian nightclub owned and operated by African Americans, which featured black jazz musicians and allowed blacks and whites to interact on an intimate and equal basis. By the 1930s, in contrast, Bricktop's emphasis had clearly shifted to attracting and encouraging a wealthy and mostly white clientele. Unlike the famous Cotton Club in New York, which featured black performers but admitted only white patrons, blacks were always welcome at Bricktop's. Yet Bricktop catered first and foremost to an international elite, and in the early 1930s that elite was overwhelmingly white. Whereas she may have seen her nightclubs as a study in elegance and cosmopolitanism, many of these wealthy white patrons undoubtedly viewed time spent there as a kind of slumming, adventurous forays across a color line that they ultimately had no desire to destroy. All too often, Bricktop's memoirs leave the impression of a black woman fawning over those at the top of a status hierarchy that confined her people to the bottom of society. Like Josephine Baker, Bricktop achieved success in a world that, while not usually overtly racist, nevertheless did not see people like her as the equals of those with money, social position, and white skin. To a certain extent, her club reflected and re-created the world of Harlem nightlife, offering black jazz to affluent white patrons in search of a daring night on the town.

This pandering to the tastes of white society also affected the music played in Bricktop's and many other Parisian jazz clubs. Musicians were expected to play comfortable tunes that did not disturb the drunken conversations of the paying guests. Performers visiting from the United States commented that their Parisian colleagues sounded years behind the times. Jam sessions, so often the source of new inspiration in jazz, were strongly discouraged by club owners. When customers did deign to notice the musicians, it was often to make outrageous and demeaning requests. One drummer who worked at Bricktop's in the early 1930s recalled a wealthy American woman who paid members of the band ten dollars each to play in the nude. This kind of insulting, humiliating behavior underlined the point that many of Bricktop's white clients saw jazz, and those who played it, simply as a source of amusement, not a serious art form. Jazz should be wild, but not *too* wild.

Yet any condemnation of Bricktop as servile or less than committed to racial justice would be unfair and ahistorical. While she may have gushed rather lavishly over some of the white celebrities who flocked to her clubs, her greatest affection and praise was reserved for African Americans of note. Jack Johnson's visit to Bricktop's in 1933 was a special occasion; Bricktop summed up her feelings about the championship boxer by saying, "I love him to this very day. If anybody ever made me feel proud of being who and what I am, it was Jack." The great actor and singer Paul Robeson received similar treatment when he came to Paris in 1937. Bricktop compared him with Britain's Duke of Kent in terms that left little doubt as to her preference: "Both Paul and the Duke were tall, but Paul was a little taller and had to look down on the Duke a bit." One must also consider Bricktop's tendency to downplay the importance of even her most famous white customers, as well as her insistence on being treated (and paid) like a professional. Perhaps most important, Bricktop's continued to serve as a gathering place for African Americans, both musicians and others, in Paris during the early 1930s. Arthur Briggs, who played piano in the house band, commented that "Bricktop was very intelligent and a natural hostess." Bricktop herself may have treated her white customers well, but she never lost her sense of self-respect, and never forgot who she was and where she came from.

The early 1930s were also very good to Josephine Baker. In fact, so great was her renown that she became virtually the only American in Paris of any color not affected by the Depression. The ranks of the jobless might swell from day to day and war might loom ever more menacingly on the horizon, yet nothing seemed capable of stopping Baker's meteoric career. The 1930s in general constitute a fundamental turning point in Josephine Baker's life. She had come to Paris as an unknown dancer in 1925, quickly taking the city, and soon all of Europe, by storm. Yet she had done so as an archetype, the wriggling, lusty embodiment of white French racial and sexual fantasies. After her return to Paris from her triumphal European tour in the late 1920s, Josephine Baker would move into the mainstream of the city's entertainment world. And she would set about to gather the trappings of bourgeois respectability, including a French husband and a magnificent house in the Paris suburbs. Gradually the black curiosity from Saint Louis became a French star. Baker would complete her metamorphosis in 1937 by acquiring French citizenship, thus permanently embracing the nation that had brought her such acclaim.

Baker's assimilation into French culture involved in part a rejection of the United States, as her travels during the 1930s made it clear that she could not expect the same success in America she had received abroad. Did this rejection also involve turning her back on black America? This question came up frequently in the 1930s and continues to surface in discussions of the life of Josephine Baker, raising issues that go to the heart of the African American experience. Baker's initial success came as a black star; it was a testament to her own great talents, but also forced her into limiting, even demeaning roles. Success gradually enabled her to craft a more dignified, respectable image, but at the same time she seemed to distance herself from the world of black America, becoming more and more French. This dilemma posed problems for African American expatriates in general. Many chose to go or stay abroad as a way of escaping the subordinate position of blacks in American society, yet in leaving America to settle in a white European capital they left their own culture behind as well. The creation of an African American community in Paris during the 1920s eased the pangs of this separation but could not erase it entirely. Josephine Baker's life during the 1930s continued to demonstrate the heights to which an African American in France could ascend, but it also showed that such success could exact costs of its own.

In September 1930, Josephine Baker marked a new stage in her dazzling career by opening for the first time in a show at the Casino de Paris. The Casino was perhaps the leading music hall in Paris at the time, and almost certainly the most respectable. There the celebrated French entertainer Mistinguett had reigned the previous year as the leading lady of the Paris stage. At the Casino, Baker starred in a show called *Paris qui remue* (or *Paris When It Sizzles*). The revue, a series of colonialist sexual fantasy skits, in which Baker generally played a young native girl from somewhere in the French Empire in love with a dashing young Frenchman, proved enormously popular. It ran at the Casino de Paris for a year, 481 performances, drawing on the same fascination with an empire in its twilight years which produced the hugely successful Parisian Colonial Exposition of 1931. The two events in fact mirrored each other to such an extent that Baker was asked to serve as queen of the exposition, in spite of the fact that she was an American citizen who had never set foot in overseas France.

In *Paris qui remue*, Baker performed for the first time "J'ai Deux Amours" ("I Have Two Loves"), the song that would become her signature piece and as much a part of her public presence as the banana skirt had been. As Phyllis Rose has pointed out in her biography of Josephine Baker, the song originally referred to an African girl torn between her love for a young Frenchman and her attachment to her people and her native land. However, in the course of her career, Baker gradually shifted the meaning so that it came to symbolize instead her position between France and the United States; Baker's fans first associated the second line of the song, "My country and Paris," with America, not Africa. Ultimately Baker would change the line to "My country *is* Paris," giving France an undivided loyalty that America no longer deserved. This transformation is extremely significant, for it showed how Josephine Baker was able to take typically condescending racial imagery and turn it into a simple yet meaningful comment on the paradoxes that confronted the African American expatriate in Paris.

During the early 1930s, Josephine Baker branched out into other fields of the French entertainment industry. She recorded "J'ai Deux Amours" and her other songs from the Casino de Paris show. She also starred in two French films, *ZouZou* and *Princess Tam Tam*, in 1934 and 1935, as well as singing the lead role in Offenbach's operetta *La Créole*. While none of these endeavors can be regarded as landmark artistic achievements, they reaffirmed Baker's popularity with her French audience as well as the breadth of her talents. Incidentally, they also testified to the business acumen of her lover and manager, the Italian entrepreneur Pepito, who skillfully guided her into the top ranks of French entertainers in this period.

By the middle of the decade, Josephine Baker's position in this hierarchy seemed beyond question. She and Pepito therefore decided the time was right for a tour of the United States. The young black dancer from East Saint Louis who had left for Paris a decade earlier would return to her native land in triumph as an international star. Pepito made all the arrangements, and Baker set sail for New York, arriving on a French ocean liner in September 1935. There she soon learned that while she had grown enormously over the last ten years, the United States had not. Europeans idolized her as a star, but white Americans still saw her first and foremost as a black woman, and black women were not considered star material in the 1930s. America's theater and music critics greeted her performances with tepid enthusiasm, if not outright hostility and disdain. In a particularly vicious attack, *Time* called her a "Negro wench" and claimed that "to Manhattan theatre-goers last week she was just a slightly buck-toothed young Negro woman whose figure might be matched in any night club show, whose dancing and singing could be topped practically anywhere outside France." Worst of all, she quarreled violently with Pepito, who left her to return to Paris where he died of cancer shortly thereafter. By the summer of 1936, Josephine Baker had had enough of her native land. Disillusioned and hurt, she returned to Paris where thousands of French fans not only appreciated her talent, but also considered blackness something of value.

This unhappy New York sojourn confirmed once and for all Josephine Baker's permanent separation from the United States. She would return at other times in her life, to much greater acclaim and respect, but henceforth France would remain her home. In 1929 she had become a property owner for the first time when she and Pepito bought a mansion in the Paris suburbs. This elegant stone house, named Beau-Chêne, sat on several beautifully manicured acres, which provided ample room for Baker's numerous pets. Foreign performers might live in Parisian hotel rooms, but she had achieved that goal so dear to most French men and women, to own a small portion of the blessed soil of France. Josephine Baker was not the only African American to realize this dream: a year later both Bricktop and Arthur Briggs bought houses in Bougival, a wooded suburb outside Paris and home to Mistinguett and Maurice Chevalier. In 1936, Baker would acquire an even more impressive property, a genuine (if rather dilapidated) château named Les Milandes in the bucolic Dordogne region of France. The following year, she would make a much more formal commitment to her adopted country. In 1937, Josephine Baker married Jean Lion, a young, prosperous French businessman of Jewish origin. Although the marriage lasted little more than a year, it afforded Baker the opportunity to become a citizen of France, which she did enthusiastically. Her transformation into an elegant Parisian lady was now complete.

Did becoming French mean ceasing to be an African American? Certainly Josephine Baker's growing fame and acceptance in Paris brought with it some distancing from black life in general and the local black American community in particular. In 1928, she had abandoned her Montmartre nightclub, Chez Josephine, after little more than a year to go on tour. The new Chez Josephine nightclub that Baker opened in 1937 was located not in Montmartre but in the rue François-Ier, near the Champs-Elysées, prime Parisian real estate, luxurious, fashionable, and light years removed from the colorful ramshackle neighborhood that still formed the heart of African American life in the French capital. The singers and dancers Josephine Baker performed with at the Casino de Paris and the Folies-Bergère during these years were overwhelmingly French and white, as was her life in general. Her relationship with Pepito and her move to Le Vésinet merely confirmed this shift. Although Baker still came to Montmartre from time to time, she was no longer truly a part of the neighborhood; Edgar Wiggins's newspaper columns on black life in the 1930s do not mention her at all. Black performers visiting from America, especially those who had snubbed her in New York, at times received a cold shoulder from the great diva. Even Bricktop noted that "Josephine had a bad reputation for avoiding Negroes when they came to Paris."

During the 1930s, both Bricktop and Baker learned that, even in Paris, wealth and renown were still essentially the preserve of a white world. Because Baker was ultimately the more successful of the two, her isolation from other African Americans became even more significant. She certainly enjoyed the rewards that success brought and gloried in the fame and fortune that the people of France had placed at her feet. But Josephine Baker did not always turn her back on her people. Visitors from the States sometimes found her affable, warm, and charming. She gave Duke Ellington a royal welcome when he toured Paris in 1933, and did the same for Evelyn and Ethel Sheppard, old friends from New York. As Ethel commented, "We were only in Paris for a couple of weeks, and she brightened our whole trip." Baker's return to the United States in the mid-1930s graphically highlighted her contradictory relationship to black America. During her trip to New York, she spent most of her time in midtown Manhattan, but also stayed in Harlem, where she performed incognito at the venerable Apollo Theater. If Baker's attitude toward black Americans seemed ambivalent, the reverse was also true. Some in Harlem took offense at her desire to socialize primarily with affluent whites downtown, noting that they still refused to accept her. Yet many others gloried in her fame and success, seeing her triumphs as their own. The journalist Roi Ottley praised her for daring to challenge the color line, arguing that she deserved the support, not criticism, of other black Americans. As the *Philadelphia Tribune* observed, "It might seem that in Europe where color isn't the handicap it is here, Miss Baker does not mind being known as a Negro, but over here it is something else again. And who can blame her?"

Trying to achieve success as a black woman in a white man's world has never been easy, and all the bright lights of Paris could not fully shield Josephine Baker from dilemmas that white performers never had to confront. At the beginning of the decade, Baker was visited by Noble Sissle, whom she had not seen since the days of *Shuffle Along* on Broadway several years and a lifetime ago. Comparing their respective lives, she plaintively noted in her autobiography: "Seeing Noble made me think. I was well aware of his dedication to our people, of the good he had done for colored people and colored theater. But didn't being a *black* star in a *white* show prove something too? Wouldn't it give me more power with which to fight for the cause? Admittedly, when my dresser hurried in with my coolie hat and feathers for the Tonkinese number and remarked that there were several rhinestones missing from the White Bird's ankle bracelet, it made me wonder." Josephine Baker's stunning success was not without its price, as the painful ambivalence of this passage suggests. Yet through it all, she never forgot the sufferings of her people or the terrible cost of injustice. Baker had her own ways of fighting racism, and in doing so she would demonstrate a level of courage that equaled her skill on stage.

The continued success of both Bricktop and Josephine Baker demonstrated that although the glory days of the Jazz Age had come and gone, jazz itself retained its power to charm and move Parisians, thus guaranteeing a place for a certain African American community. But the music that had taken Montmartre by storm had changed greatly since its first successes in Paris at the end of the Great War. Jazz in the 1920s, for all its popularity, had been largely consigned to the margins of the music world and French society in general. While it would certainly not become an establishment phenomenon in the 1930s, still "America's classical music" would win a greater level of acceptance in Paris, symbolized in particular by the rise of a new generation of skilled French jazz musicians. Thanks to their contributions as well as those of younger American musicians, both black and white, who still made the pilgrimage across the Atlantic, jazz in Paris developed a new maturity and self-confidence. The clubs of the French capital frequently featured a variety of jazz that was, like the drinks they served, frequently watered down. However, even though it was often obscured by the endless parade of champagne bottles that characterized Parisian nightlife, a vigorous young musical form reached for new levels of expression and creativity.

This new cosmopolitan spirit did not lessen the importance of African Americans to jazz, or the crucial role played by jazz in bringing them together in Paris. On the contrary, by opening up new vistas and opportunities for black Americans in the French capital, it further rooted that community in the life of Paris as a whole. As jazz became more Parisian, no longer a novelty but a standard part of the city's musical culture, so did the African American musicians who played it. At the same time, they learned more about different musical traditions and modes of expression that would enrich their own creations. The jazz world of Paris grew bigger than ever in the early 1930s, but black American culture remained a key part of it.

Likewise, French jazz aficionados, both critics and performers, played a key role in broadening the appeal of jazz in France during the 1930s, making important contributions to the art form as a whole. Foremost among these was Hugues Panassié, who in 1934 published *Le Jazz Hot*, the first significant study of jazz written in France. Panassié first encountered jazz as a young man in 1927 when he decided to take up the saxophone after a bout with polio. His father arranged for him to take lessons with Christian Wagner, a leading French jazz musician, who introduced him to the music and many musicians as well. Two years later another chance encounter would prove even more significant for Panassié. In March 1929, he met and became close friends with Mezz Mezzrow, the talented American clarinetist, then performing in Paris, whose association with the Frenchman would heighten Panassié's appreciation of jazz. As a Jew who mostly socialized with black musicians, even passing for black at times, he was able to introduce Panassié to the world of black music, which was a revelation to Panassié, whose previous knowledge of jazz had been mostly limited to white performers. Abandoning his attempts to master the saxophone, Panassié instead turned to writing, becoming in short order the first serious critic of jazz in France.

A man of powerful convictions, mercurial, sentimental, and at times arrogant, Hugues Panassié became a one-man cheering section for his beloved music in the early 1930s. In addition to writing *Le Jazz Hot*, he also founded and wrote for a magazine of the same name. A key innovation in promoting the popularity of jazz was the Hot Club of France, a society of jazz musicians and fans which sponsored concerts and jazz programs on the radio and enabled adepts of the music to correspond. In all his work, Panassié passionately attacked those elitist music critics who denigrated jazz by portraying it as inferior to the classical tradition. He also argued that jazz was not just for dancing, but an art form in its own right, and strove to make it accessible to ordinary listeners. *Le Jazz Hot* in particular provided a comprehensive survey of the international jazz scene in the early 1930s. The fact that one of the best books on jazz was written by a man who had learned about it entirely in France testified eloquently to the importance of the Paris jazz scene.

Hugues Panassié never viewed jazz as an exclusively black phenomenon, and always gave credit to leading white performers. Yet he consistently recognized the African American experience as the source of this musical inspiration. During the 1930s, he gradually gained a greater appreciation of black jazz, so much so that by 1942 he would write that "from the point of view of jazz, most white musicians were inferior to black musicians." At the same time, in contrast to the primitivist jazz fans of the 1920s who viewed it as a kind of African jungle rhythm, Panassié emphasized its roots in American culture. Hugues Panassié's promotion of jazz in the 1930s represents perhaps the single most important example of the impact of African Americans on the cultural life of France. He wrote: "the sources of this swing music are unquestionably Negroid. It is that expression of sadness, of the melancholy of the soul of the oppressed Negro, which gives swing music its intensely moving accent. This poetic quality is another thing peculiar to swing music, deeply comprehended only after long experience."

During the 1930s, white French musicians also began to make major contributions to jazz. A small number of French performers had been experimenting with jazz since the early 1920s, partly in response to the great demand for dance bands by Parisian nightclubs. Many sat in with African American musicians or formed their own groups. Most notable were Django Reinhardt and Stéphane Grappelli. Reinhardt, of French gypsy origin, soon established a reputation as a world-class guitar player, one of the best jazz has ever produced, and certainly the most important French jazz musician at the time. Stéphane Grappelli used the violin to showcase both technical virtuosity and improvisational insight. In the early 1930s, Reinhardt and Grappelli established the Quintet of the Hot Club of France, under the sponsorship of Hugues Panassié. The quintet played all the leading jazz clubs in Paris during the 1930s. Bricktop called them "the hottest thing in the world."

African American musicians in Paris did more than simply play tepid melodies for tipsy night owls. In the early 1930s, Coleman Hawkins, the "father of the tenor saxophone" traveled to Europe and stayed there for the rest of the decade, shuttling among Britain, France, Holland, Denmark, and Switzerland. In Paris, Hugues Panassié led him to perform with other musicians in the Hot Club of France. At the end of February 1935, Hawkins teamed up with Benny Carter, Arthur Briggs, Django Reinhardt, Stéphane Grappelli, and others to record an album, *Coleman Hawkins and Benny Carter*, which blended some of the best of French and American jazz. Long available only in Europe, the record was reissued in the United States in 1985. It immediately won high praise; one reviewer commented, "The unity of the four saxophonists and the drive with which Reinhardt backs them on guitar has made these classic jazz recordings. Grappelli . . . joins Reinhardt and Hawkins in a trio treatment of 'Star Dust' that is outstanding for its interplay between the saxophonist and the guitarist."

Even though Paris in these years boasted a vibrant jazz culture with many excellent performers, earning the French capital a place on the cutting edge of the art form, jazz remained firmly anchored in the American experience. Paris simply could not compete with Chicago or New York, or even smaller but up-and-coming centers like Kansas City, in terms of the number of musicians or the size and loyalty of audiences. Although several of the greatest American jazz performers visited Paris during these years, most notably Duke Ellington and Louis Armstrong, none of them lived there for any length of time. Many jazz musicians in Paris kept in touch by buying American albums whenever possible, and Panassié's *Le Jazz Hot* served as a guide to these records. Yet Parisian jazz was more than a transatlantic reflection of the real thing. By the early 1930s, it had transcended its roots as a black American import to synthesize the ideas and talents of both French and American musicians. African American jazz artists thus not only played pleasing dance music, but they also helped carve out new spaces and opportunities in interwar French culture.

PARIS, GATEWAY TO AFRICA

Paris helped open African Americans to a wider world in another sense, giving blacks from the United States contacts with other forms of black music. One example of this new openness was the Bal Nègre in the Left Bank's rue Blomet. First opened in 1928, the Bal Nègre quickly became famous as a leading nightspot for dancing and listening to black music. Like Bricktop's, it attracted people of all races and all walks of life with live music and dancing that continued till the wee hours of the morning. Yet unlike most black American nightspots, it was located in Montparnasse, more known for its artists and cafés than Montmartre. More important, the Bal Nègre featured orchestras from the French West Indies, not the United States, which specialized in the beguine, a popular dance of Caribbean origin. The Bal Nègre and several other nightclubs that came into existence at this time in Paris primarily catered to people from Martinique, Guadeloupe, and other islands of the French Caribbean; one newspaper reporter estimated this population at roughly one thousand in Montparnasse alone. Yet African Americans were certainly welcome at the Bal Nègre. Here in "the French Harlem," as Joel Augustus Rogers called it, African Americans could experience the rhythms of a black culture similar to, yet distinct, from their own.

> The orchestra is original French West Indian, and the music, too. No saxophone, no jazz, but banjos, horns and drums. The hip movement of the dance shows its African origin.
>
> The tempo is set by a shiny thing shaped like a cocktail shaker pierced with many holes. In it are several pebbles, which makes a strange peculiar noise as the leader shakes it with a movement as if he were throwing it away from him.
>
> As to the dancing, it is smoother and much less jerky than jazz. The music is lively and gay. The dresses of many of the colored women are also different. Their gowns have striking colors; they are flowing and reach out to the heels as in the good old days. Some wear bright-colored bandanas, tied so as to bring the kerchief to two points, which stick upward like the horns of a snail.
>
> The colored person from the United States who visits this place had better bring his interpreter with him if he does not speak French.

Many African Americans in Paris frequented the Bal Nègre and similar night-clubs. In August 1929, Eric Walrond, J. A. Rogers, Zaidee Jackson, and several others finished up a night of carousing by going there to "do a mean bit of ringing and twisting."

Paradoxically, this Caribbean dance hall seems to have attracted more black American writers than musicians, a phenomenon that reveals much about expatriate social life in Paris during these years. The small number of African Americans in Paris emphasized the common interests of both writers and musicians, and members of the two groups certainly came into contact on a regular basis. Most writers found their way to Bricktop's and other black clubs, although they certainly did not go there every night (few could afford to), and many saw Josephine Baker perform. Musicians and writers also met at social occasions, notably the party given for the cast of *Blackbirds* by the white literary agent William Bradley in 1929. Nonetheless, the two groups remained distinct, with separate lifestyles and professional concerns. Writers visited and sometimes lived in Montmartre, but the neighborhood did not dominate their lives the way it did those who earned a living there. During the 1930s, most came as temporary visitors, usually in the summers, and did not have to meet the same kinds of regular schedules as black musicians. They often got to-gether for dinners and parties, and in general did not establish a regular presence in public spaces like cafés and nightclubs. As a result, black writers usually gained a more cosmopolitan appreciation of the French capital than did black musicians; they were more likely to speak French, for example, and tended to explore both its monuments and its diverse cultures to a much greater extent. Partly because these writers lacked a strong focus, Montmartre remained the center of African American life in Paris during the interwar years. However, one can also glimpse foreshadowings of the independent black writers' subculture that would emerge full-blown in the 1950s.

Countee Cullen often visited the Bal Nègre during his frequent trips to Paris in the 1930s. One of the leading young poets of the Harlem Renaissance, Cullen had been attracted to French culture ever since his school days in New York, and eventually earned his living as a teacher of French. He first traveled to Paris in 1928 on a Guggenheim fellowship, enrolling as a student of French literature at the University of Paris. During the 1930s, he spent almost every summer in France, studying, exploring the city, and visiting friends like Henry Ossawa Tanner and Augusta Savage. The rue Blomet nightclub's at-traction for Cullen represented an interesting aspect of his time in Paris, because of all the black Americans who landed in the city at the time he was perhaps the most fascinated with classic French culture. Well versed in

French poetry, especially Baudelaire, Verlaine, and Rimbaud, he also developed an appreciation for the cultures of French blacks in Paris, meeting René Maran and a number of other Caribbean writers during his stays. As Cullen noted during the performance of Berlioz's *The Damnation of Faust* at the Paris Opera, "I don't like it . . . I'd rather be at the Bal."

The Bal Nègre is a good example of an important theme in Parisian African American life during the early 1930s: a strong curiosity about different forms of black culture from throughout the world. In particular, many members of the black American community in the city displayed a new affinity for Africa. This interest in African roots had a long history in the cultural and intellectual life of black Americans, and had most recently played an important role in the Harlem Renaissance, as poets, painters, and musicians worked to portray the unique qualities of the black experience. Its increased importance at the end of the Jazz Age reflected new levels of maturity and self-confidence among black intellectuals and artists. Black culture was a source of pride, not shame, and many thought its African source should therefore be explored and championed.

The part played by Paris in the African American rediscovery of Africa was both fascinating and deeply ironic. After all, the city was the seat of one of the world's great colonial empires, a place where anonymous French officials supervised the subjugation of millions of black Africans. French intellectuals may have appreciated Africa's art, but French leaders of government and industry appreciated her natural and labor resources much more. Yet France's role as a colonial power also brought thousands of her subjects to the French capital as students and workers. Outside of Marseilles, London, and some other British cities, one could not find a more diverse black population anywhere in Europe. More so than in the United States, even New York, African Americans found that in Paris the abstract ideal of worldwide black unity and culture became a tangible reality. At a time when Africa itself remained a distant and little-known continent for many black Americans, Paris became a place where a few of them could meet Africans and gain a deeper appreciation of African culture. While French blacks lived there during the 1920s, the city's role as an international meeting place for blacks loomed largest in the early 1930s, spurred above all by the development of the literary movement negritude. French colonialism and primitivism thus paradoxically combined to foster a vision of pan-African unity.

In 1936, Eslanda Goode Robeson, the wife of Paul Robeson, published a two-part article entitled "Black Paris" in the black American literary journal

Challenge. Based on interviews she conducted in the summer of 1932, it provided a survey of black life in Paris during the early years of the decade. "Black Paris" began with the kind of lyrical description of the many sights of the city beloved by American audiences, both black and white.

> Extravagantly wide sidewalks with splendid trees marching along the curbs; beautifully laid out boulevards, avenues, and streets with fascinating names; lovely quiet shabby sections reeking with historical associations. Sacre Coeur in the sunlight, in the moonlight. Notre Dame. Bookstalls on the banks of the Seine. Marvellous food. . . . The Opera, American Express, Thomas Cook's. Rue de la Paix, Galeries Lafayette, Au Bon Marché. Montmartre and the cabarets; Montparnasse and the sidewalk cafes.

For black Americans, as for so many others, the Paris of historical sights and tourist attractions first piqued their attention, even in the depths of the Depression. Yet Eslanda Robeson quickly went on to underline the significance of prominent blacks in making the French capital so alluring: "In such a setting, who would think of Negroes? Not even Negroes themselves. And yet Negroes form a definite part of Parisian life, and play an important and recognized role in the political, educational, intellectual, literary and theatrical life of Paris, in the ordinary every-day life, and in the night-life."

Eslanda Robeson's article is particularly noteworthy because the majority of illustrious Parisian blacks it describes are African or Caribbean in origin, not African American. Robeson discusses in greatest detail two individuals: Prince Kojo Touvalou Hovénou of Dahomey and Paulette Nardal of Martinique. "Black Paris" thus differs significantly from many of the descriptions of black life in Paris during the 1920s left by African American writers, especially Joel Augustus Rogers. Like them, Robeson emphasizes black success and the lives of the elite, but she includes in the city's black community all people with black skin, no matter what their geographical origins. The section on Prince Touvalou details the customs and culture of his native Dahomey, transforming this elegant black Parisian into a guide to Africa. Robeson's description of Paulette Nardal emphasized her interest in bringing together black writers from the United States, Africa, and the West Indies. Eslanda Goode Robeson was a visitor to Paris rather than a long-term resident, but she astutely shaped her article around themes that accurately reflected the spirit of the times.

Mercer Cook, a professor of French literature at Howard University, also played an important role in developing African American awareness of French black life in the 1930s. Like Countee Cullen, Cook made frequent visits to Paris during his summers off and got to know most of the leading French Caribbean and African writers there. In December 1938, he gave a talk at Atlanta University on black life in France. Entitled "The Race Problem in Paris and the French West Indies," it was published the following year in the *Journal of Negro Education* and amounts to one of the first major discussions of black life in France by an African American intellectual. In his speech, Cook made clear his belief in France as a color-blind nation.

> For many years France has enjoyed — and rightly so, I believe — the reputation of being the most liberal country in Europe. . . . Many of the Negroes living in Paris constitute an elite. They are, for the most part, students, teachers, professional and business men, writers, governmental officials and the like. Menials and soldiers also make up a large percentage of the number. All of these people live wherever their means permit them to live, go where they please and with whom they please. . . . In the French Chamber of Deputies, in addition to the six Negroes representing the colonies, there are two colored members elected by departments where there are probably not ten Negro voters.

In years to come Mercer Cook would work actively to bring the literature of French black Africa and the Caribbean to the attention of blacks in the United States.

The small community of African American visual artists in Paris often embraced African modes of expression during the 1930s. This trend of course did not represent a radically new departure for black American artists. In 1924 Laura Waring's cover designs for *The Crisis* had emphasized African themes. Alain Locke's *New Negro* anthology, published in 1925, had called on black painters and sculptors to highlight African artistic influences on their own work. Primitivist ideas were especially pronounced in French art circles, so that young African Americans who came to study art in the French capital often got more exposure to African art there than at home. Yet judging from the works produced by black American artists in Paris, such "Africanism" seems to have been most notable in the late 1920s and 1930s. Black painters and sculptors produced several important works portraying African and West Indian figures, vivid testimonies to a transatlantic black consciousness.

This visual Africanism was not based for the most part on direct experiences with the African continent. Although Henry Ossawa Tanner and a few others visited North Africa, none of the African American artists working in Paris traveled in the continent south of the Sahara during these years. Their contact with Africa and the wider black world was thus very much a Parisian phenomenon, based on both people and works of art encountered in the French capital. One particularly important source of inspiration was the Colonial Exposition of 1931. In order to impress the significance of the empire upon the ordinary people of France, who in all likelihood would never travel there, the French government sponsored the construction of a huge fairgrounds displaying examples of colonial architecture, cuisine, and culture. Built in the city's spacious Bois de Vincennes, the Colonial Exposition created a primitivist fantasy world, one in which people could take the subway to visit Cambodian temples, African jungle villages, and Saharan oases. The exposition scored a huge success, attracting more than thirty million visitors in six months. It was the single most important example of the fascination with the exotic in Paris between the wars, and its great popularity demonstrated conclusively the importance of such colonialist imagery to the people of France.

For African Americans in France, the Colonial Exposition reinforced the view of Paris as the gateway to Africa. Artists in particular were drawn to the visual splendor of the exhibit's portrayals of black people. Palmer Hayden, for example, painted watercolors of African dancers based on performers he had seen at the exposition. Augusta Savage sculpted an African warrior, entitled *Amazon,* which won her a gold medal. In a letter to W.E.B. Du Bois, the sculptress Nancy Elizabeth Prophet expressed her enthusiasm for the exposition: "Heads of thought and reflection, types of great beauty and dignity of carriage. I believe it is the first time that this type of African has been brought to the attention of the world of modern times. Am I right? People are seeing the aristocracy of Africa."

African American artists in Paris made numerous references to African art, both in the form and in the content of their own works. Many portrayed people from Africa and the Caribbean, often using live models. The sculptures of Nancy Prophet exemplified this fascination with Africa and Africans. *Congolese* (1931) is an elegantly simple bust of an African figure. The head's strongly African features and its contemplative, dignified gaze affirm the richness of black culture. Taken together, these and other Africanist works by black American artists in Paris testify to that city's importance as a meeting place for blacks from throughout the world. These artists came to Paris inspired by its reputation as the world's preeminent art center; in the French capital they learned to reemphasize the importance of black artistic expression.

The late 1920s and early 1930s represented a high point for African American visual artists in Paris. In contrast, after the middle of the decade the Depression made art studies in Paris even more inaccessible for black Americans. Only five came to live in the French capital between 1935 and 1940, and only two successfully established themselves as major artists. Selma Burke, originally from North Carolina, had worked as both a nurse and an artists' model in Philadelphia and New York before receiving fellowships to travel and study in Europe in the late 1930s. She is most remembered for her design of the head of Franklin Delano Roosevelt which still appears on the American dime.

Loïs Mailou Jones was the most important black American to study art in Paris during the late 1930s. A dynamic, attractive woman with an engaging smile, Jones came from an elite Boston family. In 1931, she became a professor of art at Howard University, interrupting her work to study painting in Paris during the academic year 1937–38 at the Académie Julian. Upon arrival in France, Louis Achille, a former colleague at Howard and one of the pioneers of negritude, helped her find a lovely penthouse apartment in the heart of Montparnasse, containing three levels and wall space two stories high. Living and working in a beautiful studio with a roof garden and a view of the Eiffel Tower, Jones spent the year perfecting her technique, taking inspiration from both French and African art, and simply enjoying the city. She met French and American colleagues, including Albert Smith, an expatriate painter who had come to France shortly after the war. As she later noted, "It was like being free for the first time — my paintings were exhibited . . . purely on merit."

Nonetheless, Jones worked hard in Paris and produced more than forty paintings, several of which won acceptance and praise in the Paris art world. Much of her work was modeled on French impressionism and did not address any specifically black themes. She in fact rejected any view of her as *just* a black artist. However, two of the paintings from Jones's year in Paris did borrow from black and African art. *Jeanne, Martiniquaise* (1938) portrays a Martinicuan woman, whereas *Les Fétiches* (1938) is an abstract depiction of an African mask. Not only do these two paintings use black subject matter, but the geometrical, stylized composition so striking in both refers to French cubism *and* to African sculpture. In commenting on the reception of *Les Fétiches* by her teachers, Jones noted, "When I took *Les Fétiches* to my professors to see, it didn't look like a Loïs Jones painting. They couldn't understand how I could do such a thing, because it dealt with cubism and the masks. And then I reminded them that Picasso, Matisse and Modigliani had made great use of African art, and I asked if they didn't think that Loïs Jones, whose heritage is Africa, has more right to do so. And they had to smile." Jones returned to France after the Second World War frequently from the 1940s to the 1960s.

As the example of Loïs Mailou Jones demonstrates, African American visual artists in Paris made use of a number of different styles in their work, not just those derived from African art. The most important of them all, Henry Ossawa Tanner, made no use at all of such influences in his painting. These people came to Paris for the same reasons as other students from all over the world: to learn about new techniques and sources of inspiration in the city that still remained the undisputed center of the art world. They did not need to go there to find out they were black; life in America had already made that abundantly clear. However, life in Paris did bring them into contact to a much greater extent with both African art and a cosmopolitan black population, giving theories of the African roots of black American art a new immediacy and force. As other African American intellectuals would conclude at times during the twentieth century, for many of these artists the road to Africa ran through Paris.

Although the work of black American artists in Paris provides a striking visual illustration of this phenomenon, the most important example of transatlantic black unity in the arts during the 1930s occurred in literature. In the early years of the decade, several students from French colonies in Africa and the West Indies started a new movement to revitalize and revalorize black culture. Taking the name *nègritude,* or blackness, these young writers explored in poetry and essays what it ultimately meant to be black. Negritude would become one of the most important developments in black aesthetics anywhere in the world during the twentieth century, but its heart lay in Paris. The fruit of debates engaged in by black students and intellectuals there for over a decade, it would more than anything else underline the central role played by black Parisians in creating a cosmopolitan community during the interwar years. Ironically, however, at the same time negritude further demonstrated the importance of primitivist ideas in helping define images of blacks in early twentieth-century France. In their discussions about the nature of black culture, young African and Caribbean students in Paris owed a large intellectual debt to the surrealists and other French avant-garde intellectuals.

Negritude represented a series of complex approaches to black culture, but above all it stood for an affirmation of blackness. Rejecting the assimilationism frequently espoused by upper-class mulattoes and blacks from the French Caribbean in particular, its young partisans emphasized the integrity and beauty of a culture whose roots lay in Africa. The stress on the history of African culture had a political as well as aesthetic dimension: young black writers used it to attack the colonialist idea that European rule was necessary to bring civilization to the Africans, and thus to press for self-determination for all peoples of African descent. Like the followers of Marcus Garvey in the 1920s, they condemned Western imperialism as racist and demanded African independence. The young negritude writers went further, however, in condemning European culture and capitalism in general as soulless and alienating. They stood, in contrast, for both political and cultural revolution, for the freedom of blacks throughout the world from all forms of European domination.

In March 1935, several black students in Paris launched the negritude movement by founding a new literary and cultural journal named *L'Etudiant Noir*. Two of its founders in particular would become widely recognized as the leaders of negritude: Léopold Senghor, a West African who would one day become the first president of independent Senegal, and Aimé Césaire, a poet from Martinique who would gain widespread literary recognition and eventually a seat in the French national assembly. In 1939, Césaire published a book of poetry, *Cahier d'un retour au pays natal (Notes on Return to My Native Land)*, that would become the standard-bearer of the negritude movement. A passionate attack on the oppression of blacks in Martinique and throughout the world, *Notes* also represented an aesthetic embrace of black culture, with vibrant images and allusions to the history and folklore of the Caribbean. It symbolized the unity of cultural and political self-affirmation that constituted the heart of negritude.

Although negritude was a creation of French-speaking black intellectuals, African American writers exercised an important influence on it. In fact, so significant was this influence that to a large extent negritude seemed to be a transatlantic reflection of the Harlem Renaissance. It adopted and pursued many themes, such as antiracism, interest in Africa, and insistence on the unique and valuable quality of black culture, developed by some of the talented black American writers in the decade after the Great War. In particular, young writers like Senghor, Césaire, Léon Damas, Etienne Léro, Félix Eboué, and Birago Diop closely followed the writings of Jean Toomer, Langston Hughes, Countee Cullen, and above all Claude McKay. It is no accident that all of these last four authors spent time in Paris during the interwar years, enabling African and Caribbean students not only to read their work, but also to meet them in person. Negritude thus represented another type of cosmopolitan black community in Paris during the 1930s. In contrast to the experience of African American artists there, however, America's black writers played the role of teachers, not students. Like jazz musicians, they had something unique to offer, and they found people in Paris eager to receive their ideas. The fact that those people were black French men and women meant that in the 1930s African American ideas influenced French culture and helped reshape the very nature of racial identity in modern France.

The contacts between black American and black French writers that helped create negritude did not just happen. In fact, blacks from different parts of the French Empire often held aloof from each other, so that one crucial goal of negritude was simply to bring people from different cultures and parts of the world into a unified and coherent black community. These differences shaped black life in Paris itself; as Eslanda Goode Robeson noted in her article,

> The average French Negro has no idea that there are important men and important work in Negro art in America. In Martinique the Negroes think all American Negroes are prize-fighters, because a prize-fighter once visited the Antilles; they know nothing of Negro art and Negro music in America. The Negroes from the French West Indies (Antillean) dislike African Negroes because they have an older civilization; cultured Antilleans are often sent to Africa as civil servants by the French government.

In the early 1930s students and intellectuals from the French West Indies took the lead in creating this community of black creative minds in Paris. No one deserves more credit than Paulette Nardal of Martinique. A beautiful, dark-skinned woman, Nardal came from an elite black family. Her father was an important engineer and her mother was a schoolteacher on her home island. A graduate of the Sorbonne, where she had earned a degree in English literature, Nardal taught school briefly in Martinique before returning to Paris to patch together a living as a journalist. In Paris, Nardal moved in with her cousins, the Achilles. Louis Achille, Sr., was a professor of English at a Parisian high school. His son, Louis Jr., had taught at Howard University in the early 1930s, and came to know several leading African American intellectuals. Their apartment at 51 rue Geoffroy-Saint-Hilaire, on the Left Bank near the Jardin des Plantes, became in the early 1930s a gathering place for both Caribbean intellectuals and blacks visiting from the United States.

Like so many members of the black elite in Martinique, in her youth Paulette Nardal had considered herself French; the word *black* was reserved for Africans or members of the lower classes. Life in Paris soon taught her that the French did not distinguish between blacks from different parts of the world, thus awakening in her a determination to embrace her racial identity with pride. Nardal's interest in questions of black culture and her fluency in English soon attracted her to the literature of the Harlem Renaissance. She and her sisters Jane and Andrée began hosting social gatherings that brought together black intellectuals of diverse backgrounds in Paris. As Léopold Seng-hor would later note, "It was during the years 1929–1934 that we made contact with American Negroes through the intermediary of Mademoiselle Andrée Nardal, who . . . held a literary salon where African Negroes, West Indians, and American Negroes could meet." These gatherings generally took place on Sundays, and featured not only discussions about the nature of black art and life in Africa, America, and Europe, but also dancing. The Nardal sisters were skilled musicians and would play American jazz for the enjoyment of their guests. Senghor enjoyed these parties, although in contrast to primitivist ideas about Africans he proved an uncomfortable, awkward dancer.

At the suggestion of Dr. Leo Sajous, a Haitian dentist who had tried to create a Negro Institute in 1929, Paulette Nardal decided to recast her inter-national literary salon (which she preferred to call a "circle of friends") in a broader, more enduring format. In November 1931, she and Dr. Sajous launched the *Revue du Monde Noir (Review of the Black World)*, a monthly magazine devoted to writings on international black culture. In one sense, the *Revue* was simply the latest example of a number of small journals devoted to black politics, culture, and colonial questions published by French-speaking black intellectuals in interwar Paris. Yet it made a unique attempt to cross linguistic and geographic barriers in showcasing the best of contemporary black literature and thought. Published in a bilingual French and English edition, the *Revue* featured original stories, essays, and poems by some of the most talented and renowned black American authors. Langston Hughes, Claude McKay, Walter White, and Jessie Fauset all published work in its pages. Also featured in the *Revue* were writers from the West Indies like Léon Damas, the Goncourt Prize–winner René Maran, and Nardal's cousin Louis Achille, Jr., as well as Africans such as Félix Eboué. Although the *Revue* was dominated by blacks from the French Caribbean, it self-consciously strove for the most cosmopolitan writership possible. An editorial in the first issue of the *Revue du Monde Noir* clearly proclaimed the new journal's commitment to international perspectives on black culture, declaring as its purpose:

> To give to the intelligentia [*sic*] of the blak [*sic*] race and their partisans an official organ in which to publish their artistic, literary and scientific works.
>
> To study and to popularize, by means of the press, books, lectures, courses, all which concerns Negro civilization and the natural riches of Africa, thrice-sacred to the black race.
>
> The triple aim which La Review du Monde Noir will pursue, will be: to create among the Negroes of the entire world, regardless of nationality, an intellectual, and moral tie, which will permit them to better know each other,

to love one another, to defend more effectively their collective interests and to glorify their race.

What could black people of diverse nationalities, languages, social status, and historical experiences possibly have in common? This fundamental question shaped the efforts of the writers and editors of the *Revue,* and their collective answer was black culture. Nardal and Sajous in particular argued that all peoples of African descent throughout the world shared a common culture, one based upon emotion and innate artistic creativity. They contrasted this warm, expressive approach to life with the cold, rational, and scientific civilization of the white world. European science may have conquered the world, but none could deny the value and contribution made by black art, music, and literature to human enlightenment. As Louis Achille wrote in the premier issue of the *Revue,* "Negroes are essentially artists. Since American Negro music and dance and African sculpture have been made known all over the world, this can no longer be questioned. In no other human race, indeed, is the aesthetic sense so general a gift and does it so often interrupt the activity of each individual." In publishing examples of black writing from around the globe, the *Revue* intended to demonstrate concretely this aesthetic racial unity.

The *Revue du Monde Noir* lasted for less than a year, publishing only six issues in all. Yet its themes of international black unity and essential black culture struck a chord among many in Paris, and exercised a strong influence on the negritude movement a few years later. Shortly after the death of the *Revue,* another group of Martinicuan students in Paris created *Légitime Défense.* Although this journal emphasized political rather than cultural black unity, many of its collaborators had written for the *Revue* and so it also emphasized connections with African American writers, especially Hughes and McKay. *L'Etudiant Noir* also stressed culture as the key to the international black experience. These periodicals, and the beginnings of negritude in general, demonstrated that the seeds sown by the *Revue du Monde Noir* a few years previously had found fertile soil.

Of all the African American writers who passed through Paris during the 1920s and 1930s, none had a greater influence on the negritude movement than Claude McKay. McKay's own life symbolized and embraced the cosmopolitanism of the black experience. The Jamaican-born McKay, who spent much of his youth in the United States and then traveled extensively in Europe during most of the interwar years, even briefly visited Morocco so as to establish some firsthand contact with the African continent. Few could thus claim to know the different regions and cultures of the black world better than he. More important than McKay's personal experiences, however, were his writings, in which he outlined a perspective on black culture and life that prefigured many of the key themes of negritude. Above all, his novel *Banjo*, more than anything else written by an African American in this period, embraced a conception of blackness that strongly attracted the young African and Caribbean students of Paris.

Published in 1928 and almost immediately translated into French, *Banjo* portrays the lives of several disparate black characters living in the picturesque waterfront slums of Marseilles. It is an autobiographical novel, whose main protagonist, Ray, closely resembles Claude McKay himself. McKay based *Banjo* on his own experiences living in Marseilles in the winter of 1927. Traditionally a crossroads of the Mediterranean and one of the least "French" places in France, in the early twentieth century Marseilles hosted a diverse population of longshoremen, sailors, and other port workers from throughout the Mediterranean, the French empire, and beyond. This lively and cosmopolitan port powerfully attracted McKay; as he noted in his autobiography, *A Long Way from Home*: "It was a relief to get to Marseilles, to live in among a great gang of black and brown humanity. Negroids from the United States, the West Indies, North Africa and West Africa, all herded together in a warm group. Negroid features and complexions, not exotic, creating curiosity and hostility, but unique and natural to a group."

Key to the novel is the relationship between Ray/McKay and the character named Banjo, a black American former sailor from the Deep South who is more or less permanently beached in Marseilles. Whereas Ray is a self-conscious intellectual tortured by racial, political, and other momentous conflicts, the uneducated Banjo is perfectly content to take life as he finds it, disdaining work and asking for little more than wine, women, and song. Banjo, who like several other characters in the novel, always speaks in dialect, gradually comes to represent pure black culture uncorrupted by Western rationality or assimilationist pretensions. Both he and Ray condemn those black characters who call for a more refined, "civilized," and elitist approach to black life; the novel condemns this desire to "uplift the race" as devaluing the culture of ordinary black people in favor of white standards. Ultimately Banjo becomes Ray's cultural guru, unconsciously guiding him back to an appreciation of the unique achievements of his own people.

Ray's thoughts were far and away beyond the right and wrong of the matter. He had been dreaming of what joy it would be to go vagabonding with Banjo.

Stopping here and there, staying as long as the feeling held in the ports where black men assembled for the great transport lines, loafing after their labors long enough to laugh and love and jazz and fight. . . . He had associated too closely with the beach boys not to realize that their loose, instinctive way of living was more deeply related to his own self-preservation than all the principles, or social-morality lessons with which he had been inculcated by the wiseacres of the civilized machine.

Banjo created a portrayal of black life that corresponded with the ideas of the young negritude writers in several respects. While McKay accurately represented the differences between blacks from different parts of the French empire, he nonetheless created a gritty yet romantic portrait of a community that brought together peoples of African descent from throughout the world. What ultimately united them, more even than their common exclusion from white society, were the wellsprings of African culture.

"'Beguin,' 'jelly-roll,' 'burru,' 'bombé,' no matter what the name may be, Negroes are never so beautiful and magical as when they do that gorgeous sublimation of the primitive African sex feeling. In its thousand varied patterns, depending so much on individual rhythm, so little on formal movement, this dance is the key to the African rhythm of life." *Banjo* thus presented themes of international black cultural unity that would become very influential in the development of negritude. As Aimé Césaire would note, "What struck me in the book was that for the first time one saw Negroes described truthfully, without complexes or prejudices."

Yet in calling for an authentic black culture, both McKay and the negritude writers also owed a major debt to French aesthetic and cultural influences. Just as African American artists like Loïs Mailou Jones learned about African sculpture in part through French intermediaries, so did these intellectuals draw from certain French thinkers a greater appreciation of African culture. French anthropologists, for example, played an important role in propagating new views of Africa. Black students in Paris avidly read Maurice Delafosse's *The Negroes* (1927), which portrayed in historical and archaeological detail the medieval kingdoms of West Africa, arguing that the Middle Ages in Africa and Europe had many points in common. Equally popular was Leo Frobenius's *History of African Civilization* (1936), which not only described advanced African civilizations but also linked them to that of ancient Egypt. The acclaim accorded African art by French critics, notably Georges Hardy in his book *Negro Art* (1927), also helped increase the prestige of the ancestral continent. New French literary movements during the 1920s, such as dadaism and surrealism, which rejected sterile rationality and much of traditional

European culture, likewise appealed to the young black intellectuals who created the negritude movement. In 1932, the editors of *Légitime Défense* proclaimed their loyalty to the path blazed by writers like André Breton and Tristan Tzara. When Aimé Césaire returned to Martinique during the 1940s, he founded a literary journal, *Tropiques*, that owed much to surrealist ideas.

It was thus no accident that a movement like negritude should develop in Paris. For young black intellectuals in the 1930s — not only Americans, but even Africans like Senghor — the French capital served as the gateway to Africa. This filter is both highly ironic and problematic. In accepting a vision of black culture refracted through French eyes, the negritude writers seemed at times to be merely relabeling traditional white stereotypes of blacks as positive cultural attributes. This tendency was especially notable in *Banjo*, whose very title constitutes a provocative allusion to a certain kind of Southern racist imagery. The emphasis on an essentialist and unified black culture at times uncomfortably recalled arguments about natural rhythm. As the Senegalese poet David Diop observed a generation later, "'To bring back the great African myths,' of tropical mysteries accompanied by the beat of tom toms, would be to furnish the colonialist bourgeois with the reassuring image he desires. That is the surest way to fabricate a poetry of 'folklore' which would only impress those salons where one discusses 'Negro art.'" French primitivism not only praised but also stereotyped black culture; to what extent was negritude simply a kind of primitivism in blackface?

Such essentialist views of black culture had inspired intense controversy in the Harlem Renaissance, with many of the community's leading literary figures sharply condemning such perspectives as false, stereotypical, and ultimately validating white prejudices. Major literary critics like William Stanley Braithwaite and Benjamin Brawley assailed what they considered a morbid, exoticist fascination with the black underclass. W.E.B. Du Bois argued that black writers should concentrate on the more refined, respectable aspects of black culture, those that white Americans preferred to ignore. The 1926 publication of *Nigger Heaven* by the white writer Carl Van Vechten triggered a firestorm of protest from these and many other Harlem intellectuals who considered the novel a lurid primitivist fantasy unrepresentative of black life. Claude McKay, who admired Van Vechten, also scandalized the Harlem literary establishment with his emphasis on jazz, sensuality, and the emotionality of the black working class. McKay's 1928 novel *Home to Harlem* generated the same kind of scandalized reaction as *Nigger Heaven*, and *Banjo* itself fared little better at the hands of many black reviewers, who attacked McKay for simply confirming old stereotypes in a new, more positive guise. Harlem's

Amsterdam News judged *Banjo* harshly, accusing its author of "slurring his own people to please white readers."

Certainly the prospect of Westernized intellectuals like Césaire and Senghor embracing, from Paris, a romanticized vision of black culture has its bizarre aspects. Yet ultimately one must evaluate negritude positively, emphasizing its differences from French primitivism. It proclaimed that peoples of African descent contributed significantly to the civilization of the world, and in praising the culture of a people so often deemed inferior and degraded it struck a powerful blow for racial equality and self-respect. Like the surrealists, who attacked the Colonial Exposition for glossing over the brutalities of imperialism, the negritude writers firmly rejected the racist condescension that so often accompanied European negrophilism. Their trenchant critique of European superiority and colonialism would bear fruit in Africa after the Second World War, as Senghor's own career demonstrated so dramatically. In both its positive and negative aspects, negritude and the broader veneration of African culture by blacks in interwar Paris represented a complex cross-fertilization of black and white intellectuals, and it was the cosmopolitan, brilliant character of life in the French capital that made it possible.

DEPRESSION BLUES

During the 1930s, Paris remained a special place for black culture, retaining a certain attraction for African American intellectuals and artists. Yet the thirties were above all the Depression decade, and the harsh realities of the time soon intruded into even this glamorous sphere. Black musicians in particular soon discovered that high unemployment made many French less hospitable than they'd been a decade earlier. Although the public continued to display a strong taste for jazz, French musicians began complaining more vocally about foreign competition. Veterans groups in Paris campaigned against foreign musicians, at one point initiating a boycott of all restaurants that used orchestras with non-French nationals. In October 1930, three hundred unemployed French musicians staged an angry confrontation with a music hall owner who used a Russian orchestra. The same group later distributed leaflets in Montmartre asking music fans to "Demand that nightclub owners [employ] French orchestras . . . because the French musician can compete successfully with any foreign competitor. The taste for Negro musicians and other exotics is only a simple manifestation of snobbery. People of France, help us!" This opposition to foreign music did not cause a noticeable upsurge of public antagonism against African Americans in Paris. Writers and artists living there during the thirties continued to emphasize the color-blind quality of life in France, and Montmartre continued to treat black musicians with hospitality. However, such unrest did result in fewer job opportunities for foreigners, including jazz performers from America, in Paris.

The French government responded to the plight of French unemployed musicians and other skilled workers with a series of laws designed to force foreigners out of their professions. The Law for the Protection of National Labor, enacted in August 1932, enabled French unions and employers to request quotas on the hiring of non-nationals. The music industry established a quota system requiring nightclub owners to hire five French musicians for every foreign one. Some did not live up to the strict letter of the law, finding various ways of circumventing it. One French club owner with an eleven-piece American band did so simply by hiring fifty-five French musicians to do nothing while the Americans played. Nonetheless, the new law certainly had an impact. In 1933, one black American journalist described this change, arguing that it hurt the Parisian entertainment world in general:

> The European unions of musicians naturally desire to corner the field, and used their power to exclude most of the American musicians. But apart from the waltz and the tango, the European orchestras cannot play good dance music — that is, the jazzy, peppy kind. . . . Business is worse than dull in Montmartre these days. The colored musicians feel that if the night clubs had the right kind of music such American tourists that have the money would come out to these clubs, but that under present conditions they stay away rather than have to suffer such music as they would not tolerate at home. The colored musicians are hoping that the authorities will see that it is to their advantage to give them a break again.

By 1933, many foreign musicians complained of the slender job possibilities in Paris and Europe as a whole. Blacks, notably Gene Bullard, still owned a few Montmartre nightclubs: a woman named Neeka Shaw owned a cabaret featuring the piano stylings of Freddie Johnson, and the trumpet player Freddie Taylor briefly ran a place named the Harlem Club. These owners still gave black musicians as much work as possible, but the majority of Montmartre nightclub owners who were French bowed before the winds of change. Some musicians still managed to put enough gigs together to eke out a living in the French capital, but their prospects had become uncertain at best, and were to remain so for the rest of the decade. It was a far cry from life in the 1920s, when even the least talented black jazz musicians found plenty of work at good wages. The Jazz Age that had so thrilled and titillated Parisians had been reduced to a mournful swan song, and its African American troubadours became simply one more group of foreigners few wanted or needed. According to the *Chicago Defender*, "Several of the old time Race musicians have returned to America, while others, who were thought to be fixtures here, are planning to return. Some of these would return at once could they swim. Bricktop, once queen of Montmartre, may migrate to Spain. . . . As for Montmartre it is dead." This article exaggerated the situation, for many black Americans stayed in Montmartre despite the hard times. Nonetheless, it did indicate the general trend in Paris during the 1930s.

In fact, even though Bricktop remained in Paris during the 1930s, her life lost much of its habitual glamour. The fall of 1933 saw business at Bricktop's considerably reduced, and the famous entertainer hosted far fewer private parties than usual. She began noticing that many of her American millionaire clients were no longer coming to Paris or, when they did, no longer spending the huge sums of money that had made her fortune a few years earlier. Some even asked to borrow money, or relied on her to guarantee their steamship passage back home to America. American tourists, especially wealthy ones, had provided an important source of income for Montmartre nightclubs during the 1920s and early 1930s, and the sharp decline of this source of income hurt the neighborhood in general. Soon Bricktop was having trouble paying her own bills and fighting to keep her club a going concern. Hard times had come to Montmartre, and not even the great Bricktop was immune. "The Depression . . . brought the people of Montmartre closer together than they'd ever been before. The entertainers, most of whom lived there, got to know the French better. There was a surprising lack of bitterness. The most commonly heard sentence wasn't 'I wish things were the way they used to be.' No, it was 'Have you got any money?' . . . We all shared what we had and looked out for one another. . . . It was a scrounging existence." Scrounging was not enough, however; in 1936, Bricktop was forced to give up her nightclub and go to work for others. She continued her role as a hostess in Montmartre music spots till the end of the decade, but the closing of Bricktop's marked the end of an era for the black American community in Paris. African Americans had put down roots in Montmartre and did not disappear immediately, but the Depression brought a permanent end to the glory days of the 1920s.

If Bricktop found life difficult in Paris by the mid-1930s, others had a far worse time of it. The troubled decade created a new image of the African American in Paris: instead of the glamorous musician or performer at the center of a brilliant social whirl, one now encountered people scrambling to keep body and soul together, listlessly spending hour after fruitless hour at the city's cafés, without direction or prospects. A young man from New York named Paul Morris unfortunately typified this new black American expatriate. Morris had originally come to Paris in the summer of 1927, having won a scholarship from New York's Cooper Union to pursue his dream of studying sculpture in the French capital. He settled down in the Latin Quarter and studied with a professor at the Ecole des Beaux Arts for two years, until his scholarship funds ran out. Wanting to stay in Paris, Morris first worked for a sculptor, then moved to Montmartre to support himself with odd jobs as a nightclub pianist and singer. He made a living that was marginal at best; by 1933, the black journalist Edgar Wiggins commented on Morris's life in Paris in the following terms:

> It is nearly three years now that Paul has "existed" in Montmartre. Occasionally he gets a job as an extra in the movies; away from that he lives as best he can.
> It is a mighty dumb man that does not know when he is beaten. And Paul can be regarded as such, as there is absolutely nothing for him to look forward to by remaining here in his condition. He gives his age as 25. Conceals his birthplace, but not the fact that he was reared and educated in New York City. His mother, Mrs. Francis Morris, owns one of the many beauty parlors in Harlem, but Paul will not accept her advice and help and return to America.
> All of our group in Montmartre know Paul, who can speak five different languages fluently, and is forever talking about great things he is going to do. Most of them say he is crazy, but the truth of the matter is, he has absorbed too much of the atmosphere that exists in the Latin Quarter. The superiority complex has gained too great a hold on him; thus converting him into another "mad genius."

This portrait of Paul Morris presents a fascinating alternative view of African American life in Paris, demonstrating how the Depression shifted perspectives on the expatriate experience. Here the black American overseas appears as a lost individual, filled with false dreams and tragically alienated from his home and family. Wiggins presents an image of Paris as a dangerous temptress, one unconcerned with the fate of those who cannot meet her challenge. The juxtaposition of the Latin Quarter and Montmartre is particularly interesting, recalling once again the relationship between Greenwich Village and Harlem. The former seems especially bizarre and alien (Wiggins titled his article "Artists Live Queer in Paris Latin Quarter"), a refuge for those dedicated to eccentricity. In contrast, Montmartre is more like home, the place Morris retreats to after his dreams have gone sour. Yet ultimately Montmartre is not really his home and cannot give him the support and encouragement he so desperately needs. Far from representing an attractive alternative to life in America, Paris in these years seemed to have little to offer.

Such tragic stories of life in Paris were certainly not unique to the 1930s; Langston Hughes was also advised to go home when he arrived in Paris in 1924, and had he stayed much longer he might well have experienced the same difficulties as Paul Morris. Yet just as Hughes's life in Paris constitutes a fitting symbol for the 1920s, so does Morris's story accurately represent the mood of the 1930s. Moreover, by the mid-1930s many of the Paul Morrises of Paris had decided to make the best of a bad situation by crossing back to the other side of the Atlantic. No definitive numbers are available, but the African American population of Paris seems to have shrunk noticeably during the course of the decade. In March 1932, for example, a letter from the American Consul General in Paris indicated that "some of the most popular jazz bands in Paris were American, but most of them have had to leave because of the widespread unemployment among French musicians." Moreover, fewer talented young African Americans came to Paris to study in these years. The Harlem Renaissance had effectively deserted France and Europe by 1935; writers like Claude McKay had gone back to the United States, and no new aspiring talents came to take their places. Only three black American artists studied in Paris after the middle of the decade, most notably Loïs Mailou Jones. With the death of Henry Ossawa Tanner in 1937, the African American community lost one of its most noteworthy members. By this time it was easy to believe that the black American expatriate presence in Paris had merely been a passing phenomenon of the 1920s, one with neither relevance to the present nor prospects for the future.

And yet the community endured. Some of its members even prospered in these years. In particular, although there were fewer opportunities for musicians, the best could still get by. As Arthur Briggs later noted, "By 1935 all the bad musicians had faded out of the picture." Like Josephine Baker, those who had integrated into French life, spoke the language, and had personal attachments to French people were the most likely to remain. Although not a talented musician, Gene Bullard possessed the business acumen and Parisian connections necessary to survive the economic crisis. By 1933, he had not only opened a new nightclub, L'Escadrille, in the heart of black Montmartre, but was also running Gene Bullard's Athletic Club in the rue Mansart right around the corner. Both enterprises seem to have done well for the rest of the decade. Willie Lewis continued to lead his jazz band at Chez Florence for much of the 1930s, and many other African Americans who had come to Paris at the start of the 1920s remained well into the Depression years. The French capital also continued to attract a few visiting black American performers on tour in the 1930s. In August 1933, for example, Duke Ellington brought his band to Paris to play three triumphal concerts at the Salle Pleyel. The great bandleader and his colleagues were amazed at how intensely and earnestly French jazz fans followed their concerts. Louis Armstrong, already well known in Europe as the King of Jazz, had performed there the year before and stayed with Bricktop while in Paris. On a return visit in 1934, he sat in with the band at Bricktop's (in the process hurting the feelings of Django Reinhardt, who idolized Armstrong, by ignoring him). The same year, Cab Calloway's band made a brief appearance in the City of Light. Even in the 1930s, many Parisians retained an appetite for jazz, enough to ensure the livelihood if not the fortunes of a few select performers.

Although in these years the African American traffic between Paris and the United States went mostly west, a few younger musicians did come to the city for extended stays. The talented trumpet player Bill Coleman represented this new generation. Born in Centerville, Kentucky, in 1904 (his birth was officially recorded in the nearby hamlet of Paris), Coleman started playing the trumpet as a child, and began working in professional jazz bands in the early 1920s. By 1927, Coleman got a job playing with the band at Harlem's famed Savoy Ballroom, and spent the next several years working in different nightclubs in New York. A slender, quiet young man, his musical skill and ability to work smoothly with other musicians brought him many opportunities. In 1933, the leader of a Harlem jazz orchestra offered him the chance to tour in France, and so he first arrived in Paris in September of that year. This brief but exciting sojourn inspired Coleman to return to Paris two years later upon being offered a six-month contract in a jazz band. Bill Coleman would end up spending much of the rest of the decade in Paris, and as he later noted in his autobiography, *Trumpet Story*, begin a romance with the city that would endure for the rest of his life.

Like so many other black American musicians before him, Coleman soon settled into Montmartre, quickly becoming an integral part of that community.

Between Boudon's and Lisieux's was a little Harlem in the early morning when all the night spots were closed. The American musicians and entertainers gathered in those bars and the stores with the "tabac" signs. . . . Other American entertainers in Paris . . . were Opal Cooper, who sang at the Melody Bar;

Snow Fisher, a dancer and drummer; Alberta Hunter, a blues singer; Glover Compton, a singer who accompanied himself on piano; Al Brown, the ex–boxing champ; Gene Bullard, who had a gymnasium on rue Mansart; Marino and Norris, singers; Cle Saddler, an ex–alto sax player; Ray Stokes, pianist; and Harry Cooper, a trumpeter who had played with Duke Ellington.

Bill Coleman's experience in Paris during the late 1930s exemplifies the continuities of black American community life there. Like many others who came to the French capital, he had worked as a jazz musician throughout the United States before achieving recognition and a position in New York, and from there had been recruited to perform in Paris. Moreover, he describes a Montmartre that even in the Depression still had a functioning African American community, linked together by a network of jazz clubs, hotels, and restaurants packed into the small neighborhood. There Coleman encountered many friends and acquaintances from the States, an indication of both the international character of jazz in the interwar years as well as the close contacts between African Americans in Paris and those at home. All in all, the Paris discovered by Bill Coleman in 1935 did not differ significantly from the city Bricktop settled in ten years earlier. Black life in Montmartre may not have been as new and exciting as it had been at the beginning of the 1920s, yet certainly, to paraphrase Mark Twain, reports of its death had been greatly exaggerated a decade later.

PARIS IN WARTIME

Surviving the Depression was one thing. Confronting the renewed outbreak of war in Europe quite another. On September 1, 1939, the armed forces of Nazi Germany invaded Poland, and in response, on September 3, Britain and France reluctantly but determinedly declared war. World War II had begun, presenting the black American expatriates of Paris with a painful dilemma. On the one hand, many had lived in Paris for the better part of twenty years, had family ties there, and in general felt much more at home in France than they did in the United States. As Bricktop noted:

> even after I knew what I should do, which was to get out, I didn't. I realized there was really nowhere for me to go. I'd built my whole career, and lived a sizeable part of my life, in France. It had become my home. Returning to America had no appeal for me. . . . So I stayed in Paris.

On the other hand, most had come to France because it offered better opportunities than the United States in the 1920s, but a country saddled with wartime restrictions and life under the threat of a Nazi invasion no longer had much to recommend itself. During the 1930s, the economic crisis was just as bad in America as in France, so that the return home did not necessarily improve one's living conditions. By 1939, however, the United States beckoned as an oasis of peace and security in an increasingly war-torn world. Few blessed with American passports could resist its appeal.

The beginning of the Second World War thus brought about the end of the community established by African American expatriates in Paris during the 1920s. A very few, like Josephine Baker, bucked the trend and remained, believing that France had become their homeland. Arthur Briggs, Charlie Lewis, and Edgar Wiggins also chose to stay in the French capital. Yet these people were exceptions, and their decisions to stay in spite of the war marked their integration into French life. In effect, they stood by France as French men and women, not as black Americans. For the overwhelming majority, Paris during wartime no longer offered a sanctuary for freedom and art. Jazz did not sound right in march time, and the easygoing spirit of the Jazz Age recoiled before the harsh realities of the impending conflict. By the time of the French defeat of 1940, black Montmartre had become little more than a memory, one that would be recalled (but never entirely revived) only after war had once again run its course in Europe.

With the declaration of war in September 1939, life in Paris changed dramatically and immediately. In a move recalling the First World War, the national government reintroduced food rationing. Fears of aerial bombardment and shelling prompted a number of measures to ensure the safety of the civilian population. The authorities distributed gas masks. They also held civil defense drills, advising Parisians to use the Metro as a shelter from bombs or poison gas. Bricktop described being so drunk during one mandatory air raid drill that the police had to carry her out of her apartment. The streets of the French capital quickly lost their remaining foreign tourists, now replaced by increasingly large numbers of soldiers in uniform.

No change had a greater impact on the life of the city than the blackout. As soon as the war started, the government banned all public nighttime lighting. Dim blue streetlamps were permitted on only a few major boulevards after sunset, and Parisians could use interior lighting only by covering their windows tightly with blackout curtains. Automobiles virtually disappeared from the city thoroughfares after nightfall. The blackout transformed Paris from the City of Light into a ghost town. It was a catastrophe for the nightclubs of Montmartre, since few Parisians wanted to wander around town in complete darkness in search of a good time. Consequently, bookings available to African American musicians dwindled even further. Unemployment and the danger of war reinforced each other in rendering Paris inhospitable.

Initially, those few black Americans who remained in Paris after the start of the war managed to maintain some of their daily routines. Bricktop continued to work in Madame Fricka's nightclub in Montmartre and also sang requests on a radio program sponsored by the French government. That fall Josephine Baker starred in a new musical show at the Casino de Paris, appearing with that other great star of the Paris stage, Maurice Chevalier. Earlier in the year, Gene Bullard had reopened the now venerable Grand Duc nightclub, and although the war certainly made a difference, he refused to admit defeat:

> Nightclubs were almost deserted and many closed. Everybody in the entertainment world was out of work, and American performers were stranded and jobless.
>
> But every night the artists, white and colored, who used to frequent my cafe, kept on coming just to get together and gossip and tell jokes and kid each other. But they did not spend any money.

Yet there was no ignoring the war, even though the bombs had not yet begun to fall. Josephine Baker volunteered for the Red Cross, providing care for the refugees streaming into the city. She also gave free weekly concerts to French troops stationed at the front, and even acted in a little-known film depicting Parisians trying to cope with the tensions and inconveniences of *la drôle de guerre*, the phony war. In a more serious vein, both Baker and Bullard were recruited to work for French intelligence in its attempts to keep track of German spies. At the start of the war, Baker was contacted by Jacques Abtey, a young officer employed in the French army's counterintelligence division. Abtey's superiors had charged him with forming a network of informants, and Josephine Baker had been suggested to him as a possibility by the theater agent Daniel Marouani. Marouani convinced the initially skeptical Abtey to approach Baker who, remembering her own glimpses of Nazism while on tour in Germany, agreed to work with him. As she commented in her autobiography, "It seemed the perfect way to fight *my* war." Baker used her various contacts in France, especially the diplomats at the Italian embassy, to furnish information about the activity of German spies in Paris. The material she collected was not always accurate, but none doubted her enthusiasm or her devotion to the cause of France.

Gene Bullard loved his adopted homeland every bit as much as Josephine Baker did, and he also found a way to participate in the war effort in 1939. At the beginning of the year, he was approached by a close friend, Georges

Leplanquais, a special inspector with the Paris police. Leplanquais asked Bullard to listen for any indications of German activities that he might over-hear in his nightclub or his gym, and report them. Bullard agreed, and Leplanquais set him up to work with an Alsatian woman, Cleopatre Terrier, code-named "Kitty," who would strike up conversations at L'Escadrille and Le Grand Duc with suspected spies. Bullard soon discovered that his old neme-sis, Justin Pereti, the Corsican gangster who had only recently put him in the hospital, was also working in counterintelligence. Gene Bullard fulfilled his charge conscientiously, during the course of the year furnishing the French with information overheard from Nazis visiting his club as part of a night on the town in decadent Paris.

Soon, however, even the last holdouts began to consider departure seri-ously. In October 1939, the American embassy in Paris called on all American citizens to leave the country, and began chartering boats for those who had not been able to procure space on transatlantic steamships. Based on the increasingly urgent warnings from both the embassy and friends, Bricktop finally decided she could stay in Paris no longer. She bought a ticket on a steamship to New York, but delayed leaving until friends insisted that she risked internment by the Germans if she remained:

> The last night I saw the Paris of Bricktop's, I was with Eddie [Molyneux], and it was just the two of us. He'd sent his car for me, because it was pouring down rain. The car drove through the dimly lit streets at a snail's pace, and I looked out at the city I loved and wondered when I would see it again. At Eddie's I tried to be cheerful and good company, but I was so depressed and worried. On the boat train I met four American musicians who, like me, were among the last entertainers to leave, and we shared our fears about going back to a country we hadn't seen for years and where we would be strangers.

Bricktop's departure signaled the definitive end of an era. Once the queen of Montmartre had left, none could doubt that the African American commu-nity in Paris had, at least temporarily, ceased to exist.

Bricktop was not the last black American expatriate to leave. Gene Bullard hesitated even longer before finally deciding he had no choice but to go, and this hesitation nearly resulted in disaster. On May 10, 1940, the long-awaited storm finally broke as Hitler launched a massive invasion of Western Europe. German troops poured across the frontiers of the Low Countries and France, outflanking their Allied opponents as they surged into the French heartland. Within two weeks it became clear that France was facing a military disaster unparalleled in its recent history. By the beginning of June, the French army had collapsed and the British were desperately trying to evacuate their soldiers trapped at Dunkirk. Authorities declared Paris an open city, abandoning the thought of resisting the Germans there. On June 10, the French government fled the capital for Bordeaux, triggering a mass panic as two million Parisians left their homes, trying by whatever means of transportation possible to stay ahead of the rapidly advancing German armies. On June 14, the Germans occupied Paris herself, and those Parisians left in the city were treated to the horrifying spectacle of jackbooted Nazi soldiers marching in triumph past the Arc that Napoleon had built, down their majestic Champs-Elysées.

The defeat of France came as a personal tragedy for Gene Bullard. More than Bricktop or virtually any other black American in Paris, he had effectively renounced America and identified wholeheartedly with his adopted country. By 1940, he had lived in France for close to thirty years. While his marriage to a Frenchwoman had not lasted, he had two French children, not to mention numerous close friends and associates. On May 28, as the magnitude of the disaster became clear, the French government ordered all men of fighting age out of Paris. Bullard was forced to flee the capital, leaving his two daughters behind in a convent school. At the age of forty-six, he joined the French military for the second time in his life, signing up as a volunteer with an army regiment stationed in the Loire valley city of Orléans. There he heard General Charles de Gaulle's stirring June 18 radio broadcast from London calling for continued resistance. Unfortunately, Bullard was wounded the same day; given both his inability to fight and the virtual certainty of an imminent French defeat, his commanding officer advised him to flee toward the south. "Major Bader said I was too badly disabled to be any use, and that anyhow the whole regiment would almost certainly be captured (which proved true later). If I were captured with them, I would not just be interned. I would certainly be executed not only because of my color which put me in at least as much danger as Jews, but also because the enemy must by now know that I had worked against them in the Underground as well as being a foreign volunteer in two wars."

Gene Bullard's last act of solidarity with the French people in 1940 was his participation in the heartbreaking exodus of millions south in a desperate and futile attempt to escape the Nazi tide. Like many, he was forced to walk much of the way, hitching rides from trucks and wagons when possible. He made it as far as Angoulême, 150 miles to the south, before collapsing in a hospital. Fortunately for Bullard, the chief doctor, H. C. Devaux, had known him in Paris and remembered with gratitude the free concerts he and other African American musicians used to give at the American Hospital. He patched

Bullard up, gave him supplies for his journey, and strongly advised him to continue. "He told me it would be dangerous for me to stay in Angoulême and certain death to return to Paris. He advised me, as a war-wounded American, to get out of France as fast as possible." So Bullard struggled on, sleeping by the side of the road and limping south during the day. Recognizing his uniform and his wounded condition, a French soldier kindly gave him a bicycle, enabling him to proceed much more rapidly. On June 22, the day the French government signed the armistice with Nazi Germany, Bullard reached the resort town of Biarritz at the Spanish frontier. Appealing to the American consulate, he succeeded in securing passage on a liner bound for the United States at the end of the month. He would not see France again for fourteen years.

For the next four years, Paris lived on German time. After the French surrender, German authorities divided the country into an occupied zone, including Paris, northern France, and the Atlantic and Channel coasts, and an unoccupied zone, ruled by a collaborationist French government headquartered in the resort town of Vichy. Stripped of most of its interwar glory, its citizens hungry and dispirited, the French capital had no room for American expatriates. Even long-term residents like Gertrude Stein and Alice B. Toklas were forced to spend the war in the French countryside. Sylvia Beach chose to remain in the city, but was arrested and interned in a concentration camp for six months. Afterward she returned to Paris and spent the rest of the war years in hiding. Her situation simply underscored the fact that even before the United States and Germany went to war in December 1941, the Nazis had divested Paris of its lingering American presence.

A few African Americans also saw the inside of German internment camps during the war as a result of their reluctance to leave Paris in 1940. Unlike most members of the black community in Montmartre, the pianist Arthur Briggs stayed on in Paris after the French collapse, and as a result found himself arrested by the Germans and sent to an internment camp in the suburb of Saint-Denis on October 17, 1940. During his nearly four years of imprisonment, Briggs remained active musically as a way of keeping up his spirits. He started both a trio with an African and a black Englishman who sang spirituals, and a twenty-five piece classical orchestra. As a reporter noted in an article about Briggs shortly after the liberation of Paris in 1944, "The orchestra became a source of much happiness and comfort to the 2,000 internees of the camp. The German commandant became so interested that he not only attended their concerts, but rehearsals as well. . . . There were about 50 colored men in the camp and Briggs told me that there were no manifestations of color prejudice. Briggs himself was well respected by every member of the camp." The pianist Charlie Lewis suffered a similar experience. Having come to Paris in the late 1920s with the jazz band of the violinist Leon Abbey, Lewis also established roots in the city which ultimately prevented him from leaving when necessary. Both discovered that their American citizenship, which had been a major asset during the interwar years, now suddenly became a serious liability, and having black skin made the situation worse.

Only one African American is known to have lived undisturbed in Paris during the German occupation. Born in Illinois in 1861, Charles Anderson had first come to Paris in 1884 and had remained in France ever since. A twelve-year veteran of the French foreign legion who saw service during the Great War, Anderson was an elderly man living quietly in Montmartre when the Nazis marched into Paris. Like most other people in France, during those tragic years he did his best to live as normally as possible, even though the office employing him had officially shut down.

So each morning, through the four-year-long Occupation, Charles Anderson boarded the subway and rode to the transport office. There he sat, each day, in his familiar chair, read the newspapers, or read good books, while the booted Germans marched outside. Each evening, at the regular closing time, he folded his newspaper, carefully locked the door of the deserted building, and rode the subway home. And each month, in the mail, there came to Charles Anderson from the South of France a check from Monsieur de Brosse, the proprietor — 11,000 francs; Anderson's "salary."

Anderson saw the German soldiers every day; they were stationed in a house across from his apartment building. "They never gave me any trouble," he says. "I think I was too old." Anderson says he never saw another Negro in Paris during the Occupation.

Most Parisians, of course, did not have the option of relocating to the United States or anywhere else. After France and Germany signed the armistice, the panic of June gradually subsided and the millions of Parisians who had fled the city slowly filtered back to their homes, trying to make sure that their loved ones were safe, their property and jobs were secure, in general reestablishing the routines of daily life. Yet it soon became clear that there would be no return to normal under Nazi occupation. The presence of German soldiers everywhere in the city constantly reminded Parisians of their defeat and humiliation. German-language signs were posted on all the city's major thoroughfares, stamping Germany on the map of Paris. During the first year of the occupation in particular, the Germans celebrated their victory over France in an unrestrained and ostentatious manner, gorging themselves on the legendary delights of the French capital.

> Nothing was too good for them. They drank beer and champagne in copious quantities. They formed lines outside the houses of prostitution which had been requisitioned and classified and which were open from early afternoon to late at night. They established guards around the municipal markets and requisitioned the best foods for their military restaurants and their officers' messes. They thronged into the department stores, the clothing stores, the tailors' shops — buying whatever they could lay their hands on. Officers of high rank disputed and almost came to blows over bolts of woolen goods or pieces of silk.

During the occupation years, Paris once again became a moveable feast, but only for the privileged representatives of the enemy.

If German soldiers seemed to be ubiquitous, everything else was in woefully short supply. Thanks to the requisitions of the German army as well as the numerous other occupation "costs" levied by the victors (not to mention the presence of large numbers of French farmers in German prisoner-of-war camps), food rations in particular soon dried up. By the spring of 1941 butter was virtually nonexistent in the French capital, and the little milk available was reserved for children, nursing mothers, and the infirm. Treats like sugar, chocolate, cigarettes, and coffee became precious luxuries. Heating fuel was also hard to come by, especially during the winter months, and many Parisians had to wash and bathe (using synthetic soap) in cold water as a result. Taxis soon disappeared from the streets of the city altogether for lack of gasoline. They were eventually replaced by pedicabs, bicycles attached to the back halves of dilapidated automobiles and powered by strong legs. France had been colonized by Germany, and that ultimate colonial symbol, the rickshaw, had appeared in the national capital.

The most notable, and sinister, new policy introduced into Parisian life by the German occupation was racism. As elsewhere in fascist Europe, Jews soon became the number-one target of both the German authorities and their local collaborators. Jews were banned from certain professions, and subjected to humiliating restrictions, such as being kept from using park benches. Particularly vulnerable was the large foreign Jewish population in Paris. Not only did French authorities refuse to defend or assist these unfortunates, but they actually took the initiative in rounding them up for deportation to the death camps of Eastern Europe. These roundups began in 1941, cresting in July 1942 with the notorious "rafle du Vel d'Hiver" that collected more than twelve thousand Parisian Jews. Few of these people ever saw Paris again, ultimately joining the nearly 100,000 Jews from France to be murdered in the Holocaust.

Because they did not occupy a central role in Nazi ideology, and because their population in France was so small, blacks in occupied Paris did not face the murderous racism that threatened the city's Jewish communities. Nonetheless, they also found themselves discriminated against. Like Jews, blacks were banned from much French professional life, in particular from performing in the theaters and nightclubs of the city. German authorities also decreed they could not move between the occupied and unoccupied zones of France. Jazz was classified as decadent music and forbidden during the occupation. Hugues Panassié managed to keep playing jazz on his radio station only by translating the English titles of his records into French so that the German censors would not recognize them, in this way, for example, Louis Armstrong's "Saint Louis Blues" became "La Tristesse de Saint Louis." A few jazz clubs did remain open in Paris and other parts of France during the war, staffed almost entirely by French musicians. In the spring of 1944, for example, Django Reinhardt starred at a club in Montmartre's rue Pigalle which catered primarily to an oddly matched group of Gestapo agents and British spies; the band even frequently honored requests to play the British national anthem, "God Save the King." Yet blacks were effectively excluded from the city's musical life. In Nazi eyes, the black presence in interwar Paris symbolized everything decadent and despicable about French culture, something they would not tolerate while they remained in control.

The occupation also reduced the options available to the negritude writers. As French citizens, even black ones, they were allowed to live freely, but the occupation shattered much of their prewar unity. Léopold Senghor was captured while fighting with the French army in 1940 and not released until a year later, while Aimé Césaire spent the war years in Martinique. Senghor and other black French intellectuals continued to meet in Paris during the war, but the threat posed by Nazi and collaborationist authorities forced them to choose their words carefully. The situation of René Maran was particularly interesting. The great author remained in his Paris apartment throughout the war, and in 1941 published a novel, Les Bêtes de la Brousse (Beasts of the Bush), subtly criticizing Nazi rule. However, under German pressure he also wrote a pamphlet criticizing the treatment of blacks in the United States. After the liberation, Maran told the black American reporter Roi Ottley that he "lived in daily dread, every knock at the door a tug at [my] heart — for this article is one of the most inspiring pieces written of the Negro's aspirations, accomplishments, and [my] immense hope in the U.S."

The restrictions upon black life in Paris imposed by Nazi occupation authorities hardly affected African Americans for the simple reason that virtually none remained in the city, or in France, by the summer of 1940. But they could not get rid of Josephine Baker, who became the only African American to take part in the French resistance. Like Bricktop, at the beginning of the war she had resolved to remain in France, identifying the French cause as her own. She held fast to this decision, and as a result found herself caught in Paris during the tragic weeks of May and June 1940. Like most other Parisians, Baker fled south, but unlike them she had a splendid hiding place to receive her: the fairy-tale château of Les Milandes in the peaceful French countryside. "I left Paris by car, taking along what I could: a refugee Belgian couple, my faithful aide Paulette and those of my animals I couldn't leave behind. Destination: my chateau in the Dordogne." Baker would not see Paris again until the liberation of 1944.

Josephine Baker spent the summer of 1940 in Les Milandes, taking shelter there from the storms of war now blowing furiously across the Continent. There she heard de Gaulle's radio broadcast, inspiring her with the belief that the cause of Free France was not entirely lost. She was soon joined in Les Milandes by the irrepressible Jacques Abtey, now traveling in disguise as the American Jack Sanders. Baker greeted "Sanders" by saying, "Foxy . . . when are we going to join him . . . *our* General de Gaulle!" Abtey made contact with Colonel Paillole, head of military counterintelligence in Marseilles, who instructed him to proceed, with Josephine Baker as his cover, to neutral Lisbon, where he would transmit information about German troops in France to England. So the two set off for Portugal in November 1940, ostensibly en route to a South American tour, with the precious information written on the back of Baker's sheet music in invisible ink. As Colonel Paillole later noted, "It can fairly be said that the destiny of our Allies and consequently of the Free French was written in part on the pages of 'Two Loves Have I.'"

From Lisbon, Josephine Baker returned to France, proceeding to Marseilles on the orders of the de Gaulle's London-based Free French organization. Marseilles lay in the unoccupied zone of France, but no one knew when the Germans might change their minds and send in their storm troopers. In order to hide her real reasons for coming to the Provençal port, namely to contact Paillole, Baker announced that she was going to star in a production of Offenbach's *La Créole*. Putting on a lighthearted operetta in a city at war and full of people desperately trying to escape the Nazis and Europe was more than a little peculiar, but it served to explain the presence of the great entertainer. Baker did actually begin rehearsals for the show, which opened on Christmas Eve, 1940, but this clumsy subterfuge simply highlighted the fact that a public figure like Josephine Baker could not operate effectively as a spy in wartime France. Upon further instructions from London, in January 1941 Baker and Abtey flew together to Algeria. Josephine Baker would spend the rest of the war in North Africa as a lieutenant in the French army, working toward the day when she could return to a liberated Paris in triumph.

After the war, Josephine Baker would be heralded as a hero of the resistance after the war. Yet her life during the war underlined the fact that Nazi Paris had no place for African Americans, and little tolerance for blacks of any nationality. She did not manage to stay in the French capital for the duration of the occupation, nor, with the exception of Charles Anderson, did any other blacks from the United States. Her struggle demonstrated the strong attachments a few African Americans had formed with France, and they and others would ultimately provide a sense of continuity for black life in the city. Nonetheless, war and Nazi occupation killed the black American community in Paris, and its rebirth would have to await the dawn of a new day in Europe.

During the 1930s, black American expatriates in Paris built upon the foundation they had established during the previous decade. In spite of the vicissitudes of the times, they managed for much of the decade to maintain a stable, if at times reduced, community presence in the French capital. The economic crisis and the end of the heady days of the Jazz Age made it more difficult for black Americans to win a foothold in the city, and those without special talents or a firm commitment to life there soon left. Yet those who stayed constituted a hard core for whom Paris was no longer just an exotic, elegant foreign city but simply home. Only the worst calamity imaginable, the Nazi defeat and occupation of 1940, could force them to abandon it.

More so than in the 1920s, African American life in Paris during the Depression decade revealed complex and paradoxical attitudes toward the very nature of blackness. Ultimately life in Paris meant isolation from the mainstream of black life in the United States, neither a problem nor even a possibility for most black people back home. Musicians like Arthur Briggs could compensate by conscientiously listening to the latest jazz recordings from America, but such efforts could not replace direct day-to-day experience. Moreover, black expatriates in Paris lived in the midst of a white culture that had its own ideas about race. Josephine Baker achieved her phenomenal success in part by pandering to them. Even the vision of Africa offered by Claude McKay and the negritude writers was mediated through French eyes. Both white and black Parisian intellectuals could agree that blacks had a highly developed artistic sense, jointly praising the products of African culture.

Yet life in Paris also offered black Americans a more sustained level of contact with Africa and blacks from other parts of the world, fostering an expansive, cosmopolitan black identity. In part, such experiences were secondhand, as the case of visual artists particularly demonstrates. But Paris was home to many blacks from the Caribbean and Africa, as well as the African American community. The relatively small size of all these communities, as well as their exile status, facilitated interchanges that were more difficult in areas of the world where one or the other group was dominant. The one thing all these people had in common was black skin, and their interest in discovering the essential commonalities of blackness arose from that simple fact. Moreover, the fact that the French themselves often made few distinctions between blacks from the United States and other parts of the world also helped promote feelings of kinship with Africa on the part of African Americans.

These contradictions were part and parcel of the black American experience as a whole. African American culture has always developed in the context of a broader white society; a "pure" black American experience completely immune from white influences has never existed. The lives of the Parisian expatriates underscored this fact, showing that even when racism was muted or absent black life in the midst of a white population had its own peculiar difficulties. While not a substitute for life in America, the existence of a coherent black community in Paris, American but increasingly open to blacks from other parts of the world, alleviated the pangs of exile and isolation. It enabled the expatriates to maintain their identities as both blacks and Americans, to succeed in the opportunities presented by a great foreign city yet have something familiar close at hand. Consequently, in the interwar years the African American community of Paris not only embraced the spirit of black cosmopolitanism, but also became itself a potent symbol of that spirit.

LIFE ON THE
LEFT BANK

EVEN THE WORST NIGHTMARES must come to an end, and in 1944 Paris awoke from four long years of brutal enemy occupation. The French capital was liberated from the Nazis on August 25, and the following May, World War II came to a triumphant end with the utter destruction of the Third Reich. The city that had played such a brilliant host to African Americans during the 1920s was once again free to do so, and by the end of the 1940s a new community of blacks from the United States had settled into its cafés, hotels, and nightclubs. Jazz, driven underground during the occupation, proved more popular than ever in the postwar era, and black American musicians continued to be in demand. The renaissance of this musical form in Paris after 1944 gave proof of the continued importance of the African American community to the life of the city. Paris returned to normal, and part of this normalcy was the presence of black visitors and residents from the other side of the Atlantic.

The next decade and a half in particular witnessed one of the most creative and interesting periods of African American life in the French capital, in some ways even more illustrious than that of the 1920s. There were certain continuities between the two eras, most notably the French fascination with jazz and the formidable personalities of Bricktop and Josephine Baker. But most American blacks who settled in Paris during the late 1940s and 1950s had not seen the city before the war, nor had many prior contacts with those who had. The sense of new beginnings that characterized postwar black life in Paris went beyond individuals. The blacks who came to Paris after 1944 were not only different people, but frequently different *kinds* of people. Those engaged in creative endeavors still typified the community as a whole, but whereas during the 1920s and 1930s musicians predominated, in the postwar years writers became the central African Americans in the French capital. Black literature now assumed pride of place in representing black culture abroad. In a word, the true equivalent of and successor to Josephine Baker during the 1940s and 1950s was not Sidney Bechet but Richard Wright. Even the urban geography of black life in Paris reflected this shift. Black Montmartre did not survive the war; while a few scattered outposts endured, the center of African American life crossed the Seine to the Left Bank and now thrived in the bustling ancient streets of the Latin Quarter and Saint-Germain-des-Prés.

If black expatriates had changed, so had the city that continued to welcome them. The drunken gaiety that exploded in Paris at the moment of liberation faded fast, revealing the deep scars left by Nazi occupation and the all too frequent French collaboration. These scars, material, political, moral, would take years to heal, their memory ensuring that Paris would never be the same. The years of the Fourth Republic, from 1946 to 1958, brought new opportunities to the people of France, but also new problems. Parisians had to get used to living in a world in which Europe was no longer the center, but rather the plaything of two hostile superpowers armed with weapons of total destruction. World War II may have ended in 1945, but peace remained an elusive concept for France during the next fifteen years. Not only did the cold war loom menacingly over the entire period, but the nation also became embroiled in a series of colonial conflicts, futilely trying to resist the postwar worldwide collapse of European imperialism. By the end of 1946, France was engaged in war in Indochina, a war it would lose in 1954 only to become immediately involved in the even more tragic and hopeless conflict in Algeria. Although these wars took place outside Europe, their consequences became increasingly manifest in Paris itself, especially as the Algerian war threatened to unravel the very fabric of the nation. While the city regained its traditional sophistication and glamour during these years, it continued to live uneasily under the shadow of war.

Although not unaware of such troubles, the African American habitués of Paris were able to lead their lives without being directly touched or fundamentally disturbed by them. More important were blacks' changing attitudes to America. To a much greater extent than during the 1920s, blacks who moved from the United States to Paris after World War II often did so as an overt protest against American racism. The postwar years thus reflected a new level of consciousness for the black American community in Paris, introducing a new model of that experience: the African American as political exile. In contrast to the largely apolitical jazz musicians and vacationing artists and writers of the interwar years, blacks living in Paris during the 1940s and 1950s often considered themselves refugees from Yankee bigotry. For many, the flagrant contrast between America's triumphant crusade against world fascism and its continued relegation of blacks to second-class citizenship proved even more galling than had the violent spasm of racism after World War I. Black writers in particular transformed their resentment into a reason for exile, so much so that during the 1950s Paris became the literary capital of black America. Although no more immune than were their predecessors a generation earlier to the delights of Parisian life or the glorious traditions of French literature, individuals like Richard Wright, Chester Himes, and James Baldwin chose Paris primarily as an escape from the United States. More than anything else during the postwar years, this conscious sense of political exile, of rejection of America for Paris, represented a significant new departure for the African American expatriate community, providing abundant material for both reflection and action in the years to come.

PARIS IN THE AGE OF EXISTENTIALISM

Like the 1920s, for Parisians the late 1940s and 1950s were shaped above all by the twin blessings of peace and victory. With the end of war in both cases came periods of spectacular cultural and intellectual creativity, so much so that much of the romantic imagery of Paris held dear by Francophiles throughout the world to this day dates from these two postwar eras. Yet in significant ways the mood of Paris after World War II differed sharply from that prevailing after World War I. The sparkling gaiety that had so charmed foreigners during the 1920s gave way to a more somber, philosophical mood. The Second World War eclipsed the First in the amount of suffering and tragedy it caused, and in the sheer depths of evil it revealed in the human spirit. No amount of champagne or dance music could make Parisians forget the occupation, or ignore the stark specter of the concentration camps. Victory had been achieved, but the war against Nazism had merely been replaced by a new cold war between the United States and the Soviet Union. This new danger not only continued to divide Parisians, but ultimately threatened to bring about the end of all humanity in a nuclear cataclysm.

Such sobering reflections made existentialism the avant-garde order of the day in postwar Paris. In these years, existentialism came to mean many things, but broadly speaking it was a philosophy that focused on the analysis of human existence, emphasizing both the isolated, desperate condition of individual existence, and the necessity for man to struggle ceaselessly, if hopelessly, to master his own destiny. Existentialism, of course, has a much longer history, traceable to the writings of the nineteenth-century Danish philosopher Søren Kierkegaard. During the interwar years the German scholar Martin Heidegger had become its leading exponent, influencing a number of young French intellectuals, most notably Jean-Paul Sartre. Thanks to the influence of novels like *Nausea* and the massive philosophical tome *Being and Nothingness*, Sartre and his companion and fellow writer Simone de Beauvoir were hailed in the years immediately after the liberation as the leaders of the latest Parisian intellectual fashion.

The existentialism of postwar Paris, though, was less a strict philosophy than a cultural phenomenon, harbinger of an era that would soon witness an explosion of mass culture and faddism. Those who had never read Heidegger could still become "existentialists" by imitating the lifestyle of Sartre and de Beauvoir. Young Parisians frequented the neighborhood that became famous as existentialist ground zero, Saint-Germain-des-Prés. Sartre and his friends had moved into the quiet Left Bank *quartier* shortly before the end of the war, living in its plentiful cheap hotels and writing for hours at a time in cafés along the boulevard Saint-Germain. Paris cafés have long served as refuges from the miseries of crowded, uncomfortable housing; in the immediate postwar years, when heating fuel was scarce and expensive, Parisians could settle into the warmth of a local café for hours for the price of a cup of coffee. The cafés of Saint-Germain-des-Prés were thus ideal spaces for Parisian intellectuals to read, write, and discuss their work. The area was soon "discovered," however, and by the early 1950s cafés like the Deux Magots and the Flore had become the tourist haunts they remain today, filled with young people from around the world, wearing berets, smoking Gauloises, and looking suitably depressed.

The existentialist mood resonated powerfully in a city where so much suffering had occurred and whose future remained uncertain, yet it was not the only important cultural influence in Paris after the war. The United States, having helped liberate the city and lead the way to victory over Hitler, became once again the object of Parisian fascination. When the Americans returned to Paris in August 1944, they brought with them not only impressive military might, but also a seemingly inexhaustible supply of coffee, candy, cigarettes, chewing gum, and of course nylon stockings into a city that had been starved of such luxuries for more than four years. For the rest of the decade, Americans stationed in or visiting the French capital seemed to live better than anyone else, making America a symbol of both youthful optimism and material prosperity. Cast-off American clothing became a prized commodity on the city's black market, foreshadowing the popularity of blue jeans in the 1960s. Parisians pulled out their old jazz recordings and started going to the new music clubs springing up around the city to hear American performers. By the end of the 1940s, the French government, urged on by the French Communist party, was engaged in a struggle with the Coca-Cola company to ban sales of Coke in its territories, hoping to prevent what was already becoming known as the "Coca-colonization" of France.

On the surface, few views of the world could have seemed further apart than worldly existentialist angst and America's confident vision of a consumer paradise. The fact that Sartre and most Parisian intellectuals firmly identified with the political Left, usually the Communists, further distanced the two. America's use of the atomic bomb to devastate Hiroshima and Nagasaki prompted horrified reactions on the Left Bank, and many leading cultural figures in France, Communist or not, argued that the United States was by far the greatest danger to world peace after 1945. Yet despite its difficult abstract reasoning based in European philosophy, there was something rather American about the culture of existentialism in postwar France. The contradiction between its vision of the lone individual and its creation of a popular fad could have sprung from the desk of a Madison Avenue advertising executive. The young habitués of Saint-Germain-des-Prés wore American-style clothing and haircuts, read detective novels, and flocked to jazz clubs. Critical of the politics and world role of the United States, many young Parisians avidly embraced its culture and its consumer products. In spite of existentialism's clear identification with the Left, the French Communists condemned the new philosophy as "the expression of a rotting bourgeoisie."

African Americans and African American culture played a central and paradoxical role in this relationship between the Parisian intelligentsia and American popular culture. Both because of its intrinsic qualities and because its condemnation by the Nazis during the occupation made it a cultural symbol of antifascism, jazz enjoyed a spectacular rebirth in Paris after the war. Like the surrealists before them, the existentialists always championed jazz, regarding it as an emotional, complex symbol of modern life. Indeed, after much existential despair, Sartre's novel *Nausea* concludes with its antihero, Antoine Roquentin, achieving a sort of spiritual resolution by listening to a blues song, musing, "The Negress sings. Can you justify your existence then?" His spirits bolstered by the soulful music, Roquentin resolves to write a novel, hoping to win from others the same respect and admiration he feels for the blues singer: "they would think about my life as I think about the Negress's: as something precious and almost legendary." Parisian intellectuals would also embrace black writers, especially Richard Wright and Chester Himes. As existentialism became more interested in decolonization and third world struggles during the 1950s, Sartre, de Beauvoir, and others lent a receptive ear to the eloquent protests against American racism voiced or penned by the black American expatriates in their midst.

In contrast to the years after World War I, Parisians viewed African Americans foremost as Americans, not Africans, during the 1940s and 1950s. Primitivism was no longer in fashion, blacks were no longer a novelty in Paris, and American culture had to a certain extent replaced African culture as an object of fascination for the city's intellectuals. At the same time, the rapidly escalating conflict between the United States and the French Left after 1945, and the tendency of American soldiers in France to behave like conquerors in a defeated country, reinforced Parisians' criticisms of the great wartime ally. Opposition to the racism of the United States, in particular the treatment of black soldiers in France, was reinforced by the political climate of anti-Americanism. More generally, the idea of black-Americans-as-Americans suited the Parisian mood of the late 1940s much more than interwar primitivist fantasies. Whereas images of sensual, spontaneous Africans fitted the devil-may-care atmosphere of *les années folles*, the bitter conflict between black and white symbolized by the African American experience was much more appropriate to the looming Manichaeanism of the cold war. Far more than before 1939, the Parisian Left now regarded black Americans as a symbol of ideological consciousness, not good times. The increased politicization of the African American community in Paris after the war would flow in part from this broader French context.

Au Pays du Bon Dieu (In the Land of the Good Lord), a 1947 novel by Yves Malartic, a translator specializing in American literature, illustrates this new perspective on black Americans. It relates the story of Phoebus, a young black soldier from Harlem serving with the U.S. Army in Marseilles immediately after the war. In the novel, Malartic neatly reverses the comparison established by interwar writers like Paul Morand between an overcivilized Europe and emotional, primitive black culture. Marseilles, and by extension all of France, here appears an impoverished wasteland populated by petty hustlers, black marketeers, and ragged children demanding chewing gum. In contrast, Phoebus is presented as a young man of some education interested in the finer things in life; instead of rejecting European culture, like any American tourist he in fact longs for it. *Au Pays du Bon Dieu* is a novel of the loss of innocence, but Phoebus is disillusioned not so much by the poverty of postwar France as by the virulent white racism of the American army. In Malartic's Marseilles, white Southern soldiers beat and murder black GIs on a daily basis, whereas Frenchwomen who consort with African Americans are harassed by the military police. The end of the novel finds Phoebus all alone, dreaming futilely of deserting and finding freedom in France after the departure of the American army. Far from portraying its black soldier as a genial, happy African, *Au Pays du Bon Dieu* represents him as a troubled American betrayed by his own country.

In brief, a fascination with the African American experience became the perfect expression of the complex love-hate attitude of the postwar Parisian avant-garde toward the United States. This paradox was not entirely new, but the cold war and the increased worldwide influence of America sharpened its importance. For many Parisians, not just the recognized literati, jazz symbolized what was best about America, while racism represented its worst aspects. Blacks could claim intimate kinship with both; they were victims of American brutality and heralds of the New World's choicest offerings. Such attitudes ensured that black expatriates from America would continue to find a place in Paris in the years after the liberation.

FROM MONTMARTRE TO THE LEFT BANK: BUILDING A NEW BLACK COMMUNITY

The fiftieth anniversary celebrations of the Normandy landings in the summer of 1994 gave little acknowledgment to the blacks who also participated in this campaign; the process of commemoration succeeded all too well in restoring America's World War II self-image, complete with its neglect of the accomplishments of people of color. African Americans, in fact, played a significant role in the struggle to liberate France from the Nazis in 1944, renewing a presence established by soldiers in another war a generation earlier. In some ways, the impact of French culture on the black troops of the 1940s was less dramatic than upon those of 1917 and 1918. France was not the only battlefield to engage African American soldiers during the Second World War, or the only country to demonstrate that racial hostility was not a universal value. More soldiers saw combat in Italy, North Africa, and the South Pacific. Many were stationed in Britain during the war, and there learned that whites could treat blacks with respect. Most important, an African American presence had already existed in France, so that the black GIs of 1944 and 1945 came not as pioneers but as the second generation of a robust tradition.

America entered the Second World War, as it had the First, firmly committed to maintaining the black soldier at the bottom of the military hierarchy.

Blacks were largely excluded from the navy and air force, and in the army served in segregated units, usually commanded by white officers. As in World War I, military leaders tended to look upon blacks as laborers rather than fighters; in 1943, the army proposed using trained black troops to help pick cotton. Racial brawls, even riots, pitted African American soldiers against both white soldiers and civilians in numerous military camps throughout the States, especially the South. The racial climate in wartime America as a whole began to resemble that of 1919, as serious rioting broke out in New York, Detroit, and Los Angeles during the summer of 1943. The African American press and organizations like the NAACP criticized continued discrimination against blacks, pressing hard for their full inclusion in the war effort as dignified and equal members of the national community. From the point of view of many, however, it seemed that the nation had learned little about racial equality since 1917.

In spite of America's reluctance to accept their contribution, African American soldiers played a remarkable role in the liberation of France. By June 1944, close to 700,000 blacks were serving in the U.S. Army; as in the First World War, most served in noncombatant positions as laborers. Blacks took part in the D day invasions of Normandy as members of port battalions, unloading war material from supply ships onto the beaches in the face of enemy fire and bombardment. The 452d Anti-Aircraft Battalion, widely considered one of the best, was stationed in Normandy on June 23, 1944. Black soldiers attached to the army's 333d Field Artillery Group landed in France on June 29, pushing the Germans back across northern France for the rest of the year. In the Battle of the Bulge in December, many African American soldiers, especially the 761st Tank Battalion known as the Black Panthers, were the first black armored units to see combat in Europe. Black truck drivers also played a crucial role in keeping American forces supplied through the famed Red Ball Express, a series of truck convoys driven by blacks from August to November 1944.

After the liberation of Paris in August 1944, the French capital became a place where black American soldiers would go for rest and relaxation, redeployment elsewhere in Europe, or demobilization and transfer back home. A place of gaiety made all the more intense by its proximity to the abyss of war, the city reverted to the role it had played in World War I. Black soldiers were also stationed in Paris as orderlies, military police, and other officials in the vast bureaucracy of the American army behind the lines. African American troops in Paris benefited equally from the warm reception given by Parisians to Allied troops in the fall of 1944 and, as in the years of the First World War, these soldiers responded with the gift of music. The American army brought its own bands back to Paris in 1944, and these groups reintroduced African American jazz to the city. Edward Toles, a war correspondent for the *Chicago Defender* in Europe, described the city's lively atmosphere shortly after the liberation.

> Paris is still Paris and swing music, banned by the Germans, rings from the jam sessions in Montmarte [*sic*] once more.
> All over the city one sees Negro musicians fresh from internment camps now playing in orchestras. . . . In this newly-liberated city I found people still kissing GIs, throwing flowers and everywhere giving our men a warm-hearted reception. Here is a sense of space whose clean perfumed air gives few evidences of bitter fighting and makes one feel at home.

The black American soldiers who saw Paris at the end of World War II did not simply fit into an already established community. The African American presence in Paris during the 1920s and 1930s had been destroyed by the war, and now waited to be renewed. As in the aftermath of World War I, a few black World War II veterans, enchanted by the prospects of life in the French capital, would choose to stay on after their demobilization, or would return to Paris after hopes for improved postwar conditions in the United States had turned sour. While owing much to the heritage of the 1920s, this new black community would settle in Paris primarily because of the city's attractions, Parisians' color-blind attitudes, and continued racism at home.

African American war correspondents like Toles witnessed the GIs' creation of a new black community, while also contributing to its rise. Writing for several black newspapers, especially the *Chicago Defender* and the *Pittsburgh Courier*, journalists Toles, Rudolph Dunbar, Roi Ottley, Ollie Stewart, and Ollie Harrington not only explored black life in Paris during and immediately after the war, but also became some of the first African Americans to settle there in the postwar years. The primary activity of black war correspondents, at a time when white newspapers tended to downplay or ignore the achievements of black soldiers, was to report on the lives of their brothers in uniform. They accompanied America's conquering armies across Europe, getting to know African American soldiers and making sure blacks at home learned of their accomplishments. At the same time, these writers became familiar with life in Paris and other parts of the Continent after the liberation. Black war correspondents were therefore ideally suited to link survivors of the prewar black community with the newcomers in uniform. Roi Ottley interviewed René Maran about black life under German rule and the attitudes of French blacks toward America. Shortly after his arrival in the city, Edward Toles met with Edgar Wiggins who had been interned there during the war years as an enemy alien. Rudolph Dunbar went to the Flea Pit, former center of black Montmartre, comparing its previous glories with its dilapidated state in 1944. "Its windows are boarded now where once brightly hued glass panes rested; its walls are marred with breaks in spots and in fact everything is changed but somehow one can sit and think of the place it once was while feeling proud Paris is free again."

But not only neighborhoods had changed; the war had also given Parisians a heightened awareness of American racism. Just as in the First World War, black American soldiers in France during the 1940s were amazed and delighted to see that they were accepted everywhere, and that the French greeted them with warmth and sympathy. This attitude was even stronger in World War II, representing not only Parisians' traditional disdain for America's treatment of blacks, but also a conscious identification of racism with Nazism. If during the war pro-Jewish sentiment stood for antifascism, after the war pro-black feelings both caused and arose out of anti-Americanism. For black Americans, the willingness of white women to associate with African American men represented the absence of the ultimate racial barrier, convincing Americans that the French knew no racism whatever. Richard Wright noted this association during a visit to France in May 1946. In an article for the French press entitled "In Paris, Black G.I.s Have Come to Know and Love Freedom," Wright commented on the absence of racism in the French capital.

I saw my first black G.I., walking arm in arm with a beautiful girl. I went up to him and asked him how he was doing. "Very well," he responded in a calm, pleasant voice, then introduced me to the young girl, who was small, blond, and pretty. They informed me they were going to get married. I congratulated them.

And where are you from? I asked.

From Saint Louis, he said.

Where do you plan on living when you go back to the U.S.A.?

Saint Louis, he replied without hesitating.

I looked at him in amazement. Had he then forgotten what kind of city Saint Louis was? Didn't he know it would mean death for him if he returned there accompanied by a white woman?

As gently as I could, I told him: Things are not going so well back home, from a racial point of view, don't you know that?

No, he said.

And I understood completely. This nice boy, this good black American *had forgotten*. . . . Living in Paris for two years, he had come to know and to love freedom.

As some African Americans discovered, one could easily experience the difference between American racism and French tolerance in Paris. As during the First World War, the American army command in France looked askance at fraternization between its black soldiers and Frenchwomen, fearing the transfer of such attitudes across the Atlantic. In Cherbourg, for example, the army assigned black and white soldiers to segregated whorehouses, greatly amusing the French prostitutes who continued to work in both. White MPs and other soldiers frequently harassed black soldiers, and as American tourists began returning to Paris they brought with them their racial attitudes and expectations. Roi Ottley described one such incident shortly after the war.

A French girl, daughter of an admiral, had consented to show me a bit of Paris. We had attended Mass at the cathedral of Notre Dame, celebrated by His Eminence Francis Cardinal Spellman of New York, where my appearance with her had caused not one ripple of notice.

We were idly walking back along the rue de Rivoli, still under the spell of a ritual symbolizing a God aloof from racialism, when a white man unexpectedly emerged from a café and deliberately jostled me. He eyed my companion severely. "Where I come from," he spluttered suddenly, "white women ain't seen with niggers!" The French passersby stood aghast. The girl, a trifle annoyed, replied, "M'sieur, please, what business is it of yours, if I am with a Negro!" I was embarrassed for my countryman. But she afterwards observed that neither a Negro walking the streets with a French woman, nor even the marriage of a French film star to a Negro, is sufficient reason for racial apoplexy in Paris. As far as I could see, the French are scarcely surprised at anything.

Despite the freedom of association Paris promised, it has never been an easy place for foreigners to earn a living, and in the immediate postwar years the city offered few opportunities. Fortunately for those African American veterans enamored of the French capital, the GI Bill of Rights opened a way to stay. Enacted at the end of the war, the GI Bill extended a wide range of benefits to the young men and women who had served in America's armed forces during the war. In particular, the GI Bill gave World War II veterans full educational benefits, paying the tuition and living expenses of those who chose to go to college after demobilization. Millions took advantage of these benefits, revolutionizing American higher education and laying the foundation for the mass-based universities of the 1950s and 1960s. The GI Bill also contributed indirectly to the development of the postwar black community in Paris because its benefits could be used at U.S. government–approved schools and universities overseas. In the late 1940s, the bill paid $75 a month, or roughly twice the average wage of a French worker, for school fees and living costs. By the end of the decade, close to five hundred African American veterans were pursuing studies in Paris in a wide range of subjects, subsidized by the U.S. government.

One black ex-GI who settled in Paris after the war was Wendell Jean-Pierre. Today a professor at Rutgers University, Jean-Pierre served in the American army during the Second World War, afterward returning home to his native New Orleans. Disenchanted with life in the postwar South, Jean-Pierre sailed for France in 1950, intending to use his GI Bill benefits to study and live there. On the ship he happened to meet J. A. Rogers, the African American historian and Paris correspondent during the 1920s, who told him of black life in Montmartre during that era. Wendell Jean-Pierre loved Paris immediately, enrolling in French-language classes at the Alliance Française, where he studied for two years. He also sang at nightclubs, including the Latin Quarter's Chez Inez, and met Richard Wright and many other black expatriates in the city. Jean-Pierre stayed in Paris for three years and also spent a year in Nice on the Riviera. In 1954, his educational benefits depleted, he was forced to leave Paris and return home with fond memories of what had been a special time in his life.

More than any other group of African Americans in Paris, black artists went there in the postwar years as beneficiaries of the GI Bill. In order to take advantage of the bill's provisions, American veterans had to study at an approved school, either in the United States or abroad. Several art schools in Paris met this qualification, especially the Ecole des Beaux-Arts and the Académie Julian, the alma mater of Henry Ossawa Tanner and Gwendolyn Bennett. The Académie de la Grande Chaumière, where Aaron Douglas and Augusta Savage had studied during the interwar years, also attracted American students in the late 1940s. By the beginning of the 1950s, more than two hundred veterans had used their GI Bill benefits to study art in the French capital, including black artists like Herbert Gentry, Bill Rivers, Romare Bearden, Robert Colescott, Pal Keene, and Harold Cousins. The experience of African American artists in postwar Paris thus provided a prime example of the ways in which ex-soldiers renewed the black community in the French capital after 1944.

AFRICAN AMERICAN ARTISTS RETURN TO PARIS

So, I met old Harris in the Cafe Select, one of the places in Paris, and he said, "Look, man, I'm going to be at the Grande Chaumière. I'm going to be an artist." So I said, "Well, that's alright. That's great." So, sure enough, he showed up. He had asked the brothers, "What do you do when you go to the Grande Chaumière?" "The first thing," he was told, "you buy a beret. Then you get some paper and some charcoal and a board to place on a chair and you watch and do what everybody else is doing," which is what old Harris did.

More than in music or literature, Paris had led the Western world in the visual arts during the early twentieth century, so that a stint in the French capital had become *de rigueur* for American painters and sculptors. By the end of the 1940s, a new generation of artists from the other side of the Atlantic began to pose a stiff challenge to Parisian dominance. Many artists had fled France before the Nazi onslaught in 1940, the most fortunate of them finding refuge in the United States, so that the war temporarily transferred the best of French art to New York. After 1945, many young artists in the American metropolis turned away from the cubist styles that still constituted the heart of the Paris school, favoring more abstract, theoretical forms of visual expression. In 1949, a Manhattan exhibition, "Intrasubjectives," brought together paintings by Willem de Kooning, Jackson Pollock, Mark Rothko, Hans Hofmann, and several other representatives of the new avant-garde. With the beginning of the new decade abstract expressionism had become a formidable movement, one that would soon shift the leadership of the art world from Paris to New York.

Given that the French capital remained the home of Pablo Picasso, Georges Braque, Henri Matisse, Fernand Léger, and Constantin Brancusi in the postwar years, it could hardly be considered an artistic backwater, and it remained the overseas destination of choice for many American artists after the war. The growth of the New York school shifted the significance of such sojourns, however, especially for African Americans. During the 1920s, black Americans came to Paris to learn from the French masters; life in France was not exile, but an integral part of the road to artistic success in America. Thirty years later such a French apprenticeship was no longer essential, and in fact could prove detrimental by calling into question one's avant-garde status. Life in Paris to a greater extent represented a rejection of the American artistic establishment. Whereas during *les années folles* African American jazz performers and visual artists had crossed the Atlantic for diametrically opposed reasons, the two groups now found a more unified identity as American expatriates, searching for an alternative to the constraints still placed upon black life in the United States.

In contrast to musicians like Kenny Clarke and Miles Davis, however, black American artists in Paris did not represent the latest avant-garde styles from the United States. Their work did not fit into any single mold, but rather took themes from both the Paris and New York schools. In general, the paintings and sculptures they produced in France were more abstract than the largely representational work of interwar black artists. Yet no single approach dominated their art. Rather, Paris seemed a city that left them free to pursue whatever artistic direction appealed to them. African American artists could showcase black themes, or they could work in other modes, without being necessarily stereotyped as black artists. Many chose to experiment with more than one style, like Ed Clark, who composed cubist-style paintings (for example, *Portrait of Muriel*, 1952), and grand abstract expressionist canvases. While Paris was no longer the world's undisputed art capital, black American artists nonetheless found in the city a haven that not only provided top-notch art schools, but also the space to develop their own talents as creative individuals.

One of the most important postwar African American artists in Paris was Herbert Gentry. Born in Pittsburgh in 1919, Gentry had begun his artistic career in Harlem during the 1930s, working for the Federal Artists Program of the Works Progress Administration. He served as a soldier in Europe and North Africa during the war, first coming to Paris during the heady days of the liberation in 1944. After his demobilization and return home at war's end, Gentry decided against pursuing his art studies at New York University, opting instead to go back to Paris as a civilian in 1946 and study at the Académie de la Grande Chaumière. Looking back on those years, Gentry fondly observed, "We were very free. . . . We had a wonderful time. We were just going out and looking at the city. . . . We went to the Louvre, we went to the Musée Moderne, we went to every museum in Paris. . . . You know, it wasn't easy to go to Europe right after World War II because everything was rationed in most of the European countries, especially in France. . . . But it didn't matter to us, because we were young, the city was exciting, that city was so beautiful. The odor, I can smell it now." As the Hemingwayesque tones of this passage suggest, even if the artistic dominance of Paris was coming under fire, it still remained a place of magical beauty for young African American artists after the war.

Following generations of artists before them, the black Americans tended to settle into cheap hotels and studios in the Left Bank, especially Montparnasse. Like other African American exiles, they found themselves drawn to the existentialist milieu of Saint-Germain-des-Prés, listening to jazz and rubbing shoulders with the city's literati. But Montparnasse, center of French art in the twentieth century, continued to exert a special fascination. American artists, both black and white, frequented celebrated cafés like the Closerie des Lilas and the Coupole along the boulevard du Montparnasse, stimulated by cheap wine and abundant conversation. As Herbert Gentry later noted, "It was the Americans who really made Montparnasse."

This was the climate for artists in Paris that attracted Romare Bearden in 1950. By the end of World War II, Bearden was widely recognized as one of the leading black artists in America, an equivalent of Richard Wright in the visual arts. A very light-skinned black man with a broad face and a winning smile, the North Carolina native had graduated from New York University in 1935. During the 1930s, he lived in Harlem and collaborated with a number of black artists, including Gwendolyn Bennett, Jacob Lawrence, and Ernest Crichlow in the "306" group. Skilled in a variety of different techniques, including cartoons, collages, and oil paintings, Bearden became one of the most important visual chroniclers of the Harlem Renaissance. He soon came to the attention of New York's white art world, and in the early 1940s became one of the few African American artists whose work was displayed in Manhattan's prestigious downtown galleries. Romare Bearden served in the army from 1943 to 1945, then returned to New York to pursue his craft.

As a veteran, Bearden was entitled to the educational subsidies of the GI Bill, and in 1950 he decided to use them to study in France. Like many Americans, he still viewed Paris as the capital of modern art, regarding it as a place where one could live cheaply in beautiful and intellectually exciting surroundings. He was inspired both by friends' tales of life there during the 1930s, and by the return of figures like Richard Wright and Herbert Gentry. Bearden arranged from New York to study at the Sorbonne with the noted French philosopher Gaston Bachelard, and in March 1950, Bearden sailed to France complete with letters of introduction to Picasso, Braque, Matisse, and other leading members of the Paris school. He discovered, though, that life in Paris was not always the stuff of dreams; his rudimentary command of French made his studies difficult and he was surprised to see that Parisian nightlife shut down at midnight, much earlier than in New York. Yet in spite of these inconveniences Romare Bearden developed a strong affection for the city. He found a comfortable studio in the rue des Feuillantines, a few blocks from the center of Montparnasse, for forty dollars a month, including meals and laundry. More important, he soon formed a close circle of friends, including James Baldwin, Constantin Brancusi, and the French painter Jean Hélion, and even traveled to Juan-les-Pins to meet Pablo Picasso. Like Herbert Gentry, whom he came to know quite well, Bearden soon fell under the city's spell. In a letter to his friend Carl Holty in New York, the artist commented:

Now at last I'm beginning to understand some of those things you used to talk about — and try indirectly to make me understand of life here in Paris. I've begun to love it here — the strangeness is wearing off & I'm getting used to the tempo. . . . I really began to enjoy Paris one day last week when I went to an exhibition of medieval Jugoslav frescos. It was an amazing job of presentation. . . . I came out of the museum perspiring and shaking and had to take two cognacs in an effort to collect myself. Then I was saved by the breathtaking Champs de Mars — and a good walk along the Seine. . . .

So the other night I came home late and drew with charcoal, something I've never heretofore been able to do — and I drew very well, with rich tones and nice passages felt all over the paper. I'll be able to work in Paris from now on.

In fact, Romare Bearden never was able to paint in Paris. He reacted to the city somewhat like the proverbial child in the candy store, fascinated by all the diverse riches it had to offer. Nine months after his arrival in France, Bearden's GI Bill benefits ran out and he regretfully returned to America, hoping to come back to Paris the following year as a Fulbright scholar. This opportunity failed to materialize, however, and in New York he found that his Parisian experience had placed him somewhat at odds with the new champions of abstract expressionism. The harsh reality of life in New York, perfectly expressed by the direct, bold themes of the New York school, tended to turn Bearden's memories of Paris into an alluring, aqua-tinted fantasy. He returned for a few months in 1951, and for much of the rest of the decade dreamed of resuming his life on the Left Bank. Yet unlike Richard Wright, Romare Bearden would remain in New York, his dreams of Paris destined to remain a pleasant reverie without substance.

Bearden's departure, unwilling as it was, highlighted the limitations of Paris as a center for African American expatriate artists. One could survive adequately as a student on the GI Bill for a while, but broader, more lucrative opportunities to sell one's work in the city's art world remained elusive. Artists did not have access to the money-making opportunities of jazz musicians, so their sojourns in Paris tended to be brief, even when they wanted to stay longer. Nonetheless, a small but steady stream of black artists came from America to Paris during the 1950s. Some had the good fortune to receive fellowships, while others got by on savings and subsidies from home. Bob Blackburn won a Whitney fellowship to study engraving in the French capital in 1953. Both John Wilson and Richard Boggers came to study with Fernand Léger in the early 1950s. The painter Larry Potter, who had studied art at New York's Cooper Union, came in 1956 for three years, then returned in 1961, remaining in Paris until his death in 1966. Ed Clark and Sylvester Britton

arrived in 1952, enrolling as students at the Académie de la Grande Chaumière. Clark, who lived in a studio in the rue Delambre, in the heart of
Montparnasse, for the next four years, called Paris the "freest of cities and a
true magnet for artists."

Although several of these artists stayed for only a few years, others succeeded in putting down more durable roots. The painter Beauford Delaney
was a prime example of these long-term expatriates. Originally from Tennessee, Delaney, like many others, had felt the pull of the Harlem Renaissance,
arriving in New York in 1929. He stayed in Harlem during the 1930s, participating in the same artistic circles as Romare Bearden and Jacob Lawrence,
and painting portraits of great black figures like W.E.B. Du Bois and W. C.
Handy. During the early 1940s, Delaney followed the trail of Bohemia to
Greenwich Village, where he began his lifelong friendship with the young
James Baldwin. His connection with Baldwin seems to have prompted his
move to Paris, where he arrived in 1953. After an initial stay at Ed Clark's
building in the rue Delambre, Beauford Delaney moved into a studio that
James Baldwin found for him in the Paris suburb of Clamart. Baldwin made
sure to introduce his newly arrived friend to the people he knew in Paris,
especially those who might buy his paintings. By the time Delaney moved
into a studio in Montparnasse's rue Vercingétorix, he had become an established figure in the French capital's art world. He painted both portraits and
abstract studies glowing with color. As a writer for Le Monde once characterized him, "Those who approach this soft man with the deep preacher's
voice experience the same feeling. Beauford Delaney elicits fraternity."
Beauford Delaney never returned to America, dying in Paris in 1973.

Most African American artists journeyed to the French capital as students,
supported by either the GI Bill or their own resources, but they soon also
began exhibiting their work in the city's art galleries. In 1949, Herbert Gentry's
paintings were featured in exhibitions at two Parisian galleries. Ed Clark
succeeded in having his work shown publicly during each of the four years he
lived in Paris, including a 1953 exhibition at the Galeric Craven near the
Ecole des Beaux-Arts, one of the city's first American art galleries. Beauford
Delaney joined Clark at the 1954 Salon des Réalités Nouvelles, and exhibited
his work at several other Parisian galleries during the decade. The Raymond
Creuze Gallery near the Champs-Elysées frequently showcased the work of
black American artists like Ed Clark, as did the American Center for Students
and Artists.

In general, the work of African American artists encountered a mixed
reception among the city's art critics, for reasons having less to do with their

individual merit than with their general approach to art. More than black writers, black American painters and sculptors were usually considered American first and black second. Most did not highlight specifically black themes in their work, or concentrate on portrayals of African American life in either Paris or the United States. Few incorporated in their painting or sculpture the kind of political reflection so typical of Richard Wright's prose, or tried to embrace a consciously black aesthetic. Therefore, although individual African American artists might receive favorable reviews (in 1954, for example, *Le Monde* praised the work of Ed Clark), on the whole Paris's art world saw little to distinguish their work from that of other Americans. This lack of attention to race charmed many expatriates, but it also meant that French critics included black artists in their disdain for the New York school and American modern art in general. As Ed Clark commented, "In 1956, in Paris, all American painters, Black or White, were considered barbarians."

Perhaps the most famous African American artist to settle in Paris after the war was the great cartoonist Oliver Harrington. "One of the all-time top five editorial cartoonists in U.S. history," Ollie Harrington grew up in New York in the 1920s, moving to Harlem after his graduation from high school in 1929. There he began to work as a free-lance cartoonist for the black press, and in 1935 developed the satirical character of Bootsie, a comic-strip antihero whose antics would become familiar to black readers from coast to coast. Harrington's cartoons enabled him to pursue his education at Yale University's School of Fine Arts, where he earned his bachelor's degree in 1940. He first went to Europe as a war correspondent in 1944, and over the next few years the glimpse of racial equality he encountered there made white America's postwar love affair with bigotry harder to tolerate. He left America in 1951 to settle in Paris, inspired both by a loathing for American racism and by the hope of continuing his art studies abroad. Like many others, Ollie Harrington began studying art at La Grande Chaumière, which featured small classes and individual instruction that gave the art student as much or as little direction as he or she desired. Harrington later described it as "a wonderful place in the development of French art history. Practically everyone at some time or another had been through La Grande Chaumière." At the same time he continued to produce his Bootsie comic strip, selling it to the *Chicago Defender* and the *Pittsburgh Courier*.

More than any of the other black American artists in Paris, Ollie Harrington embraced the expatriate lifestyle that united African Americans in the French capital during the 1950s. Shortly after his arrival in Paris, Harrington met Richard Wright in the Café Tournon, and the two soon became the best of friends, a relationship that would only grow closer until Wright's death in 1960. The cartoonist quickly became one of the central figures in the Left Bank expatriate community, widely known as a man who knew how to enjoy Paris to the fullest. His good friend Chester Himes once described him as looking like a brown-skinned version of Spencer Tracy, with broad shoulders and twinkling eyes:

> Ollie became my best friend at the Café Tournon. He was the best raconteur I'd ever known; he kept large audiences entertained and drew people to the Tournon to hear him. We could sit all night ad-libbing and never miss a cue. We used to keep audiences entranced.
> The proprietors, M. and Mme. Alazar, loved Ollie and he was a sort of accepted leader for all the blacks of the Quarter, who in turn attracted all the black Americans in the city. It was really Ollie who singlehandedly made the Café Tournon famous in the world.

Ollie Harrington lived the life that many expatriates in Paris have only dreamed about, one full of excitement, comradeship, and sexual adventure. Harrington had a lot in common with Himes and Richard Wright. He worked actively to promote justice for the black people of America, placing this struggle in the context of the international fight against fascism, and espoused a firm commitment to the political Left. Like Wright, Harrington used his art as a political weapon, to challenge and mobilize opposition to racism and other forms of oppression. At the same time, he was a born conversationalist whose warmth and openness, his ability to relate to both artists and writers, made him a natural leader of the Parisian community of black expatriates during the 1950s. Above all, the city enabled him to transcend the limits imposed upon blacks in America, to approach life first and foremost simply as an artist. As Harrington later recalled, "The art community in Paris, for example, is a completely open one. The only criterion is, are you a good artist? Or at least are you working like hell to become one? Such a criterion induces an atmosphere of camaraderie, a sharing of ideas, techniques, and often soup, all of which seem indispensable in the making of the artist. I never even remotely experienced anything like that at 'home' except perhaps in Harlem."

Ollie Harrington played a key role in the life of Paris's postwar black American community, bringing together both artists, writers, and musicians in the cafés and hotels of the Left Bank. In general, the African American artists that came to France in the late 1940s and 1950s, like their predecessors during the 1920s and 1930s, saw themselves as part of a broader black intelligentsia in exile. There was some geographical distinction between the different groups of black exiles, in line with French custom; whereas writers and musicians tended to settle in the Latin Quarter and Saint-Germain-des-Prés, artists clustered together in Montparnasse. Yet the short distance between the two neighborhoods (roughly a fifteen-minute walk) did not prevent artists from participating fully in the broader life of the African American community in Paris.

Honey Johnson, for example, worked both as a painter and a jazz singer, performing in Paris with Rex Stewart's band. She was also married to Herbert Gentry, who in 1947 opened a combination art gallery and nightclub in Montparnasse's rue Jules-Chaplain to showcase her talents. Called both Chez Honey and the Club Galérie, it displayed the work of African American and other young artists by day. At night it became a jazz club featuring live music by a host of top-notch performers including Don Byas, Kenny Clarke, Duke Ellington, and Lena Horne. They often played with French musicians, attracting a variety of listeners, including Jean-Paul Sartre, Simone de Beauvoir, Eartha Kitt, Orson Welles, and Marcel Marceau. Chez Honey lasted only a few years, but it symbolized the ability of expatriates in Paris to dissolve professional boundaries, embracing instead a broader sense of fellowship and community. "It was a special club," described Herbert Gentry. "Artists were invited there to express themselves and to meet other artists, mostly Americans, but also Danes, French, Swedes, who would come there to discuss art and music, and to exchange ideas. . . . You had to be hip and sensitive."

After 1945, African American visual artists succeeded in reestablishing a small but secure place for themselves in the French capital. Although a few who came to Paris during these years put down permanent roots, the majority did not. Ed Clark went back to New York in 1956, while Herbert Gentry moved on from Paris first to Denmark and then to Sweden by the end of the decade. Ollie Harrington found himself in East Berlin when the wall went up in 1961 and elected to remain there. Yet others, especially Beauford Delaney and Larry Potter, chose to stay, and in the 1960s they were joined by a new generation of black artists leaving America to find inspiration in the City of Light. The postwar expatriate artists thus ensured that the tradition of Parisian exile represented by Henry Ossawa Tanner and others would continue into the late twentieth century.

One of the more notable aspects of life in Paris immediately after the German occupation was the return of exiled Parisians, those who had either been taken as prisoners or forced laborers to Germany and those who had successfully sought refuge in Britain, America, or elsewhere. Among their number were a very few black Americans who had known life in the city before the Nazis marched in, and now came back to see if Paris had kept its magic. While providing a certain sense of continuity for the African American community, these people also proved that a new black generation had come to the city. Those who returned found that not only Paris, but they themselves had changed greatly in the intervening years; either they found a new place for themselves in the French capital or they did not stay for long.

The most illustrious of these returnees was of course Josephine Baker. During the 1920s and 1930s she had gradually made the transition from sexy black dancer to music hall star, becoming more respected and accepted as a part of French life. The war completed her metamorphosis, transforming Baker into a heroine of the French resistance. She spent most of the war years in North Africa working for the cause of Free France. There in 1943 she met France's leader in exile, General Charles de Gaulle, who presented her with a small golden Cross of Lorraine, symbol of the movement. Awarded an honorary position in the national air force, Lieutenant Baker returned with the Free French to French soil in 1944, landing at Marseilles in October. From there she made her triumphal way back to Paris. The black American musician and soldier Buddy Smith later described her return: "[There were] a million people up and down the Champs to see her when she came in. It was a glorious day, as big as the day they liberated Paris. She was in a big Daumier, and that car could only crawl about three miles an hour, so many people were out there. She was in the back, with all the flowers — people were throwing these flowers."

Josephine Baker's work for the resistance was singular to the French because so many other leading entertainers had collaborated during the occupation. Arletty, the star of Marcel Carné's film *Children of Paradise,* had taken a German lover, while Maurice Chevalier had ostentatiously posed for photographers drinking a bottle of Vichy water and later gone on a singing tour in Nazi Germany. In October 1946, France recognized Baker's contribution to its war effort by awarding her one of its highest decorations, the Medal of the Resistance.

Josephine Baker was back in Paris, but such a dynamic personality could not simply return to business as usual. In sharp contrast to her indifference to questions of racial justice during the 1920s and 1930s, the veteran performer now took her place in the fight against discrimination. She continued to perform on stage during the 1940s and 1950s, starting with a 1945 concert at the Theatre des Champs-Elysées almost exactly twenty years after her debut there with the Revue Nègre. Baker also toured widely around Europe and the world, most notably in the United States, where she finally won the recognition and acclaim that American critics and audiences had so long denied her. Moreover, she did so on her own terms; having long since abandoned primitivist symbols like the banana skirt for the costliest, most sophisticated Parisian costumes, Josephine Baker came to America in the 1950s as a proud representative of French elegance. During these years, she spoke out forcefully against segregation and racism in the United States, refusing to play before segregated audiences in Miami and Atlanta, and embracing the cause of Willie McGee, a black man falsely convicted and executed for the rape of a white woman in Mississippi. Baker's wartime experience had taught her that she could use her talent and fame to fight injustice, a lesson that she did not forget upon her return to the stage. Her postwar activism perfectly embodied the politicization of the African American community in Paris as a whole.

This heightened social awareness transformed Josephine Baker's personal life as well. In 1947, she married once again, this time to a young French bandleader named Jo Bouillon, who proved to be the most supportive of Baker's four husbands. With him she embarked on the most ambitious project of her life, the creation of the Family of Man. She decided to turn her château, Les Milandes, into a model international community inhabited by children of different nationalities and all races, a living demonstration of human brotherhood and peace. As she remarked to Bouillon, "We're going to be so happy with our children, Jo. We'll show the world that racial hatred is unnatural, an emotion dreamed up by man; that there *is* such a thing as a universal family; that it's possible for children of different races to grow up together as brothers."

After several years engaged in renovating the château (and in touring to raise money for the renovations), Josephine began assembling her model family, soon named the Rainbow Tribe, in the mid-1950s. They eventually numbered twelve, from places as diverse as Venezuela, Japan, France, Ivory Coast, Finland, and North Africa. For Josephine Baker, raising this international family in a fairy-tale castle in the French countryside fulfilled a dream. All too soon mounting debts and general financial mismanagement would turn the dream into a nightmare, but for the rest of the 1950s at least, Les Milandes could claim to be an oasis of peace and harmony in a troubled world.

Caring for her twelve charges increasingly took up the lion's share of Baker's time. Consequently, during the 1950s she staged a number of highly publicized "farewells" to the Paris stage. Most spectacular was her April 1956 concert at the Olympia, in which singers and dancers from most of the major theaters of Paris performed in her honor. Baker herself sang both her old songs, such as "J'ai Deux Amours," and some new ones, especially "Dans Mon Village," a salute to the Rainbow Tribe. Her farewells were inevitably followed by comebacks, both to raise money for Les Milandes, and also because she was a performer, born and bred, who simply could not give up the stage. Josephine Baker would never completely desert Paris, but the 1950s nevertheless marked the end of the central phase of her career. She had become both an international star and an activist deeply concerned with the fate of all humanity, and even the French capital was no longer big enough to contain her vision.

Bricktop, the other great African American diva of interwar Paris, also returned after the war to the city of her earlier triumphs, and quickly learned that one could not turn back the clock. She had spent the war years first in New York, then in Mexico City, where she had established a thriving night-club. Visa problems with the Mexican government led her to return to New York in 1949, where friends convinced her that Paris was ready and waiting for her. In the summer of that year, Bricktop once more crossed the Atlantic and after a brief sojourn in Italy returned to the city that had made her internation-ally famous. It quickly became evident, however, that 1949 was not 1924. As she later recorded in her memoirs,

> Montmartre looked like a wreck. It hadn't looked all that great by daylight even in the Twenties, but now it wasn't just shabby, it was almost slummy. The hotel I went to, which I remembered from the old days, wasn't the same. The atmosphere just wasn't the same. At night the atmosphere didn't get much better. The places on the Rue Pigalle and Rue Fontaine closed up either at midnight or at one a.m. That was sad. In my day, things were just getting started at that time.
>
> There were other sad things about post-war Paris. There was a lot of resent-ment toward Americans — YANKEE GO HOME signs all over the place. At the same time, the Parisians had started picking up some distinctly American attitudes toward Negroes.

Like Yves Malartic, Bricktop emphasized the bigotry of white American soldiers and their hostility toward their black fellow citizens. However, she also pointed out that these prejudices at times rubbed off on French people as well. This ripple effect was reminiscent of the impact of white Americans on Paris in the 1920s, leading some hotel and café owners to ban blacks for fear of offending their moneyed clients from the United States. Racism had reared its ugly head in Paris after the war, brought by white soldiers and middle-class tourists, "average Americans, not the quality of Cole [Porter] and his crowd." Bricktop recalled hearing even a Parisian prostitute use the word *nigger*, claiming to have learned it from a white American musician, and cited a case in which a French judge had upheld the right of a hotel owner to run a whites-only establishment. Such incidents merely reinforced Bricktop's impressions of Paris as tawdry and déclassé. Unlike many African Americans first visiting Paris after the liberation, she was not impressed by the egalitarianism of her hosts, regretfully concluding that color-blind France was just a memory.

In spite of such depressing realities, Bricktop decided to reestablish herself in the Paris nightclub business. She secured financial backing from old friends and found a club to rent in the rue Fontaine, the heart of the prewar Montmartre jazz scene. Despite nightmarish battles with the French bureaucracy, the new Bricktop's opened for business in May 1950. Opening night was a huge success, as both old friends and denizens of Montmartre competed with younger people curious to see a legend of Parisian nightlife. Bricktop appeared in Schiaparelli gowns and feather boas to sing all her old favorites and bring a bit of *les années folles* back to life:

> Thanks for the memories, of Paris in the spring,
> The Cole Porter songs we'd sing,
> Of the old Grand Duc and onion soup
> And other priceless things.
> I thank you so much.

Bricktop's new nightclub attracted the same mix of wealthy expatriates, tourists, and titled nobility that had made its fame before the war. Even the Duke and Duchess of Windsor came back, and when they threw a housewarming party in Paris Bricktop was invited to perform.

In spite of the fond, enthusiastic reviews she received, Bricktop's new club represented an exercise in nostalgia rather than the renewal of a tradition. Those who remembered the old Bricktop's were loyal customers, yet they could not by themselves guarantee the success of the new venture. More important, Montmartre no longer possessed the community of African American musicians who had furnished both performers and clients for Bricktop's in the years before the war. And Bricktop did not seem to have much luck in attracting a new generation of fans. Jazz in Paris had changed, shifting from the sprightly rhythms of the New Orleans style to the cool, abstract tones of bebop. Its geographical center had moved from the Montmartre that Bricktop knew so well to the *caves* of Saint-Germain-des-Prés, now the favorite rendez-vous for both black expatriates and young Parisians. Many of these had never heard of Bricktop, or at best knew of her as a symbol of the vanished years before the war. As Bricktop herself noted, "We were fooling ourselves, trying to re-create the old Paris days. It was like putting Humpty Dumpty together again." After a less than successful summer season in Biarritz, Bricktop returned to Paris to reopen the club for the fall season, but she experienced the same problems she had the previous spring. By November, she was ready to call it quits. The following month, she left Paris to open up a new nightclub in Rome, turning her back once and for all on the city that had originally made her reputation but no longer seemed to have any room for her. Bricktop remained an international star in the nightclub business for most of the rest of her life, but her legendary Paris years now became a fond memory.

In very different ways, the postwar careers of both Josephine Baker and Bricktop demonstrated how much Paris, and the place of African Americans in it, had changed since the 1920s. Baker had become a bigger star than ever by transcending the racial imagery surrounding her initial success; now she was not only a legend in her own time but a French patriotic icon too. Moreover, her new-found adoption of the cause of racial equality reflected the tenor of the times and the all-important legacy of the war. Bricktop, in contrast, had remained attached to the role of the black American as a symbol of festivity and wild parties, at a time when the prevailing mood in Paris tended to emphasize quiet, somber reflection. Her fondness for innocuous jazz and wealthy aristocrats had little to offer a new generation energized by the political Left and vitally concerned with global issues of war and peace. By the 1950s, African Americans had come to play a somewhat different role in the French imagination, symbolizing complex tragedy rather than primitive joy. Both Baker's series of farewells and returns and Bricktop's definitive abandonment of the French capital constituted an implicit recognition of the fact that the Jazz Age would never be seen again.

The experiences of Josephine Baker and Bricktop in postwar Paris illustrate another important difference between the 1920s and the 1950s: the changed role of African American women. Whereas Baker and Bricktop had dominated the interwar black community, the black American expatriate presence in Paris after the Second World War was an overwhelmingly male one. In contrast to black men, very few black women served in the armed forces during the war, and thus were not able to use the benefits offered by the GI Bill. No famous African American women writers participated in the literary circles of the Left Bank, nor did many black women work as artists alongside the black men of Montparnasse. The legends of Baker and Bricktop may have inspired young black women in the United States to look for stardom in Paris, but during the 1940s and 1950s none achieved the success of their illustrious foremothers.

Yet there are always exceptions, and a few African American women did settle in Paris after World War II. Like black men, some black women stayed in France for reasons of the heart, having fallen in love with and married Frenchmen. In an era when the wife generally followed the husband, such couples were in fact more likely to stay in France than African American men married to Frenchwomen. In 1952, the novelist William Gardner Smith described this phenomenon: "More American Negro women than men, it seems to me, have in the last few years married Europeans and set up their lives on this side of the Atlantic. They come from all parts of the United States, but primarily from the Eastern Seaboard: they are alike in their dislike of 'special' publicity (from writers like this one); most seem perfectly satisfied with their marriages, and do not regret the fact that they may seldom, if ever, see the United States again."

Many other black American women came on their own, however. Some first saw Paris as performers briefly passing through the city. Some came as fashion models, working in one of the city's greatest industries. Others arrived as students or tourists. More so than black men, most African American women stayed in Paris for a relatively short time, and few carved out a lasting place in the French capital. Yet as small as their numbers were, the black women who left America for Paris in these years proved that the legacy of Josephine Baker was not dead, and that the dream of life in France was not necessarily for black men only.

The experience of the singer Eartha Kitt is an important example. A petite, dark-skinned, beautiful woman with a sultry, gravelly voice, Kitt has established one of the most durable and impressive careers in theater, film, music, and dance of any African American woman in recent times. Born in South Carolina, Eartha Kitt grew up in Harlem during the waning years of its renaissance. The career that would later make her one of black America's leading musical and film stars began in her teens, when she won a scholarship to study dance at Katherine Dunham's school in New York.

Soon after Kitt began her studies in 1946, she was performing in Dunham's dance troupe, the most important company of African American dancers of its time. During the next two years, the young dancer toured widely with the Dunham Troupe across the United States and Mexico, and in 1948 her work with them took her to Europe for the first time in her life. After touring around Britain, the Dunham Troupe moved on to Paris, where it performed for three months to enthusiastic audiences. As the French critic and jazz musician Boris Vian noted in a 1950 review, "There is the great Katherine . . . who has known how to combine with infinite talent choreographic and ethnological science, elements of authentic folklore transposed through art, her very real 'presence,' and a taste for colors, materials, jewels, and attitudes, that only belongs to people of her race." Of Eartha Kitt, Vian noted that she was one of the most beautiful women in the world, with a voice that would damn all the wooden saints of France. Kitt found Paris fascinating, a city of mystery and romance, but also of hard work and opportunity. As she later noted in her autobiography, *Thursday's Child,*

> Opening night in Paris was fantastic. More silks, satins, sables, and lace than I had ever seen before. . . . If we never danced before, we did that night for Paris. . . . Maybe it was because it was Paris — the beautiful woman with a controversial reputation. The one everyone wanted to make love to but few would accept for a bride.
> For three months we went to bed at dawn. It was inevitable that I was awakened practically every morning by a bottle of perfume, champagne, flowers, or just a date for lunch. I got so tired I hated Paris and everything she stood for. I was too worn out to care. Of course I could have refused a lot of dates and hospitality, but I didn't want to miss anything.

From Paris the Dunham Troupe went on to tour the Riviera, Belgium, Italy, Switzerland, and Sweden, coming back periodically to the Paris Theater for return engagements. During one of these runs, the owner of a nightclub just off the Champs-Elysées offered Eartha Kitt a job singing there for $245 a week, quite an increase from her current $90 salary. After much trepidation, Kitt resigned her position in the Dunham Troupe to take the job at Carroll's to begin her solo career as a singer.

> I looked at myself in the mirror, thinking I looked innocent enough for a cabaret act. As I was about to go on stage, Frede came in, took one look at me, and declared, "Mon Dieu, where do you sink you are going like that?" Rip went my angelic dress up the left leg to the middle of the thigh. Before I could say Jack Robinson, I was pushed on stage as the music blared up and I was being announced. "Ladies and gentlemen, we present to you a new discovery, Miss Eartha Kitt."
> My sense told me I was standing in front of people, that I should give a reason for my eccentric behavior, or excuse myself and leave. My only excuse

was to sing, as I could see, so I opened my mouth and out came a sound called singing. The applause after each number was soul-satisfying, as it told me I was accepted.

Eartha Kitt spent the better part of the next year in Paris, working as a nightclub singer. She had a brief engagement with Bill Coleman and Don Byas at the club Perroquet, which a decade later would become Régine's celebrated discotheque. Kitt acted with Orson Welles in his 1951 Parisian production of the play *Faust*. At the end of 1951, Eartha Kitt returned to New York, where her success in Europe had created a new interest in her. After some initial difficulties, Kitt found acceptance and soon fame as a solo performer back in her native land. Like Josephine Baker before her, Eartha Kitt had come to Paris as one member of a dance troupe, but she left as a star.

At the end of the decade, another native of South Carolina would settle in Paris for a time. Like Eartha Kitt, Vertamae Smart-Grosvenor originally came from the South but grew up in a northern city, in her case Philadelphia. As she later noted in her memoirs, *Vibration Cooking*, "Being tall and digging the theater was what made me go off to Paris in '58." Often feeling out of place in high school, Smart began to think of herself as a Bohemian, identifying with a culture that would not reject her but instead value her artistic inclinations. As a teenager, she attended a lecture by Raymond Duncan, brother of the famed dancer Isadora Duncan, who confirmed Smart's attraction to an avant-garde way of life and focused it on Paris, the capital of Bohemia. At the age of nineteen, Vertamae Smart booked passage to Europe on the SS *Rotterdam*, arriving in the French capital in February 1958, without any contacts or knowledge of the French language. As she wrote to a friend, it immediately became clear that Paris was a long way from Philadelphia.

> Right by the Café Dupont a brother from Senegal came to me and said "My sister my sister," and I said *oui*. He invited me to have coffee in the café with him and his friends . . . I couldn't believe my luck. In Paris for only two hours and I had a gang already. We had coffee and after a while they asked if I wanted to go to an African night club . . . The owner was a friend of "my new gang." He asked what do you do and I said, "Ah ah ah CHANTEUSE," so he announced to the whole club that Mlle. Kasmin (that's the name I used) from Harlem (in Europe people always say that black people are from Harlem or Mississippi) will chant for us Negro spirituals. I was shocked but I had made my vow so I sang "Swing Low, Sweet Chariot." They loved it.

The owner offered her a job singing at the club for $5 a night. Smart wisely turned down an offer to tour Beirut with the house band, and several months later the nightclub owner was arrested for participation in the city's "white slave" trade.

While she might not have known Pablo Picasso and Jean-Paul Sartre, Smart found that Paris in the late fifties lived up to her hopes and expectations. Like so many young foreigners, she gravitated to the Left Bank, sharing a room in the rue de Fleurus, the street made famous in the 1920s as the home of Gertrude Stein. She learned French, became familiar with the local cafés, and shopped for fresh vegetables daily at the outdoor market on the rue de Seine. More important, Smart met a wide range of interesting and talented people from all parts of the world, including her future husband. While life in Paris meant learning to live in one small room and cook meals on an alcohol burner, it also meant participating in the kind of Bohemian community the young woman had left Philadelphia to find.

The Parisian experiences of Eartha Kitt and Vertamae Smart-Grosvenor offer contrasting images of expatriate life in the 1950s. Kitt went to the city by chance, as a result of her dancing career, and there found professional opportunities that induced her to stay. Smart chose to go to Paris as an adventure and an escape, drawn by the city's reputation for avant-garde elegance. One experience looked back to the trail blazed by Josephine Baker, the other anticipated the life of American exchange students in Paris during the 1960s. Yet their lives had much in common. Both women enjoyed the beautiful, cosmopolitan mystique of the city. Both took part in a diverse circle of disparate individuals, including but certainly not limited to other black Americans. Finally, both Eartha Kitt and Vertamae Smart spent time in Paris at crucial points in their lives. The city enabled Kitt to go from a chorus line dancer to a solo performer, while it transformed Smart from a self-conscious teenager into a confident young woman. Paris was no longer the city that had made Josephine Baker a star in the 1920s, but black women like Eartha Kitt and Vertamae Smart found that life there still had much to offer.

Although Bricktop may have found postwar Paris a disappointment, other black American musicians who had seen the bright lights of the capital during the interwar years successfully made the transition to the new era. Arthur Briggs was one of the very few who worked consistently in Paris during both the prewar and postwar eras. Having refused to leave the city in 1940, Briggs had been placed in a German internment camp on the outskirts of Paris during the war. As Allied troops neared the French capital in August 1944, the Nazi authorities fled Briggs's camp, although the inmates suffered a final bombardment from retreating German soldiers. On August 26, the day after the liberation, Briggs rented a cart and together with a friend in the camp used it to push his belongings back to Paris, where he was joyfully reunited with his wife after a separation of nearly four years. Arthur Briggs resumed his career as a trumpeter in the new jazz clubs springing up on the Left Bank. He remained in Paris, and in 1968 was elected a member of the French Academy of Jazz. Arthur Briggs could point to a career playing jazz in Paris that spanned forty years. Unlike many African American musicians in the city, Briggs had learned to avoid the seductions of alcohol, drugs, and easy money, and to carve out a stable life for himself and his family. His wartime imprisonment underscored the fact that France, not the United States, was now his home.

Bill Coleman, another jazz trumpet player and friend of Arthur Briggs, also came back to Paris in the late 1940s. However, unlike Briggs, Coleman was still a relative newcomer to the city, having played there on and off during the 1930s. During the war, Coleman had performed with different bands primarily in New York and had also toured widely, even playing in American-occupied Tokyo in 1946. Shortly after returning to New York, Coleman met Charles Delaunay of the revived Hot Club of France and told him that he wanted to go back to Paris. By the end of 1948, Delaunay had arranged a contract for Coleman to perform at a Parisian nightclub and on December 12 Bill Coleman once again set off for Paris, this time on an Air France jet, a symbol of a new era in transatlantic travel. Although no longer the young man who had first discovered France a decade earlier, the intervening years had graced the slender musician with an air of distinction suitable to a veteran of his craft. Coleman's reintroduction to Paris jazz happened more quickly than expected, for upon landing at Orly Airport in the morning after a fifteen-hour flight he was told he would be playing a concert that afternoon! "I was surprised how hip these fellows were to the styles being played in the USA! They were not at all behind the times as I had sort of expected the French jazz musicians to be. . . . I was also surprised at the large following that jazz had. The theater was full."

Back in Paris, Bill Coleman gravitated to the places he had known in Montmartre during the 1930s, especially Boudon's and the Tabac in the rue Fontaine. The area that he had described as "a little Harlem" in the 1930s had lost much of its animation, however, and Coleman missed the sight of old friends. He stopped going to Boudon's restaurant after Arthur Briggs told him the proprietor had collaborated during the occupation, denouncing Jews and blacks to the authorities. Yet even though the Paris he remembered from the 1930s had largely disappeared, Coleman soon carved out a place for himself on the Left Bank in the postwar years.

Unlike Briggs and Coleman, most black Americans who settled in Paris during the late 1940s were newcomers to the French capital, having been brought there by the war, by disillusionment with postwar America, or both. One of the most notable was Leroy Haynes, a former Atlanta University football star and art student who came to Europe with the American army at the end of the war. Gifted with a powerful physique and an expansive personality, in 1949 Haynes decided to move to Paris from his army base in Germany, ostensibly to pursue doctoral studies in sociology at the Sorbonne. He soon found that even in Paris, however, one must first find a way of keeping body and soul together. So shortly after his arrival, Leroy Haynes opened Haynes restaurant in the rue Manuel, a few blocks away from the traditional heart of black Montmartre. Like Louis Mitchell's restaurant in the 1920s, Haynes catered to a diverse clientele, including other black Americans, white American tourists, and curious Parisians. Haynes, one of the first soul food restaurants in Europe, quickly prospered and has survived to this day, now proudly claiming to be the oldest American restaurant in Paris. A fellow black expatriate, Ollie Harrington once described the atmosphere of this uniquely American establishment in the French capital: "Naturally a Paris boulevard is just about the last place to ever think of singing the blues and so the Black exile does the next best thing. He takes the Metro to the foothills of Montmartre where he will find Leroy Haynes, himself an exile, who will fix any brother or sister with generous helpings of chitlins with collard greens, red beans and rice, and even corn bread!" Haynes's restaurant quickly became one of the key establishments of African American life in postwar Paris, one referred to in several novels and memoirs of the time, and a worthy successor to those jazz clubs and cafés that served the same community in the same neighborhood a generation earlier.

The same year another African American expatriate, Inez Cavanaugh, opened her own restaurant in the rue Champollion, a short and narrow street in the Latin Quarter one block from the Sorbonne. Cavanaugh was a jazz singer who had worked in New York and managed Duke Ellington. Before the war she had married a wealthy Danish baron, Timme Rosencrantz, who had come to New York in 1933 and had soon become a knowledgeable insider in the world of black jazz musicians. In the late 1940s, they moved back to Europe and opened Chez Inez, a restaurant featuring fried chicken, jazz, and blues, often sung by Inez herself. While not as successful or as long-lived as Haynes, Chez Inez did become a place that attracted many in the new postwar black American community in Paris. Ollie Stewart mentioned the restaurant in his guidebook for African Americans, *Paris Here I Come*, as a place to go in the evening for entertainment. As the journalist William Gardner Smith observed in the *Pittsburgh Courier*,

It's six years ago that Inez Cavanaugh, of New York, came over and decided to open a night spot; six years since she served her first order of corn muffins and home fried chicken to eager Frenchmen who had never tasted the like. Since that time the club, and the woman who ran it, had become a Left Bank institution; it was inconceivable to come through Paris without stopping, at least once, at Chez Inez's.

During the winter, it was a club haunted by students, mostly Negro, from the University of Paris. They came to hear the delicate piano playing of Aaron Bridgers, the shouted blues of "Fats" Edwards and the softer blues of Inez herself. . . . In spring and summer, Chez Inez was the hang-out of American and Scandinavian tourists, who wanted to appear "in the know" about jazz. Inez knew how to make these tourists feel that they owned the place. . . . She sang real blues, and she sang songs whose words could never be published in the Readers' Digest.

In 1952, Inez Cavanaugh closed her restaurant for financial reasons and moved back home to America.

Other Parisian restaurants and jazz clubs also catered to the recently developed black American clientele, such as Tom's Barbecue near the Madeleine; the Ringside in the plush rue d'Artois (between the Champs-Elysées and the rue du Faubourg-Saint-Honoré), which later became famous as the Blue Note; or the venerable Boeuf sur le Toit nearby, opened by Jean Cocteau in 1921. Yet Haynes's restaurant and Chez Inez provide a particularly interesting glimpse of the African American community in Paris during the late 1940s and 1950s. Both succeeded as black-owned businesses and meeting spots for African American expatriates; although others of all races and nationalities were certainly welcome, they served primarily as the heart of the black American community in Paris. In the years after World War II, restaurants assumed a new importance as community gathering places for the city's black expatriates. Prewar Montmartre had featured several nightclubs, notably Bricktop's and Chez Florence, owned by black Americans. In contrast, virtually all of the jazz establishments in postwar Paris were French-owned. Restaurants thus became the only places in Paris controlled by black Americans, and as such the new centers of black sociability in the city. Jazz clubs remained important as places to work and to meet other blacks, but black restaurants represented the attractions of home.

The different locations of the two restaurants exemplified another significant change, the postwar shift of that community's center of gravity from Montmartre to the Left Bank. Leroy Haynes opened his restaurant close to the heart of interwar black Paris a generation earlier; had he been open for business in the 1920s, many of his customers could probably have walked there from the hotels where they lived, or the nightclubs where they performed. In the years after the war, however, those who frequented Haynes often had to make a long trip by taxi or subway to taste his cooking. Haynes remained a success due partly to the quality of that cooking, partly to the larger-than-life personality of Leroy Haynes himself. Yet thanks to the changing urban geography of black life in Paris, his restaurant soon became the symbol of a community that was already centered elsewhere when it first opened its doors.

Chez Inez, in contrast, found its location in the area now favored by black Americans, the Latin Quarter. While the restaurant never became the equivalent of Bricktop's on the postwar Left Bank, it still did well for a while, and its address must have helped facilitate its success. Most of the black Americans who settled in Paris in the late 1940s and 1950s, including veterans living on the GI Bill, took up residence in the cheap hotels among the Latin Quarter, Saint-Germain-des-Prés, and Montparnasse, building a community life just as richly textured as that of the interwar years. By 1950 even Bill Coleman, for whom Montmartre had *been* Paris in earlier years, had bowed to changing circumstances and "emigrated" across the river. "Lily [his wife] and I moved in to the Hôtel Crystal, right across from the Club St.-Germain. This was at the time of the fame of St.-Germain-des-Prés. . . . Boris Vian played trumpet at the Tabou, the Club St.-Germain was jumping, and Sidney Bechet officiated at the Vieux Colombier."

Why did Montmartre lose favor with black American expatriates after the Second World War? The transition from Right to Left Bank illustrates more clearly than any other change the differences in Paris and in its African American community after 1945. The war had stripped Montmartre of its glamour, revealing more clearly the shabby white working-class neighborhood that had always lain beneath. In the harsh conditions of the late 1940s, the prostitution that still abounded in the area around the Place Pigalle seemed more desperate than daring, symbolizing poverty rather than uninhibited sexuality. An incident in March 1947 cast the postwar quality of Montmartre life in sharp relief. That month the fashion industry staged a photo session in the neighborhood's rue Lepic marketplace to publicize Christian Dior's heralded New Look. Local housewives, outraged by the sight of models flaunting luxurious clothing at a time when the basic necessities of life were still hard to come by, attacked the session, beating one model and trying to strip the clothes off her back. At such a moment, the prewar splendor of Bricktop's must have seemed very far away.

As important, though, was the changing nature of the black community itself. Unlike the interwar years, after 1945 literary figures became the leading examples of black Americans in Paris, and it was natural for them to settle down in the Left Bank neighborhoods favored by their French colleagues. Parisian intellectuals had abandoned Montmartre before the First World War, when Montparnasse had emerged as the new literary and artistic center of the French capital; the colonization of Saint-Germain-des-Prés by Jean-Paul Sartre and his friends during the 1940s was only the latest example of this phenomenon. By moving from Montmartre to the Left Bank, therefore, black American expatriates were in a sense playing catch-up with the prevailing trend among the Paris intelligentsia, and the move illustrated a new relationship between the two groups. The French literary elite had far more contact with African American writers after 1945 than during the interwar years, predisposing its members to view black Americans as colleagues and fellow intellectuals rather than exotic specimens of a primitive culture.

In the postwar years, therefore, the African American community in Paris became increasingly attached to the city's intelligentsia. While Parisian intellectuals had certainly taken a keen interest in black Americans before the war, as Jean Cocteau's sponsorship of Panama Al Brown demonstrated, blacks had achieved success primarily as a new phenomenon in popular culture. Parisians in the 1920s loved jazz because one could dance to it, not because of its inherent musical qualities. After 1945, however, jazz maintained its popularity as a sort of existentialist accessory, played in dim basements on the home turf of the intellectuals, Saint-Germain-des-Prés. Finally, the shift from Right to Left Bank had an important political dimension. Unlike interwar Montmartre, which owed more than a little of its glitter to tourist dollars, the postwar haunts of Parisian intellectuals on the other side of the Seine were dominated by the political Left, which often took a sharply anti-American tone. For both African American musicians and writers, therefore, life on the Left Bank during the 1940s and 1950s symbolized a shift from the carefree expatriate days of the 1920s to a more conscious, at times bitter, rejection of the United States and the subordinate position it continued to reserve for its black citizens.

JAZZ IN SAINT-GERMAIN-DES-PRÉS

While black writers furnished the text for expatriate life in the 1950s, black jazz musicians provided the melody and the beat; were this experience a musical, it would advertise words by Richard Wright and music by Sidney Bechet. During the years after World War II, jazz formed an integral part of African American life in Paris, and of Bohemian Left Bank circles in general.

Yet the 1950s did not simply represent the return of *les années folles*; both Paris and jazz had changed too much to make nostalgia a going concern, as Bricktop discovered. Jazz was now well rooted in Parisian life, with many native performers and a significant French musical establishment. More important, some of jazz's leading exponents were now producing a very different kind of sound from that first heard by Parisians a generation earlier. Emphasizing complicated melodies, subtle rhythms, and a cool, detached pose, bebop had become the latest postwar trend in jazz. This new musical style revolutionized the jazz world, and found a ready audience in Paris. Bebop contributed to the general revival of Parisian jazz without displacing more traditional forms. Together the old and the new music would create a golden age for jazz in the French capital during the 1950s.

Saint-Germain-des-Prés became the center of both jazz and existentialism at the same time, the years immediately after 1945. More so than Montmartre during the 1920s, however, the jazz of the Left Bank was the creation of white French musicians. This shift resulted both from the increased maturity of French jazz, and also from the lingering effects of the war. Although the Nazis had banned black music in France and chased its African American performers out of the country, jazz itself had not disappeared during the Occupation. French musicians continued to meet, hold concerts, and stage amateur festivals in Paris. Consequently, the war helped promote the "Frenchification" of Parisian jazz, through no fault of its practitioners. The rise of existentialism after the war created new opportunities for this music. Sartre himself was a fan of jazz, having attended performances by Charlie Parker and Coleman Hawkins in New York's celebrated Fifty-second Street jazz clubs during the war. More important, the thousands of young Parisians who flocked to Saint-Germain-des-Prés in the late 1940s viewed jazz as part of the existentialist culture they so admired.

The combination of the revival of French jazz and the popularity of existentialism produced a new type of nightclub, the famous *caves* of Saint-Germain-des-Prés. These *caves* were basement rooms, usually small and often very crowded, that featured live music and stayed open until the wee hours of the morning. Dimly lit (thanks to postwar fuel shortages) and smoke-filled, they fit perfectly into the postwar climate of the Left Bank. The tradition of listening to jazz below street level actually began at the Hôtel des Carmes in the Latin Quarter, where the French orchestra Les Lorientais played the best live jazz in the city right after the war, but by 1947 the *caves* had moved west to existentialist territory. First to open was the Tabou Club, a small basement room located in the rue Dauphine which kicked off the fad for jazz in

Saint-Germain-des-Prés. At the end of the war, the Tabou was one of many struggling bistros in the neighborhood when it obtained the fortunate authorization to remain open after midnight. As the last resort for local night owls, it soon attracted an illustrious Parisian clientele of writers, artists, and other intellectuals, including both Jean-Paul Sartre and Albert Camus. In the spring of 1947, the owners decided to cash in on their sudden success by turning the Tabou's basement into a nightspot, and on April 11 the Tabou Club was born. It became an immediate sensation, a place where people could dance the jitterbug to the latest music, at first recorded but soon performed by a live French jazz band. Boris Vian, leader of the Tabou's band, left the following atmospheric description of the club at the height of its popularity:

> Seen from the outside it was a dingy bistro, with dirty brown walls and the word Tabou written in yellow letters on the facade. . . . One entered through a glass door, encountering a crowd as soon as one pushed aside the curtain. Twenty people surrounded the grand master of the stairway, the person who checked and gave out membership cards. Once admitted — and you needed contacts to get in! . . . one descended a tortuous stone stairway (guaranteed to bang the head of anyone over six feet tall), ending up in a long vaulted passage, like a subway station only much smaller and dirtier, bordered on one side by a stage decked out like a straw hut and on the other by an oak bar and a little nook designated as the cloak room. It took some time to make all this out, since the cigarette smoke produced a fog of London-like proportions and the uproar was so intense that one reacted by not seeing anything . . . Every night ten celebrities and thirty very well known people preside over the festivities.

A May 1947 article in the popular Parisian newspaper *Samedi-Soir* ensured the notoriety of the Tabou Club by labeling its habitués "troglodytes" and portraying their "existentialist" activities in lurid tones. Given the tremendous reputation, crowds, and profits of the Tabou Club in 1947, it was only natural that other nightspots soon sprang up in imitation, creating an archipelago of Saint-Germain-des-Prés jazz clubs by the end of the decade. One of the founders of the Tabou Club, Frédéric Chauvelot, left after disagreements with the bistro owners and in June 1948 founded a new *cave*, the Club Saint-Germain, in the rue Saint-Benoît a few blocks away. Others soon followed, including the Rose Rouge later that year and the Club du Vieux Colombier in 1950. Although all these nightspots carefully cultivated an existentialist air, the amateurish, spontaneous spirit of the Tabou Club gradually gave way to a more routine, systematic atmosphere, one in which professional jazz musicians occupied a central position.

At the center of all this activity, reigning for a few brief years as the veritable prince of Saint-Germain-des-Prés, stood the mercurial figure of Boris Vian. Perhaps no French man or woman in the twentieth century has embodied a closer attachment to African American culture than this handsome, slender young Parisian. Vian was a brilliant, intense young man whose creative genius burned like a bright flame in postwar Paris. He wrote ten novels, seven plays, forty-two short stories, four hundred songs, fifty articles, and many other creative works in the years from the liberation to the end of the 1950s. When he died of a heart attack in 1959 at the age of thirty-nine, he became a symbol of postwar youth in revolt, one whose "live fast, die young" legacy would anticipate figures as disparate as the Teddy Boys in Britain and Hollywood's James Dean. Boris Vian first became interested in jazz as a teenager before the war, when a concert by Duke Ellington inspired him to learn to play the trumpet and join the Hot Club of France. During the war, in part as a way of earning money to support himself, his wife, and infant son, Vian began playing trumpet in the jazz orchestra of Claude Abadie. He continued to play after the war, and began writing articles on jazz both for *Le Jazz Hot* and for *Les Temps Modernes*, published by his former teacher and fellow jazz fan Jean-Paul Sartre. Boris Vian led the orchestra at the Tabou Club and then moved on to the Club Saint-Germain in 1948, where he welcomed Ellington in his first postwar visit to the French capital. He also organized a jazz club for Parisian university students in 1946, the first French festival of jazz films in 1948, and many other concerts and conferences in the years immediately after the war. In 1950, Vian completed the guidebook *Manuel de Saint-Germain-des-Prés*, which confirmed his leadership of those who sought the intersection of jazz music and existentialist thought.

Boris Vian's affinity for black American culture spilled over into his literary work as well. Jazz musicians appear in several of his short stories, most notably "Cancer" and "Blues for a Black Cat." In 1946, Vian passed along to a publisher friend the manuscript of an American detective story, claiming to have discovered the author, Vernon Sullivan, and translated his work. The book, a story of the murder of two rich white women by a black man in exchange for the lynching of his brother, was published in November under the title *I Shall Spit on Your Graves*. Its combination of violence, racial conflict, and explicit sexuality soon made it a runaway best-seller in France, especially when the world learned that Boris Vian had himself written it, in fifteen days no less. A Parisian salesman's murder of his mistress in clear imitation of Vian's novel only increased the book's popularity, until the French government slapped the young author with a stiff fine and banned it outright. A clear reworking of themes made famous by both Richard Wright and Chester Himes, the novel not only demonstrated the interest of the French public in American race relations, but also made clear that Vian's own fascination with African American life was not limited to music. Like Jean Cocteau in the 1930s, he represented the sophisticated and dramatic Parisian intellectual who found in the culture of blacks from the United States a powerful new way of looking at the world. In 1953, he wrote, "It is annoying for the Americans to owe to blacks the only artistic contribution that the Unitedstatesians have been able to make to our old Europe."

By 1950, the great vogue of Saint-Germain-des-Prés had come to an end, a pleasant yet potent memory that would inspire similar outposts of Bohemia from Munich's Schwabing to Greenwich Village to Haight-Ashbury. But the jazz clubs remained, making the neighborhood the capital of Parisian jazz during the 1950s. French fans eagerly followed African American jazz and enthusiastically welcomed those musicians who came to France, either as visitors or as permanent residents. In fact, jazz almost certainly enjoyed much more popularity in Paris during the 1950s than it had in the 1920s. The *caves* soon began showcasing American bands, making them more attractive to black Americans and French jazz fans alike. Just as the hero of *Nausea* had found new meaning from a blues song, so would the existentialists discover in postwar jazz a vitality and depth that at times could make the pains and disappointments of the nuclear era seem very far away.

The postwar existentialist fad made Saint-Germain-des-Prés the center of Parisian jazz in the 1950s, but it was not the only factor in reviving French interest in this uniquely American art form. The Hot Club of France had continued to operate during the war and sprang into renewed action after the liberation, still headed by Hugues Panassié. In 1946, the organization's secretary Charles Delaunay, also a renowned scholar of jazz, published *Hot Discography*, the most complete guide to jazz recordings yet written. As during World War I, the arrival of the American army in France in 1944 brought new American musicians and greater access to recordings from the United States. The white American jazz musician Sim Copans began a weekly radio program, "Panoroma of American Jazz," at the newly established Odéon Cultural Center, providing many young Parisians with their first real taste of American jazz. By 1948, jazz in France was vigorous enough to support the first full-scale festival since the 1930s, held in Nice. During March, French musicians like Django Reinhardt, Stéphane Grappelli, and Claude Luter played alongside African Americans like Louis Armstrong and Coleman Hawkins.

As a result of such activity during the late 1940s, black American jazz musicians began returning to France, either on individual tours or for festivals. Some of those who came to Paris as visitors would decide they liked the city and end up staying, thus renewing the community of black jazz artists. The saxophone player Don Redman led the first African American orchestra to play in Paris after the war, stopping there at the end of 1946 as part of a European tour organized by the Hot Club of France. One of the band's most illustrious members was the tenor saxophonist Don Byas, an outstanding young New York reedman who would end up staying in Paris permanently. Louis Armstrong came to Paris to play a concert in March 1948, after his appearance at the Nice festival, and large crowds at the city's Gare du Nord greeted the postwar return of Duke Ellington that July.

Two events in particular symbolized the renewal of black jazz in Paris after World War II. The first was the February 1948 concert in the city by that enfant terrible of bebop, the trumpeter Dizzy Gillespie. During the war, jazz musicians in America had started experimenting with new forms, rebelling against the traditions of swing and big band music to create complex, abstract new harmonies and rhythms. In part a reaction against the increased commercialism of big band jazz, bebop was also an extremely urban (and urbane) phenomenon. Centered in Manhattan, both at Minton's Playhouse in Harlem and in the vibrant network of jazz clubs along Fifty-second Street downtown, bebop was far removed from the black South. New York produced many talented young performers, but none enjoyed greater acclaim than Gillespie and the saxophonist Charlie Parker. Gillespie's 1948 tour of Europe, which had been cut off from the evolution of this new style by the war, was therefore an event of the first magnitude in jazz history. Parisians had first heard bebop right after the war, and whereas the young existentialists delighted in the new cool sound, many fans of New Orleans–style jazz reacted with horror. In 1947, the Hot Club of France formally and bitterly split over the issue, with Charles Delaunay leading the reformers while Hugues Panassié upheld the standard of traditional jazz.

Gillespie's 1948 concert was the first important live performance of bebop in France, and it came as a revelation to many. Appearing on February 20 in the capital's venerable Pleyel theater, the king of bebop performed before an appreciative audience with an orchestra of sixteen other musicians. In a review published the next day, Boris Vian described the concert in triumphant terms.

Dizzy Gillespie and his orchestra played last night at the Pleyel before a packed crowd, in an extraordinary atmosphere of enthusiasm and excitement. . . . In an indescribable ambiance, Gillespie attacked his first piece, and it immediately became apparent that while most of his listeners, essentially composed of young people already used to this style so different from traditional jazz, reacted perfectly, a fraction of the same audience were completely disoriented by the rhythm section, so far removed from that of classical jazz orchestras, and only recovered their equanimity listening to the slow pieces.

A huge success therefore for Dizzy. . . . We should also note Gillespie's remarkable utilization of African and Cuban rhythms, performed in extraordinary fashion by his bongo drummer, Pozo y Gonzalés.

With Dizzy Gillespie, be-bop, latest stage of jazz music, has conquered Paris.

Kenny Clarke, Dizzy Gillespie's drummer on the tour and a leading expatriate jazz musician during the 1950s, later noted of that concert, "It was fantastic! It was an overwhelming success. They had never heard that kind of music before in Europe. They were just stunned, they could not believe it. When they heard that kind of music they just went crazy." In short order, bebop became *the* music of Saint-Germain-des-Prés. Whereas the lively rhythms of the swing era had suited interwar gaiety, the postwar existentialists found in the cool abstractions of bebop a perfect accompaniment to their own pensive mood.

The other key event that brought black jazz back to the French capital in the 1940s was the International Paris Jazz Festival, May 8 to 15, 1949. Paris had never before played host to a world-class gathering of jazz musicians, and the 1949 festival became a landmark in the city's postwar cultural life. Charles Delaunay organized the event, traveling to New York early in the year to sign up musicians. As the two leading stars of the festival, he chose Sidney Bechet and Charlie Parker, a diplomatic nod to both traditional jazz and bebop. In addition, America was well represented by musicians like Hot Lips Page, Bill Coleman, Tadd Dameron, Don Byas, Kenny Clarke, and (for the first time in Europe) Miles Davis, while French musicians included Jack Dieval, Hubert Fol, Claude Luter, and Pierre Braslavsky. Jazz artists from five other European nations also took part, making the festival the largest jazz event Parisians had ever seen. The concerts and impromptu jam sessions attracted large and enthusiastic crowds, and in spite of some tensions between partisans of the two schools of music the festival was a great success. More than a week's affair, the festival gave a shot in the arm to Parisian jazz in general.

Gillespie's 1948 tour and the 1949 jazz festival helped renew Parisian jazz in two different ways. Not only did these events give the city's people firsthand experience with the music, especially bebop, that black artists were playing in the United States, but it also reintroduced African American jazz musicians to the opportunities offered by the French capital. By 1949, a small group of black jazz artists had settled back into Paris, including Arthur Briggs, Rex Stewart, Honey Johnson, Big Boy Goudie, and most important Don Byas and Bill Coleman. After the jazz festival, more would decide to stay, most notably Sidney Bechet and Kenny Clarke.

Sidney Bechet was no stranger to the French capital, having originally traveled there with Josephine Baker and the Revue Nègre back in 1925. Bechet had immediately taken to Paris and settled into the jazz life of 1920s Montmartre, but his notorious gun battle with Mike McKendrick caused his deportation from France in 1929. After a brief sojourn in Berlin and an even shorter return visit to Paris in 1931, Bechet had gone back to the United States in the early 1930s, where for the rest of the decade he worked with various jazz orchestras, including Noble Sissle's big band. The jazz revival of the early 1940s found Sidney Bechet well placed and well known as a premier exponent of the traditional music from his native city, New Orleans. Based in New York during the war years, he performed widely around the country as the leader of various jazz ensembles, and in the late 1940s played for a while at Jimmy Ryan's club on Fifty-second Street. By the end of the decade, he had made numerous popular recordings, including a multivolume anthology of his music on RCA records, and was generally recognized as one of the jazz world's best soprano saxophonists.

When Charles Delaunay recruited him to come to Paris, therefore, Sidney Bechet was already an established performer at the center of the jazz world, New York. His trip to the 1949 festival was his first return to the French capital since 1931 when he had been one of many Montmartre performers. Now he came back as an international star. Parisian jazz fans were well acquainted with Bechet's music, and he clearly enjoyed the energetic welcome they gave him. In fact, Sidney Bechet was so popular that local music stores reported record sales of soprano saxophones while he was in town. Thrilled by his reception, Bechet returned home to New York and Jimmy Ryan's. However, he kept in touch with Delaunay, exploring ways of returning to Paris for longer. Delaunay both warmly encouraged him to return and made the necessary arrangements, so that at the end of September the jazz master boarded the *Ile de France* and crossed the Atlantic once again, arriving in the French capital on October 1, 1949. Bechet was so committed to staying in France this time that he even had his Cadillac shipped overseas.

Upon arrival in Paris, Sidney Bechet was greeted by a party in his honor at a jazz club on the Champs-Elysées, and then began performing nightly at the Edouard VII theater. While in Paris, he began a collaboration that would last for the rest of his life with the young French clarinet player and bandleader Claude Luter. Luter, winner of *Le Jazz Hot*'s annual best-musician poll in 1948, had a big following among the jazz aficionados of Saint-Germain-des-Prés, where he performed at the Vieux Colombier. In October, he and Bechet recorded an album that would become a classic of French jazz, *Les Oignons*. After touring through France and Switzerland, Sidney Bechet returned to the United States in November, but as he commented in his autobiography, *Treat It Gentle*, this visit marked the real beginning of his life in postwar France:

> I felt when I settled in France that it was nearer to Africa, and I suppose too that being there is nearer to all my family and brings back something that I remember of Omar [Bechet's grandfather] and my father too. So I started to record some lovely Creole tunes that I remembered from when I was young and some I made myself out of the same remembering. And the same month — I think it was October — there was a lot of American musicaners in Paris at that time and I got them together and we had ourselves a time recording a few numbers.

Before returning to America, Sidney Bechet made a short visit to London, where his numerous fans gave him a tremendous reception. These experiences in Britain and France made life in New York seem like a letdown; as one of his friends pointed out, "Even after his triumphs in Europe in 1949, back in the States he was just another jazzman scuffling." Bechet soon began making plans to cross the Atlantic again. The following June saw him in France once more, this time for good. Bechet moved back to the Vieux Colombier to play with Claude Luter, and until his death in 1959, he made the Left Bank jazz club his home base. He began his French exile by moving with Luter to the Vieux Colombier's summer retreat in the idyllic town of Juan-les-Pins. For the following three months, he got used to working with Luter and his band amid the glorious sun and seascapes of the French Riviera before returning to Paris (like millions of vacationing French men and women) at the start of September. Mistinguett, the great music hall star and rival of Josephine Baker, heard him perform: "As I sat sipping my 'pastis,' an old Negro with stubby jewelled fingers put his saxophone to his lips and began to play. . . . It was a sad tune and everyone was looking at me. Then before I knew it my eyes filled with tears. The Negro was called Sidney Bechet. He was playing *Mon Homme*. I put on my dark glasses. Others were crying too, pretty girls, who leaned their faces on their hands as they sat listening."

During the 1950s, Sidney Bechet reigned as Paris's unofficial king of jazz.

While his musical style had evolved over the years and remained in many ways unique, it continued to draw its essential strength from the traditions of New Orleans jazz, full of lively rhythms and catchy tunes. He was acclaimed by both critics and ordinary jazz fans who knew his records, and his presence in Paris after 1950 increased his popularity until it took on cult dimensions. On returning that fall, Bechet gave a series of concerts in Paris which invariably attracted overflow audiences. The demand was so great that in one instance fans stormed a theater box office, lifted it up, and carried it down the street, in spite of protests by the terrified ticket seller inside. By 1953, Bechet's reputation led French merchants to seek his endorsement for their products. A 1955 free concert at the Olympia theater in Bechet's honor produced a riot in the streets, requiring numerous police reinforcements, as fifteen thousand fans struggled to gain admittance to a space that held only three thousand. By the following year, Sidney Bechet had sold well over one million records in France, and Parisian admirers organized a Bechet fan club that October. As one American noted while visiting the French capital, "Sidney could have become mayor of Paris if he wanted to. Crowds of people followed him through the streets. I was never so surprised in my whole life as when I discovered that a compatriot, whom I had barely heard of, had become the darling of the French."

Sidney Bechet owed his Parisian celebrity to hard work, an expansive personality, and the great esteem his particular brand of jazz received in France. He settled in Paris at the zenith of his career, and in some respects his years there were the most productive of his life. The Vieux Colombier remained his home base, and Parisian jazz fans grew accustomed to his performances with Claude Luter as one of the staples of the city's music life. He would also take up regular summer residence at Juan-les-Pins. Bechet toured widely throughout France and Europe during his years in Paris. In 1952, for example, Bechet traveled with Luter's orchestra to Belgium and Switzerland, toured North Africa, and played a concert aboard the USS *Coral Sea* in the Mediterranean. In addition to his frenetic performance schedule, the veteran jazzman made numerous recordings during his Paris years, and briefly ran his own jazz club, Chez Sidney Bechet, just off the Champs-Elysées. Thanks to this ceaseless activity, Bechet carved out a place for himself in the French capital equaled by no other African American since Josephine Baker.

Sidney Bechet was not always the easiest man to work with, and had a notoriously fiery temper. Yet he liked to be with people, have a good time, and share his musical talent with those who appreciated it and him. He was very friendly and solicitous toward the younger French musicians who came to hear him perform or, if lucky, sat in with the master. Bechet also went out of his way to welcome American musicians visiting the city, although he jealously guarded his own turf, once threatening an American who dared to play the soprano sax at the Vieux Colombier by ostentatiously polishing his revolver. Above all, he treated his fans well, becoming for many Parisians the very symbol of the black jazz musician. As Charles Delaunay once observed, "Sidney never became big-headed with the people. He liked to be recognized by them as he walked down the street, and when anyone shouted greetings to him he always shouted a friendly message back. People loved to hear him talk in French, even though it was always Creole. . . . If he was in a bar he'd start up a conversation with anyone. Oh yes, he had great appeal for the general public."

Like other talented African Americans before him, Sidney Bechet found life in Paris very agreeable indeed. His income from performances and record sales enabled him to live very comfortably, even lavishly. Shortly after his arrival in France he bought a pleasant house at Grigny, in the countryside near Paris, where he could go fishing and keep his large dog, Yank. Although removed from the center of American jazz, Bechet had good friends, numerous colleagues, and thousands of enthusiastic fans. A rolling stone for much of his life who never lacked for female companionship, in France Sidney Bechet finally settled down and got married. He had met Elisabeth Ziegler in Frankfurt in 1928, lost touch for over twenty years, then fortuitously met her during a 1951 tour in Algiers. They were married that August in Cannes before four hundred guests in a spectacular wedding ceremony. The newlyweds paraded through the streets in an open carriage, heralded by the release of scores of doves. They were accompanied by jazz bands and several floats, including a twelve-foot model of a soprano saxophone. The two remained married for the rest of Bechet's life, but like many Frenchmen Bechet soon took a mistress, a Frenchwoman named Jacqueline Pekaldi, who in 1954 gave birth to his son, Daniel. Bechet in effect maintained two different families, Elisabeth at the Grigny house and Jacqueline and Daniel in a house north of Paris, and spent time with both. He even composed pieces named after both women. Far from being a slave to his work, Sidney Bechet established a personal life in exile that was complex but ultimately rich and satisfying.

At the heart of Bechet's popularity in France, however, lay his music itself. By the 1950s, Sidney Bechet was one of the grand old men of jazz. Not all Paris jazz fans saw themselves as existentialist *rats de cave*, and many treasured the kind of swinging sound that Bechet had helped make popular. Yet although primarily a traditionalist, Bechet did not condemn the new avant-garde styles of jazz out of hand. Not overly fond of Dizzy Gillespie, he did note that bebop was valuable in bringing a whole new audience to jazz. This ability to embrace different styles was crucial in France, where the split between traditional jazz and bebop had widened into a chasm. By the 1950s, Hugues Panassié and Charles Delaunay were no longer speaking to each other, and would remain antagonists for the rest of their lives. However, since Delaunay, the chief advocate of bebop in France, also managed Bechet, the veteran jazzman was able to remain in touch with a younger audience as well as retaining the loyalty of those who regarded him as a symbol of the golden age of jazz. Many of the young existentialists who cheered the bebop revolution were also quite happy to listen and dance to Bechet's mellow melodies in the *caves* of Saint-Germain-des-Prés.

The French loved Sidney Bechet because to a certain extent he became one of them. His French last name and Creole heritage helped, of course, but more important was the fact that he played with French musicians and contributed to the development of jazz as an art form in France. Bechet genuinely liked the French and believed in French jazz. At one point he described the history of jazz by saying, "The rhythm came from Africa, but the music, the foundation, came from right here in France." His long collaboration with Claude Luter reached beyond the Vieux Colombier to produce an important body of recordings that have remained keystones of jazz in France, and his willingness to work with young French musicians helped shape the generation to come. Sidney Bechet also learned from the French, and his years there gave his music a different quality from that played in the United States. Like Josephine Baker before him, Sidney Bechet did not live in isolation in Paris, but instead worked to unite the best that French and African American culture had to offer.

More so than Baker, however, Sidney Bechet remained very much the black American to the end of his days. At times he seemed ambivalent about life in France, once declaring that he lived there only because he couldn't earn a decent living back in New York. Given the difficulties experienced by many jazz musicians in the United States, even the very best, during the 1950s, there may have been some truth to these words. In any case, Bechet never showed any signs of returning home after 1950, and after his 1951 tour of the United States, a friend wrote, "Sidney's return to his native land has been anything but pleasant for him. After the calm and comparative quiet of Europe, Sidney says he finds the restaurants too brightly lit, and the streets too crowded and noisy, and although he always gets homesick, when the cards are on the table it is still France he prefers." Life in Paris had its charms, enough

Top: African American soldiers attacking German lines with hand grenades, France, World War I

Bottom: Officers of the 367th Infantry Regiment with a French friend

This page: Two cartoons from the *Chicago Defender* contrasting American bigotry with French lack of prejudice.

Opposite, top: A black infantry band returning from service in France

Opposite, bottom: Harlem's "Hell Fighters" parade up Fifth Avenue upon their return to New York.

Above: A group of African American performers arriving at a Paris railway station, circa 1925

Left: Two African American musicians, Turner Layton and Tandy Johnstone, strolling down the Champs-Elysées, 1929

Right: Bricktop on a street in Montmartre, 1924. She signed the photograph for her friend Langston Hughes, "Bless you, Brick."

Below: "A Christmas bash — every year I invited all the Negro musicians in Paris to a big party at Bricktop's."

Left: Josephine Baker performing in the show *Folie du Jour* at the Folies-Bergère, Paris, 1926 to 1927

Opposite: Two cartoons relating the exploits of "Bungleton Green," an African American in Paris

Below: Arthur Briggs (third from the left) with his band in Paris, 1935

BUNGLETON GREEN :-: :-: :-: :-: :-: :-: :-: By L. Rogers

AT LAST I HAVE FOUND MY JACQUELIN, AND THIS IS THE DAY I AM TO MEET HER AT THE CAFÉ DE LIBERTE!—

FRANCE AND LIBERTY!!

I CAN'T IMAGINE ANYONE HAVING THE NERVE TO CRITICIZE THIS COUNTRY!!!—

VIVE LA FRANCE!

A-AHH-H HERE SHE IS.

DARLING, I HAVE CROSSED THE OCEAN AGAIN TO SEE YOU, AND—

OUI?

SAY, I'M FROM THE SOUTH IN THE U.S.A., AND I'M NOT ACCUSTOMED TO THIS!!!

LISTEN, BUZZARD, THIS IS FRANCE NOT AMERICA.

YOU—KK?£—

BUNGLETON GREEN :-: :-: :-: :-: :-: :-: :-: By L. Rogers

WELL, SINCE I'VE BEEN HERE IN FRANCE I'VE MET MY OLD "SWEETIE," JACQUELIN, AND I'M LIVING GREAT—

FRANCE IS THE NEAREST PLACE TO HEAVEN OF WHICH I KNOW—

I'VE GOTTA MEET MY OLD FRIEND, PIERRE.— HE AND I WERE BUDDIES DURING THE WAR—

AND HE PROMISED TO BREAK ME INTO PARIS SOCIETY— HERE HE COMES NOW!

HOPE I AM NOT LATE MEESTER GREEN—

AHH-H, BY ZE WAY MEESTER GREEN, I HAVE JUST MET A GENTLEMAN FROM AMERICA.— MAYBE YOU LIKE TO MEET HEEM.

COME MEESTER GREEN, AND I NTRODUCE YOU TO DEES AMERICAN GENTLEMAN

SURE!

MEESTER GREEN, MEET MEESTER REDNECK FROM AMERICA.

SO YOU'RE FROM THE STATES— GLAD TO MEET YOU—

I DON'T THINK MUCH OF THIS "FROG" FOR INTRODUCING ME TO YOU,— I'M FROM MISSISSIPPI, AND—

HUMPH-H— IN AMERICA WE IGNORE YOUR FOLKS—

YOU— *@#!m!* ☆☆

Loïs Mailou Jones's studio in Montparnasse, 1937

INVADERS ON A FRENCH BEACHHEAD

A group of Negro soldiers resting on a beach in France during recent invasion. They were among the first to land and are now busy getting supplies to the American and British soldiers.—Acme photo by Bert Brandt.

African American soldiers on the beach in Normandy during World War II

Above: Loïs Mailou Jones painting Notre-Dame, 1947
Opposite, top: African American tourists at the Luxembourg Gardens.
Opposite, bottom: A group of black Americans in a Parisian café. The woman on the far left is Inez Cavanaugh.

Richard
Wright at a
Paris café

Below:
Dancing at
Bricktop's,
1950

James Baldwin in
Saint-Germain-
des-Prés

Below:
Sidney Bechet
at the Vieux
Colombier,
Paris, 1955

Left: Poster for Josephine Baker in *Paris Mes Amours* at the Olympia Theater, Paris, 1959

Opposite: Beauford Delaney in his Paris studio, 1961

Below: Duke Ellington and Beauford Delaney in the Café Tournon

Above: The Golden Gate Quartet on
the banks of the Seine, 1960

Right: Advertisement
for the Rib Joint,
Paris, 1994

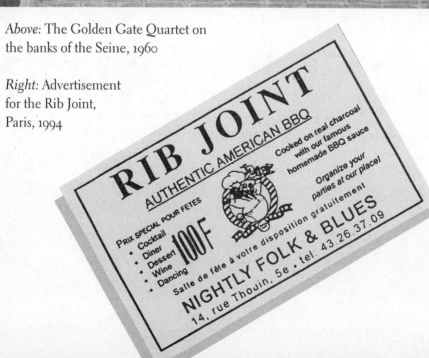

to outweigh longings for one's native soil. The French treated Bechet well and enabled him to live in comfort doing what he liked best. They rendered to him the homage he felt he had earned after a lifetime in jazz. As Sidney Bechet noted in his autobiography, this respect for his life's work and life's blood counted for more than anything else.

> So I played at the Olympia, where I'd played a lot before and since — and I don't know whether I'm glad or sorry that there were terrible scenes outside. The people there were so anxious to get in that the police had to be called and there were scuffles and arrests and everything. I'm sorry that these people who love the music should have got into trouble, but . . . hell, I'll play for them whenever they want me. I'm getting on now, but, like I've said I've lived for the music; I won't play when it's wrong, but I'll play any place, anywhere, when it's right. It's the music and it's the people that's made what I've got to say in this world worth while. And as long as I'm around and as long as I can get that instrument up to my mouth that's what I want to do.

Like Bechet, Bill Coleman had first seen Paris before the war, and had long considered returning before Charles Delaunay brought him back at the end of 1948. During 1949, Coleman toured France and Germany, playing in a jazz band that included Don Byas, and took part in the Paris Jazz Festival in May. After the festival, Coleman went back to performing in various clubs and theaters throughout the city. With Delaunay to arrange bookings for him, Bill Coleman settled easily into the Paris music scene and kept very busy playing one gig after another. In 1950, for example, he not only played several concerts in the French capital, but also toured extensively in Switzerland and Italy. The following summer, Coleman replaced Sidney Bechet at the Vieux Colombier in Paris while Bechet worked in Juan-les-Pins, and that fall began a stint at the rival Club Saint-Germain-des-Prés. While he never achieved the fame of Bechet, by the beginning of the 1950s Bill Coleman had become a valued member of the jazz community in Paris. He had liked the city when he first saw it during the 1930s, and now he had returned for good; as he noted in his autobiography, "I was so happy about being in France that I celebrated every day with a fresh bottle of cognac which I kept in my room, and I was drinking 15 to 20 cognacs in bars."

Paris became Coleman's permanent home, and life there gradually transformed him from a rootless vagabond into a settled, stable family man. Like many musicians, when he first came to Paris Coleman led a very transient existence, moving from one anonymous hotel to another and enjoying a social life centered around the clubs where he and his friends performed — a life that led at times to alcohol abuse, an all-too-frequent problem for many jazz artists. It did not take Bill Coleman long, however, to develop more permanent attachments. While performing in Bern, Switzerland, at the end of 1949, Coleman met a young Swiss woman named Lily. Communication was difficult because neither spoke the other's language, but a common love for jazz seems to have made that irrelevant. Lily later joined Bill Coleman during his engagement in Rome, and they began a relationship that would last for the rest of his life. The two returned to Paris where they took up housekeeping together. In October 1953, they were married at the American Church in Paris, proceeding after the ceremony to a reception at Leroy Haynes's restaurant and then to a party at the Ringside jazz club, where Lionel Hampton and other guests played for hours.

Bill Coleman's work life also became more stable by the mid-1950s. Since his move to Paris, he had never lacked for jobs, but unlike Sidney Bechet had had no long-term engagement. In 1954, however, he began playing at a new club in the Latin Quarter, the Trois Mailletz. Although the golden age of Saint-Germain-des-Prés had long since passed, the idea of the basement jazz club had remained popular, and places like the Trois Mailletz represented the plush, updated version of the old *cave*. As Coleman described it, "It was a beautiful cellar, very well preserved, from the twelfth century. The famous French poet François Villon had been imprisoned there. One floor below was another cellar that had been a torture chamber and was now a museum. When a prisoner had died after being tortured, the body was thrown into the well and came out into the Seine river." After touring in Europe during the early months of 1955, Coleman returned to the Trois Mailletz in August, becoming a regular performer there for the rest of the decade. Thus both he and Sidney Bechet now had their "own" Left Bank jazz clubs. In 1956, Bill and Lily Coleman rented their first Paris apartment, located on the rue de Condé in the heart of the Latin Quarter. Three years later, the couple bought a two-room residence in what had become the center of African American life in Paris, the rue Monsieur-le-Prince, just down the street from the home of Richard Wright. A property owner for the first time in his life, Bill Coleman had come to France to stay.

If Sidney Bechet represented the glories of traditional jazz in postwar Paris, Kenny Clarke symbolized the genius of avant-garde styles. The great drummer was born in Pittsburgh in 1914 and grew up searching for broader horizons than those offered by his working-class community. Like Gene Bullard, Clarke became interested in life overseas at a very early age; as he later noted in an interview, "I wanted to go to France. I had read about it. I kept thinking

about it: France, Paris, must be nice. I was twelve." At the same time he began
to play the drums, starting his career as a professional musician by the time he
turned eighteen. Kenny Clarke soon became a fixture on the Pittsburgh jazz
scene, and in 1936 moved to New York, recording his first record album the
following year. Clarke's new, rapid-fire style of drumming soon attracted admirers, most notably Dizzy Gillespie, whom he met when they played together at Harlem's Savoy Ballroom. By the early 1940s, Kenny Clarke was
jamming regularly with musicians like Gillespie, Thelonious Monk, Coleman Hawkins, and Lester Young as one of the pioneers of bebop.

After his army service in World War II, Clarke returned to New York and
joined Dizzy Gillespie's band, taking part in its triumphant 1948 tour of
Europe. By this point, Kenny Clarke had established an international reputation as one of the best drummers in jazz, with decades of experience and
numerous recordings under his belt. This renown only grew when in 1952
Clarke joined the pianist John Lewis, the bassist Percy Heath, and the vibes
player Milt Jackson to form the Modern Jazz Quartet. One of the most
successful (and certainly most durable) groups in jazz history, the Modern
Jazz Quartet specialized in tight ensemble playing, usually from printed sheet
music. A jazz equivalent of the string quartet, it represented a move away from
both improvisational bebop and traditional swing music, toward a more classical style. The quartet was a huge success, making Clarke one of the leading
jazzmen of his day.

Yet in 1954 Kenny Clarke quit the Modern Jazz Quartet and two years later
moved to Paris, where he would reside for the rest of his life. He left the
quartet in part because he disliked its increasing enamoredness with European forms of music, a trend noticeable in American jazz as a whole at the
time. To an important extent, however, this surprising and ironic decision
reflected a broader disenchantment with life in America. The jazz scene in
New York was rigidly run by an elite of primarily white music promoters, who
decided who would or would not play the city's leading clubs, and kept black
jazz performers firmly under their control. One such promoter allegedly
threatened to blacklist Kenny Clarke in New York after Clarke accused him of
stealing music from Dizzy Gillespie. At the same time, many musicians,
notably Charlie Parker, were succumbing to the burgeoning heroin trade.
The postwar explosion of illegal drugs confirmed the end of the Harlem
Renaissance, transforming the neighborhood into a crime-infested wasteland,
and hit the music community particularly hard. As far as Clarke was concerned, drugs merely represented another type of manipulation of his people.
For example, white club owners would pay musicians in drugs rather than

money. The problem ultimately was white control of black music, and by the 1950s exile from America seemed a way to escape this control. "The music has gotten into the wrong hands," wrote Clarke. "Musicians everywhere are sitting home by the telephone waiting for a white man to call them for a gig, and I don't see any future in that. I've been playing the drums for forty years, and the only future I see in our music is for black people to have their own thing going; otherwise it's no use."

Kenny Clarke left America at the height of his career as a self-conscious refugee from racism, disheartened and disgusted by the powerful white establishment's mistreatment of his music and his people. Yet this decision was not just a negative one, for Paris also beckoned. By the time he moved there permanently in 1956, Clarke had come to know the city well. He first visited on tour in 1937, immediately responding to Paris's beauty and the enthusiasm of its inhabitants for jazz. He returned in uniform during the war; unconsciously renewing the tradition of James Reese Europe and other black musicians who had introduced jazz to the French capital in World War I, he formed a band and played a concert in the city shortly after the liberation. But his performances during 1948 and 1949 in Paris are what left the strongest impression on Kenny Clarke. Thrilled by his adoring reception at the jazz festival, Clarke stayed on in Paris after it ended, playing with other musicians at various venues around town and giving drumming lessons to French musicians. As Dizzy Gillespie noted, "The French acted more wisely and they stole Kenny Clarke from me . . . I felt sure Kenny would do very well when we left for the States and he stayed behind." Clarke remained in Europe for nearly two years before returning to New York in May 1951.

Like Sidney Bechet and Bill Coleman, Kenny Clarke went to Paris as an invited guest. The composer Michel Legrand invited Clarke to join the big band led by Legrand's uncle, Jacques Helian, and sent him a first-class ticket aboard the *Liberty* to cross the Atlantic in style. Although that opportunity soon fell through, Clarke's fame and popularity in France were enough to ensure him as much work as he needed. He soon settled into the comfortable position of house bandleader at a Parisian jazz club, first the Club Saint-Germain-des-Prés, then the Blue Note, an important nightspot in the late 1950s. Clarke also performed at concerts and jazz festivals throughout Europe, recorded widely, and played music for television shows and films by directors like Roger Vadim and Marcel Carné. In 1958, he met Daisy Wallbach, a Dutch woman who would become his wife four years later. The couple bought a house in Paris and in 1964 had a son, Laurent. As far as Kenny Clarke was concerned, life was both easier and more profitable in France than America. "My income was much greater in Europe than in the U.S. Plus, in the U.S., they tell you when you have to work and how you have to work and whom you have to work with and all that."

In short, like the hero of the Joni Mitchell song, Kenny Clarke had become "a free man in Paris." Although he did not return to the United States until 1972, he remained in touch with friends and fellow musicians like Dizzy Gillespie when they came through France. Life in the French capital could present some drawbacks; in the 1960s, for example, French musicians began to demand restrictions on the number of foreigners allowed to play in France, limiting opportunities for African American jazz artists. But that lay in the future: during the 1950s, Kenny Clarke was able to enjoy a good living and, most of all, prestige and respect doing what he liked to do best. Freed from an oppressive jazz establishment in America, Clarke's life in Paris represented exile of the most productive and privileged sort. It gave him the ability to work and develop on his own terms, and jazz fans everywhere would benefit.

No survey of postwar jazz in Paris would be complete without considering the case of Miles Davis. Like Duke Ellington and Louis Armstrong, Davis traveled to the French capital several times during his long career, but never chose to settle there. As an artist who felt that life in Paris, however sweet, was not conducive to his art, Miles Davis therefore represents an important countertheme to the history of black expatriates in France. The embodiment of cool, Miles Davis is one of the great figures of American jazz, a talented trumpet player who came of age musically during the golden age of bebop and spearheaded the transition to jazz-rock fusion in the 1960s and 1970s. Davis was born in Alton, Illinois, in 1926 and grew up in East Saint Louis, a city whose black inhabitants still vividly remembered the race riots of a generation earlier. He grew up in an affluent home, one that encouraged his precocious interests in music. Miles Davis started taking music lessons at the age of nine, and playing the trumpet soon became the obsession it would remain for the rest of his life. He got his first job with a band at the age of seventeen, and a year later left East Saint Louis to study at New York's Juilliard School of music. His real education, however, took place at Minton's Playhouse in Harlem, where he got to know Milt Jackson, Dizzy Gillespie, and other great figures of the bebop revolution. There Davis began his long and fruitful association with Charlie Parker, one that would fundamentally reshape his own approach to music.

The great trumpeter was in his early twenties when he came to Paris to participate in the 1949 jazz festival, and immediately found the city to his taste. "I had never felt that way in my life. It was the freedom of being in

France and being treated like a human being, like someone important. Even the band and the music we played sounded better over there. Even the smells were different." Davis not only met Sartre and Picasso, but fell in love with Juliette Greco, a singer and symbol of the existentialist generation. In his autobiography, he describes the feeling of falling in love in a glamorous, foreign city, of long hours spent talking in cafés and jazz clubs, in a passage that fulfills all the romantic stereotypes of April in Paris. Moreover, in Paris the young musician learned that not all whites were the same, and that some were capable of treating blacks with humanity and respect. Yet in spite of such wonderful experiences Davis decided to go back home after a few months. Both Kenny Clarke and Jean-Paul Sartre urged him to stay, but in vain. Returning to the United States so depressed Miles Davis that he became addicted to heroin, spending the next four years in a self-destructive fog.

In 1956 and 1957, Davis went back to the French capital while playing concerts in Europe. There he renewed his friendships with Greco and Sartre, as well as expatriate musicians like Bud Powell and Don Byas. In 1957, he played at the Club Saint-Germain with Kenny Clarke and Pierre Michelot. He also met the filmmaker Louis Malle, who recruited him to write the musical score for his film *L'Ascenseur pour l'Echafaud* (which played to American audiences as *Frantic*). Yet, unlike his friend Kenny Clarke, Miles Davis ultimately decided that his future lay in the United States. As he commented in his autobiography,

> while I didn't love being in America all the time, I never thought about moving over to Paris. I really loved Paris, but I loved it to visit, because I didn't think the music could or would happen for me over there. Plus, the musicians who moved over there seemed to me to lose something, an energy, an edge, that living in the States gave them. I don't know, but I think it has something to do with being surrounded by a culture that you know, that you can feel, that you come out of. If I lived in Paris, I couldn't just go and hear some great blues, or people like Monk and Trane and Duke and Satchmo every night, like I could in New York. And although there were good, classically trained musicians in Paris, they still didn't hear the music like an American musician did. I couldn't live in Paris for all those reasons, and Juliette understood.

During the postwar era, African Americans in Paris became expatriates, a concept that took some getting used to. For most Americans, the term referred to those white writers who had settled in Paris during the 1920s, members of the nation's elite who had chosen to come home after sowing their wild oats in foreign fields. The prospect of America's despised and downtrodden opting to leave their native land angrily and permanently troubled many whites, as did their acceptance in the city that more than any other represented the height of sophistication and style. In an essay on Richard Wright, Oliver Harrington commented on the racial and political undertones of the term. "Wright pointed out that F. Scott Fitzgerald was an expatriate and Hemingway is an expatriate but they are white and a white writer has a right to be whatever he wants, expatriate or ex anything. But a Negro has to go to the good white folks and ask 'Please, Mister Boss-man, kin I please be an ex somethin', suh?'" At the same time, some black Americans in Paris considered the label expatriate inappropriate, arguing that because the United States had never really accepted them or been their home in any fundamental sense, they should not be considered exiles from it. As Beauford Delaney noted, "One must belong before one may then not belong. I belong here in Paris. I am able to realize myself here. I am no expatriate."

The desire to belong was crucial, for, far from rejecting America, many blacks in Paris felt it was America that had always rejected them. Paris, on the other hand, offered them at most success and acclaim, at least tolerance and the ability to seek their own paths in life unmolested. Moreover, the creation of a black community in exile enabled them to leave racism behind without also forsaking black culture. From Leroy Haynes's restaurant to the cafés of the Latin Quarter and the jazz clubs of Saint-Germain-des-Prés, this culture flourished in the late 1940s and 1950s, producing a rich creative interchange between French and African American intellectuals and artists. Finally, by the 1950s the French capital could claim a tradition of welcoming black Americans which stretched back over several decades. Those who came after World War II continued and built upon the legacy of those who had come after World War I. The result was to create a space in Paris where one could be black and free at the same time, a powerful and alluring vision that would continue to beckon African Americans dissatisfied with the restrictions imposed upon them by their native land.

5

THE GOLDEN AGE OF
AFRICAN AMERICAN
LITERATURE IN
PARIS

THE POLITICS OF EXILE

IN THE TEN YEARS after the liberation, a number of leading black American writers left the U.S. to live in Paris, creating an outstanding African American literary community there. This exodus marked the advent of one of the most exciting and productive periods in the history of American blacks in the French capital. Just as Josephine Baker and other entertainers symbolized the African American presence in Paris during the 1920s, so equally did Richard Wright and his fellow writers represent to both contemporaries and historians black American life there during the 1950s. With the possible exception of New York, no city in America could rival the collection of black literary talent along the banks of the Seine during these years. Moreover, these black writers constituted the most important American literary group of any color in the French capital after the war. If the 1920s were the era of Fitzgerald, Hemingway, and Stein, then the 1950s belonged to Wright, Baldwin, and Himes.

Richard Wright, whose novel *Native Son* (1940) had made him one of the most important and influential black writers in the United States, crossed the Atlantic in 1946. In part following Richard Wright's lead, James Baldwin also made the one-way flight from New York to Paris at the end of 1948. Wright's expatriate existence in the French capital prompted at least two other important black writers to move there: the young writer William Gardner Smith in 1951, and Chester Himes, a well-established writer of detective fiction, in 1953. Their reasons for leaving the United States to take up residence in a foreign city were as varied as they were themselves. The physical beauty and intellectual excitement of the French capital constituted a powerful lure, much as they had for creative spirits throughout the world for decades. In his unpublished essay "I Choose Exile," Richard Wright rhapsodically declared, "To live in Paris is to allow one's sensibilities to be nourished by physical beauty . . . I love my adopted city. Its sunsets, its teeming boulevards, its slow and humane tempo of life have entered deeply into my heart." William Gardner Smith decided to opt for Parisian exile out of a love for French literature, especially that of Balzac and Zola, as well as a fascination with the experiences of Ernest Hemingway. Even the poverty of postwar Paris was attractive because it meant that Americans could live there very cheaply.

More important, however, and more unique, was the sheer desire to escape the United States. By the late 1940s, James Baldwin, trapped between the white and black worlds of New York and not fully at ease in either, was looking for a way out. The suicide of his friend Eugene Worth, later fictionalized in the novel *Another Country*, crystallized his feelings of desperation. Paris appealed because it was inexpensive and he knew some American writers there, but as Baldwin noted, "I wasn't really choosing France, I was getting out of America. I had no idea what might happen to me in France, but I was very clear as to what would happen if I remained in New York. I would go under like Eugene."

Chester Himes expressed the reasons for his move to France in similar terms:

> I received a deluge of letters from Dick [Wright] . . . First he wrote of how pleasant and stimulating life was in Paris; then of how cheaply one could live. That was my first experience with black expatriates who have become self-appointed civic boosters for their favorite European capital. All this I took with a grain of salt; I didn't expect any utopia and I had always found white people much the same wherever I had been in the United States. I didn't expect the Europeans to be greatly different. After all, Americans were their descendents. I just wanted out from the United States, that was all. I had had it.

In the context of the times, the phenomenon of a number of black American writers rushing to leave their native land must have seemed peculiar to many. An island of prosperity in a world struggling to recover from the most destructive war in human history, the United States stood at the zenith of its power and influence in the late 1940s. The *Time* magazine publisher Henry Luce had proclaimed the dawning of the American century, and refugees from Europe and Asia pleaded for admission to the New World. But for

Richard Wright and others, America's stubborn refusal to treat its black citizens with dignity and respect overshadowed all else. Wright framed the issue clearly at the outset of "I Choose Exile," saying, "I live in voluntary exile in France and I like it. There is nothing in the life of America that I miss or yearn for. . . . There is in the entire United States of America!"

These were strong words to address to Americans at the beginning of the self-satisfied 1950s, and in fact Wright's essay was never published in the United States. Yet they expressed a point of view widely shared among the African Americans who called Paris home in the fifteen years after the end of the war. One who stated this perspective most forcefully was Ollie Harrington, a writer and cartoonist who became one of the central figures among black expatriates in Paris during the 1950s. As a war correspondent for the *Pittsburgh Courier*, Harrington first went to Europe in 1944, reporting on the exploits and experiences of black soldiers in the war, and noting how the experience of combat tended to bring GIs together across the color line in spite of prejudiced attitudes. However, Harrington's hopes that this spirit of racial tolerance would continue into peacetime were soon dashed upon his return. Traveling through the South shortly after the end of the war, he came up against the same kind of virulent determination to maintain the racial status quo that had produced so much hatred and violence in 1919. In a speech, "Where Is the Justice?" given at an October 1946 forum in New York on "The Struggle for Justice as a World Force," Harrington assailed the treatment of returning black veterans. He graphically outlined horrible instances of discrimination, such as the army office in Birmingham, Alabama, which offered to hire a veteran with a master's degree as a janitor; the refusal of many veterans' hospitals to accept black patients; or the more than nine lynchings of black veterans, all unpunished, in the year since V-J Day. Harrington's work with the NAACP publicizing lynchings after the war earned him a reputation as a political radical, possibly a Communist. In 1951, after being warned by a friend of an impending investigation by army intelligence, Ollie Harrington left the United States for Paris and permanent exile.

The failure of the United States to address the problem of racial discrimination in the years after World War II had thus alienated a small but prestigious and influential group of African American intellectuals. Members of this group were convinced that even after the world victory over fascism, America's determination to deny its black citizens equal rights remained unshaken. Blacks had experienced a similar bitter disenchantment after the First World War, but that did not produce a comparable literary expatriate phenomenon. Although most leading black writers of the 1920s traveled to Paris and spent some time there, none (with the significant exception of Claude McKay) took up permanent residence, or described themselves as self-conscious refugees from American racism, even though the racist backlash of 1919 was much bloodier. Although the individual personalities and circumstances of men like Wright, Harrington, and Baldwin explain part of this sharper rejection of American racism after 1945, there were also broader differences between the two postwar eras. The simple fact that the late 1940s constituted the *second* time in a quarter century that blacks had returned from fighting for freedom for white Europeans overseas to renewed discrimination at home made the experience even less tolerable, convincing some of the hopelessness of any realistic prospects for racial equality in the United States.

In addition, the mounting cold war of this period led many white Americans to consider protests against racism as somehow linked to Communism, partly because both represented vague threats to the status quo, partly because Communists abroad delighted in fiercely attacking America's racial injustices. Of the major exiled writers, only Richard Wright had any formal ties (long since renounced) to the Communist party, yet their forthright antiracist declarations and activities, combined with their involvement in progressive (and interracial) milieus in places like Greenwich Village, easily fostered suspicions of anti-Americanism. In contrast, Paris beckoned with a vibrant intellectual community sharply critical of American racism and the American perspective on the cold war in general. Given a world that demanded such starkly opposed choices, the decision for exile, while certainly not easy, had a forceful and undeniable logic.

THE ROMANCE OF CAFÉS AND CHEAP HOTELS

By the time Chester Himes arrived in Paris in 1953, he was able to fit into a flourishing black literary colony in the heart of the Left Bank. His choice of the areas around the Latin Quarter and Saint-Germain-des-Prés was not deliberate, but made sense. Richard Wright moved there in order to be close to friends. He met both Gertrude Stein and Sylvia Beach during his first visit to Paris in 1946, and the two famous expatriates impressed upon him the numerous attractions of the Left Bank. The postwar vogue of existentialism also attracted Wright, and while not necessarily comfortable with its tenets he had met and admired Jean-Paul Sartre in New York, and would become a good friend of Simone de Beauvoir. After living in Left Bank hotels for two years, Wright moved with his wife, Ellen, and his daughter, Julia, into a comfortable apartment in the rue Monsieur-le-Prince in May 1948.

Richard Wright and his family were somewhat unusual among black Amer-

ican expatriates in having their own apartment. Most members of the community made do with rooms in hotels of varying quality scattered throughout the
Latin Quarter and Saint-Germain-des-Prés. Decent housing in the French
capital has always been scarce, and many expatriates were simply finding the
best lodgings they could in such establishments. Hotel rooms were cheap,
often costing only a few American dollars per night, so that even those without
much money could prolong their stays on the Left Bank. Some carried this
asceticism to extremes: long after Chester Himes had achieved an impressive
level of professional renown and material comfort, he continued to move
from one hotel to another while he was in Paris, never setting down permanent roots. Yet life in hotels also represented a kind of vagabond freedom that,
in contrast to the increasingly suburban stolidity of American society, had a
certain appeal, and black Americans had picked up this symbol directly from
the intellectuals of Sartre's circle, who made a practice of this lifestyle. A few
in particular became favorites of the African American community, often
ones that had been colonized earlier by the existentialists. The more upscale
Hôtel Louisiane in the rue de Seine was a prime example, a place where
Jean-Paul Sartre and Juliette Greco were followed by several black American
jazz musicians, including Lester Young and Bud Powell in the 1950s. The
Hôtel Pont Royal in the rue Montalembert, a refuge for Sartre and de Beauvoir from the tourists of Saint-Germain-des-Prés, became James Baldwin's
favorite residence in Paris after 1968. Other addresses of note included the
Hôtel Tournon in the street of the same name, the Hôtel Crystal in the rue
Saint-Benoît, and the Hôtel California in the rue des Ecoles.

Life in such hotel rooms was spartan, to say the least. The furniture often
consisted of little more than a bed and a chair, perhaps a sink with (usually
cold) running water. Plumbing, the eternal despair of Americans in France,
was typically ancient, with a bathroom equipped with a "Turkish toilet" located in the hallway. In short, such hotel rooms constituted a roof over one's
head but little more. As James Baldwin once noted in an essay on student life
in Paris, "The sordid French hotel room, so admirably detailed by the camera,
speaking, in its quaintness, and distance, so beautifully of romance, under-
goes a sea-change, becomes a room positively hostile to romance, once it is
oneself, and not Jean Gabin, who lives there."

Like their Parisian hosts, African American expatriates reacted to such
conditions by seeking out the comforts and comradeship of the city's cafés,
where they could settle down at a small table in the corner and work for hours,
or meet their friends and associates to discuss matters both weighty and ar-
cane. If all else failed, they could find endless entertainment by observing the

constant crowds passing in the street. A place at a Parisian café was like a box seat at the theater, only much less expensive. In contrast to the increasing privatization of American society, these cafés gave black expatriates both a warm center for community life and a window on the wider world. In his 1955 essay, "Equal in Paris," James Baldwin succinctly characterized the role of the café in Parisian intellectual life: "The moment I began living in French hotels I understood the necessity of French cafés. This made it rather difficult to look me up, for as soon as I was out of bed I hopefully took notebook and fountain pen off to the upstairs room of the Flore, where I consumed rather a lot of coffee and, as evening approached, rather a lot of alcohol, but did not get much writing done."

It has long been customary for Parisians to choose "their" cafés, always going to the same place for a drink or meals, and the black Americans who lived on the Left Bank after 1945 soon adopted this local custom. One gradually got to know the proprietor and staff, who would always be ready with a customer's favorite beverage and even perform small services like receiving mail. Many patrons would not only frequent the same café, but always at the same time and at the same table, thus endowing a public spot with the familiarity of one's living room. African Americans sampled Parisian café life widely in this period, but the two undisputed favorite locales of the black community were the Tournon, downstairs from the hotel, and the Monaco, in the rue Monsieur-le-Prince, near its intersection with the main street of the Left Bank, the boulevard Saint-Germain. The Monaco was the first to become popular, thanks to the influence of Richard Wright. After moving into his apartment in 1948, Wright began looking for a nearby café suitable for working and meeting friends, following the French tradition that reserves the home for family life. As Wright later observed, "At the outset of his sojourn in Paris a foreigner does not at once select his favorite café. The determination of a café in which to spend one's hours of relaxation is a delicate problem, a matter of trial and error, tasting, testing the nature and quality of the café's atmosphere." Not satisfied by many of the well-known establishments like the Flore and the Deux Magots, which were too noisy and full of tourists, Wright soon began frequenting the Monaco, which offered both anonymity and proximity. He introduced his friends and associates to the café, and the Monaco soon became the place to meet not just Richard Wright, but also other black expatriates. There people like Ollie Harrington, William Gardner Smith, and many others would sit for hours talking about life, art, and the problems of America and the world.

Like many cafés favored by Parisian intellectuals in these years, the Monaco had two faces. On the surface, it was a very ordinary place, no different from many other neighborhood gathering spots throughout the city. As Ollie Harrington later described it, "The Monaco was a typical French working-class cafe which noisily raised its sheetmetal shutters at seven when the local clientele, butchers, bakers, hairdressers and little craftsmen, would begin drifting in looking for their cafe au lait, laced with cognac. They would look in again four or five times during the day for some additional fuel — usually vin blanc or rouge — until knocking-off time." Since the Latin Quarter was not a typical Parisian neighborhood, however, it also welcomed outsiders from all over the world, who could rejoice in experiencing the "real" Paris. About half of these foreigners were American, including roughly twenty African American men, while the rest came from England, Sweden, Senegal, and other parts of the world. The two groups of people seem to have gotten along amicably if not necessarily closely, benefiting from the live-and-let-live spirit that so attracted Americans to the French capital.

While the Monaco remained popular, in the early 1950s African American intellectuals and artists in Paris also began gathering at the Tournon. Located across the street from the beautiful Luxembourg Gardens in the heart of the Latin Quarter, it was "discovered" by William Gardner Smith, who described it in his novel *The Stone Face* as "a garish splash of green, yellow and red. It was crowded, noisy, smoke-filled, with huge murals of the Luxembourg Gardens on the walls." The Tournon was located only a few blocks from the Monaco and attracted a similar mix of working-class locals and expatriates from America and other parts of the world. Black writers, artists, and other members or hangers-on of the expatriate community would gather in the back of the café to chat, catch up on the latest news, write, or play pinball, a postwar novelty in Parisian cafés. Chester Himes, who visited frequently, described evenings at the Tournon with Ollie Harrington in *My Life of Absurdity*:

> The evenings I went to the Café Tournon and exchanged jokes with Ollie. In front of that vast white audience I could not restrain myself any more than he could. We were fantastically absurd, all of us blacks. But Ollie was funny. I could always follow Ollie's lead. The absurdity of the other blacks was ofttimes hurting. But ours never, it was only entertaining. During that spring the Café Tournon became the most celebrated cafe in all of Europe, and from there one could select entertainments of all types.

Life as a struggling writer in Paris was often difficult. It frequently meant running short of money and learning to do without all but the basics. The city offered a rich public life, but writing was essentially a hard and lonely profession, sometimes made even more so by the distance far from home. In describing his daily routine in Paris, the writer William Gardner Smith made clear both its hardships and the crucial sociability offered by the cafés to those without other social ties. The young expatriate had a small, simply furnished room on a lively, noisy street; consequently, the roar of Parisian traffic echoed day and night. Smith would wake at about 10:30 in the morning and start writing. He would work until about 2:00 in the afternoon, then go eat lunch for about seventy-five cents at a local restaurant. After lunch, Smith would go to the Tournon, staying until about 4:30 or 5:00, then return to his room to work for a few more hours. Evenings he usually spent visiting friends, at the Tournon or other cafés.

The importance of cafés like the Monaco and the Tournon underlined several important characteristics of black American life in Paris after 1945. The expatriates' use of cafés as both workplaces and social centers revealed their close ties with Parisian intellectuals, especially those of Jean-Paul Sartre's circle; the two groups often frequented the same locales. Simone de Beauvoir would engage Ellen Wright as her literary agent later in the 1950s. Richard Wright in particular met and at times worked with many of France's leading intellectuals, including Albert Camus, Maurice Merleau-Ponty, and Jean Cocteau. More than once, he took Sartre and de Beauvoir to meet Herbert Gentry at the painter's nightclub, Chez Honey. In modeling their social life on that of their French peers, whether by conscious design or in response to small, poorly heated hotel rooms, African Americans in Paris displayed a greater willingness to adopt French cultural practices than in the interwar years. During the 1920s, they had often come as teachers, but now they were learning to do as the French did. At the same time, French intellectuals seemed more interested in getting to know black American writers than in the 1920s and 1930s, now regarding African Americans as peers rather than symbols of exoticism.

Most important, the café culture of black Americans on the Left Bank demonstrated the solidity of the community that formed in the years after the war. Probably at no point during the twentieth century have African Americans in Paris been more closely interconnected than during the fifteen years after the end of World War II. Black Americans of all descriptions, from tourists to GIs on weekend passes to students, soon learned that one could go to certain cafés to meet both well-known figures like Harrington or Wright, or simply one another. The Tournon and the Monaco symbolized and reinforced, but did not create this strong sense of community. The rejection of the United States so strong in those years created feelings of shared alienation and

exile, which prompted many to seek contact with their fellow expatriates. Yet
any community is but the sum of the interactions of individual personalites, so
that ultimately a study of the African American community in postwar Paris
must consider in detail some of the leading individuals who composed it.

RICHARD WRIGHT: EXPATRIATE AND WORLD CITIZEN

Richard Wright stood at the center of this community, so much so that one
could use his name to characterize the entire postwar expatriate phenomenon. Not only was he the most famous and prestigious African American
intellectual in Paris (and one of the most renowned anywhere), but he personally assisted many of the other blacks who came to the French capital in those
years. Wright also provided the most important link between that expatriate
community and the wider world of the Parisian intelligentsia. In the history of
black American expatriates in Paris, only Josephine Baker's fame matched his.
Whereas Baker came to Paris as the embodiment of French primitivist fantasies, Wright symbolized the political engagement of Parisian intellectuals
after the liberation. He introduced a new dimension to the history of black
Americans in Paris: the expatriate as refugee from racism. Yet ironically,
Wright's rejection of American racism and his principled refusal to live in the
U.S. ensured a continued connection to the other side of the Atlantic. Unlike
Josephine Baker, he never manifested any signs of becoming French, but
instead remained vitally concerned on a day-to-day basis with the affairs of his
native land. For all his rejection of the United States (or perhaps because of
it), more than anyone else, Richard Wright created the model of the African
American in Paris.

Born into the dire poverty of the sharecropping black South in 1908, Richard Wright exemplifies both the proudest traditions of American upward
mobility and the unique dimensions of such individual success for black
Americans. Exposure to the harsh racism and poverty of the South in the early
twentieth century shaped in Wright a fervent desire to become a writer as a
way of both chronicling and transcending the brutality he saw around him.
This desire took Wright first to Memphis and then, in 1927, to Chicago. He
spent the next ten years, a crucial period of his life, in the midwestern metropolis. In Chicago, he became a writer, producing poetry, short stories, and
essays depicting the lives of black people in both the rural South and the
ghetto North. Richard Wright belonged to several interracial literary groups
and published his work in radical newspapers and magazines like *The New
Masses* and *Left Front*. Wright also became a political activist, like many other
young black intellectuals in Chicago, joining the Communist party to work

for racial equality. For him, as for many other American writers who came to maturity during the Depression, the literature and politics of black life in America could not be separated; this was the central lesson of his Chicago years and would shape his work for the rest of his life.

If Richard Wright became a writer in Chicago, he became a famous writer in New York. Moving there in 1937 to work on the Federal Writers' Project, the New Deal agency that funded so many young literary talents during the Depression, Wright easily settled into an interracial community of progressive intellectuals centered in Greenwich Village. There he completed his magnum opus, *Native Son*, which was published to near universal acclaim. The searing, tragic drama of black life in Chicago completed the transformation of Richard Wright from the son of poor sharecroppers to one of America's most respected and admired young authors. Two other important events from these years would leave a lasting imprint on Richard Wright's life. In 1939, he met Ellen Poplar, a young New Yorker and party member of Polish Jewish origin; the two married in 1941 and remained together for the rest of Wright's life. A year later, in angry response to its subordination of struggles for racial justice to the needs of the war effort, Wright left the Communist party. While he would remain committed to progressive causes until his death, Wright's rejection of the milieu that had done so much to shape him as both a writer and a political thinker confirmed his independence of spirit and determination to fight for his own vision of peace and social justice.

Both Richard Wright's political struggles and his personal life shed light on his resolve to leave America permanently for Paris in 1947. Wright's decision astonished many, and for good reason. After all, the novelist was a success story in every sense of the word, living in a nation of unequaled wealth and power. The year before he had published his autobiography *Black Boy*, which had brought him further praise from America's critical establishment. Yet the discrimination that Richard Wright continued to face brought home to him the bitter truth that in the United States a successful black man was still just a black man. When the Wrights purchased a comfortable home in the heart of Greenwich Village in 1945, they were able to do so only by using a white lawyer who never mentioned the race of his client. Discrimination also prevented them from buying a farm in Vermont. In particular, Richard Wright's marriage to a white woman, a transgression of America's most sacred racial taboo, made him and his wife the targets of bigoted insults. The Wrights' hopes that life in the tolerant Village would shield them from such problems had proved illusory, and they especially feared the impact of growing up in American society on their three-year-old daughter, Julia.

Moreover, Richard Wright's direct statements about racism and other political issues made life in New York increasingly difficult. During a radio broadcast in May 1945, for example, Wright declared, "Whites can no longer regard Negroes as a passive, obedient minority. Whether we have a violent or peaceful solution of this problem depends upon the degree to which white Americans can purge their minds of the illusions that they own and know Negroes." As a result of such statements, Wright found himself the subject of investigations by the FBI and other government agencies. At the same time, local Communists responded sharply to his criticisms of the party, even organizing his Greenwich Village neighbors against him. Given such attacks, it was easy for Wright to conclude that the United States had no place for an independent, outspoken black man.

Paris, by contrast, offered the chance to look at America's racial dilemmas from a broader, more international perspective. Gertrude Stein in particular urged Wright to consider a move to France, and helped facilitate his decision to opt for exile. In spite of last-minute attempts by the State Department to delay delivery of his passport, on May 1, 1946, Richard Wright and his family set sail in New York, arriving in the port of Le Havre eight days later. They stayed in Europe for the rest of the year, returning to the United States in January 1947. Wright soon realized, however, that America's treatment of blacks had not changed, and after experiencing renewed examples of racial antagonism and discrimination in New York decided to return to France. On July 30, 1947, the Wrights sailed out of New York Harbor, ironically on the steamship *United States*. Although he would from time to time visit his native land, Richard Wright would never live there again.

Richard Wright spent the last period of his life, from 1947 to his death in 1960, in Parisian exile. Many of his friends at the time, both black and white, opposed his departure on principle, contending that it represented in effect a desertion of the struggle for racial equality in the United States. Another version of this point of view has been developed by some literary critics and historians, who have tended to portray these years as a sort of coda in the life of the great writer. By separating himself from the life of black America, the argument runs, Wright lost direct touch with the raw material that fueled his literary vision. Life in Paris may have been good for his family and his self-respect, but it was a sort of gilded cage that isolated him from the source of his inspiration. After all, Wright finished his best-known and regarded works, *Black Boy* and *Native Son*, before he chose exile. Although he remained productive, writing eight books during his life in France, none had the impact of his first two.

Exile, even at its most comfortable, has its price. Yet the argument that Paris cost Richard Wright his creative voice has serious defects. It ignores both the importance of the black community in Paris that Wright himself did so much to create, as well as the new, broader political dimensions his work developed as a result of life in the French capital. The existence of this black community, plus Wright's interactions with black visitors from the United States, greatly helped him keep in touch with the changing nature of African American life. At the same time, the greater exposure that Paris offered to political activists from the third world gave Wright a more sophisticated, international perspective on issues of race, class, and power in the modern world.

Richard Wright continued to pen both fiction and essays in France. The contrast between the reception of *Black Boy* and *Native Son*, on the one hand, and the novels he wrote in Paris, on the other, owes more to racial and literary politics in the United States than to the intrinsic quality of his later work. In the last decade of his life, Wright published two novels, *The Outsider* and *The Long Dream*. Both were set in the United States and continued the author's exploration of the complexities of modern racism. American critics, black and white, attacked the two books as outdated portrayals of racial conflict in their society, arguing that a writer who lived in Paris could no longer claim an intimate knowledge of the situation. Some accused Wright of failing to understand how the civil rights movement had changed the South for the better, and suggested that his views and his prose owed more to Parisian philosophers than to an understanding of African American folk culture. Yet, as the literary critic Paul Gilroy has argued, in these two novels and his Paris writings in general Richard Wright was able both to address specific aspects of the black experience and to transform it into a metaphor for the human condition as a whole.

Both Wright's fictional and nonfictional Paris works reveal this new cosmopolitanism of vision. In *The Outsider*, published in 1953, Wright addressed the plight of blacks in the United States and pondered the sufferings of mankind. In portraying the struggles of his protagonist, Cross Damon, Wright drew upon his own experiences in Chicago, Harlem, and Greenwich Village, and upon the themes of French existentialism. Damon emerges as a black Everyman who can be saved only by a transcendent, universal humanism. *White Man, Listen!*, published in 1957, approached the issue of racial discrimination from a thoroughly international perspective. In this collection of essays, Wright sought to link the racism he had personally experienced in America with the struggles of colonial peoples throughout Asia and Africa. The color line was a global phenomenon, and the black experience in the

United States provided an important perspective on bigotry and discrimination throughout the world.

At the same time, the relatively tolerant racial climate Wright found in Paris also had an impact on his ideas about racism. His relations with French intellectuals and the fact that many, notably Jean-Paul Sartre, were making the same transition from existentialism to support for third world liberation, reaffirmed Wright's view of racial conflict as essentially a political problem. This approach was not new; it had guided him during his years in the Communist party, and Richard Wright never abandoned his interest in the politics of racism. Yet Wright's life in Paris, his discussions with both white and black French intellectuals, and his increasing exposure to racial conflict throughout the world confirmed his belief that racism was not simply a matter of hatred and misunderstanding, but arose out of struggles over power. The fight against racism, therefore, was part of a larger humanist movement in which all men and women could and should take part.

While Wright's life in Paris may have lacked the sparkling glamour of Bricktop's and Josephine Baker's, it was nonetheless a very comfortable existence that fully justified his decision to relocate. In May 1948, he and Ellen moved to a spacious apartment in the heart of the Left Bank at 14 rue Monsieur-le-Prince; while not wealthy, the Wrights could afford amenities, like a car, far beyond the reach of most African American expatriates in the French capital. His family, including his second daughter, Rachel, born in Paris in 1949, prospered on alien soil. Above all, he was able to work extensively on his own writing, to travel, and to discuss ideas with people from throughout the world. As the literary critic and Wright biographer Michel Fabre has observed of this period in Richard Wright's life, "Wright also had a well-established group of friends, admirers and literary acquaintances, and enjoyed somewhat of a reputation as a *maître* to whom young writers came for advice on their manuscripts. . . . He adored discussing politics and literature with Blacks of all nationalities, or with the Scandinavian and American students in the Monaco and the Tournon, his regular cafés. . . . He was more than ever at the center of the international exchange of ideas." This portrait hardly seems to represent a man whose best days have passed him by.

Life in Paris enabled Richard Wright to put together a cozy and supportive community, composed of other black American writers and artists as well as progressive white Americans and intellectuals from France and throughout the world. He could remove himself from the traumas of daily life in the United States, yet through American newspapers and visitors still keep in close contact with changing events in his native land. Paris has always treated its great intellectuals well, and Wright found much more respect and consideration not only as a black man, but as a writer there. Thanks to his own gifts and to the privileged place the Left Bank reserved for creative spirits during the 1950s, Richard Wright was able to assemble around himself a gathering of African American artists and intellectuals unmatched since the days of the Harlem Renaissance.

Yet ultimately he rejected the very idea of a black community in Paris, going so far as to say to a reporter, shortly before his death, that "there is no Negro American colony. The Negroes associate with the French to avoid the white American colony." This statement does not contradict the fact that Wright enjoyed associating with other black Americans in Paris and even helped to bring them together. Rather, it indicates Wright's increasingly cosmopolitan outlook on life, and his insistence on being regarded as a human being, and a writer, above all. He chose to socialize with other African Americans in Paris because they shared those values, not just because of the color of their skins. But he also enjoyed getting to know French intellectuals as well as different people of all races from throughout the world. Paris did not shut black people up in a ghetto, but allowed them to luxuriate in a diverse assembly of creative individuals. The black American community that developed there embraced a vision as broad as the human imagination could reach.

Although Paris provided Richard Wright a refuge, he did not move there in order to turn his back on American racism. If anything, during his years in France, Wright spoke out even more forcefully than before against the social injustices that had caused him to flee the United States. Articles such as "American Negroes in France," "The Shame of Chicago," and "The American Problem" testify to his continuing concern, even obsession, with the plight of black Americans. These writings and others, published in both France and America, focused on racial discrimination against blacks in the United States. Even "American Negroes in France" emphasized the ways in which white Americans had attempted to export racism across the Atlantic. The numerous interviews Wright gave during his final years reveal relatively little about his life in Paris, focusing instead overwhelmingly on his views of America's racial dilemma.

Richard Wright also took direct action to fight the evils he and his friends condemned. In October 1950, Wright and the journalist William Rutherford founded the French-American Fellowship, a group dedicated to bringing together all those, black and white, American and French, committed to promoting racial equality and human freedom. A diverse assembly of Ameri-

can and French intellectuals participated including James Baldwin, Leroy
Haynes, Ollie Stewart, Jean-Paul Sartre, Claude Bourdet, and Charles Delaunay. The organization's statement of purpose was extremely broad, pledging
to fight all sorts of racism, to examine the problem of human freedom in the
industrial world, to promote the arts and the spirit of internationalism. However, it proved quite capable of taking specific actions, such as protesting
discrimination at the American Hospital in Paris, or demanding that the U.S.
government grant a visa to the Marxist historian Daniel Guérin, the author of
a critical study of American life. In 1951, the fellowship actively fought the
conviction of Willie McGee. In spite of a major campaign in America, including protests by Josephine Baker, the state of Mississippi executed McGee
in May of that year, conclusively demonstrating the continued vitality of
American racism.

The French-American Fellowship was a brief endeavor, accomplishing
little after 1951, but it provides a clear illustration of the cosmopolitan character of Richard Wright's political vision. The group not only spoke out against
injustice directed at black Americans, but also investigated other issues, such
as France's war in Indochina, and sponsored cultural events like an exhibition
of American painters in July 1951. Consistently during his Paris years, Wright
continued to speak out against injustice throughout the world. In April 1955,
he traveled to the newly independent nation of Indonesia to attend the Ban-
dung conference of non-aligned nations. The following year, he published a
report on the conference under the title "The Color Curtain," underlining
the centrality of racial difference in relations between the West and the third
world and calling on the former to renounce imperialism.

Like other black American expatriates before him, Wright also met black
people from throughout the world in Paris. During the late 1940s and 1950s,
Africa and Asia were rapidly and sometimes violently rejecting European
colonial domination and moving toward independence. It was a period of
extraordinary political ferment in what was coming to be known as the third
world, and even more than during the interwar years the French capital provided a convenient place from which to observe these momentous changes.
Although dispersed during the war, the negritude writers began regrouping
shortly after the liberation. Initially, many wished to continue the movement's
primary focus on black culture, but they soon became involved in discussions
and critiques of colonialism with an increasingly political edge. Some of the
leading exponents of negritude also became directly involved in political
action. Shortly after the war Léopold Senghor, Aimé Césaire, and Léon
Damas were all elected to the French national assembly, from Senegal, Mar-

tinique, and French Guiana, respectively. Having begun in the interwar years as a movement to validate black culture, negritude now took its place in the struggle against colonialism and for third world independence.

During his first visit to Paris in the summer of 1946, Wright met both Senghor and Césaire for the first time. A year later, Wright became one of the sponsors, along with French intellectuals like Sartre, Albert Camus, André Gide, and Pierre Naville, of the new negritude journal *Présence Africaine*, directed by the Senegalese writer Alioune Diop. Over the next several years, Wright would work closely with members of the black French literary elite in Paris, developing a greater appreciation of African culture as well as a broader political understanding of racism as an international phenomenon. He also exercised a strong influence on the younger generation of negritude writers, notably Ousmane Sembene, whose novel *The Black Docker* owed much to both *Native Son* and Claude McKay's *Banjo*.

The single most important example of Wright's ties to French black writers was the Congress of Negro Artists and Writers, which he organized along with Césaire, Senghor, Diop, and other associates of *Présence Africaine*. The congress, which took place at the Sorbonne from September 19 to 22, 1956, was an epochal event, the first organized, systematic meeting between black American and black French intellectuals. Sixty delegates from twenty-four countries participated: the members of the *Présence Africaine* group represented the French side, whereas the American delegation consisted of Horace Mann Bond, Mercer Cook, John Davis, James Ivy, William Fontaine, and Richard Wright himself. The U.S. government had prevented W.E.B. Du Bois from coming by refusing to issue him a visa, but the elderly statesman sent along a written message of support. Over the next three days, the delegates discussed a wide variety of issues, including the nature of black culture, its relationship to Africa, the impact of colonialism on blacks, and the politics of decolonization. The debates were certainly not free from discord; in particular, Aimé Césaire's Communism and his characterization of African Americans as a colonized people alienated many of the Americans present. Nevertheless, the fact that such a congress was held at all represented for the proponents of negritude a dream come true, and Richard Wright had been instrumental in its realization.

Even more so after the war, Paris represented a gateway to Africa. In 1953, influenced by other black intellectuals in Paris and London, Wright decided it was time for him to visit the ancestral continent. In 1946, during a trip to London, Wright had met George Padmore, the Jamaican political activist and fellow ex-Communist, who had introduced him to many progressive third world intellectuals living in the British capital. Wright remained in contact with Padmore, who, as political adviser to the Gold Coast's Kwame Nkrumah, arranged for him to visit that emerging African nation in 1953. Wright arrived in Africa in June, stopping first in Sierra Leone, then traveling widely throughout the Gold Coast. He published his observations in *Black Power*, the first of three travel books he wrote in Paris, the following year.

Wright went to Africa motivated both by anticolonialist convictions and a desire for self-discovery. As *Black Power* makes clear, Wright found Africa to be an alien land, full of customs and attitudes he found difficult to understand, yet also one whose culture at times strikingly resembled that of black Americans. Far from sharing an intimate bond with the Africans he met, Wright realized that many simply regarded him as a Westerner and an American. As he stated at one point, "I'm of African descent and I'm in the midst of Africans, yet I cannot tell what they are thinking and feeling." At the same time, on his first day in Africa, he noted his pleasure at discovering a land where blacks constituted the majority. At a political rally in the capital of Accra, Wright witnessed the dancing with a haunting sense of familiarity:

I'd seen these same snakelike, veering dances before. . . . Where? Oh, God, yes; in America, in storefront churches, in Holy Roller Tabernacles, in God's Temples, in unpainted wooden prayer-meeting houses on the plantations of the Deep South. . . . And here I was seeing it all again against a background of a surging nationalistic political movement! How could that be? . . . I'd long contended that the American Negro, because of what he had undergone in the United States, had been basically altered, that his consciousness had been filled with a new content, that "racial" qualities were but myths of prejudiced minds. Then, if that were true, how could I account for what I now saw? And what I now saw was an exact duplicate of what I'd seen for so many long years in the United States.

Richard Wright found Africa fascinating, but his experience there does not seem to have changed his identity in any fundamental sense. He realized that at heart he remained a creation of the West, and he showed no desire to leave Europe for a life in Africa. Yet Wright also remained sympathetic to the struggles of Africans for political independence and economic development, continuing to condemn the nefarious influence of European colonialism on the continent's affairs. Most of *Black Power* is concerned less with the relationship of African Americans to Africa than with the politics of race and freedom in a continent rapidly moving toward independence. As such, it represented a logical continuation of Wright's participation in the 1956 black writers confer-

ence, demonstrating how life abroad had developed his international perspective.

Wright's experience in Africa represents something of a landmark in the
history of African Americans in Paris. During the interwar years, many had
learned a greater appreciation of African culture, but none had actually ven-
tured to the sub-Saharan part of the continent. After 1945, however, many
black Americans would choose both Paris and different parts of Africa as
settings for exile from the United States. Richard Wright was one of the first,
and more would follow in his footsteps a decade later. Not all those African
Americans who made the pilgrimage to the mother continent journeyed via
Paris, of course, but enough did to continue the tradition of Paris as the
gateway to Africa. The fact that this shift from refracted to direct views of
Africa came in the same period as the end of colonial rule is not at all
accidental. Black Americans in interwar Paris had formed their own impressions of Africa in the context of French primitivism. Such impressions often
had a romantic quality that postwar voyages to the African continent did not
always justify. Nonetheless, direct experience in Africa enabled black Americans to judge for themselves, outside the parameters of French intellectual
tutelage. If the period after 1945 witnessed the end of European empires in
Africa, for African American expatriates in Paris it also brought a certain
decolonization of vision.

GIFTED OUTSIDERS: JAMES BALDWIN
AND CHESTER HIMES

Whereas Parisian exile made Richard Wright the universally recognized king
of a lively black expatriate community, for James Baldwin life abroad confirmed his situation as an outsider. Many ties linked the two great writers, their
success and their lives together in Paris, even their famous literary feud, a
constant source of debate among black Americans in Paris during the 1950s.
And much separated Wright and Baldwin. Two differences are crucial. In
addition to their respective insider and outsider status, the two men also
moved to Paris at different points in their personal and professional lives.
Richard Wright came to the Left Bank as an established, internationally
famous author, having already written the most celebrated work of his career.
James Baldwin, in contrast, crossed the Atlantic as a young and relatively
unknown talent whose triumphs lay in the future. To a much greater extent
than Wright, Baldwin's literary work would reflect his life in Paris. James
Baldwin thus became an American original: one of the very few blacks to

follow Hemingway's path (by now the dream of thousands of young Americans) from picturesque obscurity to literary stardom in the City of Light.

James Baldwin was born in Harlem in 1924, a year before Josephine Baker left New York for fame and fortune in France. The community he grew up in was a study in contradictions, combining the vibrant musical and literary life of the Harlem Renaissance, and the stern yet joyous universe of the black church, which gave meaning to the travails of so many of its residents. In Harlem, Saturday night and Sunday morning coexisted uncomfortably, a relationship that would provide the inspiration for much of Baldwin's literary work. The young Baldwin grew up in a household dominated by his stepfather, David Baldwin, a harsh man embittered by racism and poverty who worked in factories during the week and preached in Harlem churches on the weekend. James's childhood thus combined material and emotional deprivation, a bleak existence he learned to escape by immersing himself in the fantasy world of literature. His constant reading and his native intelligence soon brought him recognition in school, and would ultimately lead to a real and permanent escape from the poverty and humiliations of his early life.

The summer of 1943 constituted an irrevocable transition for the young Baldwin in several respects. On the day he turned nineteen, his family buried his stepfather, who had died in an insane asylum. Baldwin had graduated from high school and left home the previous year, but his stepfather's death marked the definitive end of his life in Harlem. That summer he moved to Greenwich Village on the advice of his friend, the artist Beauford Delaney, whom he would later rejoin in Paris. In the Village, he made two crucial decisions that would shape his life: to become a writer, and to acknowledge his homosexuality. Compared to his harsh upbringing in Harlem, Greenwich Village brought Baldwin into contact with a cosmopolitan, interracial milieu, allowing him to pursue both his literary craft and sexual explorations in the gay underworld. In 1944, he was introduced to Richard Wright, whose work he had treasured as a high school student.

Like Wright, however, Baldwin soon discovered that for all its vaunted liberalism the Village was still a white neighborhood in a nation that continued to treat blacks with hostility and contempt. Both the overt antagonism of white bigots he encountered there, and the sincere but uncomprehending sympathy of his white friends, made Baldwin feel like more of an outsider than ever. If he could not find a home for himself in Greenwich Village, where in America or the world could he go? By 1948, Baldwin was beginning to achieve some success with his writing, publishing essays and short stories in major publications like *The Nation* and *Commentary*. Yet he remained as alienated as ever, and in November, following the example of his idol and mentor, Wright, he moved to Paris in search of both artistic inspiration and acceptance as a human being.

Upon his arrival in the French capital, with $40 to his name, Baldwin went immediately to meet Richard Wright at the Deux Magots café. Wright welcomed him cordially and helped him find a hotel room. Yet although Baldwin thus came with the best possible connections to the African American community in Paris, he still did not feel at home. And $40 did not last long in Paris, even in the late 1940s. Lacking any other source of income, Baldwin resorted to borrowing from Wright and other expatriates, which strained relations on both sides. He was still essentially unknown in Paris, and often felt patronized or ignored by the French intellectuals who formed part of Wright's circle. As his money ran out, Baldwin left the Latin Quarter, moving into the much poorer neighborhood of Belleville. Largely populated by Arab immigrants, Belleville was the closest equivalent to Harlem in the French capital, and Baldwin's isolation during the harsh winter of 1948 to 1949 symbolically represented a second repudiation of Greenwich Village. Yet he did not cut his ties to the black and white expatriates of the Left Bank completely, continuing to oscillate between these two very different Parisian worlds during much of the 1950s.

James Baldwin's relationship to the black American community in Paris was therefore ambivalent, to say the least. Without the support offered by Wright and others, he might not have survived there, or even come in the first place. Moreover, Baldwin took an active and public role in the community's café life, and came to know the Latin Quarter and Saint-Germain-des-Prés intimately. Yet the Left Bank was not Harlem, and especially in these early years the camaraderie it offered could not compensate for Baldwin's own feelings of alienation and inadequacy. In his 1950 essay "Encounter on the Seine," James Baldwin dismissed the idea of a black American community in the French capital.

> In general, only the Negro entertainers are able to maintain a useful and unquestioning comradeship with other Negroes. Their nonperforming, colored countrymen are, nearly to a man, incomparably more isolated, and it must be conceded that this isolation is deliberate. It is estimated that there are five hundred American Negroes living in this city, the vast majority of them veterans studying on the G.I. Bill. They are studying everything from the Sorbonne's standard *Cours de Civilisation Française* to abnormal psychology, brain surgery, music, fine arts, and literature. Their isolation from each other is not difficult to understand. . . . It is altogether inevitable that past humiliations

should become associated not only with one's traditional oppressors but also with one's traditional kinfolk. . . . Through this deliberate isolation, through lack of numbers, and above all through his own overwhelming need to be, as it were, forgotten, the American Negro in Paris is very nearly the invisible man.

The final allusion here to Ralph Ellison's Harlem antihero merely confirms the autobiographical character of this psychological study of exile. The emphasis on self-imposed isolation, while certainly true of some African Americans in the French capital, owes much more to Baldwin's personal dilemmas and choices than to black life there in general. During his early years in Paris, the young author had not yet overcome the demons that had chased him from both Harlem and Greenwich Village, and even on the banks of the Seine he continued to consider himself, to a large extent incorrectly, an outsider.

James Baldwin had been in Paris for little more than six months when his famous feud with Richard Wright erupted. In June 1949, Baldwin published an essay entitled "Everybody's Protest Novel," in which he attacked politicized literature for giving a one-dimensional portrait of human character. As one of his examples, Baldwin cited *Native Son*, claiming that the figure of Bigger Thomas represented a black man defined by white anger and fear, without transcendent humanity. "Below the surface of this novel there lies, as it seems to me, a continuation, a complement of that monstrous legend it was written to destroy. Bigger is Uncle Tom's descendant, flesh of his flesh."

Fighting words indeed! "Everybody's Protest Novel" is a brilliant essay, full of complex ideas and beautifully written. Yet in criticizing *Native Son*, Baldwin chose to take on not only the giant of African American literature, but also the mentor who had helped him get established in Paris. Moreover, the timing of the article, published in the United States when many attacked Wright for his politics and for leaving America, made it seem that Baldwin was working with those in the American government and literary establishment eager to tarnish the great writer's reputation in order to promote his own. Baldwin claimed that he meant no such thing and still respected Wright enormously, but Richard Wright was understandably furious. On the day the article was published in Paris, the two had a stormy meeting at the Brasserie Lipp in Saint-Germain-des-Prés. Wright accused Baldwin of betrayal and swore to have nothing more to do with him. Efforts to resolve the feud failed, especially after Baldwin attacked *Native Son* again in his 1951 essay "Many Thousand Gone," and the two remained estranged for the rest of their lives.

Baldwin's feud with Richard Wright was something the young author would later regret, but at the time it soon became a classic example of what the French call a *succès de scandale.* It brought him to the attention of the literary worlds in both France and America, greatly increasing his publishing opportunities. Although James Baldwin had not exactly been unknown before, some now hailed him as the heir apparent to the throne of African American literature. While many of Richard Wright's friends in Paris condemned Baldwin, the controversy brought him new recognition among the black and white American literati of the Left Bank. The significance of the Wright-Baldwin feud testified to the importance not only of the two writers, but also of the African American expatriate presence in Paris. Exile politics and controversies often resemble a tempest in a teapot, violent but usually of concern only to those directly involved. In contrast, the conflict between Richard Wright and James Baldwin was a major event in American literature, closely followed by many on both sides of the Atlantic. More than anything else, it demonstrated that in terms of black literature Paris had become the Harlem of the 1950s.

During the 1950s, James Baldwin shuttled between Paris and New York, repeatedly going back home only to discover that he could not live and write there. Although when he first left for Paris in 1948 he considered his departure definitive, not until the early 1960s would Baldwin finally resolve to become a permanent expatriate. The young writer discovered that Paris was not an easy place in which to survive, but that life there did stimulate his writing. Like many expatriates, Baldwin used the cafés as places to see and be seen, as well as the sites for long work stints. During these early years, he turned out several essays and wrote his first novel, *Go Tell It on the Mountain,* composing much of the book during a stay at the Swiss home of his friend and lover, the artist Lucien Happersberger. In 1952, Baldwin returned to America for the first time since 1948 to find a publisher for the novel. At least one biographer has suggested that this prodigal's return further emphasized the contrast between him and the determined exile Richard Wright, yet like Wright before him, James Baldwin was to learn that he could not go home. He stayed with his mother in Harlem and looked up many old friends in the Village, but in general found the racial and political climate in New York as bad as ever. As soon as Knopf accepted his book, he used part of his advance to book passage for France, returning in 1953. Baldwin was living in Paris when *Go Tell It on the Mountain* came out in New York to enthusiastic, if not rave, reviews that established him as one of the leading black American writers of his time.

James Baldwin stayed in France for another four years before returning once again to America, and while he was abroad he wrote his second novel, *Giovanni's Room.* This new work differed from Baldwin's first novel in almost every respect. Whereas *Go Tell It on the Mountain* was a highly autobiographical portrait of black life in Harlem, *Giovanni's Room* was not only set in Paris, but did not feature blacks at all. The book tells the story of a young white American named David who is in love with two people, his American girlfriend, Hella, and an Italian bartender, Giovanni. It is the most Parisian of James Baldwin's novels, featuring vivid descriptions of Saint-Germain-des-Prés and the gay underworld of the city. *Giovanni's Room* testifies to Baldwin's love of Paris, both directly in terms of David's attraction to it and indirectly in that life there enabled him to transcend the socially accepted role of a black author. Yet the novel also presents a bleak vision of the French capital, a place of isolation where true love is only a bitter dream.

> My real fear was buried and was driving me to Montparnasse. I wanted to find a girl, any girl at all.
>   But the terraces seemed oddly deserted. . . . I saw no one I knew. I walked down as far as the *Closerie des Lilas* and I had a solitary drink there. I read my letters again. I thought of finding Giovanni at once and telling him I was leaving him but I knew he would not yet have opened the bar and he might be almost anywhere in Paris at this hour. I walked slowly back up the boulevard. Then I saw a couple of girls, French whores, but they were not very attractive. I told myself that I could do better than *that*. I got to the *Sélect* and sat down. I watched the people pass, and I drank. No one I knew appeared on the boulevard for the longest time.

Baldwin always rejected characterizations of *Giovanni's Room* as a "homosexual novel," preferring to consider it a tale of frustrated love. Yet paradoxically, in its story of a love affair between two white men the book offers important insights into African American life in Paris. Homosexuality was certainly an important, if often discreet, part of that experience, and not only for James Baldwin. Jean-Claude Baker's tell-all biography of his adoptive mother Josephine details her numerous involvements with other women, including Bricktop. The distinguished Shakespearean actor Gordon Heath, who settled permanently in Paris in 1948, for years ran and sang at the Abbaye nightclub in Saint-Germain-des-Prés with his lover, the white American Lee Payant. During the 1960s the Mars Club catered to a large gay clientele, including black musicians like Billy Strayhorn and Art Simmons. Like Greenwich Village, Paris in the 1950s offered a thriving gay male subculture, centered around spots like the Café Flore's upstairs room, where Baldwin and other African American men were able to find sexual contacts. More important, the city as a whole seemed a place where one's private life was one's own concern, a sharp contrast to the puritanical voyeurism reigning in postwar America. Most of all, James Baldwin found in Paris a place where he could be judged simply as an individual, not as the sum of his various social identities. There was no African American gay subculture in Paris; rather, homosexuals took part in the life of both black expatriates and the French intelligentsia. In *Giovanni's Room*, Baldwin wrote about homosexuality *and*, in an important act of rebellion for a black writer, presented a story about whites. The novel represented Baldwin's most daring transgression of the boundaries of race and sexuality in order to chronicle the innermost verities of the human experience.

Not surprisingly, *Giovanni's Room* initially met with a hostile reception from New York's leading publishers, who felt that a novel about homosexuality by a black writer could not possibly win mass acceptance. Yet when the novel was published in 1956, it received immediate acclaim from both critics and the public as a whole. James Baldwin was now a well-established literary figure, at home among the intelligentsia of both Paris and New York. At this stage in his life, having achieved many of his early goals, Baldwin began to develop the more activist concern with antiracist struggles that characterized his later years. He attended the 1956 black writers conference at the Sorbonne, and while he did not agree with all the positions of the African and Caribbean spokesmen he met, he became fascinated with their political commitment.

More important, Baldwin began to learn about the burgeoning civil rights movement in the American South, especially the Montgomery bus boycott triggered by Rosa Parks and organized by the young Dr. Martin Luther King, Jr. Compared to these momentous events, the black American community in Paris, composed of people who "spent most of their time sitting in bars and cafés talking about how awful America was" seemed like a trivial waste of time. In 1957, therefore, Baldwin left Paris once more, this time not in search of a publishing contract, but in order to participate in the struggles of black Americans to achieve the kind of freedom he had found on the other side of the Atlantic. That summer he traveled widely throughout the South, observing the conflicts over integration in cities like Charlotte, North Carolina, and Little Rock, Arkansas, and meeting Martin Luther King in Atlanta. Far more than his experiences in Paris, Baldwin's direct experience of the segregationist South would commit him to political activism for the rest of his life.

James Baldwin would return to France in 1963, eventually making his home in the idyllic Riviera village of Saint-Paul-de-Vence. He had come to Paris fifteen years before penniless and unknown, and now enjoyed success and recognition as a writer, as well as a new self-confidence. All these enabled him to, as he later put it, go back home and pay his dues by fighting the racism that had made him an exile in the first place. Baldwin was one of the first African American expatriates to recognize and act upon the realization that exile could be not only a political statement, but also a political liability, distancing one not only from the suffering of one's people but from their struggles and triumphs. This paradox would emerge as a key concern among African Americans in Paris a decade later. Yet at the same time, Baldwin's life abroad had fueled the creative genius that enabled him to take such action, making his contributions to the civil rights movement all the more effective. Whereas for Richard Wright exile in Paris provided a comfortable and stimulating refuge from American racism, for James Baldwin it helped an insecure young man develop the intellectual and personal strengths he needed to fight for a new day in the United States.

Chester Himes constitutes the third in what one might call the triumvirate of African American writers who settled in Paris during the 1950s. All three achieved a level of success and recognition in the French capital unmatched by any other African American writers, and by few Americans in general, before or since. All three left the United States in more or less overt protest against American racism and the burdens it placed upon black creativity. Also, Richard Wright, James Baldwin, and Chester Himes constitute a fascinating trio not only because of their similarities and close interconnections, but also because of their differences. Chester Himes had much in common with both of his illustrious peers. Like Wright, he came to France as a mature man and established writer, and similarly settled permanently in Europe as a repudiation of American racism. Like Baldwin he never felt completely comfortable in Paris, remaining a loner and an outsider during his time there. Yet Himes was also an original, both as a writer and as an African American expatriate. To a much greater extent than Wright or Baldwin, he severed his ties with the American literary establishment, publishing many of his works in French translation and living off the royalties paid by French publishing houses, an amazing achievement for a foreign writer. Whereas Wright and Baldwin appealed to French intellectuals, Himes's mystery novels appealed to the broader public's fascination with the popular culture of the United States. American-style stories of crime and gangsters enjoyed a big following in France, as demonstrated by the success of the *romans policiers* and *film noir*, and Himes's stylish tales of violence spoke effectively to this audience. Paris played a major role in the life of all three expatriate novelists, but more Parisians read Chester Himes than either James Baldwin or Richard Wright.

Chester Himes was born in 1909 in Jefferson City, Missouri, to middle-class parents whose accomplishments could never shield him from racism. Incidents such as a white hospital's refusal to treat his brother after a chemical accident made life more difficult and caused bitter family arguments. His very light-skinned mother, in particular, despised both whites for their inhumanity (more than once she made whites back down by pulling a pistol on them) and blacks for their timidity in accepting it. Her deep inner conflicts about race would prove a powerful legacy for her young son. In 1926, Chester Himes entered Ohio State University, registering the fourth highest score on the entrance exam of that year. Yet in rebellion against both the racism he found in college and his own middle-class background, Himes neglected his studies, choosing to spend his time in the company of gamblers, pimps, and prostitutes in the black ghetto of Columbus. His descent into the world of crime led in 1928 to his conviction for armed robbery, earning the nineteen-year-old Himes a prison sentence of twenty to twenty-five years hard labor.

Chester Himes served seven and a half years in prison and during those years became a writer, publishing his first short story in 1934 while still incarcerated. After his release in 1936, he managed to eke out a living working for the Ohio Writers' Project and publishing articles in the black press. A year later, he married a young African American woman named Jean, and in 1942 the couple moved to Los Angeles, where Himes hoped to find work as a screenwriter. Instead, like thousands of other African Americans lured by the vision of wartime California, Himes ended up working in the shipyards. A fellowship from the Julius Rosenwald Foundation, an organization that funded education for blacks, rescued him from the docks and brought him to New York in 1944. During this period, he wrote his first novel, *If He Hollers Let Him Go* (1945), a tragic story of a black man trapped between a black and a white woman. Two years later, Himes published his second novel, *The Lonely Crusade*, portraying union organizing among the kinds of black workers he had met in the Los Angeles shipyards. *The Lonely Crusade* in particular met with a harsh reception from both sides, black and white, in the literary establishment, shocking many with its explicit discussion of politics and sexuality. The *Atlantic Monthly* commented that "hate runs through this book like a streak of yellow bile," whereas *Commentary* compared it to "graffito on the walls of public toilets." Embittered by criticism reflecting a denial of America's racial realities, Himes stopped writing for five years, and began dreaming of ways to leave the United States.

Meanwhile, the young author gained a certain reputation in Europe. Both his novels came out in France and England, and in 1952 *The Lonely Crusade* was selected by Parisian reviewers as one of the top five American novels published that year in France. Unlike American reviewers, French critics praised Himes's unsparing portrayal of racism, and the ways in which it degraded both blacks and whites. *The Lonely Crusade*'s story of a protagonist who rages futilely against the injustices of a world that makes no sense fitted neatly into the existentialist view, winning its author respect and acceptance in French literary circles. Both Richard Wright and Himes's translator Yves Malartic urged him to come to Paris. In the end, the dissolution of Chester Himes's personal ties in America prompted him to choose exile. His mother had died in 1945, while in 1951 he and Jean separated. With the death of his father in 1952, Himes realized there was no more reason for him to stay in a land he despised. In 1953, he used advance money from his new novel, *Third Generation*, to purchase a ticket on a steamship to France, arriving in Paris on April 10. He would spend the rest of his life in Europe.

Like James Baldwin before him, Chester Himes saw Richard Wright as soon as he got to the French capital. Wright helped him settle into a Parisian hotel and introduced him to Ollie Harrington, William Gardner Smith, and other black expatriates. Himes quickly got to know people in the community and began spending most of his time at the Monaco and Tournon cafés. He rejected the idea that blacks should associate with one another because of their skin color, and always maintained a position on the periphery. Yet his observations of African American life in 1950s Paris, as recorded later in the two volumes of his autobiography, remain an excellent record of that time.

> Most of the brothers and sisters I found in Paris were intelligent, educated and talented. There were some rats, of course, and some brothers spying for the CIA; but most were either employed by the U.S. government in legitimate capacities, or on their own, such as writers, artists, jazz musicians, blues singers, stripteasers, students, or GIs. A few were pimps and prostitutes. There were more homosexuals than lesbians, perhaps because there were more brothers than sisters, but the large majority were heterosexual, mainly because, whether they were male or female, they found more takers than they could cover.

Himes's concluding remarks represent both his observations and his own experience. The author's early years in Paris enabled him to explore his conflicted attitudes toward white women. Symbolic both of the racist oppressor and of the forbidden fruit denied to black men by racism, white women were a constant preoccupation of the young Chester Himes. The theme of tragic miscegenation runs through his early works. Both *If He Hollers Let Him Go* and *The Lonely Crusade* revolve around a black male protagonist who is manipulated, seduced, and then destroyed by a cunning white woman. Such tortured relationships could end only in violence. *The Primitive* (1955) depicts the murder of a white woman by her black intellectual lover. Based in part on Himes's own affair with a Rosenwald employee, Vandi Haygood, the novel epitomized a period in the author's life he characterized as a descending spiral of sex and violence. Othello was alive and well, and living in America.

On the ship going to France in 1953, Chester Himes had met and fallen in love with Willa Trierweiler, a white American returning to Europe to divorce her Dutch husband. Shortly after his arrival in Paris, she moved in with him, and they spent the next year and a half together in the French capital and traveling throughout Europe. Willa Trierweiler was one of the great loves of Chester Himes's life, yet the relationship was doomed by his insecurities, their lack of money and stability, and her regrets for the family and the world she had left behind. Himes later wrote, "During her terrible grieving, all the comfort I could offer her was sex. Is sex the ultimate that a black man can offer a white woman? I wondered. I didn't want to believe it . . . [Willa] didn't want to admit failure, either. She had run off with me in defiance of her tradition and her race, leaving her husband and her children, and she didn't want to go crawling back penitent and defeated." Yet in the end that is exactly what happened. In December 1954, Trierweiler took passage on a steamship to return to New York. She and Himes parted amicably but with a sense of tragedy, realizing that flight to Europe had not enabled them to bridge the gap that separated black and white in America.

Willa Trierweiler was not the last white woman to attract Chester Himes during his years of exile. Himes's life, in particular as revealed in the second volume of his autobiography, exemplified a major theme among the African American community in Paris after the war, the close sexual relations between black men and white women. Interracial liaisons were certainly not unknown to black Americans in Paris during the interwar years, as Bricktop made clear, but they were not so universal nor so public as after 1945. Moreover, African American women pursued forbidden love every bit as much as African American men; none crossed the color line as spectacularly as Josephine Baker in the 1920s and 1930s. During the 1950s, in contrast, men dominated the African American community in the French capital, and their attraction to members of the opposite sex and race was the clearest expression of this dominance. As Chester Himes wrote:

All of the American blacks whom I knew had white women, sometimes two or three or more. Richard Wright had his white wife, Oliver Harrington was a great favorite of all the foreign white women in the Latin Quarter . . . Bertel, a black painter from Gary, Indiana, was seen in the company of numerous white girls and was allegedly living with a white Dutch girl and her mother. Frank Van Bracken, who claimed to be the Paris correspondent for *Ebony*, had several white girls whom I had heard referred to as prostitutes, and it is a fact Frank was actually arrested and served time in a Paris jail for hustling prostitutes . . . Ish Kelley, the prototype for FishBelly in Richard Wright's book *The Long Dream*, had so many white women and babies by them it was said he had a concupiscent eye . . .

I never met an American black man at that time in Paris who wasn't living with one or more white women or married to one.

Chester Himes engaged actively in sexual exploration during his first years in Paris, and all of his partners seem to have been white women. In his autobiography, he describes in steamy detail his affair with a young German, Regine Fischer, a relationship characterized by both tenderness and brutality and ended with Fischer's commitment to an insane asylum after Himes left her, weary of her increasingly obsessive behavior. In 1957, Himes met an English librarian and journalist named Lesley Packard who would become the final love of his life. The two would later marry, inaugurating a period of greater success and stability for Chester Himes. They remained together until his death in 1984.

The specific nature of relationships between black men and white women in Paris varied widely, from transient sexual encounters to long-term commitments, both with and without the benefit of clergy. With the exception of Richard Wright, most black American men came to Paris alone and became involved with women they met there, in cafés, jazz clubs, restaurants, or at the homes of friends. Most often, these were women from other European countries living in Paris who were attracted to the Bohemianism of the Latin Quarter. Relatively few seem to have been white Americans, and even fewer were French. In his memoirs, Chester Himes noted that whereas the Paris police ignored relations between black men and foreign women, if a Frenchwoman lodged a formal complaint against an African American male the gendarmes would usually expel him from the country. As in so many other ways, Paris welcomed expatriates but kept them isolated from the mainstream.

The central role played by white women in black expatriate life reveals much about the African American community on the Left Bank in the 1950s. More than professional opportunities or political activism, their presence was the single greatest difference between black life in Paris and in the United

States. Not just the prevalence of interracial relationships, but the small number of black women would have made the African Americans of the French capital unrecognizable as a black community on the other side of the Atlantic. Yet the pattern of relationships between African American men and white women in Paris was far too pronounced to result simply from a lack of alternatives. For many black men, of course, the willingness of white women in Paris to consider them as sexual partners was the clearest possible marker of the difference between American and French attitudes. Moreover, both black men and white women symbolized for each other the romance and Bohemianism of Paris. In the storied streets of the Latin Quarter, members of either group could indulge in sexual experimentation not available or allowed at home. Yet white women also represented the enemy, and in light of the frequent American tendency to confuse sex and violence some African American men saw the act of sleeping with white women as one of revenge and conquest. Chester Himes certainly saw his relationship with Regine Fischer in this light; his description of their first sexual encounter exemplified his tortured attitude. "I tried to think of some way to hurt her. I pumped, wishing I could split her open like a melon. I looked down into her blue-gray eyes with hate and fury, wishing my tool was the size of a telegraph pole."

Even in Paris, however, transgressing the boundaries of race and sex could exact an emotional cost. Relationships between black men and white women could involve sexual fantasies, racial resentment, and self-hatred, bringing to the surface an inner turmoil both social and psychological in origin. Also, if interracial sex represented a challenge to white America, it also constituted a certain rejection of the norms of black American society in general, and the black woman in particular. To some black male expatriates, black women symbolized the traditional role of African Americans that they longed so desperately to escape. A character in William Gardner Smith's novel *The Stone Face* dramatically expressed these conflicts:

> "It's a trap. . . . Most of the women they got over here are white, and I could never marry a white woman and look at myself in the mirror again. You know, when I was younger in New York . . . my mother told me: 'If you ever marry a white woman, don't bring her here in my house, you hear! You ain't givin' that satisfaction to the white man! . . . No son of mine gonna insult black womanhood by marrying a white woman and *stay my son!* You hear me?'"
>
> "You know, Simeon, I can't get those words out of my mind. Every time I sleep with a white chick I feel guilt, feel that I really hate the woman. I can't marry that."
>
> Simeon said, "Marry a Negro woman, then."

"That's the trouble. I can't do that either. . . . I can't marry her because the white man says I *got* to marry a Negro woman! In a way, marrying a Negro woman would be like accepting segregation. It's crazy, but that's the way I feel, I can't help it. I would be staying 'in my place.' Well, dammit no! I ain't gonna stay in my place!"

If the prevalence of interracial relationships between black men and white women distinguished Paris from most black communities in America, it underlined once more the similarity of expatriate life in the French capital to intellectual enclaves in the United States like Greenwich Village and San Francisco's North Beach. Such neighborhoods provided spaces where blacks and whites could find love together and expect a comparatively tolerant reaction. The lives of Richard Wright and James Baldwin in particular symbolized this transatlantic similarity. The parallel only goes so far: both Wright and Baldwin encountered prejudice in Greenwich Village, and in both cases racial conflict prompted them to leave America behind. Nonetheless, Bohemia in Paris had much in common with Bohemia in New York, San Francisco, and other American cities. For many left-wing American intellectuals, black and white, life in the United States during the 1950s represented a kind of exile, and communities like the Village isolated colonies in a strange, frequently hostile land. From this perspective, life in Paris was not radically different but rather an intensification of an expatriate experience that had already begun at home.

For Chester Himes, therefore, exile in the French capital enabled him to release the burden of racial bitterness, replacing anger at the white race with love for an individual white woman. Life in Paris also freed him from American racism in another way, by giving him recognition as a writer in France. Unlike most black expatriates, Himes came to France as an established literary presence, his first two novels already having been translated into French. During his years in Paris, he largely abandoned writing the tragic novels about interracial conflict that had launched his career in the United States, shifting instead to publishing detective stories for French publishers. This transition was at least in part fortuitous. Early in 1957, he encountered Marcel Duhamel, who had translated *If He Hollers Let Him Go*. Duhamel was directing the detective series La Série Noire for Gallimard Press, and suggested that Himes write a story for it. This offer was a valuable one, for not only did La Série Noire publish the best mystery novelists, such as Raymond Chandler and Dashiell Hammett, but it also paid very well. Himes had never written mysteries before, but Duhamel's offer of a $1,000 advance proved irresistible.

Thus began the highly successful career of Chester Himes, mystery novel-ist. Although this genre of literature was new for him, its themes of vio-lence and absurdity suited his outlook. As he notes in his autobiography, while discussing Duhamel's offer, he had thought, "I had started out to write a detective story when I wrote that novel [*If He Hollers Let Him Go*], but I couldn't name the white man who was guilty because all white men were guilty." Himes settled down to work on his mystery and in January 1957 finished the book he would publish under the title *The Five Cornered Square* (in France, *La Reine des Pommes*). For Himes, this new book repre-sented a promising turn in his career as well as independence from the United States.

> On the 22nd of January Duhamel gave me a chit for the remaining 200,000 francs of the advance and a pat on the back . . . I shook hands with Minnie Danzas, who was translating the book, and went to the cashier's office to get my money. I wrote a new ending the same day, and the next I went down to Old England men's store on Boulevard des Capucines to buy a shirt. After I had bought a shirt to please me, a tan and black checked woolen shirt to go with my brown and black sports jacket and charcoal brown slacks, I stopped in the shoe department and bought an outrageously expensive pair of English-made yellow brogues. I came out of the store walking hard and feeling proud; now I was a French writer and the United States of America could kiss my ass.

The Five Cornered Square was an immediate success in France, winning a French literary prize in 1958, and its reception led Duhamel to give Himes a contract to write eight more detective stories. Chester Himes became not only the first African American to write for a French audience and live off the royalties paid by French publishers, but also the first major African American detective novelist. He would continue to explore this literary genre, eventu-ally producing classics like *Cotton Comes to Harlem* and *Blind Man with a Pistol*. It was one more aspect of the absurdity of black American life, no doubt richly appreciated by Himes himself, that an African American had to come to Paris in order to take part in a tradition of American popular culture.

Richard Wright, James Baldwin, and Chester Himes dominated the African American literary world in postwar Paris, but they were not the only black American writers to live in the French capital during these years. William Gardner Smith left his native Philadelphia for Paris in 1951, spending most of the decade there. With the encouragement of Richard Wright, Smith settled easily into the African American community on the Left Bank, working as a reporter for the French news service Agence France-Presse and writing several essays and a novel, *South Street*.

Frank Yerby, the prolific author of historical romances like *The Foxes of Harrow*, also came to Paris in the early 1950s. One of the very few black writers to earn a decent living from the profits of his novels, Yerby came to France in 1952, and met various members of the African American literary community in Paris. Unlike Smith, Yerby chose not to stay in Paris, instead following the path laid by Claude McKay a generation earlier for Provence, where he spent the next four years before settling permanently in Spain.

E. Franklin Frazier, the leading black sociologist, lived in Paris from 1951 to 1953, working as a researcher at UNESCO. There he wrote his celebrated study of America's black elite, *Black Bourgeoisie*, often working at café tables in the best Parisian tradition. The book was published in France in 1955, two years before it came out in the United States. The fact that such a landmark work of African American social thought was written and published in Paris underlined the greater level of opportunities offered to black Americans by the French capital.

The members of the African American community in postwar Paris were tightly connected by numerous affinities, but that did not mean that they always loved each other. As in any small community, people jostled for recognition, misunderstandings erupted into quarrels, and differences of opinion degenerated into enduring hostilities. The feud between Richard Wright and James Baldwin was of course the most famous instance of this kind of conflict. But another example was the so-called Richard Gibson affair. Like William Gardner Smith, Gibson was a black American who had found work with Agence France-Presse. In 1956, Ollie Harrington had let Gibson use his apartment while Harrington went on vacation, but Gibson had refused to give it back when Harrington returned to Paris. This disagreement precipitated two fights, one a shouting match at the Café Tournon, one a physical brawl at the apartment, in which Harrington beat up Gibson but failed to oust him from his lodgings. A year later Gibson retaliated by sending letters ostensibly written and signed by Harrington to *Time* magazine and the London *Observer*. In these letters, "Harrington" warmly embraced the armed struggle of the Algerian independence movement against France, a political position that could easily have resulted in Harrington's expulsion from the country. Exposed by Harrington and Richard Wright, Gibson lost his job at Agence France-Presse and was himself forced to return to America instead.

The Richard Gibson affair cast a pall over the black community of the Left Bank because it seemed to be more than a simple question of personal revenge. Rumors quickly spread that Gibson had been a CIA agent who, with his allegations of pro-Algerian sympathy, was trying to destroy a community that had been highly critical of American policy and the United States in general. These fears were reinforced by a *Time* article in 1958, "Amid the Alien Corn," which falsely attributed to Richard Wright remarks attacking American racism. Wright had not in fact granted an interview to *Time,* and one of its Paris reporters later told him the remarks had been intended to discredit him and black expatriates as a whole. These two incidents not only reinforced the belief that white America viewed blacks in Paris as subversives and traitors, but more chillingly made it more difficult for the habitués of the Left Bank to trust one another. Whispers abounded at the Tournon and the Monaco, as the cozy solidarity of expatriate life was challenged by the suspicion and paranoia of political exile.

None of these tensions gainsaid the importance of community to African American life in postwar Paris. The essence of community is not so much mutual affection as mutual interaction; you may not love your neighbors, but your life is interwoven with theirs in many different ways. Judged by this standard, black writers in the 1950s Left Bank formed a vibrant and creative community, one that supported its members but at the same time gave them the freedom to explore wider horizons in Paris and throughout the world. Chester Himes may have held himself apart from it, and James Baldwin at times even denied its existence, but they nonetheless both relied on others within this group and in turn furnished aid to those younger and less experienced in the ways of exile than themselves. Black writers formed the most cohesive group of Americans seen in Paris since the days of Fitzgerald and Hemingway, and their lives in exile confirmed the continued importance of the French capital for those literary talents seeking an alternative to life in the United States. In the cafés and hotels of the Left Bank, these intellectuals learned both to reaffirm and transcend their identity as African Americans, becoming ultimately proud black citizens of the world.

NEW PERSPECTIVES
ON RACE

THE YEARS from 1960 to the mid-1970s represented an important new era in the history of African Americans in Paris. Neatly bounded by the death of Richard Wright in 1960, on the one hand, and Josephine Baker in 1975, on the other, it was an age of conclusions and transitions. This fifteen-year period brought two significant changes to black expatriate life in the French capital. Up until this time, African American life in Paris had been essentially a product of the two world wars. By the 1960s, in contrast, the age of great conflicts had become a distant memory. Paris remained as glamorous as ever, but its excitement and beauty now seemed more a matter of course, rather than a dramatic counterpoint to the horrors of war and racism. To a certain extent, the 1960s resembled the 1930s; blacks who had come to Paris after the wars had by this point become established in the city, gradually developing a new identity as Parisians rather than expatriates. This evolution was much more profound in the 1960s, however, without a war to cut it short. African Americans had more opportunities to get used to the city, to develop institutions and traditions that would anchor the lives of veterans and facilitate the integration of newcomers. During the 1960s and early 1970s, therefore, the black American community in Paris had the chance to ripen and mature in a way that the dramas of the twentieth century had up to that point prevented.

At the same time, the 1960s brought a reevaluation by black expatriates of the broader significance of their Parisian exile, centering around new perspectives on race. In part, growing familiarity with the French capital led some to consider the deeper meaning of their lives; no longer dazzled by the city's novelty, African Americans had the time to develop new attitudes toward life. However, the difference with previous eras lay not so much in the nature of that life itself as in its context; blacks may have gone to the same Parisian cafés and jazz clubs in 1965 as in 1955, but the larger world had changed radically in the intervening years. Two changes in particular were significant. Most important was the new position of blacks in the United States. Thanks to the civil rights movement and subsequent political struggles of the 1950s and 1960s, African American life underwent the most profound shift in a century as the downtrodden black masses of both South and North made "Freedom Now!" not just a slogan but an insistent demand. While racism certainly did not disappear, life in the United States began to offer a range of possibilities to African Americans unimaginable a generation earlier. It also became increasingly clear to black expatriates that Paris was not as immune from racial discrimination as some had believed. Traumas like the Algerian war and hardening attitudes toward nonwhite immigrant workers in France called into question the old color-blind myth. While both transformations began in the 1950s, their full impact was not realized until 1960 and after; the significance of African American exile in Paris would shift radically against this background.

From the introduction of jazz in 1917 until the death of Richard Wright in 1960, the contrast between an overtly racist America and a tolerant and accepting French capital had dominated the life of the black expatriate community in Paris. Even those who did not consciously identify themselves as exiles took advantage of the greater opportunities offered them by Paris than by their own native land. Although it did not disappear, this contrast became much less marked by the late 1960s. In spite of these changes, however, Paris continued to play host to hundreds of blacks from the United States, who for many different reasons found life there preferable to that in America. The urgency of exile may have diminished, but the mutual attraction between Paris and African Americans would endure well into the second half of the twentieth century.

THE GIANTS DEPART

Nothing signaled this transition from one era to another more than the deaths of the two most prominent African Americans to settle in Paris after the Second World War. Sidney Bechet and Richard Wright died within a year and a half of each other, Bechet in May 1959, and Wright in November 1960. Each a leader in his chosen field, the two great men had symbolized the ability of black Americans to achieve renown and respect in the French capital. Moreover, the fact that both died in Paris represented the ultimate confirmation of their decisions to renounce life in the United States and commit themselves to exile. Wright and Bechet had in different ways stood at the center of expatriate life in postwar Paris, and had contributed much to the life of the city in general. With their passing, the golden era of the Latin Quarter and Saint-Germain-des-Prés would fade.

By the late 1950s, Sidney Bechet had settled into a comfortable and fulfilling life as the leading representative of New Orleans jazz in France. He continued to play widely both in Paris and at jazz festivals throughout Europe in 1958, and off the job spent time with his wife, Elisabeth, as well as his mistress, Jacqueline, and their son, Daniel. Yet in spite of his appearance of continued vigor, Bechet was gravely ill. During tours of festivals in southern France and Italy in the summer of 1958, the veteran jazzman came down with what appeared to be bronchitis. His doctor referred him to a specialist, who diagnosed a case of advanced lung cancer, forcing Bechet to cancel the rest of his engagements for several months, including an invitation to the Monterey Jazz Festival. Bechet refused simply to disappear, however. In December, he recorded an album of Christmas music at a Paris studio, and a week later insisted on performing in the annual Jazz Night concert at the city's Salle Wagram. As the writer Kurt Mohr noted, "He managed to be his flawless, explosive self, climaxing with that old standard *Maryland, my Maryland.* Everyone on stage, and a large part of the audience, knew that these were the very last notes that were winding up the career of Sidney Bechet."

The final curtain call came a few months later. He was hospitalized at the beginning of 1959 as his physical condition began to deteriorate rapidly. By April, he was clearly beyond repair, and his doctors allowed him to spend his final days at home in Garches with Jacqueline and Daniel, where he died on his sixty-second birthday, May 14, 1959. Five days later, more than three thousand relatives, friends, and admirers, including Claude Luter and Arthur Briggs, attended Bechet's funeral at Garches's Saint Louis church to pay homage to the great musician one last time. Tributes poured in from colleagues and fans throughout the world, and the Parisian newspaper *Le Figaro* commented, "His disappearance closes a capital chapter in the history of jazz." Blue Note records took out a large memorial advertisement in *Down Beat* magazine. A month later, Noble Sissle and several other musicians sponsored a concert featuring Coleman Hawkins in tribute to Bechet's memory at Carnegie Hall in New York. Death came too early for the master of the soprano sax, yet few could doubt that his life had ended on a triumphant note.

In contrast, the final days of Richard Wright were agonized and conflicted, so that his death seemed more tragic than graceful. For Wright, the early 1950s had been a glorious period of promise, in which he reveled in the egalitarianism and cosmopolitan vistas of the French capital, but the late 1950s brought numerous disappointments. He remained productive during the last years of his life, writing both fiction and social commentary, but his efforts met with an increasingly hostile audience in the United States. Much of the bad press was clearly political; many in America's white literary establishment were outraged that a black writer who had been granted so many opportunities should choose exile in Paris, using it as a forum from which to criticize American racism. For example, while the African American papers praised *White Man, Listen!* warmly, many white American reviewers condemned it as strident and out of touch with changing racial conditions in the United States.

Parallel to his growing alienation from the literary community in America, Richard Wright became more and more isolated from other expatriates. The Richard Gibson affair and *Time* magazine's misquotation of Wright in 1958 had made Wright suspicious of other black Americans in Paris, fearing their manipulation by the CIA or other U.S. government agencies. He was well aware that spies working for the American embassy had infiltrated the French-American Fellowship and had a presence at the Café Tournon, and he commented to Ollie Harrington, "Do you know why the cafes in the Quarter are crowded up 'till the last minute. . . . it's because all those CIA informers can't leave until the one customer who ain't an agent leaves with the lady agent he thinks he picked up." As Harrington noted in his essay "The Mysterious Death of Richard Wright," "From that time [1956] Wright seemed obsessed with the idea that the FBI and the CIA were running amuck in Paris. He was thoroughly convinced that Blacks were special targets of their cloak and dagger activities."

Such fears were not entirely unfounded; at one point a check of Wright's apartment found several electronic bugs. Yet the resulting atmosphere of suspicion doomed the expansive community that Wright had created when he first came to Paris. He remained estranged from James Baldwin, as Baldwin's fame and recognition grew. He had also fallen out with Chester Himes in 1957. That year Himes wrote his short novel, *A Case of Rape,* a classic *roman à clef* about black expatriate life in Paris. The book included an unflattering and thinly veiled portrait of Richard Wright: although Himes's characterization was not completely unsympathetic, portraying a man "feverish with a desire for both personal and creative freedom," it nonetheless depicted Wright as petty, egotistical, paranoid, and ultimately ineffective. "He was also hailed by the rightist press and literary circles in France as the great genius of his race. It was not until his usefulness had passed and he had been dropped that he fully understood his position as a political figure. . . . he had been used by the French, first, to illustrate their freedom from racial bias and preconceptions and, secondly, to focus public attention on America's brutal persecution of its Negro minority." Conflicts over Willa Trierweiler also cooled the friendship of the two writers. For various reasons, they had little to say to each other in the last years of Wright's life.

This mood of isolation, suspicion, and bitterness formed the emotional context for Richard Wright's final novel, *Island of Hallucinations*. Wright worked intensely on this book during the last two years of his life, but it remained unfinished and unpublished. His only novel set in Paris, *Island* explores the life of African American expatriates as the author himself had known it. Many of Wright's acquaintances take on composite fictional form, often unflattering: James Baldwin is the character Mechanical, the homosexual grandson of a hangman who commits suicide by jumping off Notre-Dame cathedral. At one level, the novel is literary revenge. The broader theme, however, is one of disenchantment with exile. Paris appears as a fantastic, often debauched city, full of prostitutes and criminals. As Michel Fabre has argued, "The primary question explored in 'Island of Hallucinations' was not, in Wright's opinion, that of how the black expatriates practiced their little games of espionage or indulged in petty quarrels, but rather why their exile, which was generally a liberation, did not change their lives, which continued at best like a daydream and at the worst like an obsessive nightmare." As such, the novel should be considered not as an overview of Richard Wright's life in Paris, but rather an insight into his troubled final years.

In 1960, Wright died of a heart attack while hospitalized at the Eugène Gibez clinic in Paris. The great author had been in poor health for some time, having suffered a violent attack of dysentery in the summer of 1959 which kept him in a weakened state for several months. He had largely recovered by the beginning of 1960, but renewed intestinal problems prevented him from regaining his health completely. In early November, Richard Wright came down with a case of the flu that laid him low for two weeks. He then checked into the Gibez clinic for further examinations and monitoring on November 26, and over the next two days his health seemed to improve. His sudden death on November 28, at the young age of fifty-two, came as a shock to his family and friends.

Many of those who mourned Wright refused to believe that he died of natural causes, and rumors spread that he had in fact been assassinated by the

American government. The author's ostensibly good health, his death in an obscure clinic, and the absence of an autopsy all fed this idea, not to mention Wright's own belief that agents from the United States were out to get him. Both Ollie Harrington and Chester Himes, for example, thought that Wright had been murdered. Harrington once stated, "I've never met a Black person who did *not* believe that Richard Wright was done in." According to one theory, Wright had been visited in the Gibez clinic by a mysterious woman of Hungarian refugee origin, who had injected him with a drug that had caused his heart attack, then disappeared, never to be seen again. Both Michel Fabre and, more recently, James Campbell have rejected this suspicion as unlikely if not impossible, pointing to a lack of evidence and arguing that Wright simply did not pose enough of a threat to American policymakers to warrant his execution.

Such conclusions are well founded, leading inexorably to the belief that Richard Wright's untimely death was tragic but natural. Nonetheless, the idea of assassination, while not literally true, retains a metaphoric importance. Wright was an outspoken black man who increasingly devoted his public persona to combating American racism. To do so by rejecting America for exile in Paris, and choosing to place his grievances before the court of world opinion, especially when the civil rights movement at long last promised to bring an end to bigotry at home, was extremely daring. Moreover, to place America's racial dilemmas in an international political context at the height of the cold war constituted for many an unforgivable sin. In an era of international relations seemingly based on paranoia, Richard Wright's suspicions are not so hard to understand. Harshly criticized by many in the United States and the subject of surveillance by government agencies, it is not surprising that many of Wright's friends concluded that his sudden death was unnatural. In a sense, Wright's demise foreshadowed the very real assassinations of Medgar Evers, Malcolm X, and Martin Luther King later in the decade. The myth of Wright's assassination represented a logical conclusion to an increasingly politicized life of exile. In criticizing America from Paris, Wright had crossed the Rubicon.

The deaths of Sidney Bechet and Richard Wright deprived Paris of two of its most eloquent African American voices, and symbolized the passing of a luminous era. Parisians and foreign tourists still listened to jazz in Saint-Germain-des-Prés nightclubs, but the area had lost its dominance in this field as other *boîtes* opened throughout the city. The special synthesis of jazz, existentialism, and popular culture symbolized by the *rats* of Saint-Germain-des-Prés had long since passed, and its leading exponent, Boris Vian, died a month after Bechet. Similarly, the unique constellation of literary talent that Richard Wright almost single-handedly brought to Paris in the early 1950s lost much of its cohesion after his death. In 1961, Ollie Harrington left Paris for East Berlin, having been offered a contract to illustrate a new series of books by a local publisher. He was there when the Berlin Wall went up and remained in Germany until his death several decades later. Harrington had been Richard Wright's closest friend in Paris as well as one of the key figures in the black expatriate community, and his permanent departure from the city further underlined the end of a singular age.

Still, by 1960 the African American community in Paris had a rich history that went back several decades, and it would have taken more than the deaths of two individuals, even as illustrious as Wright and Bechet, to bring an end to it. Musicians like Arthur Briggs, Bill Coleman, and Kenny Clarke continued to prosper in the Latin Quarter, Saint-Germain-des-Prés, and other neighborhoods during the 1960s, ensuring the ongoing presence of African American jazz in the city. Artists like Beauford Delaney and Larry Potter still lived and worked on the Left Bank. And even though black writers were not so interconnected as during the 1950s, several former members of Richard Wright's circle could still be found in the cafés and nightclubs of the Latin Quarter. Both Wright's wife, Ellen, and their daughter Julia chose to stay in the French capital; now a young woman, Julia had decided to transfer her studies from Cambridge University to the Sorbonne shortly before her father's death in order to be closer to him, and afterward remained in Paris. William Gardner Smith still worked as a journalist at Agence France-Presse, and Leroy Haynes's restaurant continued to dish out soul food and conversation to black expatriates, foreign tourists, and curious Parisians.

The 1960s introduced a new level of maturity, a more settled quality, to black American life in Paris. While the city would continue to attract the young and adventurous, it now also featured many African Americans who had been there for years. Many of those who had come in the late 1940s and 1950s were now entering middle age, and had gradually learned that life in Paris consisted not just of long nights in jazz clubs or endless café discussions, but also concerns about finding decent dwellings, seeking the best schools for their children, or developing their careers. For people like Beauford Delaney, Kenny Clarke, and Leroy Haynes, Paris remained a wonderful place to live, but ceased to be the dazzling revelation of their youth. The aging process did not represent stagnation, however. As a result of it, the African American community in Paris became more diverse than it had been in the 1950s, including more people in their middle years and more children. Greater familiarity with life in Paris also brought a more nuanced, matter-of-fact perspective on the city, helping to undercut the romantic myths of earlier years. Moreover, during the 1960s some blacks in France developed a broader vision of the expatriate condition, seeing not just Paris, but ultimately the entire world as a place where they could find alternatives to American racism.

The increased stability and rootedness of the postwar African American expatriate community is perhaps best illustrated by the careers of James Baldwin and Chester Himes. Life in the French capital had enabled both to write effectively, bringing them fame and material comfort, if not fortune, by the start of the 1960s. Because of this success, however, both Baldwin and Himes had in a sense transcended their earlier lives in Paris. Both still retained a connection to the city during the new decade, Himes in particular, but their lives were no longer circumscribed by its boundaries. Paris had enabled them to go beyond the limits of America, but now they could expand beyond Paris as well to become citizens of the globe.

Although James Baldwin spent much of the 1960s in Paris, he never settled there for long, developing a very different life than he had in his lean and hungry days a decade earlier. The man who briefly returned to the French capital in 1959 after an absence of two years in the States was a radically different individual in two important respects. James Baldwin had now achieved universal recognition as one of America's leading black writers and spokesmen. During the late 1950s and early 1960s, he published several essays and two landmark books, the collection entitled *Nobody Knows My Name* and the pathbreaking and popular novel *Another Country*. No longer the struggling outsider, Baldwin was now a part of America's literary establishment, one whose opinions on race relations and black literature were eagerly solicited and read.

At the same time, Baldwin had embraced the civil rights movement, becoming a political activist for the first time in his life. On returning to the United States in 1957, he had traveled to the South to witness the drama unfolding there, and was deeply moved, after meeting Martin Luther King in Montgomery, by the great man's commitment to racial justice and nonviolence. Although living mainly in New York, Baldwin made several trips to the South, both as an observer of the civil rights struggles and increasingly as a participant. He also traveled throughout America, speaking out against racism and its victimization of his people. Far from sitting on the sidelines of the movement in Europe, he now plunged headlong into it.

Baldwin's writing during these years reflected his new commitment to political engagement *within* the United States. Although its characters include both a Frenchman and an American former expatriate, *Another Country* is set almost entirely in New York. The novel explores racial tensions between blacks and whites in the Bohemian circles of the American metropolis, portraying the attempts of lovers, black and white, gay and straight, to transcend the barriers that divide them. Although Paris appears as a place where such transcendence is possible, the novel makes it clear that escape abroad cannot substitute for the honest, painful confrontations necessary to overcome intolerance. The majority of the essays collected in *Nobody Knows My Name* deal with racism and the condition of blacks in the United States. In the first essay, "The Discovery of What It Means to Be an American," Baldwin argues that his Parisian sojourn led him to embrace his own national identity. Several others deal with his perceptions of the South and the civil rights movement, including a sharp attack on William Faulkner. The essay that deals most with Baldwin's Paris days is "Alas, Poor Richard," his eulogy of Richard Wright. In it, Baldwin regrets his break with Wright, yet reaffirms the reasons for his disagreement with his mentor.

The final contrast between the two great black authors, Richard Wright dying in Paris and James Baldwin returning to America to join the struggle for civil rights, illustrated the width of the chasm between them. There were many reasons for their famous feud, including ideological differences, Baldwin's deep-seated conflicts about father figures, and the old tradition that prompted young writers and intellectuals to establish their reputations by attacking their predecessors. Yet perspectives on Paris and the desirability of exile played a key role in the break, as well as shaping the reactions to Wright and Baldwin in both France and America. If the French, especially the French literary Left, used Wright as a symbol of American racism and iniquity in general, the American literary establishment used Baldwin to attack Wright and uphold a more hopeful vision of the United States. At the same time, the big story in American race relations was the civil rights movement, and it was Baldwin, not Wright, who could claim a firsthand knowledge of contemporary events in the South. Richard Wright's untimely passing placed the conflict in the starkest possible terms: death in Paris or life in America.

Paris remained the scene of many youthful triumphs, but James Baldwin, now in his late thirties, was no longer young, and his relationship to the city began to take on a nostalgic quality. Far from a place where he could observe and write undisturbed, the city now represented merely another locale where he was well known and in demand. As it had for Romare Bearden, the French capital became a place for Baldwin to enjoy life and old friends, but not to create. Since Paris no longer offered either an exotic isolation that inspired his literary efforts, or the most useful venue for involvement in the struggles of black people, Baldwin's stays tended to be brief, more like visits than renewals of residency. His trip there in 1959 established and typified this pattern. Feeling in need of some respite from his growing visibility in New York, Baldwin obtained an advance from his publisher and sailed to France in July. He spent a month at Beauford Delaney's Clamart studio, then moved into an apartment of his own in Saint-Germain-des-Prés. Although James Baldwin worked productively during these months, writing several essays, he found himself inundated by old and new friends and lovers. He left Paris to return to New York in January 1960; over the next few years he would travel widely, to Africa, Israel, and Istanbul, in search of the solitude and inspiration that Paris had once offered him but that his own celebrity and success had destroyed.

Nonetheless, the French capital retained a special place in his heart. In 1965, he began negotiations to buy an apartment in Paris, a process that took years, involving considerable time, effort, and money. He was in Paris that year when his play *The Amen Corner* opened to glowing reviews from Parisian critics, and went on to enjoy a much more successful run than it had had in New York. Written in 1953, the play depicts life in the kind of Harlem storefront church so central to Baldwin's childhood, condemning the narrow-minded religious intolerance exemplified by his stepfather. By the late 1960s, James Baldwin had achieved the kind of renown in Paris enjoyed by Richard Wright a decade earlier; as one friend noted, "In France he had become a giant figure, a bigger celebrity than a movie star, a man generally admired."

At the end of 1970, health problems led him to convalesce in the medieval village of Saint-Paul-de-Vence just inland from the bustling Riviera. Baldwin fell in love with the beauty and tranquility of the community and bought a large ramshackle farmhouse on ten acres of land, complete with a view of the Mediterranean in the distance. Baldwin had finally found a place where his soul could rest, and Saint-Paul would serve as his home base for the rest of his days. The villa represented the conclusion of James Baldwin's transformation from poor, agonized child of the Harlem streets to a man of property and prestige in France, and no place had played a greater role in that metamorphosis than Paris.

Whereas both Richard Wright and James Baldwin addressed the choice between Paris and America as a fundamental conflict, Chester Himes increasingly left both alternatives behind in the 1960s. Unlike Wright, Himes felt no essential sympathy for or loyalty to the French; unlike Baldwin, he felt no moral or artistic imperative to resume residency in the United States. By the beginning of the decade, Himes had also achieved a measure of fame and financial security as a writer living abroad, and Paris remained his home during the decade. Yet Himes also traveled widely in those years, never settling down in the city in the manner of Richard Wright, Beauford Delaney, or Kenny Clarke. He made extended trips to France, Europe, and also Mexico, and returned frequently (albeit usually briefly) to the United States. In 1960, Himes began living with Lesley Packard in her apartment in the Latin Quarter's rue de la Harpe, staying there while in Paris for the next several years. In 1964, the couple moved into a flat near the enchanting Place de Fürstemberg, and later rented other lodgings in the Left Bank. Himes noted, "That was what we most disliked about Paris: we didn't have a permanent home there like Herbert Gentry and Ollie Harrington and it kept us moving. Yves Malartic once said about me, I was like a snail with my home on my back."

Himes maintained his posture both as an expatriate and a man on the margins of Parisian society; yet at the same time he experienced a great deal of success and acceptance. In 1963, his novel *A Case of Rape* was published in Paris by a small French press. The only one of his novels set in France, the book brought Himes much notoriety with its unsentimental view of French racial mores. *A Case of Rape* prompted hostile reactions from many Parisian critics who labeled the book anti-French. It tells the story of four African American men in Paris wrongfully convicted by a French court of raping a white woman. A fascinating exploration of the politics of justice, Himes's novel expressed his own lack of faith in the racial tolerance of the French (or, for that matter, any whites). Chester Himes had never believed in the myth of color-blind France, but his novel's theme of French bigotry also reflected a more general disenchantment with French racial attitudes during these years.

Dividing his time between Paris and the south of France for much of the decade, Himes wrote prodigiously, turning out his famous series of nine detective novels set in Harlem. All but one was published originally in France. They include *A Rage in Harlem* (1964), *The Real Cool Killers* (1966), *All Shot Up* (1966), *The Heat's On* (1967), *Run, Man, Run* (1968), and *Blind Man with a Pistol* (1969). Life in France thus enabled Chester Himes to become a true American original, a black mystery writer who pioneered a genre only recently resumed by writers like Walter Mosley. Featuring two black New York Police Department detectives, Coffin Ed Johnson and Grave Digger Jones, as their intrepid heroes, Himes's thrillers forcefully depict the violent underbelly of Harlem, ranging from bars to back alleys to storefront churches. Like Mosley after him, Himes presents a gritty, unsentimental portrait of black life, one that largely abstained from racial polemics yet showed how Harlemites were constrained by the subordinate position of blacks in American society. Himes's violent, realistic novels displeased many blacks who criticized him (like Claude McKay a generation earlier) for writing lurid tales to cater to white stereotypes. His experiences in the 1950s had gradually taught him to sublimate his own racial pain into an art form, laying the base for his creative flowering during the 1960s.

This literary success, in both France and the United States, also brought increased recognition. Himes commented in his autobiography that "I had become a celebrity. Thousands of bums in the Latin Quarter swamped down on our apartment to see me." When he and Lesley Packard moved to Aix-en-Provence in 1966, local real estate agents vied to sell him luxurious villas, assuming (quite erroneously) that such a famous author must also be quite wealthy. In particular, the publication of *A Case of Rape* brought Chester Himes fame almost overnight.

> I went back to Paris and found *Une Affaire de Viol* was still making bubbles. My name had become a byword. It seemed as if everyone in Paris came to my house. I forgot about my detective stories. I forgot about the film I had been so anxious to make the year before. I forgot about the reportage that Présence Africaine and *Die Welt* were publishing. I thought only about all the snubs and injustices I had suffered all of my years abroad. At last I felt recognized. I felt I had become more famous in Paris than any black American who had ever lived. Maybe I was right.

Ah, the sweet, intoxicating smell of success.

For all his recognition and renown, Himes still felt and reacted like an outsider. His writings frequently displeased both whites and blacks, and throughout his career Himes showed himself more than willing to criticize people of all races. He therefore often felt alienated from friends and associates, happiest in the solitude of a provincial village. A trip to Stockholm in 1965 caused him to miss the Paris funeral of Larry Potter. Chester Himes responded by lamenting, "Larry was one of the most popular blacks in Paris and from what I learned afterwards people were struggling to get into the church, but no one invited me though I wanted to go. That made me know more than anything else that I was not very popular with the black community."

Eventually Himes, like Baldwin, chose to settle down permanently in the countryside. In 1970, he and Lesley left Paris for good, moving into a comfortable villa in the small town of Moraira on Spain's sun-kissed Costa Blanca. He wrote no more novels, but worked on the two volumes of his autobiography, the first of which was published in 1972. While under no illusions about

Spain, which he called a racist country, Himes enjoyed the peace and quiet of his small village, frequently receiving visiting writers and other intellectuals. He stayed there, only returning to Paris for short visits, until his death in 1984. Paris had given him the impetus to write, but in Spain he finally found balm for his tormented soul.

After 1960, the three African American writers who symbolized Parisian expatriate life in the postwar era had left Paris behind: Richard Wright had died, and Chester Himes and James Baldwin had moved out of the country. Their absence deprived the city's black American community of some of the illustrious closeness it had known during the 1950s. No longer could one simply drop by the Tournon or the Monaco and meet its patrons for the price of a cup of coffee. More significant, Paris could no longer claim to be the literary capital of black America; African American literary expression, like African American political protest, anchored itself firmly in the United States during the new decade. African Americans in Paris became a broader, more diverse group that better represented black American life as a whole. A new generation of black expatriates came to France in the 1960s, both attracted and contributing to a vibrant American community far from home.

A NEW BLACK COMMUNITY

No one bridged these two generations more fully than William Gardner Smith. A writer and journalist, he had served in the U.S. Army just after the Second World War, when he was stationed with the American occupation forces in Germany. In 1951, he moved to Paris, drawn like so many others by the example and encouragement of Richard Wright, and soon became a fixture in the expatriate community of the Latin Quarter. In keeping with the times, he considered himself an exile from racism and McCarthyite political repression, and saw a refuge in the French capital. After spending a few years living a marginal existence in cheap hotels, Smith secured a position in 1954 with Agence France-Presse, the leading French news agency, and would work for the company for nearly his entire life. Smith traveled briefly back to America in 1967, but Paris was now his home. He ended his days in the Parisian suburb of Thiais, where he died of cancer in November 1974, at the age of fifty-seven.

The life of William Gardner Smith in Paris encapsulates many of the themes common to black expatriate life in the French capital after the war. After years of scraping by, he obtained the kind of job usually out of reach for blacks in the United States. His early days in the city were characterized by cheap hotels, long sessions at cafés, numerous sexual involvements, and other traits of Bohemia, but Smith gradually settled down into a relatively bourgeois existence.

For much of the 1950s he lived with a woman named Musy Hafner; at one point the couple resided in the Tournon hotel in a room so dilapidated that the owner had to prop up the ceiling to keep it from collapsing. In 1961, Smith married Solange Jovey, a young Frenchwoman he met in a Left Bank hotel, and the couple moved into a three-room apartment in the working-class neighborhood of Belleville. William and Solange spent nine years together, producing two children, before he divorced her in 1970 to marry Ira Reuben, a Jewish woman of Anglo-Indian descent working at the Indian embassy in Paris, with whom he spent his final years.

The two novels Smith wrote in Paris reflect not only his own personal evolution, but also key themes of the black expatriate experience in France during the 1950s and 1960s. *South Street* (1954) takes place entirely in the black ghetto of South Philadelphia, where the author had grown up, and explores the many subtle ways in which poverty and racism doomed the lives of African Americans. In a sense, the novel represented a sort of personal farewell to America, enabling Smith to confront and overcome the traumas of his own upbringing. Whereas one of its main characters dreams of escaping to Canada, Smith had realized that dream in his own life in Paris. In contrast, William Smith's next and final novel, *The Stone Face* (1963), is set entirely in the French capital. A highly autobiographical story, it gives a vivid portrait of black expatriate life in the 1950s, portraying both its attractions and its disillusionments. *South Street* not only constituted a rejection of America, but it helped establish Smith as a writer by earning him royalties the same year Agence France-Presse hired him as an editor. *The Stone Face* reflected a new view of the city, typical of Smith and younger black expatriates, in which the author's initial romanticism was tempered by a more balanced assessment of its problems and prospects. The book ends with the hero's departure from Paris, leaving open, however, the possibility of return.

This ambivalence likely arose from Smith's own divided feelings about life in Paris during the 1960s. He left France twice in that decade, first to live in Ghana from 1964 to 1966, then to return briefly to America, for the first time in sixteen years, during the summer of 1967. Both times, however, Smith came back to Paris, drawn by his love for the city, his family and friends awaiting him, and by his skepticism about alternatives elsewhere. His attachment to the French capital spoke for that of many African Americans who had come there in the aftermath of the Second World War and stayed on. Most had come as young people (Chester Himes, who settled in France at the age of forty-four, was an exception), and by the mid-1960s had crossed over into middle age. In the 1950s, Paris provided the opportunity to sow one's wild oats and hurl defiance at American racism; a decade later it had become for those who stayed simply their home. As Arthur Briggs, Gene Bullard, and others discovered during the 1930s, even in Paris, people with families, children, and steady jobs tend to come home earlier at night. Paris remained for them a wonderful place to live, and if they occasionally dreamed of far horizons, years of accumulated habits sufficed to keep many anchored to the banks of the Seine.

As William Gardner Smith symbolized continuity among writers in Paris, so did figures like Kenny Clarke and Art Simmons represent it among musicians. The new decade found Clarke easing gracefully into middle age, a dapper, dark-skinned man with a short mustache and a fondness for pipes and tweed jackets. Like Smith, Clarke had become a family man by the 1960s with the birth of his son in 1964. In 1961, he started a new band with the Belgian pianist Francy Boland. A big band in the style of the classic jazz orchestras of the 1930s, the Clarke-Boland ensemble brought together musicians from twelve different countries, including African Americans like the reedmen Johnny Griffin and Nathan Davis, and the pianist Kenny Drew. The band toured widely throughout Europe during the 1960s, recording thirty-seven albums in eleven years. Clarke also continued playing in Parisian nightclubs and worked with many different musicians, including the brilliant pianist Bud Powell in the early 1960s. All in all, during these years Clarke continued to enjoy life in Paris very much and showed no inclination to return home. His first visit back to the States did not come until 1972, after a sixteen-year absence, and then he stayed only a few days. Not until 1979 did he return for a longer time, going back home triumphantly to teach jazz for a semester as a visiting professor at the University of Pittsburgh. Like William Gardner Smith, he found that Paris had become his home.

The pianist Art Simmons also chose to remain in Paris after 1960, becoming one of the African American community's central figures during the new decade. Described by one writer as "a man of medium build with *café au lait* skin, prominent cheekbones, [and] an infectious laugh," Simmons had come to Europe in 1946 as a member of the U.S. Army's Special Service Band stationed in occupied Germany. He then moved on to Paris in 1949 to study, first at the Paris Conservatory for a year, then at the Ecole Normale for three. By the early 1950s, Simmons was playing the piano solo or with other musicians at the city's various jazz clubs, and spending time off relaxing with others at cafés like the Tournon. At times he performed with the veteran French bassist Pierre Michelot and Don Byas at the Ringside, or accompanied Honey Johnson at Herbert Gentry's Club Galerie in Montparnasse, enjoying his expatriate life to the fullest. Talking with Wright, Baldwin, Harrington, Smith, Gordon Heath, Larry Potter, and others at the Tournon, Simmons provided an example of the benefits of escape from the United States: "I know a cat from the States who was wearing glasses when he arrived here. Had been wearing glasses for years in the States. After six months in Paris, he was so relaxed psychologically that he took the glasses off and suddenly discovered he didn't need them. He had never really needed them from a medical point of view. Just all that tension had affected his eyes."

By the 1960s, Art Simmons was a fixture in Parisian jazz circles. He performed regularly during the early years of the decade at the Mars Club, a popular new nightspot on the Right Bank. There he frequently alternated with Aaron Bridgers, a pianist who had come to Paris after the war to work for the United Nations and stayed on as a musician. Simmons also worked at the Living Room, a French-owned club located off the Champs-Elysées on the rue du Colisée which soon became his major venue in the city, and a sort of home away from home, not only for him, but for the black community in general. Top-notch musicians like Myriam Makeba, Archie Shepp, Milt Jackson, and Lionel Hampton appeared there during their visits to the French capital. But Art Simmons, playing alone or with his trio, was its main attraction.

Like Bricktop before him, Art Simmons presided at the Living Room over a place that was not just a nightclub, but a community center for African Americans in the French capital. The pianist kept a file of addresses of African Americans in Paris, so that people in search of someone there would often consult him for assistance.

Individuals like William Gardner Smith, Kenny Clarke, and Art Simmons soon found themselves regarded as elder statesmen in the Parisian African American community, by virtue of their experience and their success in making it in Paris. They also found themselves in a minority as a new generation of blacks arrived, either on short visits or, more rarely, permanently. These newcomers, unlike the expatriates who had arrived by circumstance in the aftermath of the world wars, often came with more deliberate intentions. Those who came to Paris in the 1960s were the first generation to arrive in jet planes, not ships, cutting the transit time down from over a week to less than a day. Air travel not only made getting to France easier, but it significantly lessened the sense of isolation from people and events back home; if need be, one could leave Orly Airport in the morning and be back in New York in time for dinner. Now a trip across the Atlantic was more likely to be part of a mundane tourist itinerary than a voyage from one world to another. Some initially came to Paris as tourists, liked what they saw, and tucked away their return tickets. By 1960, the mythic image of the black American expatriate in Paris was firmly established, drawing people who wished to walk down a path already well trodden.

Moreover, Paris had become a different place from the city celebrated by Bricktop or even Richard Wright. For France, as for the United States, the 1960s represented a period of unprecedented economic prosperity and growth, increasingly giving its citizens opportunities to indulge in the same kind of consumer goods Americans had enjoyed for years. Paris became more chic and upscale, losing some of the tumbledown charm remarked upon by American tourists in earlier years. André Malraux, the minister of culture under de Gaulle, launched a massive project to clean up and restore many of the city's monuments, and even indoor plumbing and American-style toilets were now becoming common. But such new affluence had its price: unlike the postwar years, Paris now became quite expensive, and holders of U.S. dollars could no longer rejoice in their ability to buy anything they wanted for a song. The city might still be the stuff of dreams, but in the 1960s dreams did not come cheap. As a result, for black Americans who came to Paris in those years, just getting by sometimes posed more of a challenge than it had before.

In spite of these difficulties, however, African Americans maintained a presence in Paris during the 1960s and 1970s. In fact, the number of black expatriates increased; whereas Richard Wright estimated the population at roughly five hundred in the early 1950s, various reports counted approximately 1,500 black Americans living in the French capital a decade later. As in earlier years, these Americans abroad came from many different walks of life, and had come to Paris for a number of reasons. Although a few followed their careers to the city, the majority chose Paris as a refuge from the United States, one offering both racial tolerance and a more genial way of life. Some found that life in Paris, far from offering wealth and fame, at times entailed sacrifices and a lower standard of living than that available in America. While few in Paris experienced the dire poverty so much a part of the black condition back home, nonetheless during the 1960s the success of a Josephine Baker or a James Baldwin was clearly the exception, not the rule. As a study of African American expatriates published in 1968 observed,

> There is a Paris most American visitors never see. . . . It is the world of those
> expatriates, black and white, who are employing every scheme, dodge and

hustle known to Western man to survive in the City of Light. . . . It is a daily round of jagged uncertainties, in which black con men rush from café to snack bar to bistro seeking that action, whatever comes, that will snare enough elusive francs for another meal, a bottle of wine, a thin wedge of insulation against the chill specter of a vagrancy arrest and deportation. They live at the other end of the line from the well-fed opera singers, the respected professors, the coddled GI's. Yet theirs, too, is the realm of the black expatriate.

For example, some African Americans down on their luck would gather around Art Simmons at the Living Room, hoping the generous musician would stand them a drink or even a meal. Simmons treated them so regularly that one State Department employee took to calling them "Art's leeches." The story of the exiled foreigner struggling to survive was an old, old one in Paris, and more than a few blacks who had crossed the Atlantic with visions of glory eventually found themselves in that position. As a minister at the American Church in Paris commented, "They put up a good front of being happy. . . . But the fact of the matter may be that they had no breakfast or lunch, that they haven't showered for a week, and may have only 5 francs in their pocket."

Most African Americans who settled in Paris during these years did not conform to this description. The majority of black expatriates were neither wealthy celebrities nor impoverished hangers-on, but solid, hardworking individuals who for one reason or another found life abroad more to their taste. In addition to musicians and writers, blacks in Paris worked as scientists, insurance salesmen, restaurant owners and employees, fashion models, secretaries, and taxi drivers. Edward Barnett provides a characteristic example of African American expatriate life during the 1960s. A photographer originally from Detroit, Barnett had always loved to travel and first visited Paris in 1960 during a trip through Europe. He stayed in Paris after finding a job selling newspapers, and although he had not intended to become an expatriate, remained there for several years. By 1966, Barnett had established a permanent life in the city, living in a small apartment in Montparnasse, married to Kerstin, a Swedish woman, and working as a free-lance photographer. Although his living conditions had been much better in America, where he'd had a sports car and a much bigger apartment, Barnett remained in France, declaring, "The French tend to leave me alone so I can live my life as I see it."

Not all African Americans in Paris were artists or writers. Cliff Johnson, a biochemist from New Orleans, held a steady job and lived in a four-room apartment with his wife and four children in the countryside outside the French capital. Thirty years old when the *New York Times* interviewed him in 1966 for an article on American expatriates, he had been in France for five years. In 1969, James Browne worked in Paris as a computer engineer for an American company. Thirty-six years old, he lived with his wife, Louise, and their three children in a modern apartment in the Parisian suburb of Bou-logne-Billancourt. The Brownes in particular contradicted the classic image of black expatriates in Paris. A married African American couple, they had come to France for professional reasons and lived in a style not too different from that of middle-class blacks in America. James and Louise Browne lived in Paris for two years, but at the time of their interview they clearly anticipated returning home.

As in earlier years, a variety of institutions brought together African Americans living in the French capital. Jazz clubs like the Living Room and the Mars Club served as important community centers, places where the new-comer from the United States could meet other black Americans and find a little bit of the atmosphere of home. Restaurants also remained central to African American life in Paris. Haynes continued to prosper during the 1960s, so much so that visiting blacks frequently referred to it as "Soulsville in Paris." Buttercup Powell, the wife of Bud Powell, ran a restaurant in the early 1960s called Buttercup's Chicken Shack. Located in Montparnasse, for a few years it also served as a gathering place for blacks from the United States. Like Art Simmons, Mrs. Powell often helped those new to town find rooms, friends, and a sense of belonging in France. One journalist referred to her as "mother confessor to the unemployed, the lovelorn, and the homesick among the 1,500 Negroes" in Paris. Certain cafés at times also attracted an African American presence, such as the Café de Seine near Saint-Germain-des-Prés, or the Café Sélect in Montparnasse.

In contrast to the interwar years, black American social life in Paris did not occur just in black-owned institutions. Most jazz clubs in the city were French-owned, and only soul food restaurants like Haynes continued the tradition of African American entrepreneurialism. Increasingly, blacks from the United States met each other in many different kinds of settings. During the 1960s, institutions organized by the American community in Paris as a whole attracted a significant number of blacks. The growing presence of the United States in the French capital, and the decline of rigid customs of racial segregation at home, enabled African Americans to take advantage of organizations dominated by their white fellow citizens. Many blacks interested in the arts spent time at the American Center in Montparnasse, a gathering place for both Americans and others interested in the contributions of the United States to music, art, dance, and theater. The American Library in Paris also attracted many blacks from the United States. The American military still provided an important space for African Americans in Paris to meet. The NATO offices in Paris brought a small black population from the United States during the early 1960s. African Americans met at the American Legion Hall, near the Champs-Elysées, on Friday nights to socialize. Their growing presence in such multiracial settings reinforced blacks' cosmopolitan sense of community in Paris. At the same time, blacks were open to people of many different backgrounds.

The black expatriate community in Paris remained vibrant and diverse in the second half of the twentieth century, featuring a range of individual talents and interests. Although the cohesion of the Richard Wright circle did not survive his death, those working in the creative arts still played a central role in the collective life of African Americans in the French capital. Black artistic expression had long since ceased to be a novelty in France, and the high cost of living generated by postwar prosperity raised new obstacles to those in search of life on the Left Bank. A new generation of writers, artists, and musicians still came to Paris in the 1960s. The same prosperity both enabled some blacks to accumulate the funds to make the trip, and to survive in France, often on part-time work. The racial climate in the United States might be improving, yet true equality remained a distant vision. Consequently, escaping American racism still provided a key motivation for many black Americans who moved to Paris. Moreover, the city now had an image not just as a color-blind society, but as a place that sheltered an important African American community. The French capital was known far and wide in black America as the home of Josephine Baker and Richard Wright, inspiring many young people to attempt a similar success overseas. By the 1960s, therefore, the concept of the black American in Paris had become a powerful myth in its own right, one whose allure ensured its own continuity.

Although the black expatriate community in the 1960s did not achieve the recognition and fame of a decade earlier, a new generation of African American writers nonetheless made its presence felt in France. One of the most notable was Ted Joans, a musician, painter, and poet, who arrived in Paris in 1960. Originally from Illinois, Joans earned a degree in music from the University of Indiana, then moved to New York, settling into the Bohemian milieu of Greenwich Village. He discovered the philosophy of surrealism while taking courses at the New School for Social Research and concluded (like the negritude poets before him) that this revolutionary approach to art and life constituted an appropriate metaphor for black culture and the black condition. Surrealist concepts soon permeated both his painting and poetry, and in 1960 Joans set off for Paris as the homeland of his new muse.

In France, Ted Joans became a central figure of black expatriate life, and although he has traveled widely, Paris has remained his home down to the present day. Shortly after arriving, he met the patriarch of surrealism, André Breton, who took him under his wing and proclaimed him the only black American surrealist. During the 1960s, Joans wrote prolifically, crafting poetry that both prefigured and represented the artistic, political upsurges of that turbulent decade. A true cultural revolutionary, Ted Joans saw both surrealism and jazz as art forms that broke the mold of status quo complacency, and in his work he sought to bring them together. More than most black expatriates, therefore, he worked consciously and effectively to fuse French and African American artistic forms.

Another black artist whose work defied easy categorizations was the writer and filmmaker Melvin Van Peebles, the father of actor and director Mario Van Peebles. Producer and director of one of the landmark black films of the modern era, *Sweet Sweet Back's Baadaass Song* (1971), Van Peebles settled in France in the early 1960s, financing a shoestring existence in Paris by working haphazardly as a literary critic and cartoonist for French publications. He soon succeeded in getting his own work published; his first book, *A Bear for the F.B.I.*, came out in 1964, followed by his autobiography, *An American in Hell*, a year later. By far his most Parisian work was the collection of vignettes entitled *Le Chinois du XIVe (The Chinese Man of the 14th District)*, published in 1966. The book portrays the lives, hopes, and dreams of a disparate group of people who frequent a café in a working-class neighborhood. A sort of modern *Canterbury Tales*, it represents one of the most authentically French creations of any African American, demonstrating the extent to which black expatriates had become integrated into Parisian café culture.

After publishing that book, Van Peebles turned to his true love, film. He directed his first movie, *The Story of a Three Day Pass* (1967), while living in Paris. The tale of a brief romance between an African American soldier on leave and a young Frenchwoman in Normandy, the film was chosen by the French government as its official entry into the 1968 San Francisco Film Festival. This exposure brought him offers from American studios, prompting Van Peebles to return to the United States at the end of the decade, where he directed his classic satire of American race relations, *Watermelon Man* (1970). As with James Baldwin and Eartha Kitt, exile in Paris had enabled Melvin Van Peebles to write his own ticket back to America.

To a much greater extent than a decade earlier, African American women achieved prominence in Paris during the 1960s. Carlene Polite drew upon the feminist writings of Simone de Beauvoir to examine her own ideas about race and literature while living in the French capital. Like Melvin Van Peebles, she published her first novel in France. Entitled *Les Flagellants* (1966), the book dealt with the trials of an interracial couple trying to find shelter from the storms of American racism. Barbara Chase-Riboud, like Ted Joans and Melvin Van Peebles, has worked in more than one artistic medium. Originally from Philadelphia, Chase studied art as a young woman at the Tyler School of Fine Arts, and went on to earn a master of fine arts degree from Yale University in 1960. In 1961, she came to Paris on a weekend visit from London and never left. There Barbara Chase met and married the French photographer Marc Riboud. The couple set up housekeeping in Paris, and Chase-Riboud has continued to work as an artist. A Parisian gallery sponsored an exhibit of her drawings in 1966, and since then her work, primarily sculpture, has been featured at other galleries and art museums throughout Europe and America. Barbara Chase-Riboud has also fashioned a literary career for herself, having published both novels and poetry. Her first collection of poems, *From Memphis to Peking*, appeared in 1974, and in 1981 her novel *La Virginienne*, based on the life of Thomas Jefferson's black mistress Sally Hemings, was published in France.

Paris remained a magnet for black artists after 1960. Both Beauford Delaney and Larry Potter called the city home until their deaths there in 1973 and 1966, respectively. Parisian galleries prominently displayed their works, and the Galerie Lambert staged a major one-man show devoted to Delaney in 1965. This new acceptance of African Americans by the Paris art establishment signaled both a growing appreciation of abstract expressionism, and the results of years of hard work in France by black artists, rather than a recognition of their work as a specifically black art form. Newcomers included Bob Thompson, a painter from Kentucky who journeyed to Paris in 1961 to study on a Gutman fellowship, then settled into a studio in Montparnasse. He stayed in Paris for two years, then traveled around Europe before dying in Rome at the tragically young age of twenty-nine. Although originally from Texas, Bill Hutson lived and worked for years in the San Francisco area, where he developed his skills as a painter and photographer. He lived overseas for fourteen years from 1963 to 1977, moving first to Amsterdam, then to Paris in 1965, before returning to America to take up residence in New York. While in France, he participated actively in the Parisian art world, exhibiting his own works at the Galerie Cazenave in 1968. Sam Middleton lived in Amsterdam for most of the 1960s, but from 1961 to 1963 he kept a studio across the street from the Montparnasse cemetery and maintained close contacts with black artists. Of him, Ted Joans has written, "Sam Middleton was, once-upon-a-time, the (and I do mean THE) Afro-American *numero uno* modern artist in Europe."

African American arts as a whole had begun to enjoy greater acceptance and celebrity. In 1965, the American government sponsored a conference in Paris on black American literature. The first of its kind ever held in France, the conference starred Langston Hughes, who had been dreaming about settling in Paris for years, as well as the young novelists Paule Marshall and William Melvin Kelley. In 1969, the American Center in Paris sponsored a showing of works by Bill Hutson, Ed Clark, and Sam Middleton called "3 Noirs USA." Both were staged by American organizations in Paris, who in doing so acknowledged the contributions made by blacks to the culture of the United States. During the angry expatriate years such events would have been hard to imagine; now they signaled a new day for American race relations on both sides of the Atlantic.

Although the postwar symbiosis of jazz and existentialism now lived only in memory, the French capital retained its status as one of the jazz centers of Europe. No musical revolution comparable to the introduction of bebop in the late 1940s took place among Parisian jazz musicians. Instead, performers felt free to adopt a variety of musical styles, from traditional New Orleans sounds to the new experiments in "free jazz" pioneered by Ornette Coleman and Don Cherry in New York during the early 1960s. Some of the clubs from the postwar years, notably the Club Saint-Germain and the Trois Mailletz, continued to draw the crowds during the new era, supplemented by newer spots like the Blue Note, the Chat Qui Pêche, the Mars Club, and the Caveau de la Huchette. These clubs continued to provide a venue for both veteran African American musicians and newcomers. The saxophone player Nathan Davis met Kenny Clarke while he was a soldier stationed in Europe during the late 1950s. After Davis's discharge in 1960, Clarke invited him to Paris to join his band, and he stayed there for most of the decade, returning to America in 1969 to teach at the University of Pittsburgh. His fellow tenor sax player Johnny Griffin, a veteran of Art Blakey's Jazz Messengers, came to Europe on tour in December 1962, and ended up living in Paris for ten years before moving to a small village in the Netherlands. These musicians and others, together with the many performers who continued to come through the city on tour, ensured the presence of African American jazz artists in Paris during the second half of the twentieth century.

Probably the most important black jazz musician to settle in Paris during the 1960s was the great trumpet player Donald Byrd. Born in 1932 in Detroit, Byrd grew up in the kind of striving black environment that emphasized education, hard work, and responsibility. Son of a college-educated minister who also worked as a garbageman, Byrd as a young man was encouraged to study hard and apply himself diligently to his piano lessons. His mother's brother, Uncle Calvin, had a jazz band and first set young Donald on his career path by giving him a trumpet for Christmas when he was ten years old. By the time he left high school at the age of seventeen, Byrd was committed to the trumpet and to the life of a jazz musician. Even during a three-year stint in the air force, he was able to continue playing and studying jazz, and afterward, in 1954, he gravitated to New York, where he soon became a fixture in the city's nightclub scene. A year later, he began playing with the Jazz Messengers and went on to work with leading musicians like Max Roach, Thelonious Monk, Sonny Rollins, and Lionel Hampton. By the end of the decade, Donald Byrd was one of the top trumpet players in jazz, having performed with virtually all of the major artists and produced several recordings. In 1955, he created his own group, the Donald Byrd Quintet, which lasted until 1970.

For Donald Byrd, the idea of life abroad had a complex appeal. As a child he had been inspired by his father's belief that life overseas, either in Europe or Africa, held out better prospects for black people than life at home. Byrd first visited Europe in 1958, a year after his father's death. Like Kenny Clarke and Sidney Bechet, he came to Europe as a name performer, and found many doors open to him as a result. Initially there on a two-week tour of Paris, Brussels, and Cannes, Byrd stayed on for six months in Paris to perform at the Chat Qui Pêche nightclub in the Latin Quarter, playing for $50 a night. Romance, in the form of a Frenchwoman named Denise Genillon, brought Donald Byrd back to Paris in the autumn of 1963. He settled there for the next four years before returning permanently to the United States.

Byrd's life in Paris differed significantly from that of many other black jazz musicians. Most either came through the city on tour and quickly departed, or else settled there more or less permanently, putting down roots and basing their private and professional lives in the French capital. Byrd's four years in Paris gave him an in-depth appreciation of the city and the French people, but did not sever his ties to the United States. More important, Donald Byrd did not come to Paris to work in the city's jazz clubs. Thanks to his success in America, he was able to live off the proceeds of his recording contract, plus the hefty fees he charged for occasional public appearances. In contrast even to leading expatriate musicians like Clarke or Bechet, Donald Byrd lived in Paris as a man of independent means, free to explore whatever intrigued his imagination. He spent a great deal of time with Genillon in the city's unparalleled museums, further developing an appreciation of art that would eventually make him a major collector. While in France, he also spent two years studying music theory with Nadia Boulanger, the world's leading teacher of music theory whose former pupils included many of the great names in twentieth-century classical music. Byrd's life in Paris thus resembled that of a writer or artist who had crossed the Atlantic to learn from the French, rather than that of the typical musician who earned a living there playing for jazz aficionados.

Donald Byrd also differed from many of his peers in Paris by taking a much less romantic and favorable view of the French and the opportunities they offered jazz musicians. His first visit to Europe had not fully lived up to his (or his father's) dreams, and he never formed the emotional attachment to the French capital felt by many other African American musicians. Byrd's relative lack of enthusiasm also reflected changing conditions for black musicians in Paris during the 1960s. By that time, jazz was once again well established in France, and African Americans had long since ceased to be a novelty in Parisian nightclubs. France now had a whole new generation of French jazz performers, some of whom viewed black musicians more as competition than inspiration. Nathan Davis recalled a challenge from one such musician: "Yeah, I remember one time I came off the bandstand. . . . This one saxophone player came up to me, blocked my path, and said, 'You're taking work because you're black.'" Responding to such feelings, in 1965 the French musicians union sought to limit foreign performers in Paris by reviving the 1932 law establishing a 10 percent quota. Club owners like Madame Ricard of the Chat Qui Pêche, and Ben Benjamin, manager of the Blue Note, threatened to close their operations rather than comply with such regulations, and the quota system was never strictly enforced. Nonetheless, some musicians like Aaron Bridgers lost their jobs and in general Paris became a much less hospitable place for American performers.

Such restrictions did not affect Donald Byrd personally, but confirmed his belief that Paris offered no sacred refuge from racism. His years abroad taught him that although in Europe different peoples may have occupied the place at the bottom of society reserved for blacks in America, these nations were by no means immune from bigotry. Moreover, he contended that black jazz musicians were exploited in Europe just as in America, albeit in different ways. He felt that even Kenny Clarke, a man he admired and the most successful African American musician in Paris during the 1960s, did not receive the respect he deserved: "The thing with European musicians was, as soon as they stole the Afro-American musician's stuff, especially Kenny's, they would go out playing like black cats, and then they would try to keep the blacks from working." In addition, Byrd argued that black musicians tended to come to Europe when they could not face the competition in America, stagnating there and reliving past glories. This theory put a new twist on Miles Davis's argument that Paris lacked the critical mass of leading jazz musicians crucial to innovations in the art form. Although life in France had its charms, the action was in the United States, and that is where Byrd wanted to be.

In short, while Donald Byrd enjoyed his years in Paris, he never conceived of himself as an expatriate or set down roots. He did not play in the city's jazz clubs, and except for Nathan Davis associated little with other African American musicians. Byrd was no hermit, however; he did appear on French television and at occasional jazz festivals. Moreover, like many other black American musicians he was able to realize opportunities in France still closed to him in the United States. While in Paris, he started writing musical scores for European radio and television orchestras, which he continued to do well into the 1970s. The costs involved in America made this venture virtually impossible for all but leading composers. However, Byrd's success in America enabled him to experience the French capital on his own terms, enjoying life there while he chose to, then returning to America once he had gotten what he wished.

In a very different way, Bud Powell's life in Paris also ran counter to the romantic myth of the expatriate jazz musician. Bud Powell was one of the greatest and most tragic figures of postwar jazz, the most influential and creative artist of the modern jazz piano. Born in New York in 1924, Powell became an active participant in the city's jazz scene by the 1950s, playing with figures like Dizzy Gillespie and Charlie Parker. Powell's genius at the keyboard won him renown but did not save him from the ravages of schizophrenia and alcoholism, which at times forced him into mental institutions. A severe pistol whipping at the hands of a Harlem nightclub bouncer left him physically and mentally shattered, and when French admirers offered to bring him to Paris to work Powell accepted, arriving in 1959. The next three years represented the last flowering of Bud Powell's artistry, as his emotional troubles abated somewhat and he worked regularly in Paris jazz clubs. For example, he formed a trio with Kenny Clarke and Pierre Michelot. In 1962, however, Powell contracted tuberculosis, forcing him to stop working for the next two years. He returned to New York in 1964 with the intention of returning to Paris after a brief visit, but his mental and physical state continued to deteriorate. Paris had helped restore Bud Powell but could not save him, and the great pianist died in a Brooklyn hospital in July 1966.

Although neither Donald Byrd nor Bud Powell embraced life in the French capital, many others did. New nightclubs might come and go, but the city always offered a place to listen to the wail of a saxophone or the cool stylings of a jazz piano. A steady stream of African American musicians played in these clubs alongside colleagues from France and other countries. By the 1960s, the figure of the black American entertainer in Paris had assumed the proportions of a myth, one suggestive of freedom, exoticism, sophistication, and romance. In 1957, the white American writer Harold Flender published a novel about the life of a black jazz musician in Paris. Entitled *Paris Blues*, the book portrayed the attractions of the expatriate experience while ultimately characterizing it as unsatisfying. In 1961, the novel was made into a Hollywood movie of the same name, starring Paul Newman and Sidney Poitier, and featuring an appearance by the great Louis Armstrong. Whereas the novel focused on a black musician, the movie highlighted the life of a white expatriate, with the black man reduced to the role of sidekick. As such, the film both documented the experience of African American musicians in Paris and also symbolized the reasons why the city remained a refuge from America.

It is ironic that the image of the black musician in Paris achieved greater recognition at a time when the reality was becoming more inaccessible. The campaign by French jazz musicians to limit foreign competition certainly played a role in restricting opportunities for African Americans in Paris, but other factors intervened as well. University exchange programs and the era of mass tourism had increased the number of Americans, including blacks, able to come to Paris. Although the city's jazz scene remained vibrant, it could not accommodate all those who dreamed of finding renown in a smoky *cave*. As Art Simmons commented, "It's no longer a novelty to be a Negro in Paris. That's all finished now. They've seen good, they've seen bad — you have to *produce* as a performer. Before, you were a Negro first. Now you are a Negro second."

As Simmons's remark reveals, only the most talented black Americans were able to make a go of it in Paris. Opportunities might be more limited than in the early 1920s or 1950s, but they still existed for a gifted and fortunate few. In the 1960s and 1970s, the image of life in Paris reached more black Americans than ever before, transmitted by both newspaper and magazine articles, and the personal reminiscences of returning tourists. These various accounts transformed the experience of African Americans in France from the concrete reality of a few into a fantasy shared by millions.

The 1960s thus brought some important changes to the world of black American jazz in the French capital. Although there were as many jazz clubs in Paris as ever, few if any were owned by black Americans. A notable difference from earlier eras was the relative absence of African American women. Although the actress Marpessa Dawn (star of the 1959 French film *Black*

Orpheus) had moved to Paris, and the young Nancy Holloway was beginning to make a name for herself in the city's nightclubs, during the 1960s no black women from the United States achieved the success of Josephine Baker or Bricktop. Yet jazz remained important to Parisian life, and although it was not an exclusively black phenomenon it continued to offer a space for the best African American performers. Donald Byrd may have felt that Kenny Clarke did not receive his due from the French, but Clarke himself clearly thought otherwise. Paris was no longer an easy place to make it, but for those who did, the rewards could still make the struggle worthwhile.

African American life in Paris during the 1960s and 1970s retained a strong sense of black community, while at the same time cultivating a cosmopolitan outlook that encouraged interaction with the tremendous variety of peoples and experiences available in the French capital. The city still attracted black Americans from numerous backgrounds, including but not limited to those active in literature, music, and the visual arts. As in the 1950s, the Left Bank, especially the Latin Quarter and Saint-Germain-des-Prés, remained the focal point of the community. However, expatriate centers thrived elsewhere, notably Haynes restaurant in Montmartre and the Living Room off the Champs-Elysées, and individuals lived and worked throughout the city. Blacks felt free to pursue a life where they were recognized as individuals, following whatever interests they desired, but at the same time could take advantage of a reflection of the collective spirit so important to black life in the United States. Art Simmons, himself a focal point of this phenomenon, summed up its contradictions neatly with the following observations:

> There is no Negro "community" here as such. . . . Just because we all know each other doesn't mean we're a community. I know many of the white Americans here too. But, at the same time, don't think we Negroes don't make it our business to know where we all are. I guess that's kind of a safety valve to have in case something goes wrong. After all, why do I buy *Ebony* Magazine over here? Because I want to know what my people are doing, that's why. . . . We need each other — and we call on each other. . . . I suppose there *is* a community!

This new era had brought changes to the expatriate community in Paris. For the first time in the twentieth century, black newcomers did not arrive in Paris in uniform as a result of the hazards of war. Musicians still decided to stay in the city after coming through on tour, but they generally had much more knowledge about it than those who settled in France during the 1920s. The myth of the free black in Paris lured more than ever before, but black expatriates often found it difficult to secure a place. The possibility of success on the scale of Josephine Baker might still tantalize, but more important was the refuge the city still seemed to offer from the racial traumas of the United States. Even after the charm of life in a small room on the sixth floor without an elevator had worn off, one could still contend that material deprivation was a small price to pay for freedom.

Yet the contrast between a racist America and a color-blind Paris, which had always lain at the heart of the black expatriate experience in France, lost some of its sharpness in the 1960s. Back home in the United States, segregation and racial discrimination were confronting a challenge of unprecedented scope by black people and their white allies in the South, a challenge so powerful that many assumed full equality between the races was just a matter of time. In Paris, however, some observed new and disturbing manifestations of racism. The horrors of the Algerian war underlined the discrimination and hostility faced by France's Arab minority, and the increasing population of immigrant workers from North Africa, black Africa, and the Caribbean suggested that America was not the only country with a racial caste system. Although these changes on both sides of the Atlantic had begun in the aftermath of the Second World War, during the 1960s they achieved fruition and began to affect African American views of life in Paris. Taken together, shifting racial realities in both France and the United States cast the experience of Paris's black expatriates in a new light.

A DISTANT THUNDER

From the early 1950s to the mid-1960s, the series of legal and activist strategies collectively known as the civil rights movement fundamentally reshaped life, for both blacks and whites, in the South and the United States as a whole. Seen from the vantage point of over a quarter century later, at a time when many of its achievements are taken for granted and some find it more fashionable to speak of "reverse racism" against whites, it is easy to forget the dramatic impact of the movement on the nation's soul, or the sacrifices and courage of those who took part in it as both leaders and foot soldiers. Yet at the time, the civil rights movement inspired both tremendous hope and fear among the black people of the United States. Not since the end of slavery had blacks dared to imagine, let alone demand, such a thoroughgoing revision of their condition in America. The prospect that blacks in the South might *soon* enjoy basic rights like the vote, decent schools, or even non-segregated public restrooms, that the daily diet of public humiliation at the hands of whites, reinforced by the occasional beating or lynching, might come to an end, struck many as nothing less than epochal, almost too wonderful to be believed. At the same time, those blacks who lived in or knew the South did not underestimate the segregationists' determination to resist change to the bitter end, violently if need be. As the Ku Klux Klan, White Citizens Councils, and other racist organizations mobilized to fight the civil rights crusaders with cross burnings, police beatings, and murder, many wondered in anguish how many more dead it would take to bring racial apartheid to a long overdue end.

The civil rights movement began in the 1950s with a series of challenges that would have seemed unimaginable a decade earlier. On May 17, 1954, in response to a case brought by the NAACP Legal Defense Fund, the Supreme Court declared school segregation by race unconstitutional. The historic *Brown v. Board of Education* decision fueled the determination of those blacks who since the end of the war had regarded segregation as an anachronism whose time had come. In December 1955, Rosa Parks refused to sit in the black section at the back of a Montgomery, Alabama, bus, triggering the boycott that would desegregate the city's transit system and catapult the young Martin Luther King to national prominence. In 1957, at a time when civil rights leaders were already becoming the targets of gunshots and bombings, King, Bayard Rustin, Ralph Abernathy, and other activists came together to create the Southern Christian Leadership Conference, which would spearhead the movement over the next decade. The same year, in response to the recent Supreme Court decision, President Eisenhower reluctantly sent federal troops to Arkansas to support the right of black students to attend all-white Central High School. By 1959, major civil rights organizations stood poised and ready to issue a frontal challenge to institutionalized segregation and racial discrimination in the South.

Yet the heart of the movement, involving both its most aggressive actions as well as the bloodiest and most determined white resistance, took place during the first half of the 1960s. On February 1, 1960, four black students from North Carolina Agricultural and Technical State University sat down at a whites-only lunch counter in Greensboro and refused to leave until they were served. Their action triggered a wave of sit-ins, first in Greensboro, then throughout the South, a strategy of popular actions to force the immediate desegregation of public facilities. A year later the freedom rides began: integrated busloads of volunteers traveled from the North throughout the South in open defiance of local racial policies. The riders encountered mob violence along the way, but these attacks failed to halt what was now a massive popular struggle. College students and other volunteers, both black and white, staged marches, boycotts, and other actions defying the racial status quo. The Student Nonviolent

Coordinating Committee, founded in 1960, initiated a project to register black voters in the South, striking directly at the political basis of segregation. By 1963, the civil rights movement had not only spread throughout the South, but also became a nationwide issue, attracting volunteers from across the United States and emerging as a central concern for the presidential administration of John F. Kennedy. The impact of the movement on American life was made graphically clear by the March on Washington of August 28, one of the largest demonstrations held up to that time in the national capital. On that hot summer day, some 200,000 people, roughly 75 percent black and 25 percent white, reaffirmed the national commitment to racial equality while listening to Martin Luther King deliver his classic speech, "I Have a Dream."

Such moments of triumph were accompanied by many tragedies, consecrating the civil rights movement with the blood of martyrs. Segregation had long established a climate of fear in order to maintain itself, and it confronted the peaceful protesters with escalating acts of violence. Volunteers frequently suffered beatings at the hands of both white counterprotesters and of the white policemen whose word often represented the only law in small Southern towns. Demonstrators, blacks and whites, men, women, and children, were attacked with police dogs, nightsticks, and pressurized water hoses. In a region that still used lynching to resolve threats to the racial status quo, segregationist violence did not stop short of murder. James Meredith, the first black student at the University of Mississippi, was shot down during his "Walk Against Fear" across the state in 1965. Meredith survived, but others were not so lucky. The civil rights workers Viola Liuzzo, James Chaney, Michael Schwerner, Andrew Goodman, and others were murdered by white vigilantes. Medgar Evers, the leader of the Mississippi NAACP, was shot and killed outside his home. The most atrocious incident of all occurred in September 1963 when terrorists in Birmingham, Alabama, a center of violent resistance to desegregation, bombed a black church, killing four young girls during Sunday school services. Coming a mere two weeks after the March on Washington, the bombing bloodily illustrated the determination of white supremacists to prevent integration.

The early 1960s were thus a time of hope and a time of sorrow for black Americans, but above all a time of historic, unprecedented change. What did such events mean to African Americans living an ocean away in Parisian exile? Their people were engaged in an enormous struggle that involved tremendous effort and sacrifice, yet at the same time held out the prospect of a truly egalitarian America. In an era when tens of thousands of Americans of all colors risked jailings, beatings, and even death to fight for racial equality, how effective, or justified, was Parisian exile as a protest against racism in the United States? How could black Americans in Paris contribute to the struggle, or were they doomed to remain outsiders looking on as great events transpired across the ocean?

Such questions fostered intense debate and soul searching among black expatriates. No matter what one thought of the movement, it could not be ignored; not only did it dominate the black periodicals that many received from America, but it received ample coverage in the French press. Many African Americans in Paris had relatives in the South who kept them informed. In December 1963, for instance, Beauford Delaney received a letter from his brother S. Emery Delaney of Knoxville, Tennessee. Commenting on the recent assassination of President Kennedy, he expressed the hope and anguish of the times: "We have all been saddened by the death of our Beloved President, a dedicated man and loved by so many millions of people, millions passed his bier sorrowfully, to me the greatest tragedy in my lifetime, a personal loss. I was only a few ft away from him when he was here as candidate at the airport where he spoke, we have had quite a time here the last 2 years our people fighting for equal rights as yet no legislation, I pray the day is near, the future looks dark."

Virtually all realized the significance of the civil rights movement not only for black Americans in general, but for their own exiled condition in particular, yet their reactions were not uniform. For some, the violent resistance that greeted the civil rights marchers, as well as the lackluster support offered by the federal government merely confirmed the racist character of white America and their own wisdom in leaving the United States behind. When William Gardner Smith asked one black writer in Paris if he felt that blacks should return to America to participate in the struggle, the writer responded, "The United States for me no longer exists!" In Harold Flender's novel *Paris Blues*, the expatriate saxophonist Eddie Cook expressed similar pessimism about the prospects for change in America. "How many lynchings have there been there recently? . . . How many more murderers have been let off after beating little Negro kids to death? How many more homes have been blown up? It's a great country!"

Such arguments, validated by centuries of bitter experience with American racism, evoked two responses. The first was that the atrocities committed by white Southern segregationists during the civil rights movement represented the last gasp of a dying beast, that in fact racism was on the defensive and life was getting better for black people in America. The active participation of thousands of whites in the movement seemed to support the belief that

American attitudes toward race were undergoing a fundamental change for the better. In general, few African American expatriates were moved or convinced by this position. For those who saw themselves as refugees from racism, feeling it necessary to cross the Atlantic to escape its effects, it was difficult to be optimistic about the chances for true racial equality. Most had moved to Paris from the North, not the South, and the kind of de facto discrimination they had experienced there showed little likelihood of disappearing. Throughout the 1960s, African Americans who settled in France continued to emphasize the more tolerant atmosphere they found in contrast to the United States. America might be changing, but in the opinion of many expatriates it still had a long way to go.

The second response, however, carried much more weight. This position argued that African Americans everywhere had a moral imperative to take part in the struggle of their brothers and sisters in the South for freedom. By the early 1960s, the civil rights movement had assumed the dimensions of a crusade, and failure to participate could be and was seen by some as dereliction of duty. After all, how in good conscience could one enjoy the ease and comfort of a Parisian café while black children, *children*, were bravely facing white mobs or being blown up in their own churches? Exile was justified as a protest against racism only so long as the possibility of reforming conditions at home remained remote. The civil rights movement, however, offered just such a possibility, forcing many black expatriates in Paris to reevaluate their reasons for being there.

The film version of *Paris Blues* (1961) featured a dialogue that encapsulated the increasing pressure on African Americans to return home and take up the struggle. In both the novel and the movie, Eddie Cook falls in love with a black schoolteacher from Chicago, Connie Mitchell, who is visiting Paris as a tourist. Although the story ends ambiguously, it implies that Cook decides to return to America, drawn by his love for Mitchell. Unlike the book, however, the film addresses the issue of the civil rights movement, and its claim upon all blacks, in depth. In a key interchange, Mitchell uses the example of the movement to question Cook's attachment to exile. In response to Cook's assertion that he loves Paris because there nobody cares about his race, Mitchell argues, "There isn't a place on the face of the earth that isn't hell for somebody, some race, some color, some sex." Whereas Cook dismisses America as a racist hell, Mitchell asserts that "things are much better than they were five years ago and they're gonna still be better next year. And not because Negroes came to Paris, but because Negroes stay home, and with millions of white people they work to make things better for everybody in America!" Debuting four years after the novel, the film *Paris Blues* picked up on a theme increasingly central to the life of African Americans in France.

During the 1950s, black expatriates in Paris had often defined their choice as a political act, a rejection of racism; by the mid-1960s, for some it represented instead an avoidance of political commitment: the expatriate as escapist rather than refugee. Members of the city's African American community often responded angrily to this charge. Toward the end of his life, Richard Wright had been labeled out of touch with events in America, including the civil rights movement, by both black and white critics, and some in France considered the accusation of sitting out the struggle merely another way of calling black expatriates uppity niggers. Nonetheless, the feeling remained among blacks in Paris that they should do something to support the movement, and as the fight for black equality moved from South to North during the 1960s this feeling intensified. Or as James Browne put it, "I don't think any American black man should live permanently overseas while we're fighting so hard for justice in the U.S. We've enjoyed Paris these last two years but we've got to get back to where black people are on the move — we must be a part of it."

Browne's words illustrated another important reaction of blacks in Paris to the political movements of the 1960s. For some, the civil rights struggle inspired not just a sense of obligation but also a feeling of great excitement, a belief that the era of liberation so long hoped, wished, and prayed for was finally imminent. The question, therefore, was not so much whether one should stay in Paris, but why one would even want to? The city might be charming, offering racial tolerance and an appealing black community life, but, ironically enough, compared to the historic drama unfolding in the United States it seemed a backwater, peripheral and isolated. It might afford, as Richard Wright pointed out, an important international perspective on questions of race, but presented few opportunities for the kind of direct involvement that many craved.

Desire as well as duty thus shaped the reactions of many African Americans in Paris to the civil rights and Black Power movements of the 1960s, and played a role in motivating those who chose to leave France for America. James Baldwin established the model for this kind of homeward pilgrimage when he left Paris in 1957 to work with Martin Luther King in the South. A decade later, William Gardner Smith traveled back to America for a month as a correspondent for Agence France-Presse, charged with covering the racial crisis during a long hot summer in which black ghettos in Detroit, Newark, and many other cities exploded into flames. For Smith, the voyage was both a journalistic investigation and a homecoming, one that he later described in his book *Return to Black America*. The same year, Donald Byrd ended his four-year sojourn in Paris to resume life in the United States, motivated by many of the same reasons that had inspired Baldwin ten years earlier.

> I remember Klook [Kenny Clarke] and everybody was saying, "What the hell do you want to go back to the States for?" . . . I did not want to run away from that. Everyone over there felt, what are you going back to that shit for? That's where I am supposed to be fighting. What should I do, hide over there? . . . The ones who did not come back, they kept themselves away from a refreshing period of hope here. Their rationale was that it was some whitey shit: "I don't want to be bothered." But by them not becoming involved they also lost a valuable experience. That is something that they can't experience anymore. It will never happen again. They were completely out of it.

No one knows how many black Americans chose to leave Paris for the United States (or, for that matter, chose not to leave the United States for Paris) as a statement of personal commitment to black political struggles during the 1960s. Donald Byrd's remarks, however, make the important point that they were a minority; most black expatriates decided to stay put. There were of course many reasons for remaining in Paris, both personal and structural. The role played by inertia in human affairs has often received less attention than it merits. Many African Americans in France were stirred by news from home and probably toyed with the idea of returning, but simply never got around to it. Others had families, jobs, and established lives in Paris which they did not want to disrupt. Having in effect become middle-aged residents of France, not young expatriates, people like William Gardner Smith were not willing to start over again; for them, moving to the United States represented a new expatriation as much as a return home. While undeniably sympathizing with black struggles in the United States, they were not ready to turn their lives inside out for them.

COLOR-BLIND FRANCE?

For centuries, the presence of people of color in France had been intimately related to the establishment of French colonial possessions in Africa, Asia, and the Caribbean. The empire sent hundreds of thousands of its subjects, blacks, Asians, and Arabs, to France during World War I, where they fought in the trenches and worked in munitions plants and on farms. At the end of the conflict, the French government sent most back home, deciding that France was "not ready" to become a multiracial society. A few managed to stay, however, settling into marginal neighborhoods in cities like Paris, Marseilles, and Bordeaux. During the 1920s, a small but steady stream of workers, students, and political activists from the empire settled in France, primarily Paris, of whom the negritude writers were only the most prominent examples. World War II and the Nazi occupation temporarily cut France off from its colonies, but even in those years Paris retained a certain nonwhite presence.

If the First World War began the decline of Europe's overseas empires, the Second World War completed it. By 1965, twenty years after the surrender of Nazi Germany, virtually all the colonies in Africa and Asia had achieved formal independence. The French empire was shaken by these winds of change as well, yet tragically France chose to resist the inexorable wave of decolonization, fighting to hold on to its possessions to the bitter end. As a result, the nation became embroiled in major colonial wars from 1946 to 1962. During the Second World War, France had lost control of Indochina to the Japanese as that nation shattered the old European empires in East Asia. The French hoped to regain power there upon Japan's defeat in 1945, but the real heirs of Japanese rule turned out to be the Vietminh, the powerful Communist resistance movement led by Ho Chi Minh. During the war, the Vietminh had proclaimed their intention to create an independent Vietnam free from both France and Japan, and they stuck to their guns even after Tokyo's surrender. The French refused to accept this declaration and went to war against the Vietminh in 1946, an eight-year disaster that culminated in the spectacular defeat of the French army at Dien Bien Phu in 1954. France sued for peace, and by the end of the year the French empire in East Asia had come to an inglorious end.

The loss of Indochina represented a serious setback for France, coming at a time when the nation was trying to assert its great-power status in a world increasingly divided between the United States and the Soviet Union. Yet the defeat did not touch most French people personally: Indochina lay on the other side of the world, and the majority of the soldiers who fought for France had not even been French nationals. In contrast, the war in Algeria became a national trauma for the French people, in many ways even more divisive and devastating than America's experience in Vietnam. Algeria had been a French possession ever since 1830, and by 1945 was considered not a colony, but an integral part of the French nation, home to a million white French settlers. Yet the overwhelmingly Arab population of Algeria had few political rights or economic opportunities, with the result that since World War II the Arabs' desire for independence from Paris had grown rapidly. In November

1954, the Arab activists of the National Liberation Front, or FLN, set off a war against French rule, inspired in large part by the success of the Vietminh earlier that year. For the next eight years, Algeria was embroiled in a horrifying conflict that dragged on until the French finally agreed to accept its independence in 1962.

Even by the bitter standards of the twentieth century, the war in Algeria was particularly vicious, marked by bloody massacres of thousands of people, the widespread use of torture against soldiers, rebels, and civilians, and the internment of large sections of the Muslim population in concentration camps. Both the FLN and the French army committed numerous atrocities, including the torture and murder of women and children. Out of a population of ten million, roughly one million Muslim Algerians died during the war. In contrast to Indochina, however, the French homeland was not shielded from the violence occurring in this part of its empire. Algeria lay on the other side of the Mediterranean from France; Marseilles was as close to Algiers as to Paris. Most of the French soldiers who fought there were French citizens, so it was not long before families throughout France were mourning the loss of their loved ones. The large French settler community in Algeria, which viewed the FLN revolt as insubordination by its servants and inferiors, adamantly rejected any consideration of Algerian independence and insisted on waging war against the FLN by whatever means necessary.

By the end of the 1950s, the escalating violence and terror in Algeria had spread to metropolitan France, especially Paris, as the different parties to the conflict sought to increase pressure on the French government. The French army, supported by the white settlers, was edging closer to open revolt against what it saw as the government's tendency to negotiate a settlement with the Algerian rebels. In 1958, the French Fourth Republic collapsed under the strain of the war, giving way before the return to power of the wartime hero Charles de Gaulle, whose support by the army made his victory seem like a semilegal coup d'état. Yet even de Gaulle soon realized that a military solution was impossible, disenchanting his army and settler supporters, who in response created the Secret Army Organization, or OAS, a terrorist group that promptly launched a bombing campaign against supporters of Algerian independence in both Algeria and France. Targets included Jean-Paul Sartre, whose Paris apartment was bombed twice, and other members of the small but growing antiwar movement in France.

France was also home to a large Algerian population, which was becoming increasingly active in the struggle over French policy in its homeland. By 1961, it was not uncommon to see the bodies of Algerians floating down the

Seine through the middle of Paris, victims of the French police, the OAS, or factional fighting within the independence movement. The Algerians were generally the poorest people in France, working the worst jobs with the lowest wages, and living in urban slums or suburban shantytowns known as *bidonvilles*. Their very presence in the country graphically refuted the idea that the French did not discriminate on the basis of skin color or nationality. With the growing impact of the war on France itself, the Algerians residing in the country came to symbolize both racial discrimination and colonial oppression.

The black American expatriates who settled in Paris during the 1950s were not unaware of the Algerian question, both the war overseas and their low status in France. When writing about his first apartment in Paris, for example, James Baldwin noted, "I lived mainly among *les miserables* — and in Paris *les miserables* are Algerian." Even as his fame and fortune grew, Baldwin returned to this neighborhood from time to time, his own self-conception as an outsider making him feel at home. His short story "This Morning, This Evening, So Soon," published in *The Atlantic Monthly* in 1960, reflected the author's growing distance from the city's Arabs as he became more accepted into French society. By the late 1950s, it was impossible to ignore the war in Paris, as terrorist bombings multiplied along with rumors about a possible coup d'état. In *My Life of Absurdity*, Chester Himes observed that in 1959, "The Algerian war was at its greatest intensity, and racial prejudice in France was as intense as it has ever been." For Himes, who had never been seduced by the myth of color-blind France, the war and resulting racial tensions merely confirmed his cynical view of whites.

Yet the Algerian question had little impact on the life of African Americans in Paris during the postwar years. For all their disheveled charm, neighborhoods like Saint-Germain-des-Prés were actually some of the more affluent parts of the city, increasingly so during the 1950s, and few Algerians or other immigrants of color lived there. Caught up in the heady feeling of being accepted, even sought after, by numbers of white people in a glamorous foreign capital, it was easy for blacks in Paris to pay little attention to the racism directed against another minority group. For African Americans, racism had always meant first and foremost prejudice against blacks, and it took some adjustment to get used to the idea that in a different setting whites would treat blacks fairly while viewing other people of color with hostility and contempt.

Most important, however, black expatriates were acutely aware of their status as guests of the French. Throughout the twentieth century, the French government had welcomed foreign political exiles on the implicit assumption that they abstain from involvement in French politics. Activism around issues concerning the exile's own country might be tolerated, but any expatriate who dared question conditions in France itself risked speedy and permanent expulsion from the country. Consequently, whatever their actual feelings about the Algerian war, Richard Wright and other expatriates felt they had little choice but to keep quiet about it if they wanted to stay in Paris. The 1956 Gibson affair was so contentious precisely because the forged letter purportedly from Ollie Harrington denouncing French policy in Algeria put Harrington (and by extension, the African American community in general) in danger of crossing over the line. Richard Gibson himself later commented, "There was a lot of sympathy for the Algerian national struggle among the American writers, but the problem was, how could you speak out and still stay in France? People wanted to criticize the war, but they wanted to stay in France, so they were caught in a bind."

Among the black expatriate community, William Gardner Smith devoted the most attention to the Algerian war and the broader question of French racism. Gibson blamed Smith for initiating the idea of sending forged letters attacking France's Algeria policy, and Richard Wright believed Gibson. Although that specific charge did not seem to be true, Smith's well-known sympathy with the plight of Algerians in both Algeria and Paris made it plausible. Even before the start of the war in Algeria, William Smith wrote columns for the *Pittsburgh Courier* depicting the poverty and oppression of Arabs in the French capital.

> And that night, dressed, comfortable in your own security, you sit on the terrace of the famous Cafe Flore and listen to the chatter of American tourists. An Arab comes by, selling hand-woven rugs. "Buy a rug, lady? Buy a rug?" No one buys, and he walks off, to the next cafe.
>
> And the American woman, in a new, expensive Paris dress, says to her companions: "He's an Arab, isn't he? They're filthy, aren't they? I hear they're all thieves and racketeers!"
>
> A bell rings somewhere in your head. Echo from another land. You finish your beer and go home, tired, to bed.

With the beginning of the Algerian struggle for independence in 1954, Smith soon became a firm, if discreet, supporter of the FLN's fight for liberation. His 1963 novel, *The Stone Face*, is not only a blunt denunciation of French racism against Algerians, but also provides a penetrating exploration of the ways in which African American expatriates in Paris confronted this question at the beginning of the 1960s. A highly autobiographical novel set in the black community of the Latin Quarter, *The Stone Face* tells the story of Simeon Brown, a young black man from Philadelphia fleeing the violence and racism of his native land, who finds solace in the French capital's black expatriate community. He immediately falls in love with Paris, presented as a beautiful, tolerant city where a black man can hold his head high. As Simeon soon learns, however, there is a serpent in this racial Garden of Eden. While leaving a jazz club, Simeon notices a policeman beating up an Arab, an incident that triggers memories of his own conflicts with the Philadelphia police. Gradually he comes into contact with Algerians in the city, learning of their own oppression and resentment of the French. One afternoon he ends up talking with four Arabs in a Left Bank café after one hails him with the bitter comment, "Hey! How does it feel to be a white man?" This man, named Hossein, proceeds to contrast French treatment of him and Simeon in trenchant terms: "We're the niggers here! Know what the French call us — *bicot, melon, raton, nor'af.* That means *nigger* in French."

Much of the rest of the novel concerns Simeon's growing awareness of prejudice against the Algerians and resultant disenchantment with the French and their racial attitudes. A French student explains the feelings of his people toward the Arabs in their midst by saying, "I wouldn't rent a room to an Arab because he'd probably rob the whole apartment while I was out. That's a fact. But it's not racism." Simeon's conflict between his angry rejection of American racism and his growing awareness of similar problems in Paris assumes the dimensions of a classic moral dilemma. It is all the more agonizing as Simeon deeply loves the French capital. Yet at the same time he becomes disturbed by the complicity of his beloved Parisians in the horrors of the Algerian war and their treatment of the city's Arab minority. Even more troubling is the attitude taken by many of the African Americans in Paris, who try to ignore the whole issue or else argue that it's not a black problem. Babe, Simeon's oldest friend in exile, takes this position: "'Forget it, man. Algerians are white people. They feel like white people when they're with Negroes. . . . A black man's got enough trouble in the world without going about defending white people.' But he was not convincing, even to himself. He too wanted to hold onto the new peace, the new contentment." So does Simeon, but in the end he simply can't.

The novel culminates dramatically, with a stunning explosion of racial violence in the center of Paris. In October 1961, Simeon's Algerian friend Ahmed and his associates take part in a demonstration declared by the FLN to break a curfew imposed by the French government on Algerians (but no one else) living in Paris. Thirty thousand Algerians descend upon the city's

wealthy central districts, publicly demanding independence for their homeland. The French police react with savage and unprecedented brutality, indiscriminately assaulting men, women, and children. In the course of one night,
more than two hundred Algerians are shot or beaten to death, including
Ahmed. Caught up in the violence, Simeon is himself arrested and thrown in
prison. Thanks to his American status he is quickly released, but life in Paris
has lost its joy for him. The book ends with Simeon's return to America.

More than any other document from the 1960s, *The Stone Face* sets forth
the parallels between racism in America and in France. Harlem and the Arab
quarter both lie on the northern edges of their respective cities, bombings
inspired by racist anger explode in both Paris and the South, policemen in
both nations viciously beat and kill those seen as racial inferiors. In his depiction of the October 1961 demonstration, William Gardner Smith wrote more
as a journalist than as a novelist, for that event occurred almost exactly as he
described it. The massacre represented the single worst example of civil strife
in France, possibly Western Europe, since the Second World War, and because news of it was suppressed by the Paris police few people in France to
this day know that it even happened. Nothing that occurred in the South
during the struggle for civil rights took such a toll in human lives. The parallel
is all the more powerful precisely because Smith acknowledges the many
charms of Paris, playing on the contrast between French treatment of American blacks and of Algerian Arabs. Ultimately the city appears as an illusory
paradise, confirming the idea that blacks have no homeland and that there is
no escape from racism.

Even after the end of the Algerian war, pervasive discrimination against the
many nonwhite immigrants in Paris tended to contradict the old color-blind
myth. Contrary to the belief of many Americans, France has long been a very
diverse nation, the crossroads of Europe. During the 1920s, in part because
America drastically restricted its former open door policy, France had been
the world's leading recipient of immigrants. This practice continued after
1945, but with a crucial difference. Before the Second World War, most
foreigners in France were Europeans, people from Spain, Italy, Portugal, and
Poland in search of a better standard of living. After 1945, however, the nation
began to receive large numbers of people of color, who by the end of the 1960s
constituted a majority of immigrants in France. Arabs from Algeria, Morocco,
and Tunisia formed the largest group, but many blacks from the French
Caribbean and the former French colonies in Africa also came to work in
France. By the 1960s, therefore, France had become a multiracial nation, one
in which nonwhites, as in America, found themselves firmly relegated to the
bottom of society.

Most African American expatriates in Paris during the 1960s were aware of France's growing population of color and the discrimination it faced. Edward Barnett called Algerians the Negroes of France and observed that the Senegalese in Paris mostly worked in menial jobs. Vertamae Smart-Grosvenor was disenchanted with Paris upon her return there in 1968, noting, "Man, when I arrived and saw those black cats sweeping the streets I knew that the third world has got to happen." Such observations did not prevent African Americans from continuing to settle in and enjoy Paris. Most still felt that the French treated blacks better than the Americans. But the old belief that Paris was a city without prejudice lost much of its power. Instead of Richard Wright's optimistic Francophilia, many expatriates now preferred the cynicism of Chester Himes, who never expected much from the French and was therefore not disappointed.

If not Paris, however, what about Africa? If faith in the color-blind attitudes of the French gave way to disillusionment, could not black people hope to find true equality in the new black nations that were their ancestral homelands? *The Stone Face* initially ended with Simeon leaving Paris for Africa; Smith changed the ending in hopeful response to civil rights actions during the summer of 1963. Attempts by black Americans to renew contact with the mother continent have a long history, from the creation of Liberia by repatriated slaves in the early nineteenth century to Marcus Garvey's Back to Africa movement in the 1920s. During the 1960s, the emergence of proud new independent black African nations and the growing black consciousness movement in America prompted many African Americans to consider the idea of leaving the United States for Africa, and a few did settle there as expatriates.

Ghana in particular, which under the charismatic Kwame Nkrumah in 1957 became the first black African colony to achieve independence, attracted a number of African American expatriates. America's greatest black intellectual, W.E.B. Du Bois, led this new black movement to Africa. Although opposed to Garveyism, Du Bois had supported and figured prominently in international pan-Africanism for most of the twentieth century. In 1961, he left the United States to settle in Ghana at the invitation of Nkrumah. The leading African American statesman ended his life as an expatriate in Africa, dying in Ghana in 1963 at the age of ninety-five. His widow, Shirley Graham Du Bois, remained there at the center of a small group of American black expatriates that at times included Maya Angelou, Martin Kilson, Leslie Lacy, and Julian Mayfield.

For many African Americans, the lure of Africa was a powerful one, and its pull extended to those living in Paris. Why exchange life in one white country for exile in another when the mother continent beckoned? More concretely, the prospect of living in a nation where blacks were the majority and in control was something few African Americans had ever experienced, and that Paris could not offer. Perceptions of increasing French racism only reinforced this attraction. In *Return to Black America*, William Gardner Smith described a conversation with a black musician, Jesse Harris, about France and Africa. Watching an African worker sweeping the streets in front of their café, the two expatriates pondered the place of blacks in France.

> Jesse sipped his coffee . . . "A black man. Got nothing but Africans sweeping the streets of Paris these days. Job's too lowly for a Frenchman, got to import African slaves. . . . Same old thing. Here or in the States. The white man rules, he's a racist, and he exploits black people . . ."
>
> Jesse looked at me and said, "What the hell are we doing here? What the hell are you and me, black people, doing in this white world? . . . Only fit place for us, only fit place for a black man, is where we're at home — Africa. I'm going to end up there. Black Power in the States or not. I'm going to die there."

African Americans living in Paris had already torn up their roots in the United States and chosen exile. To some, it therefore made sense to continue this flight from racism all the way back to the source of black culture.

During the 1960s and later, Paris became once again a gateway to Africa for a number of black Americans. In contrast to the interwar years, when black expatriates had been content to learn about African art along the banks of the Seine, several now chose to visit the ancestral continent in person. Ted Joans, while retaining his base and contacts in the French capital, became a frequent traveler to Africa and around the world. His fellow poet Melvin Dixon, who first came to Paris in 1972, found that the contrast between the beauties of the city and the lowly condition of its black and brown residents inspired in him an increased interest in the third world, leading him to visit Africa at the beginning of the 1980s. Paris also became a place that African Americans visited on their way to or from Africa. Malcolm X made two brief stopovers there during the mid-1960s, as did the writer Alex Haley, whose book *Roots* would soon revolutionize the way blacks in the United States looked at their homeland.

Like Richard Wright, most black Americans who traveled from Paris to Africa did so with round-trip tickets, eager to discover this new black world but not yet ready to move there permanently. However, a few liked what they saw and decided to give life in Africa a try. Bill Sutherland, a middle-class African American with a long history of political activism, first traveled overseas in 1951 when he visited Paris and toured Europe. In France, he met African leaders who inspired him with a desire to see their homeland. Sutherland lived in Ghana for four years during the 1950s, returning in 1961. After several years, he moved on to Tanzania, obtaining a position in the government of Julius K. Nyerere. By the late 1960s, Sutherland had spent much of his adult life on the African continent and could claim to be one of the few African Americans who had successfully made the transition back to the historic homeland.

The experience of William Gardner Smith, on the other hand, was much less positive. Both the disillusionment with French racial attitudes expressed so eloquently in *The Stone Face* and a feeling that his creativity needed a change of scene impelled the writer to listen to the dreams of Africa voiced by so many of his friends in both Paris and America. In 1964, Smith received an invitation from Shirley Graham Du Bois, then head of Ghana Television, to come to Accra and work in the news department. Smith moved there with his wife, Solange Royez, and his infant daughter, Michele, in September, settling into a large house overlooking the sea, which was lent to them by the Ghanaian government. William Gardner Smith was thrilled by his first encounter with Africa, from the prospect of living in a nation where all the officials and leaders of society were black, to his immediate feelings of kinship with its people. "Moving along an Accra boulevard, I felt, sometimes, as though I were walking down a street in South Philadelphia, Harlem, or Chicago. These black people in their multicolored robes, with their laughter, with their rhythmic gait, were my cousins. It was a joy to fade into their midst." The small African American colony in Accra was the center of expatriate life on the continent, and fully shared in the sense of being present at the creation of a newly liberated black world. Smith quickly settled into the rhythms of life in Ghana's capital city. The birth of his son, Claude, in July 1965 seemed to cement his ties to the new nation.

Yet William Gardner Smith soon discovered that his dream of freedom in Africa, like the dream that had brought him to Paris, was more than a little illusory. He realized that for all its proud political independence, Ghana and all of black Africa was still very dependent economically on the West, relying both on unequal trading relationships and on patronizing financial aid. He was disturbed both by the rampant corruption among Ghana's officialdom and by the sharp contrast between the lives of the rich and poor in the country. Moreover, Smith came to realize that in important ways Africans and African Americans have fundamentally different outlooks on life. In particular, not having lived as an oppressed minority in a mostly white society, Africans did not emphasize racial solidarity in the same way. Smith wrote,

"The idea of American black nationalists, summed up in the phrase, 'We are black, therefore we are brothers,' is incomprehensible in tribal societies where the hereditary enemies have, precisely, been black." Like Richard Wright before him, Smith found in Africa both many cultural similarities with his own people, but also learned that Africa was not simply black America unchained.

Smith left Ghana in 1966, but not of his own volition. He gradually became aware of the problems and mounting opposition faced by the Nkrumah government. The business and military elites of the country opposed Nkrumah's socialistic economic policies and attempts to limit corruption. On February 24, 1966, they sprang into action, unleashing an armed coup d'état that deposed Nkrumah in a matter of hours. The impact on Smith and other members of the black American colony in Ghana was drastic and instantaneous. Smith was arrested and ordered to leave the country immediately. He and his family had no choice but to comply, and within a few days they found themselves on a plane bound for Switzerland. After briefly staying with Solange's parents in France, the family decided to return to Paris. Smith wrote his mother at the time, "I am very sad to have had to leave Ghana . . . I want to return to Africa eventually. But for the moment, I must reestablish my family here."

Aside from brief trips as a journalist, however, Smith never did return to Africa. He refused to go back to Ghana even after the military regime offered him a job if he "cooperated." Toward the end of his life, the writer started work on a new book, one focusing on a black American who, as a result of living in both Paris and Africa, loses all sense of belonging anywhere. Far from leading to the discovery of a new, more accepting homeland, flight from one's own native country brought only further alienation. Smith's death in 1974 prevented him from finishing the novel, but the fact that he died in Paris confirmed his own life history as a tale of disenchanted exile.

The prospect of a return to Africa has remained a dream for many black Americans down to the present day, drawing its force more from continued racism and alienation in the United States than the concrete realities of African life. To a certain extent, as a dream it replaced earlier visions of life in France. However, Africa did not replace Paris as an alternative to the United States for blacks in the 1960s, due partly to conditions in Africa itself. The overthrow of Nkrumah effectively destroyed the black American expatriate community in Ghana; although some continued to live there, the dream of Ghana as forging new paths toward black liberation was tarnished beyond repair. Nkrumah's fall from power came at a time when the first rush of enthusiasm that greeted the rapid decolonization of Africa and Asia was giving way to a more sober assessment of the economic and political difficulties facing the third world. In 1965, both Sukarno in Indonesia and Ben Bella in Algeria fell victim to similar military seizures of power; like Nkrumah, they had led their nations to independence and symbolized the militant developing world on the march. A month before the coup in Ghana, the Nigerian army overthrew that nation's civilian government. In the face of such political turmoil, the vision of third world liberation was something easier to admire from afar. Even after the effective end of the French empire in Africa by 1960, Paris remained a crossroads for African students and diplomats, and as such an excellent window on the affairs of that continent.

The new shape of international race relations in the 1960s, then, did not bring to an end the African American expatriate community in Paris. American blacks came to Paris for a variety of reasons, including but not limited to flight from racism, and as long as they continued to do so and sought one another out in the French capital, the black community would endure. At the same time, although black expatriates did not always embrace a politicized vision of exile, their experience in Paris, and the continued survival of the black community, underlined the fact that racism was still a problem back home. The civil rights movement changed American life in important ways, especially in the South, but it certainly did not bring an end to discrimination or make blacks and whites true equals in the United States. By the late 1960s, the movement's shift from battling the legal segregation of the South to confronting the de facto economic discrimination of the North tended to emphasize not how far the nation had come in redressing its heritage of bigotry, but rather how far it still had to go. The disenchantment and frustration that fueled the Black Power movement reconfirmed the idea that white Americans would never accept blacks as equals. At the same time, the myriad daily reminders of racial tension that suffused interactions between blacks and whites in the United States remained inescapable. Throughout the 1960s, African Americans who moved to Paris were continually struck by the absence of such tension, by their own ability to relax and live without thinking about race. As Ollie Stewart commented in 1969, "In America I would spend 75 per cent of my time thinking about color — here color is nothing to worry about." Even after the 1960s, therefore, Paris continued to promise the heady feeling of living not as a black person, but just as a person, something still not possible in America.

To charge African Americans who chose to live in Paris, in spite of French racism, with hypocrisy is to miss the point. It is certainly discouraging that more did not follow the example of William Gardner Smith in publicly condemning French bigotry. Like most people, however, black expatriates chose the best life they could, one that happened to be abroad, without necessarily choosing to validate the problems of their host society, problems for which they were not responsible. Few accused blacks who remained in America of supporting a racist society by living there. One difference, of course, was that blacks in the United States had, as citizens, much more ability to fight against racism than as exiles in France. African American expatriates could do little about the ills of French racism without risking deportation. They did, however, have the ability to take some actions in support of the struggles of their own people back home. As a result, the heightened black American political activism of the 1960s produced an echo on the other side of the Atlantic. Continuing and building upon traditions established during the 1950s, the black expatriate community in Paris organized to show that they remained close to the movement for justice and equality in America.

EXPATRIATES AND POLITICAL ACTIVISM

The French capital has a long tradition of welcoming, or at least tolerating, political exiles, and has frequently witnessed activities staged by such groups in support of the ongoing struggles in their homelands. Although most black Americans in Paris were not political refugees in the strict sense of the term (they could return home if they chose), the civil rights and Black Power movements of the 1960s inspired some to take advantage of Parisian hospitality. Expatriates held meetings, circulated petitions, and gave interviews to the French press about the changing racial situation in the United States, hoping to contribute to the struggle for justice. In part, expatriates who "got involved" did so for the same reasons as African Americans living at home; this fight was theirs, and they were moved by examples of those who gave so much to make black people free. It is also true, however, that organizing protests in Paris served to show that black expatriates had not necessarily sold out and deserted the struggle by leaving America. Even though they had themselves escaped the burden of American racism, they had not forgotten those left behind. Finally, following the example of Richard Wright in the 1950s, some blacks felt that their presence abroad could serve as an asset for the struggle for black liberation. Living in an international media capital, they could inform the world about the evils of American racism and thus help mobilize the court of world opinion to force change. During the 1950s, many expatriates (and their critics) had viewed the act of leaving America as a political protest in and of itself. In the era of civil rights, however, simply emigrating no longer sufficed. Even for those in Paris, the time had now come to stand up and be counted.

As in the United States, black college students in Paris often took a leading role in initiating political activity. The tradition of African Americans studying in Paris goes back to the early nineteenth century, when affluent Creoles from New Orleans would send their sons to France to polish off their classical educations and acquire Continental chic. Many of the expatriates in Paris in the 1950s had initially settled there as students on the GI bill. Like other young blacks from the United States in earlier eras, the black expatriate students in the 1960s came to France out of a desire to see Europe and experience French culture. These newcomers, however, differed in important ways from earlier generations of African Americans. Whereas previously many had used fellowships for study as a way of coming to Paris, often looking for other means of staying when the money ran out, these new students often came on summer or junior-year-abroad programs, intending to go back to finish up their college degrees after a brief sojourn in France. In general, they appear to have been younger than the artists who won fellowships to study in Parisian art schools during the 1920s, or the veterans of the late 1940s, and there were simply more of them than in the past. In the United States, postwar prosperity and the huge expansion of higher education had created a massive new undergraduate population, its impact extending even to black students in Paris. Like their peers, black and white, back in America these young people conceived of their university status as a social and political identity, not just a matter of registration; they were *students*, not just people who studied. In Paris, African American students mingled with other black Americans but at the same time had their own rituals and habits. As a result, they became an increasingly important voice of the black community in the French capital.

It was only natural that students should take the lead in organizing this community to act in solidarity with black struggles in the United States. Throughout the 1960s, black college students were in the forefront of these movements, from the sit-ins to the strikes that rocked many predominantly white campuses by the end of the decade. African Americans studying in Paris came out of this politicized atmosphere, and were not likely to stop thinking about such issues once they left American soil. Moreover, their relatively temporary status in France encouraged a sense of connection to events back home. Students usually had much more personal experience with freedom struggles than older black expatriates in Paris, and more than a few regarded their time in the city as merely a brief furlough before they returned to take part. As the *New York Times* observed in 1969, "While black American students are [in Paris], they are among the Negro community's most outspoken militants. They and the artist-writer group conduct a variety of programs, including fund-raising for the Student Nonviolent Coordinating Committee and for the Black Panthers, to demonstrate their support of and identification with the movement at home."

One black student who took an active part in political organizing during her stay in Paris was Bette Woody. Now a professor at the University of Massachusetts–Boston, she spent several years in the French capital during this period. Originally from a middle-class background in rural Ohio, Woody attended Antioch University in the late 1950s, and in 1959 spent her junior year in Paris. After her return to America and graduation from Antioch, she moved to New York for two years, then moved back to Paris in 1962 for another two years, working as a researcher and translator. Like many other African Americans at the time, her interest in traveling to Paris was shaped both by the general reputation of the city and ideas about black life there; the Parisian legacies of both the impressionists and jazz artists like Bud Powell created an alluring vision of the French capital. During her junior year in Paris, Woody enrolled in the Ecole des Beaux-Arts, finding lodgings in nearby Saint-Germain-des-Prés. She found herself in the heart of the black expatriate colony in the city, a position that enabled her to experience the city's jazz clubs and meet famous individuals like James Baldwin and Richard Wright.

Bette Woody's student days in France were heady ones. She studied lithography at the Ecole, hung out in cafés and jazz clubs, took part in a lively, avant-garde arts scene, and met other Americans and people from around the world. She soon discovered that in Paris student life and politics went hand in hand. French students took political issues seriously, including struggles around the political significance of art. More strikingly, the city was full of foreign students from throughout the third world, many of whom kept close ties with liberation movements at home and used their time in Paris to mobilize support for them. Cafés were the perfect spot to meet other students and discuss international political affairs. Many of the black students in Paris, especially when Woody returned in 1962, had already worked for civil rights back home, so it was only natural to continue this involvement in a supercharged, politicized atmosphere. The ever more traumatic impact of the Algerian war reinforced students' activism. In some ways, this activism represented a break with the older generation of African Americans in Paris who had settled there after World War II. In remembering her years in the French capital, Woody described a meeting with Richard Wright that summed up this contrast:

The challenge for us was asking him about the civil rights movement and about where he stood as far as black rights, what was he doing about it. He was so famous and important. He was very bristly about the civil rights stuff in America, I think a little defensive about his position. This was an older man being confronted by some silly people who were big risk takers. . . . We didn't have any memories of lynchings in Mississippi, and so our idea was that civil rights were civil rights were civil rights, and you just had to go out and demand them! . . . I don't know enough about Wright's philosophy and his politics, but my sense was that he was kind of naive in a way, he didn't really know that much about the growth of the civil rights movement in America as a broader movement, and he certainly didn't know anything about black students.

These encounters reveal much about the changing nature of black American life in Paris during the 1960s. Richard Wright certainly never saw his exile in France as a retreat from politics or the concerns of blacks in the United States; as the essays in *White Man, Listen!* demonstrated, he spoke out more forcefully than ever against discrimination. However, he approached activism essentially as an intellectual, using his published writings to attack bigotry. For the black students who challenged him, however, simply speaking out was no longer enough. Some had participated in demonstrations and sit-ins for civil rights back home, and their idea of political involvement was riding in an integrated bus through the South, not condemning racism in a novel. The students were fired not only by commitment but by youthful optimism, a belief in the possibility of change *now*, which not all of their elders could share. Two different conceptions of African American politics, and two different generations of African Americans, thus confronted each other across Parisian café tables.

Bette Woody and her friends did not simply criticize their elders for their failure to take direct action, however. Especially after she returned to Paris in 1962, Woody and others got involved in organizing support for civil rights in the United States. Her first stay in France had introduced her to the model of international student politics and the role foreign students could play in their own countries, and she applied this model to black student life in Paris. After 1962, Bette Woody became a part of a group of black Americans, mostly students, who met to discuss the situation in America and consider what African Americans in Paris could do to raise awareness of the issues in France. Organized in part by Richard Wright's daughter, Julia, as well as the student leader Carlos Moore, the group of ten to twelve black men and women met on a regular basis in the Wrights' apartment to plan strategies. The group's major accomplishment was to organize a visit to Paris by Malcolm X in February 1965, as it turned out a few weeks before his death.

Bette Woody's portrait of black American activism in Paris during the 1960s emphasizes the concern black students had about the changing racial situation in America, their desire to discuss it with one another as a way of keeping in touch, and their wish to undertake supportive actions of small practical import but tremendous symbolic significance. But students were not the only African Americans in Paris to search for ways of demonstrating their commitment to the struggle. Perhaps the most important example was the meeting held in solidarity with the March on Washington in August 1963. A few days beforehand, James Baldwin and the actor William Marshall published a notice in the *New York Herald Tribune,* distributed in Paris at the time, calling on all interested Americans to come to the Living Room on Saturday, August 17, to discuss the upcoming march. As Baldwin commented to the *New York Times,* "We want to serve notice we are part of this revolution in the United States." About fifty people answered the summons, including African Americans and white American sympathizers like Anthony Quinn and Ralph Nader. The next morning, the group proceeded to the American Church of Paris, where organizers spoke before an overflow crowd in support of the civil rights movement and circulated a petition affirming the goals of the Washington demonstration. The petition stated: "We cannot physically participate in this march, but we, like the rest of the world, have been tremendously stirred by so disciplined an exhibition of dignity and courage and persistence."

The following Wednesday about eighty people staged a silent march across the Seine to the U.S. embassy, where they submitted the petition, signed by almost three hundred Americans, to government officials. By nightfall, the embassy had received five hundred more statements of support by mail. As Art Simmons later described the event, "It was a beautiful thing, very dignified."

The August 1963 march was the only time that blacks in Paris actually staged a public march for civil rights, but there were other activities that could and did permit African Americans in France to act in solidarity with the struggle back home. Expatriates formed overseas chapters of black American organizations like the Student Nonviolent Coordinating Committee, the Black Panthers, and Malcolm X's short-lived Organization of Afro-American Unity. These groups distributed information from home among the black community in Paris, and got musicians to play fund-raising concerts whose proceeds would be sent back across the Atlantic. Black Americans in Paris also helped arrange the visits of movement leaders from the United States touring Europe to raise international awareness about the continuing plight of their people. Martin Luther King stopped in the city on his way back from Stockholm, where he received the Nobel Prize in 1964. In 1966, Stokely Carmichael spent ten days in the French capital, speaking to groups of French and African students, as well as meeting with members of the African American community. Scheduled to speak in favor of the Vietnamese National Liberation Front, Carmichael was detained at the airport by French police, and was released only after President Charles de Gaulle personally intervened.

Malcolm X was not so lucky. The star speaker of the Nation of Islam passed through France twice, both times near the end of his life when he had already broken with Elijah Muhammad and the nation's leadership. The first visit, in November 1964, took place as Malcolm X was returning from his second trip to Africa. En route back to the United States, he stopped off briefly in Paris and London, the two former capitals of colonial Africa which now played host to large groups of African students and intellectuals. While in Paris, he gave a speech at the Salle de la Mutualité, a large hall in the Latin Quarter, and was interviewed by Melvin Van Peebles. As Chester Himes noted in his autobiography, the fiery black leader already had quite a following among expatriates in France: "There were a lot of young American blacks in Paris at that time who were devoutly interested in Malcolm X, who had returned from Mecca. Some claimed to be his followers and more or less worshiped him, others wanted to know him to become his followers; the black women oldtimers on the Paris scene were all trying to seduce him. There were scores of black men who claimed to be watching Malcolm for the CIA."

Whereas this trip proceeded without incident, the second erupted in controversy. In February 1965, Malcolm X returned to London to speak before African activists. Bette Woody's group arranged for him to make a detour to the French capital, where he was scheduled to talk about the Western intervention in the Congo and Vietnam. When he arrived at Orly Airport, however, he was immediately detained by police. Informing him that his presence was "undesirable in France," they placed him on an Air France jet bound for London, officially deporting him from the country. Recriminations exploded immediately as to who was responsible. The French government claimed that Malcolm X would have endangered the public order in Paris. A rumor soon arose that the French had acted to prevent an assassination of Malcolm X by the CIA, or at least stop it from happening on their soil. Malcolm X himself believed that State Department officials had inspired his deportation from France, wanting to prevent his criticisms of U.S. foreign policy from reaching an international audience. Bette Woody's recollection of this incident tends to support such allegations of American involvement. "The day he was supposed to come we went to the airport to pick him up . . . everything was all set. Malcolm X was coming to town! We got to the gate where he was supposed to come out . . . and he was about to go through customs, and two FBI guys —

these are FBI, speaking English, looking American — came and got him and pulled him back into a room . . . and we never saw him again . . . the conclusion was that basically the Americans decided that they were just going to do this on their own." The rally went on as planned, with Carlos Moore speaking in place of the absent Malcolm X. A month later, the great tribune was dead, the victim of assassins' bullets in New York.

For politically concerned African Americans living in Paris, as well as for those in the United States, Malcolm X symbolized the transition from the civil rights movement of the early 1960s to the Black Power consciousness that dominated the latter years of the decade. The splintering of the movement in the late 1960s and 1970s and the despair that followed the assassination of Martin Luther King in 1968 prevented any one group or issue from organizing significant activities in the French capital. For some, the turn to the right in American politics symbolized by the election of Richard Nixon to the presidency in 1968 once more gave exile a political significance in and of itself. If America had become a fascist state, then expatriates were again political refugees. Yet many blacks in Paris did keep in touch with African American political movements and organizations at home. The Black Panther party in particular attracted a lot of interest. For some African Americans, especially young people, the murder of the apostle of nonviolence in April 1968 meant that "picking up the gun" was the only viable response left to stem American racism. The Panthers, with their paramilitary uniforms and their willingness to challenge the white police, captivated the imaginations of many. By the beginning of the 1970s, several black expatriates espoused the militant ideology of the Black Panthers and claimed direct connections with the organization in the United States. Rumors circulated of black GIs who had deserted their army bases in West Germany for the French capital before using their military skills to bring the revolution back to the States. Increasingly, the Panthers espoused an ideology of third world revolution, in large part based on the writings of Frantz Fanon, the black French author of *The Wretched of the Earth* and leading theoretician of liberation struggles. This internationalist perspective proved especially attractive and relevant to African Americans living far from home.

The connection became even closer after 1969, as the Black Panther party itself became to a significant extent a movement in exile. The attack on the Chicago Panthers and the murder of Fred Hampton by the Chicago police in December 1969 convinced many black activists that the American government had declared war on them, leaving them little choice but prison, death, or escape abroad. Black Panther members thus became political refugees in a far more concrete sense than the circle around Richard Wright, for many of those who left could not, or at least believed they could not, return to America as free men and women. Yet Paris was not the first choice for black radicals fleeing the United States. Visions of the revolutionary third world beckoned, offering the opportunity to experience nonwhite socialism in power. In 1968, Eldridge Cleaver, the leading Panther ideologue who had just run for president on the Peace and Freedom ticket, fled California for Cuba, arriving in Havana on Christmas Day. He soon organized a Black Panther party in exile, consisting of eight individuals who had hijacked commercial airplanes to the Caribbean nation in order to join the revolution. Relations with Cuban authorities soon soured, however, leading Cleaver and his followers to seek a new host country. In 1969, the Cubans deported Cleaver to Algeria, where he set up a center for Black Panthers and sympathizers which lasted for the next three years. Yet Algiers, like Havana, ultimately disappointed these apostles of third world revolution. As Cleaver noted later in an interview, "This is no place for an Afro-American liberation movement."

In January 1973, Eldridge Cleaver left Algiers for Paris, leaving behind the dwindling colony of Black Panthers in exile. The Black Panthers had supporters among the left-wing intelligentsia of France, and Cleaver soon applied for asylum as a political refugee. His wife, Kathleen's, knowledge of French made the city a reasonable choice, as did the cosmopolitan character of its population. As Cleaver observed in *Soul on Fire*:

> The heavy pedestrian traffic between the Metro station and the hospital, including workers, patients, and visitors, provided a perfect atmosphere of anonymity, ideal for someone living illegally in Paris, with a false I.D. and an assumed name. Many of the workers, patients, and visitors at the hospital were black — immigrants from former French African colonies, most of them French citizens. Among the passers-by were Arabs and many French citizens from Martinique, now officially a part of France. Some of the people of color who passed my house were of a polyglot mixture that defied all classification, the results of hundreds of years of French colonialism and the march of French armies around the globe. You could meet anything there and no one took a second look. I was just another *noir*.

In effect, Paris represented the third world without the messiness of third world politics.

Eldridge Cleaver's move from Algeria to France signaled a decisive and permanent ideological turning point. In leaving Algiers, Cleaver abandoned his romantic view of third world anti-imperialist socialism, opting instead for the liberal-democratic "repressive tolerance" of a Western capital city. The move was the first step on a path that would soon lead the black revolutionary to reject decisively the Left as a whole, allowing him to return to the United States as a repentant true believer in capitalism and the American Way. Instead of the French capital becoming a place where blacks from the United States could gain a greater awareness of Africa, in this case it enabled an exiled African American weary of Africa to find his way back to the United States.

The Cleavers' years in Paris, from early 1973 to late 1975, were far from happy, resembling less the lives of most African Americans in Paris than conditions experienced by the city's political exiles for generations. During 1973, the couple resided illegally in the country while a galaxy of French celebrities, ranging from Jean-Paul Sartre and Simone de Beauvoir to François Mitterrand, pleaded with the government to grant the notorious international revolutionary political asylum. The Cleavers rented modest lodgings in working-class neighborhoods, waiting for legalization of their resident status so they could bring their children, currently staying with relatives in America, back to live with them in France. The appeals of their supporters eventually succeeded in persuading the government of Valéry Giscard d'Estaing to grant their petition, so by 1974 the family was once again united and living legally in the country. Yet the prospect of living out his life in obscure, impoverished exile in Paris held little appeal for a man by now used to action and the glare of public attention. The Black Panther party in America was in shambles, with both Huey Newton and Bobby Seale subjecting Cleaver to bitter attacks, so that few black radicals looked to him for leadership or inspiration.

The Cleavers lived an isolated life in the French capital, making few contacts with other African Americans. Other Panthers had followed Eldridge Cleaver to Paris, but the French government sternly forbade them from engaging in any political activity, preventing the kind of black radical politics in exile that had flourished briefly in Algiers from resurfacing on French soil. Instead, Cleaver had to confront the prospect, like so many refugees before him, of his children gradually growing up French and forgetting all about the struggles to which he had dedicated his life. The bitterness of exile, of having to spend one's mature years paying for the headstrong choices of one's youth, transformed the initial excitement of acceptance by the French into feelings of regret and despair. "I was getting sarcastic and cynical: sarcastic about the minor league gloating of the Europeans, and cynical about my own attempts to create a meaningful philosophy of life . . . I looked around at other exiles and saw that they were slowly being bent into the French mold. I felt doomed."

By the end of 1974, Eldridge Cleaver had begun to speak openly of returning to America in the very near future, and his political orientation shifted dramatically. Cleaver now praised American democracy and condemned Communism as both destructive and racist. Newspapers in the United States began to feature stories about the "new" Eldridge Cleaver, a man who had clearly realized the error of his ways while in exile and had learned to love again what he had formerly taken for granted. In 1975, Cleaver manifested his abandonment of radical politics in another way, by starting a new career as, of all things, a clothes designer. Clearly, exile in the world's fashion capital had changed the man's life in more than one way. In the fall of that year, Cleaver came out with a line of "codpiece" pants, designed to display male genitalia prominently. As an October ad in *Rolling Stone* declared, "You'll be Cock of the Walk with the New Fall Collection from Eldridge de Paris." In the same month, Cleaver decided finally to bite the bullet and return to America. After negotiating terms with the American embassy in Paris, the erstwhile Black Panther leader flew to New York on November 18, 1975, where he was promptly arrested by federal agents and sent to California for trial. Cleaver was interned in a San Diego federal prison, where he converted to Christianity, before being released on bail in August 1976. Now the darling of conservatives, from William F. Buckley to Pat Boone, Eldridge Cleaver went on the lecture circuit to trumpet his newfound faith in both God and America. The prodigal son was home for good.

Eldridge Cleaver's departure in 1975 marked the end of any significant African American political mobilization in Paris. This exit did not mean that the black expatriate community in the French capital simply dropped all political concerns. The persisting plight of African Americans in the face of racism and economic equality has continued to elicit concern and occasional activism. Nonetheless, as in the United States, the hopes for an imminent end to American bigotry retained little force by the mid-1970s; the "sixties" were clearly over and the Reagan era loomed on the political horizon. Those who considered themselves political activists did not necessarily reject the ideals of their youth as Cleaver did, but few failed to recognize that the days of strident protest had passed, at least for the time being. Moreover, the idea of exile in Paris as a political statement no longer seemed so compelling. Instead, the city remained what it had been for most of the twentieth century, a pleasant place for African Americans to live.

W. Somerset Maugham once commented that the white American expatriate Henry James wasted much of his life going to English garden parties in the late nineteenth century, thereby missing out on the greatest story of the age, the emergence of modern America. Did African Americans in Paris during the 1960s exercise a similar lack of judgment? Do the charges of escapism and hypocrisy, so eloquently expressed by William Gardner Smith in *The Stone*

Face, ring true? In part, certainly. Many black expatriates in Paris valued the sense of personal liberation that life in the city could bring, caring little that they could do less for civil rights and black equality there than back home. Many did not take part in the solidarity activities that other expatriates organized. But this neglect should not serve as a condemnation of the black American community in Paris as a whole. Some black expatriates chose to ignore the discrimination against Arabs and other people of color in France, but many more were shocked and disturbed by it. African Americans abroad could play a useful role in focusing world attention (and moral pressure) upon the mistreatment of black people in the United States. As William Gardner Smith observed to the *New York Times* in 1969, "I've talked to many black people coming to Paris and they say, 'Stay where you are — let Europe and Africa know how it really is for the brother in America.'"

It is significant that most criticisms of black Americans in Paris came from within the community itself, from those who felt guilty about their fortune in escaping American racism when so many others could not. Such feelings of desertion deprived life in France of some of its glamour and special quality, reinforcing the disadvantages of exile abroad. They prompted some individuals, notably James Baldwin and Donald Byrd, to go back home for good, and others to regard Paris as only temporary. Others continued to enjoy life in the city, but with a sharper awareness of the complexity of exile, that most choices involved both gains and losses. William Gardner Smith, always the most attentive of African Americans to such concerns, summed up the problem succinctly in *Return to Black America*:

> The black man who established his home in Europe paid a heavy price. He paid it in a painful tearing of himself from his past. . . . He paid for it in guilt: for, no matter what the rationalization, no matter whether he cooperated with the black movement from abroad, he could never escape the conviction that the real fight was *there*, on the spot, on the battleground. He paid for it, finally, in a sort of rootlessness: for, seriously, who were all these peculiar people speaking Dutch, Danish, Italian, German, Spanish, French? . . . what did they know about the black skin's long, bitter, and soon triumphant odyssey? The black man, no matter how long he lived in Europe, drifted through those societies an eternal "foreigner" among eternal strangers.

STUDENT POWER IN FRANCE: MAY 1968

Not all the political challenges faced by African American expatriates in France during the 1960s revolved around race. The massive student revolt that erupted spontaneously in Paris during the spring of 1968 did not for the most part address issues of racial discrimination or the experience of black Americans living in Paris. Yet the young French insurgents had much in common with the black Left in America, and its representatives and sympathizers in Paris. Both condemned Western imperialism and looked to third world liberation movements for inspiration. Both were broadly anticapitalist and frequently viewed the American government as the world's greatest enemy of human progress. In addition, French student rebels and American black militants shared many heroes, especially Frantz Fanon and Mao Tse-tung. Those who took to the Parisian streets in 1968 had often been inspired by black American struggles for freedom, and had flocked to listen to speeches by visitors like Stokely Carmichael and Malcolm X. Few in 1968 would have predicted that a revolution modeled on liberation struggles in Asia and Africa would arise in the heart of a Western capital city, yet for a few weeks in May exactly that seemed to be happening. In May 1968, black American expatriates in Paris found the city they had become accustomed to briefly but radically transformed in a way that shook the very pillars of French society. Some supported the movement, others tried to ignore it, and a few even opposed it. Yet France's May crisis not only made itself directly felt in the lives of this group of Americans, but also, by hardening French attitudes toward politically active foreigners, changed their own position in Paris. It was a powerful reminder that expatriates who neglect events in their host nation do so at their peril.

The year 1968 was one of the most turbulent of the twentieth century, not just in the United States, but around the world. At the center of this political turmoil marched the international student movement, whose shock troops laid siege to the materialistic complacency of the postwar West. The May 1968 movement in Paris dwarfed all other student uprisings by virtue of its size and impact on French society. The crisis began earlier in the year at Nanterre, a relatively obscure suburban campus of the gargantuan University of Paris, where student radicals had sought to mobilize around a number of political issues, including imperialism and opposition to America's war in Vietnam. The movement soon shifted from the isolation of Nanterre into the heart of Paris's Latin Quarter, setting up operations in the central courtyard of the Sorbonne itself. Administration attempts to shut down the Sorbonne in turn merely prompted students to occupy its buildings, turning the venerable university into a twenty-four-hour-a-day popular debating society on how to make the revolution. When the authorities brought in riot police, the students fought back, staging the largest street battles in Paris since the liberation of

1944. French workers began responding to the call of the student Left and walking out on strike, expressing their frustration at low pay, high unemployment, and especially feelings of alienation on the job. Members of various professional groups throughout the country began demanding more autonomy at work and reform of often rigid bureaucracies. Even soccer players joined in, occupying the central offices of the National Soccer Federation and calling for "le football aux footballeurs!" By the last week of May, France confronted the largest strike in its history up to that point: ten million French men and women, 20 percent of the entire national population, had joined the spontaneous protest. Much Parisian life came to a dead stop. Mail was not delivered, trash accumulated in the streets, long lines formed at gas stations as fuel deliveries became more and more haphazard. Leading politicians began negotiating to see who would succeed de Gaulle, whose downfall now seemed only a matter of time.

As with most other residents of the city, the rapid escalation of events in May took most African Americans in Paris completely by surprise. Many lived or socialized in and near the Latin Quarter where most of the violence took place, often witnessing firsthand the clashes between students and police. Even those who had lived in the city a long time suddenly became tourists again, venturing out to stare at a Paris transformed. William Gardner Smith, ever the assiduous reporter, wrote about the battles on the Left Bank. He witnessed the confrontations along the rue Gay-Lussac, where roughly one thousand students and teachers battled the police behind barricades improvised from paving stones, wrecked cars, and fallen trees. Comparisons with Afro-Asian liberation movements were not lost on Smith, who observed that the insurgents hailed Che Guevara, Ho Chi Minh, Stokely Carmichael, and Malcolm X as their heroes. To complete the third world analogy, Smith noted that the battle ended with the students vanishing into the surrounding community, just like the Vietcong.

As Paris and the entire country descended into chaos, one no longer had to search for the revolution. Even those who were not necessarily interested in or sympathetic with the movement found themselves affected when all public services ground to a halt. Dean Ferrier, an African American woman who had come to Paris as a student in the late 1950s and stayed, recalled being stranded in the city because all the trains had stopped running: "That was the beginning of the train strike and, as you know, everything went on strike . . . the post office, telephone, everything."

Chester Himes arrived with his partner, Lesley Packard, from Spain at the end of April and soon found himself in the midst of a whirlwind. The couple settled into an apartment in the sumptuous Sixteenth District of the city, far away from the turmoil of the Latin Quarter. The peace and quiet they found there did not last long, however: "Renault workers were marching into Paris from the east and the citizens had stopped organized transportation of all kinds, refused to deliver mail or collect garbage. We could hear the cannon firing on the outskirts of the city. The trains and all air transportation had stopped and the city had become physically dangerous . . . When the riots reached St.-Germain-des-Prés and the riot police broke the doors of Aux Deux Magots and the Café Flore, we began thinking of another city." Himes and Packard did leave Paris briefly for Darmstadt, Germany, unconsciously following in the footsteps of those aristocrats who had fled France for the valley of the Rhine during the French Revolution. However, they soon returned to the French capital, settling into an apartment in Montparnasse where Himes spent the summer working on his autobiography.

Although the violence that accompanied the May movement in France was frightening and the incessant strikes made daily life much more difficult, many black expatriates in Paris supported the movement. As Dean Ferrier commented, "It was a great time of *protestation*, of people trying to figure out what the other guy was [all about]." Many sympathized with the demands for greater personal liberty pressed by the students, and saw their struggle as another dimension of the worldwide fight for justice that included the campaign for racial justice in America. This affinity was powerfully reinforced by the students' own third world ideology, and in particular by their clear identification with both the Black Power and antiwar movements in the United States. Some sought to aid the young French insurgents directly. Julia Wright knew, more than most African Americans in Paris, the frustrations that often awaited students in French universities, and for her it was an easy leap from organizing support for the civil rights movement to acting in solidarity with the rebels of May 1968. She took part in the movement, helping to gather food and medical supplies for students wounded in the fighting. When Vertamae Smart-Grosvenor came back to Paris in 1968, she got swept up in the events, joining Julia Wright in supporting the young people in the streets. In a very different way from that described in travel brochures, May 1968 brought back to the young African American woman the excitement of the French capital.

The other time somebody went crazy was at the Sorbonne when I was helping Julia sell the *pouvoir noir* [Black Power] in the stall in the courtyard. It was during the occupation in '68. The whole courtyard was bustling. Everybody was selling everything. The Marxists were selling their stuff. The Jeune Nation was selling their propaganda. People were making speeches on the loud-speaker. They even had some Africans selling Billy Graham Bibles . . . I had on all my do and was feeling very good because I had been speaking only French all day and was able to talk to a lot of the brothers and sisters of the Third World who didn't speak English.

Like the Algerian war, the May 1968 crisis in France inspired one African American to write a novel, which remains the best testament to the ways in which black expatriates in Paris reacted to the events of that tumultuous year. In 1969, Frank Yerby published *Speak Now*, a tale of star-crossed lovers set amid the revolutionary chaos of the preceding year. Yerby was no stranger to Paris, and had spent some time in southern France during 1967 before returning to his home in Madrid. He based *Speak Now* not on firsthand experience of the May events, but instead on information gleaned from the French press. Nonetheless, Yerby's understanding of France, and of the lives of African American expatriates, was very well developed, enabling him to write a novel touching upon many of the reactions of that community to the French student revolt.

Like *The Stone Face*, but in a much more direct manner, *Speak Now* relates the story of a love affair between a black American man and a white woman in Paris. So central is this theme that the book's preface opens with the sentence "This is a novel about miscegenation . . ." Harrison Forbes, like the protagonist of *Paris Blues*, is an African American jazz musician who plays clarinet in a club cutely named Le Blue Note. Forbes also resembles Flender's Eddie Cook in his deeply cynical outlook on life, due in part to his experiences as a soldier with the U.S. Army in Vietnam. Portrayed as a man who expects little from other people or from life in general, Harry spends much of the novel wearily denouncing the sorry state of humanity, embodied above all by white racism. He is also tortured by self-hatred, criticizing black leaders and African civilization in general. At one point, he declares, "My people, *le Bon Dieu* pity them! What have we? Whom can we boast of?"

In sharp contrast to Simeon Brown in *The Stone Face*, however, Yerby's hero has no illusions about the tolerance of his French hosts. The novel is full of portraits of racist French people, especially French hatred of interracial relationships. It is therefore only fitting that he becomes involved, not just with any white woman, but with a wealthy young heiress from a family of tobacco magnates in the Deep South. He meets Katherine Nichols at a Parisian café while having breakfast. Kathy is penniless and confused, having just been robbed blind by a lover, so Harry buys her something to eat while she tells her story. It soon becomes a classic case of opposites attract: the skeptical Harry opens the eyes of the naive young Kathy to the problems of the world, teasing her about her own racial biases while taking care of her. In turn, Harry is himself transformed as he falls in love, a love possible only in exile. The couple gets married in Paris, at a ceremony presided over by a French official who uses the opportunity to praise his nation's liberal heritage. It is Paris in the spring, and once again love has triumphed over racism.

Speak Now presents a rather pathetic and unsettling vision of a black man turned inside out by his love for a white Southern damsel in distress, one whom he is continually rescuing even though she has far more resources than he does. Harry's feelings for Kathy run far too close for comfort to the idea of loving one's oppressor. However, the setting is not a Parisian spring like any other, and it is the description of the May 1968 student revolt that gives the novel its greatest interest. In *Speak Now*, the events of May form a constant backdrop that from time to time intervenes to change the lives of Harry and Kathy. The two first declare their love (more accurately, their lust) for each other one night during some of the worst street fighting in the Latin Quarter. Harry is performing when he gets a frantic call from Kathy that she's trapped between rioters and police in Saint-Germain-des-Prés. Harry immediately sets off to save her, and is able to get through the barricades because the students feel a black man must be on their side. Ultimately, however, the May movement brings this couple back together. After a series of (unintentionally comic) misunderstandings, the two are reunited amid a riotous night of fighting between revolutionaries and the forces of order, only to become victims of police brutality. Harry strikes a policeman and in return the police beat Harry senseless and arrest him. The novel ends in Harry's hospital room, with the couple pledging their determination to stay together and force the world to make a place for their love.

Speak Now gives an ambiguous but essentially positive portrait of the May events, closely reflecting the attitude of many African Americans in Paris toward the crisis. The initial image of the movement is one of chaos, of violence out of control that disrupts the normal course of life in the city. A swinging jazz set at Le Blue Note is interrupted when Harry leaves suddenly to rescue Kathy from the battles in Saint-Germain-des-Prés. Transit strikes make getting both in and out of the French capital a complex, arduous task. Yet in spite of himself Harry likes the students who dare to challenge the authority of the French state. Moreover, they clearly demonstrate feelings of solidarity with him as one of the world's oppressed, whereas most older French men and women treat him with suspicion or contempt. *Speak Now* ends very much like *The Stone Face*, as the protagonist realizes the link between racism in America and racism in France. In both cases, the hero assaults a bigoted policeman, and as a result is himself beaten and thrown into prison. The policeman who Harry attacks initiates the violence by striking him for having the temerity to kiss a white woman in public. In striking the racist policeman, Harry not only attacks bigotry and defends the woman he loves, but implicitly recognizes his solidarity with the young insurgents of May 1968.

Speak Now ends at the height of the May crisis, when revolution seemed imminent in Paris. Yet little more than a week later the movement was in full-scale retreat, with the venerable old warrior Charles de Gaulle once more master of the situation. By May 30, many French citizens were tired of the incessant strikes, the food shortages, and the garbage piling up in the streets, and worried about where the crisis would lead. This change in public opinion became clear when more than 500,000 supporters of the president staged a spontaneous march down the Champs-Elysées, angrily denouncing the student leaders. The government used substantial wage increases and other concessions to lure most strikers back to work. The success of this strategy became clear for all to see when the Gaullist party won an overwhelming victory in the national elections of June 1968. The elderly politician's hard realism had triumphed over the youthful idealism of the French students, handing the May movement a crushing and definitive defeat.

Although the turbulence of the student revolt had often temporarily inconvenienced African Americans living in Paris, the end of the movement affected many more directly. The riots themselves had adversely affected the city's jazz clubs, filling some with tear gas and forcing others to close for lack of clients. After the end of the crisis, the Paris jazz scene hit a dry spell, leading tenor sax player Nathan Davis and others to move elsewhere in Europe. The participation of many foreigners in the struggle, most notably the German Jewish student leader Daniel Cohn-Bendit, made French authorities and police much less tolerant of political refugees in their midst. A few African Americans who had taken the side of the students consequently found themselves deported for their pains. More generally, the new official intolerance toward foreigners affected not just activists, but anyone whose papers were not in order, especially people of color, who then as now the French police were more likely to stop and question without warning. African Americans in the country illegally did not receive any special consideration, and many were therefore forced to leave. In remembering the aftermath of May 1968, Dean Ferrier commented, "A lot of Americans — a lot of jazz musicians, a lot of painters and writers — left because they cracked down on immigration. It's just that they were asking you for your papers every three hundred meters and a lot of people didn't have them, a lot of people were living here and working on the black market . . . living and feeling free for the first time in their lives. That even happened to me."

Thus the backlash that followed the May crisis made life more difficult for the kind of black expatriates who hung on to life in the city without much in the way of prospects or resources, drawn by the city's reputation for openness and tolerance toward people of color. After May, Paris lost some of its tolerance, for expatriates and for all those in search of alternatives to the System, and in consequence offered less of a place for African Americans. Tannie Stovall (no relation), an African American scientist who moved to Paris in 1964, noted, "May '68 killed it. . . . After May '68, people became less agreeable to black Americans because some of them had the brilliant idea to associate themselves with antigovernment forces and to demonstrate against the government. After '68, few were welcome anymore."

The near revolution of May 1968 in France thus carried multiple meanings for the black expatriate community in Paris. For a few, it offered a new avenue for political involvement, reinforcing the international dimension of the struggles of the 1960s. For others, those who sympathized but did not take part in the events, it reinforced the insurgent character of the 1960s in general, forming a new connection between life in Paris and back home in the United States. African Americans tended to focus on those aspects of the May movement which emphasized solidarity with the third world, especially Maoist ideology and opposition to American intervention in Vietnam. For many, therefore, the struggles of the French students had some connection to revolts by people of color throughout the world. At the same time, however, May 1968 demonstrated some of the hard realities of life in France. The city's boulevards lost much of their beauty when filled with tear gas and burning Citroëns, when their chestnut trees were chopped down to make barricades. The ideals of the student movement, championing a society based on love, not profit, were nothing if not romantic. They became less attractive for many black expatriates (and Parisians in general) amid the stench of putrefying garbage that had not been collected for weeks, or long lines at gas stations. Above all, the violence of the riot police revealed the iron fist hidden under the velvet glove of French tolerance. All too reminiscent of the brutality directed by white Southern sheriffs against marchers for civil rights, it clearly demonstrated that, for all their vaunted tolerance, the French were capable of responding savagely to any perceived threats against the social order.

For France as a whole, the crisis of May 1968 represented a last hurrah for the social and political militance of the 1960s, and its impact on black Americans living in Paris reflected a trend. The new toughness of French police and immigration officials proved merely a prelude to the economic recession of the early 1970s, which limited opportunities for expatriates in Paris much more decisively. Although the days of the early postwar era when one could live like a king in France on American dollars had long since vanished, the booming economy of the 1960s offered a variety of job possibilities even to Americans without work permits. The oil crisis and the world economic downturn of the early 1970s brought France's era of postwar prosperity to a halt. By 1973, the nation, which had grown accustomed to full employment, counted 300,000 citizens without jobs, a number that soon climbed past 1,000,000. Such an economic climate, which has lasted to the present day, left little room for foreigners, including African Americans. The days in which a young man with few resources like James Baldwin or William Gardner Smith could move to Paris and make a living for himself had largely passed into history; the French capital now presented a cold shoulder to such youthful romantics. May 1968 demonstrated in exaggerated measure both the romance and the hard-nosed realism of Parisian life. The city would retain both, but after the early 1970s the predominance of the latter meant that Paris had little to offer would-be expatriates.

The repression that followed the May movement, and the subsequent economic recession, reinforced a new, less romantic view of Paris in the 1960s. Not only did life in the city seem to become harder, but changing racial realities on both sides of the Atlantic called into question its reputation as a refuge from prejudice. Yet black Americans continued to settle in the City of Light, if anything in larger numbers than ever before. The glamour of Paris remained a powerful lure in the 1960s, serving both to attract the curious and convince those who had fallen in love with France to stay just a little while longer. The unprecedented prosperity of the era, combined with the increased opportunities for middle-class blacks in the United States, made both options more feasible. The massive expansion of higher education and the tourist industry brought more African Americans to Paris as visitors and students. Good job opportunities enabled people to earn enough money at home to support short stays in France, and many found that once in Paris one could obtain enough work to eke out a living, albeit a modest one. Above all, the simple fact remained that in many significant ways Parisians continued to treat black Americans with much more respect and consideration than did their own white countrymen back home. Most African Americans in Paris immediately noticed a lessening of tension, a feeling that one could breathe freer and do whatever one wanted without fear of racist repercussions. The black American expatriate community in Paris during the 1960s therefore underscored, at least in part, the survival of racial difference and discrimination in the United States. As long as American blacks and whites lived in different, unequal, and hostile worlds, a few of the former would continue to seek their fortunes on the other side of the Atlantic.

AFRICAN AMERICANS
IN PARIS TODAY

BLACKS FROM THE UNITED STATES have a rich and important history in Paris, and they continue to contribute to the increasingly diverse culture of the city today. At the end of the twentieth century, the French capital remains home to a vibrant and diverse African American community, roughly one thousand strong according to various estimates. While no longer counting among its members individuals like Josephine Baker or Richard Wright who symbolize entire eras, the city's black community can still claim many talented and successful people who for one reason or another have found life there preferable to that offered by their homeland. In some respects, life in the city fails to live up to the romantic vision that so often (and not just for African Americans) surrounds it. Life is expensive in France, jobs are hard to find, and living conditions frequently much worse than in the United States. Moreover, France is now home to a powerful racist political movement, the National Front. Black Americans in Paris today rarely fail to acknowledge these problems, many offering a matter-of-fact assessment of their adopted city. Yet the romance remains, and so, for the most part, do they. Consequently, the experience of African Americans in the City of Light continues to present both a rich historical record and a vital living tradition.

Present-day black Paris differs in important ways from earlier eras. The city no longer contains distinctive African American neighborhoods, along the lines of Montmartre in the 1920s or even Saint-Germain-des-Prés in the 1950s. In addition, the proliferation of low-cost flights between France and America has further reduced the distance between the two nations. Today's African

American in Paris is more likely to be a short-term visitor, in the city on business or pleasure, than an expatriate severing ties with his native land. But black Americans continue to settle in Paris for a variety of reasons, and they establish common bonds. From the jazz clubs of Les Halles to Haynes restaurant, institutions and rituals still bring this diverse constellation of people together. The current failure of the United States to effect the full equality and integration of its black and white worlds has ensured the continued importance of black community and life abroad as themes in the African American experience. As in the past, both contribute today to maintaining black Americans as a unique presence in the storied city by the Seine.

DEATH OF A DIVA

If the 1960s began with the deaths of Sidney Bechet and Richard Wright, one must date the contemporary era from the passing of Josephine Baker in 1975; nothing better symbolizes the transition from past to present than the death of the woman whose career spanned fifty years of African American history in Paris. Unlike most other black Americans there, Josephine Baker supported the conservatives during the May 1968 crisis, going so far as to join the massive demonstration on the Champs-Elysées in favor of Charles de Gaulle. Baker's participation in the May demonstration symbolized her life during the 1960s; the political reversal it represented paralleled a much more significant reversal of fortunes. Ever since her epochal debut with the Revue Nègre in 1925, Baker's life in France had been an almost uninterrupted series of triumphs, a modern-day fairy tale. Not only did she remain popular as an entertainer during much of the 1950s, but she had become a real live fairy godmother, one whose castle sheltered orphans from around the world. The 1960s, in contrast, were a very difficult decade for the great star, one that saw many of her dreams turn to dust. The period was not a completely dismal one; Baker continued to give concerts in France and around the world, although bookings became more difficult to obtain as she grew older. An especially meaningful event for her was the 1963 March on Washington, prompting her to fly over from Paris to speak before the huge crowd. The thank-you note she received from Martin Luther King filled her with pride.

Yet such triumphs were soon eclipsed by growing difficulties with Baker's Dordogne château, Les Milandes. The idea of maintaining a large family in a lavish French castle had always been an ambitious (some said egotistical) dream. By 1962, Josephine Baker had adopted twelve children, hoping to pay for them and Les Milandes through tourist revenues. This venture was indeed a possibility, for the château did at first attract visitors, some 300,000 of them a year in the late 1950s. Yet Baker's lack of financial skills and her penchant for dramatic, expensive gestures quickly piled up debts. A turning point came with the breakup of her fourth marriage to Jo Bouillon. For years, he had shouldered the primary burden of managing Les Milandes and caring for the Rainbow Tribe while their famous mother was away on tour. By 1960, he had reached the end of his rope, fed up with Josephine's refusal to face financial realities and insistence on being in full control, so he left her and Les Milandes for good.

Bouillon had long exercised a steadying influence on Josephine Baker, and with his departure the situation at Les Milandes took a distinct turn for the worse. Debts accumulated rapidly and local shopkeepers began to refuse credit, forcing Baker to shop for food in distant Paris. Financial difficulties led Baker to return to the stage in an effort to raise money for Les Milandes. But the proceeds from her concerts never brought in enough to pay for the château's expenses, and her frequent travel made the prospect of raising twelve children by herself immensely more difficult. By 1964, creditors were threatening foreclosure, and in July the fifty-eight-year-old star had her first heart attack. Through heroic efforts and the loyalty of friends, Josephine Baker managed to hang onto Les Milandes for the next few years, but the inevitable end came in 1968. At the beginning of May, as students were taking to the streets in Paris, Les Milandes was sold at auction. Baker still did not give up, remaining to be forcibly evicted the following spring. Police carried her out of the castle, and photographers recorded her sitting forlornly on its steps dressed in a tattered bathrobe. As Phyllis Rose has commented, "She had been turned inside out by her own idealism and reduced to the poverty from which she began: the Folies star as bag lady, Josephine Baker as her own mother." Ultimately she had to be taken away by an ambulance after suffering a minor heart attack.

The image of Josephine Baker cast out on the steps of her own château summed up not only the hazards of fame, but more particularly the African American experience in Paris at its most dramatic. In this one heartrending scene, she embodied both the romantic dreams and the all too frequently harsh realities of life in exile; both those who had achieved success overseas and those who never would identified with her plight. Fortunately for Baker, the networks she had built up over a lifetime did not let her down in this tragic moment. Shortly after the debacle at Les Milandes, she was back on stage in both Paris and Monte Carlo. Her performance in Paris, at a restaurant called La Goulue, was such a success that the owner renamed his place Chez

Joséphine for the duration of her stay. Although she had lost her fairy-tale castle forever, Josephine Baker soon found another place to shelter her family. Princess Grace of Monaco had admired Baker for years, and after learning of her eviction arranged for her to move into a villa in the idyllic seaside town of Roquebrune, to be subsidized by the Red Cross of Monaco. It was not Les Milandes, but it still represented a quantum advance over the slums of Saint Louis.

By now Josephine Baker was well into her sixties, a world-famous entertainer who could look back with pride upon an unparalleled career that spanned several decades and continents. Many in her position would have been more than content to rest on their laurels and enjoy their memories, but Josephine Baker was not one to give up the footlights, not while breath remained in her body. In the last decade of her life, therefore, Baker continued to perform, squeezing her aging form into sultry costumes and singing both the old songs and the new hits. Maintaining her career was no easy feat. For many in France and abroad, her glamour belonged to the past, a pleasant memory with little relevance for contemporary audiences. Yet Baker continued to seek out bookings where she could find them, and gradually succeeded, thanks both to her own determination and a wave of nostalgia in the early 1970s, in once more resuming her rightful place on stage. In 1973, she returned to New York, performing both at Carnegie Hall and Harlem's Victoria Theater in June. In spite of another heart attack in Denmark later that summer, she returned to America in the fall, performing in California and ringing in the new year in Manhattan's Palace Theater. She continued to tour internationally in 1974, including a difficult visit to South Africa. Her most significant triumph came at the annual Red Cross ball in Monaco that summer. Starring in a retrospective show of her life entitled simply *Joséphine*, Baker put on a dazzling, youthful performance, conclusively demonstrating her continued vitality. Thanks to her success in Monte Carlo, Parisian backers arranged for the show to open in Paris, her first booking in the French capital since 1968.

Baker's return to the City of Light was to be her final triumph. She was unable to secure a commitment from the major theaters in the city whose stages she had once dominated. Instead, the show was booked into the Bobino Theater in Montparnasse, a classic old French music hall that, in Josephine's opinion, represented a back-door entry into Paris. But none of this mattered. When the show finally opened on April 8, 1975, the theater was packed, having been sold out for weeks in advance. The audience, which included luminaries like Mick Jagger, Sophia Loren, Princess Grace, and Alain Delon, welcomed her enthusiastically and appreciatively. Highlights of the evening included a message of congratulations from the French president, Valéry Giscard d'Estaing. The reviews in the Paris press praised her lavishly, recalling her long career and many moments of glory in the French theater. The next night Baker performed again to a packed house. That night, after dining with members of the show, Josephine Baker went to sleep, surrounded by newspapers featuring reviews of her success. She suffered a stroke in her sleep and slipped into a coma, dying the following day at the age of sixty-nine. Her death could not have been more perfectly arranged had it been scripted by Hollywood. Almost fifty years after her historic debut with the Revue Nègre, Josephine Baker died as she had lived, once again the toast of Paris.

Josephine Baker's funeral on April 15, 1975, formed a spectacular finale to her unique career. The French government gave her a state funeral at the city's impressive Madeleine church, the first American woman it had ever honored in this way. Parisians lined the city's rainy streets to watch as her coffin was carried in state past the Bobino Theater, where her name appeared in lights one last time, to the church where Napoleon had crowned himself emperor of France almost two centuries earlier. Twenty thousand people thronged around the church, including the mayor of Paris, the head of the Legion of Honor, and Charles de Gaulle's son-in-law. Baker lay in state in her French army uniform while the nation she had adopted as her own said farewell with a twenty-one-gun salute. An obituary in *Le Figaro* commemorated her passing with the words "Josephine Baker, like the other sacred monsters of the music hall, was more than just the 'black pearl' glistening among sequins and feathers: she was a personality, a persona, a soul." Eventually Josephine Baker was buried in Monaco, the last gift of Princess Grace. But it was only fitting that her final and most dramatic performance should take place in Paris, turning the city into a gigantic open-air theater in which she made her ultimate curtain call before an audience of thousands.

ADIEU, UTOPIA?

Did the death of Josephine Baker mean the end of the fairy tale in a broader sense, implying that Paris was no longer a place where dreams could come true? In 1993, the *Los Angeles Times* published an article on the situation of African Americans living in the French capital. Entitled "Adieu, Utopia," the article contended that Paris no longer offered blacks a refuge from the racism they faced in the United States. Increasing restrictions on foreigners and the ever mounting cost of living in what is now a very expensive city posed obstacles to would-be expatriates. In particular, the article concentrated on the rise of French racism, arguing that black Americans were no longer immune from bigotry in the City of Light: "Although many black Americans still feel that France is generally more racially tolerant than the United States, things are changing. . . . black Americans in France are beginning to encounter the kind of discrimination that the French used to reserve for Arabs."

The article went on to describe in detail both racial incidents experienced in Paris by black Americans and the larger context of conflicts between white French and people of color from Africa, the Arab world, and the Caribbean. Yet it concluded on an upbeat note, pointing out that many African Americans continue to live in the French capital in spite of the problems there. As Randy Garrett, the owner of a barbecue restaurant, the Rib Joint, notes at the end of the article, "Paris is the pleasure capital of the world."

"Adieu, Utopia" deftly summed up some of the contradictions of life in Paris for black Americans today. The capital's eternal attractions, ranging from great museums to gorgeous cityscapes, remain as powerful as ever; certainly few Americans would find it necessary to explain why they would want to live there. Moreover, the particular romantic myth of the French capital's love for black culture and black Americans, and the legendary legacies of the most illustrious expatriates, provide further incentive for those African Americans intrigued by the prospect of a new life in France. But no city can ever live up to the myths that surround it, and Paris is not paradise. Such reevaluations of the expatriate's dream are not new. Ever since the days of the Algerian war, voices in the city's black community have questioned the romantic myth of black life in Paris, and some have gone beyond raising questions to leaving France, either for other places of exile or to return to America. As the article indicates, many black Americans who criticize life in Paris still remain, and increased racial conflict has not significantly limited or challenged the community they have created.

Why? Opportunities for blacks to travel to Europe are far greater than in the past, enabling more to visit France as tourists. Many of the African Americans in Paris today initially came for brief periods, decided they liked what they saw, and stayed or returned. Also, a spirit of adventure and desire for alternatives to humdrum routines in the United States still plays an important role in prompting people to choose life abroad, and black Americans in Paris are no exception. Some stay in the city because they happened to fall in love with a French man or woman, or because they found professional opportunities not available at home. No matter their reasons, most African Americans living in Paris today recognize the imperfections of this glamorous capital. Few nurture

the illusions of their predecessors that the French do not differentiate according to skin color, and they often recognize that their American citizenship
makes them a distinct elite among people of color in France. Jennifer Bullock, a young woman working for a student exchange program, noted that
many French landlords and *au pair* employers refused to engage black students. Commenting on the comparison between racism in France and America, Bullock noted, "They say it's almost worse here [in France], and in a way
it is, because it is accepted. I mean, if you look at the street cleaners, they're all
African." Paris may not be perfect, but it is still an exciting world capital. In an
era when the very concept of Utopia is increasingly in disrepute and earlier
dreams of complete racial equality in the United States have faded, few
expatriates expect more.

Yet for all that, the African American presence in Paris retains a special
quality. More than just the end result of a series of individual decisions, the
very existence of this group still constitutes a certain judgment of race relations in America, and is thus a political symbol. The French capital still
represents for many black Americans on both sides of the Atlantic a place
where they can expect to be judged as human beings, not by the color of their
skin, even if the realities of life there may not always support such a belief.
Moreover, some feel that, although racial discrimination exists in France, it is
less systematic and institutionalized than American racism. Tannie Stovall, an
African American scientist who has lived in Paris for thirty years, shares this
view: "The fact that you have a skin color that's dark, of course that's going to
provoke some sort of reaction, sometimes negative reaction. However, to my
knowledge you've never had institutionalized discrimination here. I mean, it's
never been the law that you had to go to certain schools. It's never been the
law that you could not marry somebody that was not of your race. You had laws
like this in the United States until very recently." It follows that if African
Americans could obtain fully equal treatment at home they would be less
inclined to choose exile, even in an elegant world capital. Americans have
often pointed with pride to the desire of people throughout the world to
immigrate to our shores. The ironic fact that one group of Americans would
see *emigration* as an attractive option, especially as a way of achieving those
quintessentially American goals of individual respect and success, has the
potential to call into question not just the condition of African Americans, but
the viability of the American dream itself. Escape from racism only partially
motivates black Americans to live in Paris. Nonetheless, it is difficult not to
consider the existence of a black American community in France as a referen-
dum on the American dilemma.

Many African Americans have raised the theme of American violence as a key reason for not returning home. Randy Garrett, who never wants to live in America again, argued, "I can't handle the violence and the aggression. I'd much rather be poor over here and safe, than rich over there and ducking and dodging and waiting for people to do something crazy." Jean Stovall felt that Paris was a much safer place for her and her husband, Tannie, to raise their two children than the United States. "I remember the first time I heard the expression 'offing' somebody. . . . Other negative things. . . . Drugs decimated a lot of the youngsters and a lot of the kids. It was either drugs or violence. Comparing the two situations, I could never believe that at one time while [Tannie Jr. and Frederic] were growing up that we wished we were in the States." Others characterized Paris as a place where they could walk around late at night without fear, in contrast to American cities.

At first glimpse, this concern about violence does not appear to be a racial issue. On the one hand, the French typically (and with reason) point to the high level of violence as a prime example of what is wrong with the United States. To a certain extent, therefore, the interviewees' concern about it reflects assimilation into a French mind-set. On the other hand, in the United States blacks, especially young black men, suffer the effects of violence far more than any other group of citizens. Today a shockingly high percentage of young African American males are in prison, on probation, or on parole, and murder constitutes a leading cause of death for this group. The worries of Tannie and Jean Stovall for the fate of their sons thus make a good deal of sense, and reflect an awareness of another crucial arena in which American blacks have yet to achieve equality with American whites.

One aspect of contemporary black life in the United States that has a definite impact on the expatriate phenomenon is the condition of the black middle class. Seen from one vantage point, the growth of a large population of prosperous African Americans appears as the most hopeful development in American race relations since the civil rights movement. Over the last generation, millions of black families have succeeded in escaping the ghetto and carving out a life for themselves blessed with the middle-class trappings of new cars, comfortable homes, and college educations. Economic statistics show a clear expansion of relatively affluent blacks in American society. From 1967 to 1991, for example, the percentage of black households with incomes of $50,000 or more per year rose from 5.2 to 12.1 percent, or 1.3 million, and the percentage with six-figure incomes doubled over the same time period. Young blacks now attend college in rates not significantly different from young whites, and a large and growing black population now lives in suburban areas, not central cities.

Moreover, African American progress is not just a matter of numbers.

During much of the 1980s, *The Cosby Show* reigned as the most popular situation comedy on television. A loving and sociologically intact nuclear family headed by a doctor and a lawyer residing in a sumptuous Brooklyn brownstone, the Huxtables not only represented black success, but implied that such success would render racial conflict obsolete. After all, *everyone* could relate to the Huxtables. The show also represented the increased prominence of black entertainers in America. Its success made Bill Cosby one of America's wealthiest performers, with an income of nearly $100 million from 1990 to 1992. At the same time, black show business personalities like Michael Jackson and Oprah Winfrey achieved multimillionaire status. Such accomplishments would seem to justify the predictions of many social commentators that racism had lost much of its power in American society and that true black equality was either already a reality or soon would be.

Yet such confident assertions belied the reality of black middle-class life in America, a life structured above all by continued inequality and racial oppression. Blacks with college educations and postgraduate degrees continue to earn less than whites with the same level of education, and they are more than twice as likely to be unemployed, roughly the same ratio that applies to black and white unemployment rates in general. In spite of economic progress, most black Americans, including much of the middle class, continue to live in segregated neighborhoods or attend segregated schools. Recently the ABC news show *PrimeTime Live* featured an episode testing the significance of racism in contemporary life. The show took two middle-class men, one white and one black, and followed them as they separately applied for jobs, looked for apartments, or went shopping. Time and time again, the white man received a friendly, courteous welcome whereas the black man encountered suspicion, hostility, and rejection. The episode ended with a scene showing the two men trying to flag down a cab; the first taxi to appear sailed right past the black man to stop for the white man. In 1992, *The Cosby Show* broadcast its final episode, to national acclaim. That same evening, the worst racial uprising in American history erupted in Los Angeles and quickly spread throughout the country.

In short, while middle-class black Americans may live far better than their predecessors, racial equality remains a distant prospect at best, as they find they have to work harder than whites in comparable situations for the successes they enjoy. The response to this situation has been alienation and anger. In 1993, Ellis Cose, an African American editor at *Newsweek*, published a book on the subject entitled *The Rage of a Privileged Class*. Based on surveys and interviews with a wide range of successful professionals, Cose's book revealed a deep frustration among affluent blacks with their position in American society. Individual after individual related stories of racial insult and hostility, from the senior corporate lawyer who told of being barred from an elevator by a white junior partner in his own firm, to the female law professor who recalled being compared to Buckwheat by a white colleague. Many, employed in workplaces where they were one of a few (or even the only) blacks in a largely white environment, noted that they often censored their own opinions so as to get along with the dominant white culture. The situation of one young black woman seems all too typical. A Harvard graduate, she decided to leave her well-paid job with a major corporation. Her superior asked her why the company was encountering problems in retaining young African Americans. Rather than discuss the numerous examples of racism she experienced on the job, the woman simply noted that senior management contained no one who "looked like her," in other words, no blacks, and especially no black women. The woman concluded that the color of her skin still counted far more than the content of her character in corporate America.

The wounding effects of such discrimination are compounded by white America's refusal to acknowledge the continued pervasiveness of racism, defensively proclaiming itself a color-blind society instead. In the mid-1990s, unscrupulous white politicians have transformed this denial into a new racist political movement, seeking to destroy precisely those affirmative action programs that have enabled so many blacks in the United States to leave the ghetto behind. This combination of discrimination and denial has produced a sharp sense of outrage among many middle-class African Americans. A 1990 Gallup poll of black suburbanites on Long Island, New York, revealed that two thirds claimed to have experienced discrimination, and that many were less satisfied with their lives than lower-income whites. The following year, another Gallup survey found that 70 percent of college-educated blacks felt that the quality of life for blacks had gotten worse over the preceding decade. In fact, middle-class African Americans were if anything *more* dissatisfied with racial conditions than their less affluent brothers and sisters.

The sharp discontent of middle-class blacks in the United States, and the unwillingness of white Americans to address this discontent, is closely connected to the African American experience in Paris today. Although no definitive analysis is possible, many of the blacks who live in France either come from middle-class backgrounds or have achieved middle-class status through their own efforts. This characterization certainly applies to those I interviewed: Tannie Stovall is a scientist with a doctorate, Benjamin Davis has both an MBA and a law degree from Harvard, and Jennifer Bullock has a bachelor's degree from Barnard College. Dean Ferrier holds a doctorate in international relations and pursues a thriving career in global affairs which has led her around the world. They may not necessarily enjoy the material accoutrements of bourgeois black life in the United States, but as a group they are often highly educated and successful in their chosen professions. In part, of course, African Americans in Paris tend to be middle-class because it takes resources to get to France and survive there. Even in the days of mass transatlantic air travel, flights from New York to Paris lay well beyond the resources of impoverished Americans. Moreover, the desire to explore the world usually results from a certain amount of cultural capital, a knowledge of and experience with far horizons most often the property of those with extensive formal educations. At the same time, however, a key theme in the history of black expatriates in Paris during the twentieth century has been the ability of many to achieve success in France surpassing what they could have expected in the United States. From this perspective, then, the relative affluence of African Americans in Paris may also derive from conditions in France itself.

Tannie and Jean Stovall are prime representatives of the black American middle class in Paris today. The Stovalls first moved to the French capital in 1964, drawn both by the offer of a position in a French laboratory for Tannie, and by a desire to see the world outside America. With the exception of two years in the early 1970s, they have lived in Paris ever since. Tannie holds a doctorate in physics from the University of Minnesota and works as a senior scientist for the Department of Public Works. Jean recently retired from her career as a researcher at UNESCO. They have two grown sons: one, Tannie Jr., in his mid-thirties, and the other, Frederic, in his early twenties. All members of the family except Jean hold dual French and American citizenship. The Stovalls offer a unique perspective on life in Paris, that of a unified black family, as opposed to the more typical individual experience. They enjoy a full life, one of professional achievements and opportunities for travel and leisure, including a vacation house in Spain. Yet they remain very conscious of and concerned with the conditions of blacks in the United States, even watching CNN every day. Far from being adrift between two worlds, Tannie and Jean Stovall impress one as firmly at home in both France and America.

For Tannie Stovall in particular, Paris has been a place where, in contrast to the United States, racism did not hinder his advancement in his career. Stovall came to France as a highly trained professional and has benefited from opportunities he found there. As he commented during our interview, "I felt I had been appreciated more, strictly on a scientific level, here than I was in the

United States. Here people thought I really was a scientist . . . I have pretty good relationships with my colleagues at work, and that is something I've always appreciated here . . . I had trouble having this [acceptance] in the United States. There was always this suspicion that if I worked where I was, it probably had to do somehow or another that somebody in particular was nice to me." The Stovalls have encountered racial tolerance in other aspects of their life in Paris. Jean Stovall pointed out that "there is no place for racism in Paris if you have the money. . . . We remember places in Washington, D.C., and in New York . . . or in California or Chicago, where blacks can't, I mean *really cannot* go. . . . After knowing that, it was refreshing being in the city of Paris where they couldn't care less if you buy. There was no area reserved for whites, or reserved for anybody." While very aware of French racism toward Arabs and other peoples of color, the Stovalls argue that it lacks the entrenched structural foundation of bigotry in the United States.

Because racism in France places greater importance on social class, the idea of Paris as a sanctuary from prejudice remains relevant for middle-class black Americans. Expatriates in France continue to speak of the notable difference between racial attitudes in their adopted homeland and in the United States. In particular, many note that while prejudice exists in France, it overwhelmingly targets the poor and unassimilated from the nation's former colonies. An affluent black or Arab who speaks fluent French and understands the customs of the country will encounter relatively few closed doors. This attitude contrasts sharply with life in the United States, where in spite of their success and hard work middle-class African Americans frequently find themselves confronting the same kinds of discrimination meted out to lower-income blacks. Although some Americans argue that socioeconomic class status counts for more than the color of one's skin, this group's experience clearly demonstrates that race, and racial prejudice, continue to be the most important determinants of the quality of life of black Americans today. In America, blacks remain blacks, and therefore subordinate, no matter what they do, whereas in France blacks may go as far as talent and determination permit. As long as discrimination remains alive and well in the United States, black expatriates in Paris will symbolize escape from it.

Such attitudes persist in spite of the striking, undeniable rise of racism in France and Europe as a whole in the 1990s. Although racial hatred is no stranger to the European continent, the end of the cold war brought with it an explosion of bigotry and ethnic tensions. The most dramatic example is the former Yugoslavia, where conflicts between Serbs, Croats, and Bosnian Muslims have produced the first full-scale war on European soil since the death of

Adolf Hitler. Elsewhere in eastern Europe, the collapse of Communism has been accompanied by the multiplication of far-right political movements and an increase in anti-Semitism and other forms of racist discourse. Newly re-unified Germany has not remained immune from the contagion of racism, as neo-Nazi groups have organized openly and skinhead militants have attacked, beaten, and murdered nonwhites throughout the country. Some political observers have pointed with apprehension to the coincidence of German reunification and neoracism, but the problem is not simply a German one. Not since the 1940s has Europe as a whole experienced a comparable level of racist mobilization.

Recently, France has emerged as a prime example of the tide of racial bigotry washing across the Continent. As in earlier years, immigrants of North African, African, and Caribbean origin have found themselves the primary targets for intolerance. In the face of continuing high unemployment rates, many if not most French men and women contend that the nation can no longer afford to receive outsiders, offering them precious jobs and housing opportunities. Yet increasingly, the question of immigration has become a disingenuous stalking-horse for race and racial hostility in French life. France terminated virtually all legal immigration in 1974, so that only a very few lucky foreigners can obtain a French residence permit; while illegal immigration certainly continues, it has not reached anything like the levels confronted by the United States, or even southern European nations like Italy and Spain. When the French say "immigrant" today, they generally mean "person of color." The children of North Africans, even if they were born in France and speak only French, are often referred to as "second-generation immigrants," an oxymoron that one would never apply to the offspring of Poles or Italians. As one woman in the Paris suburbs, herself the daughter of Armenian immi-grants, recently noted, "Integration was easier before when the immigrants tended to be all white and Christian. . . . The longtime residents here have a hard time accepting people of color. They have the feeling they have been invaded." Proud of their assimilationist tradition, many people in France now see the growing nonwhite population as a group that cannot be integrated into society, posing a fundamental threat to French culture. The nation's Muslim community, for instance, now claims five million members, or nearly one out of every ten residents of the country. The prospect of minarets rising next to the spires of Gothic cathedrals troubles many, and the desire of Muslim girls to wear the veil in public school has repeatedly thrown the nation's educational establishment into an uproar.

All too often violence has shaped the response to these fears of economic and cultural competition. Clashes between French police and black and Arab youth are no longer unusual in the impoverished, polyglot neighborhoods of the Paris suburbs. As in Germany, attacks on nonwhites have escalated, not stopping short of murder. In 1992, the Parisian journalist Fausto Guidice published a book entitled *Arabicides,* in which he demonstrated that roughly two hundred Arabs in France have been killed by whites over the past twenty years. The overt prejudice against people of color which first surfaced during the Algerian war now seems to have become an endemic feature of French society. A nation where tolerance once appeared to be an unquestioned value now braces itself for violent racial conflict, its cities surrounded by ghettos all too familiar to the American observer. In an article on La Cayolle, a working-class suburb of Marseilles, the *Washington Post* portrayed the magnitude of France's urban malaise: "For the past two years, sporadic riots have erupted in similar North African ghettos around France. The French government has identified 400 'highly volatile' communities where further civil unrest is likely to occur, including La Cayolle and a half-dozen other neighborhoods scattered around Marseille."

Racism in France is symbolized above all by the powerful political movement known as the National Front, led by the flamboyant Jean-Marie Le Pen. The National Front, now one of the most important political parties in France, fits squarely into the tradition of the extreme Right in twentieth-century French politics. Le Pen himself first became politically active in the neofascist movement of Pierre Poujade during the 1950s, and served in the Algerian war (rumors still circulate about his participation in the torture of Algerian prisoners). In October 1972, he and several other ideologues founded the National Front in order to unite the French Right by running candidates in national elections. The fledgling party quickly seized upon the theme of hostility to immigration as a way of uniting its diverse factions and appealing to the French electorate as a whole. Calling for "France for the French," the National Front blamed immigrants for unemployment and other social ills, calling for the end of legal immigration and the forcible expulsion of all immigrants from the country. By the early 1980s, it had emerged as a major new force on the French political scene, winning almost 10 percent of the vote in the elections of 1981. Jean-Marie Le Pen, a man endowed with the rhetoric and physique of a barroom brawler, has not hesitated to indulge in racist and anti-Semitic speeches. He has been known to say "Racism in France today means patriotism" and to accuse "the Jewish international" of weakening the national spirit.

Yet in spite (or perhaps because) of such statements, the National Front is more popular today than ever before. Although it finds supporters throughout French society, it has won especially strong backing in southern France, where large numbers of former French residents of Algeria confront a sizable Arab population, and in the depressed and racially mixed working-class suburbs of cities like Paris, Lyons, and Marseilles. In the national elections of June 1995, the Front won close to 15 percent of the vote, in spite of the murder of an Arab teenage boy by its supporters in Marseilles a few months earlier. Le Pen's forces captured the mayoralties of three major French cities, including the port of Toulon, while a former Front member was elected mayor of Nice, the fifth largest city in the country. Although neo-Nazis in Germany may attract more attention from the world press, the French National Front has become unquestionably the largest and most powerful racist political movement in western Europe today.

While Jean-Marie Le Pen may stand as a willing and charismatic symbol of racism in France, the phenomenon goes far beyond the National Front. Increasingly, the mainstream of French politics has embraced anti-immigrant sentiment and all that it implies. The French government has moved to tighten restrictions on the entry of North Africans into the country, fearing in particular a wave of political refugees triggered by the conflict between military forces and Islamic fundamentalism in Algeria. The number of entry visas granted by France to Algerian citizens fell from 900,000 in 1988 to 400,000 in 1994. Growing racism has not targeted just immigrants, however. Minister of the Interior Charles Pasqua has proposed changing French naturalization laws, ending the practice that automatically grants citizenship to any child born in France (as in the United States). Such a move has the potential to deprive thousands of Arab and African youth of French nationality, threatening their eligibility for social benefits and rendering some effectively stateless. This proposal was recently endorsed by the former French president Valéry Giscard d'Estaing, a figure of the moderate Right opposed to the National Front. Jacques Chirac, France's president, recently commented on the plight of French workers living next to immigrants "with father, three or four wives, about 20 kids, earning $10,000 a month without working. . . . If you add to that the noise and the smell, the French worker goes crazy."

As during the Algerian war, the dramatic and disturbing escalation of racist sentiment in France during the last decade once again raises questions about the African American experience in Paris, on both concrete and symbolic levels. Why should blacks leave the United States to take up residence in another predominantly white society where people are discriminated against, physically assaulted, and even murdered because of the color of their skin?

More generally, can the capital of a nation in which racist politics increasingly assume center stage still claim a special place in the hearts of black Americans? Concretely, few American blacks who live in Paris or even visit for a short time are unaware of racial conflict and division in that society. As far as most are concerned, the myth of color-blind France is effectively dead.

African Americans have often discovered, however, that racist treatment often stops as soon as their U.S. nationality becomes clear. If the best defense against police brutality in Los Angeles is a video camera, in Paris it is an American passport. Whereas the existentialist Left of the 1940s and 1950s embraced African Americans as exceptions to (and victims of) American culture, today's nationalist Right in France tends to accept the same people precisely because they *are* Americans. As a student, I can recall having a fascinating conversation with a middle-aged Frenchman late one night in a Montmartre bar. This individual, who like Le Pen had served as a soldier in Algeria, fulminated passionately against the Islamic fundamentalists of Iran and all those who dared to reject Western culture, arguing that such people deserved death. Yet he was very friendly to me and hastened to add that this question had nothing to do with black Americans, who were civilized, after all. In sum, while "Adieu, Utopia" correctly concludes that the rise of French racism has had an impact on African American expatriates, it remains true that this impact is still relatively minor, and that in general black Americans continue to benefit from a largely positive image among the people of Paris. Above all, as a group they still feel that they are treated better in France than in the United States.

French blacks experience prejudice, and their lives provide some interesting insights into the impact of French racism on African Americans. Encounters with blacks from the French colonies and ex-colonies of Africa and the Caribbean have been a key aspect of the African American expatriate experience in Paris throughout the twentieth century. In getting to know people whose skin was the same color but who spoke a different language and belonged to radically different cultures, African Americans in France developed a broader understanding of the role played by race on a worldwide level. The interaction between the two groups has gone in both directions, as the influence of writers like Claude McKay and Richard Wright on different generations of negritude intellectuals makes clear. In at least one sense, however, relations between the two black populations have shifted sharply over the course of the century. Whereas the number of French blacks in Paris during the interwar years was relatively small and disproportionately composed of intellectuals and musicians (much like the African American community), today this group has become far larger and more diverse. More than 350,000 blacks from West Africa, mostly immigrants without French citizenship, now call France home, and more than 400,000 people from the Caribbean possessions of Martinique, Guadeloupe, and French Guiana live in the Paris area alone. The neighborhood of Barbès-Rochechouart is now an overwhelmingly African area, a little bit of Senegal in the French capital.

Unlike black Americans in the city, however, French blacks in Paris are predominantly poor or working-class. Many work in relatively low-level jobs for the French post office or other national and local government agencies, and live in the same dilapidated public housing projects that symbolize the despair of young French Arabs. Speaking in 1990, the sociologist Claude-Valentin Marie estimated that more than half the Caribbean blacks working in France did so for the public sector, and three fourths of those occupied the lowest two rungs of the civil service hierarchy. The figure of the African street sweeper remains today an accurate and powerful representation of the condition of France's black immigrants and citizens. Benjamin Davis, an African American international lawyer based in Paris, confirmed this general impression of French blacks, commenting, "As for black French people, one of the things I've never seen is a black French person who is working someplace else than the post office. You don't see black énarques [graduates of the elite National School of Administration]."

Yet the experience of the French black population today also in certain ways perpetuates the old notion that France treats blacks well. While the nation's black citizens still face discrimination and are certainly not equal to their white brothers and sisters, they nonetheless seem to receive far more favorable treatment than their Arab neighbors. In general, they are more integrated into French society and culture, often speaking better French than Arab immigrants. The bitter legacy of the Algerian war does not divide them from the French, nor does the explosive issue of Islam as a foreign cultural practice. In particular, blacks from the Caribbean have assumed, both historically and today, a privileged position among people of color in France. Martinique and Guadeloupe have been controlled by France since the early seventeenth century, longer than Alsace or Savoy. Today they are full-fledged *départements* of France, and their residents are French citizens who are steeped in French culture from birth. As a result, far more than Arabs or even black Africans, they are frequently perceived and treated as French men and women of color, not foreigners, which can sometimes have bizarre consequences. I remember witnessing a recent National Front rally in which a small delegation of blacks from Guadeloupe took part: France for the French indeed! It is still true, therefore, that blacks in France, both French and American, face less overt bigotry there than they generally encounter in the United States.

At the same time, the presence of a large black population in Paris constitutes another source of attraction for African Americans. With an estimated African and Caribbean population of more than half a million, Paris *feels* much blacker than it did in the early twentieth century, as black as many American cities. Whereas the novelty of people of color in Paris at earlier times often facilitated the acceptance of black Americans, today they can walk down the city's streets without feeling unusual or self-conscious because of the color of their skin. Moreover, Paris today is home to a rich black diaspora that, like those of the Caribbean or Brazil, fascinates many blacks from the United States looking for both exoticism and racial solidarity. As an article in the *New York Times* noted about ten years ago, "The city boasts black radio stations, such as Tropique FM and Afrique FM; black restaurants, including Le Kaissa . . . and La Savane, . . . black food shops; black discothèques, like Rex, at 3 Boulevard Poissoniere, and Ruby's, on the Rue Dauphine; black publications such as 'Jeune Afrique'; black beauty salons; even a black library." Linguistic and cultural differences often render communications between American and French blacks difficult, and many Americans complain that French Afro-Caribbeans remain just as remote from them as white French people. Some African Americans feel that the *Antillais* identify more as French than as black, embracing a racial assimilationism foreign to most from the United States. Jennifer Bullock spoke of being rejected by a young French black man at a party when she said she identified as black, not *métis* (mixed race). Commenting on the experience, she observed, "I think that English[-speaking] blacks . . . are a little bit more conscious or socially advanced about racism and those things, than the *Antillais* people that I've met."

Nonetheless, African Americans can eat at African and Caribbean restaurants, or dance in nightclubs featuring black French performers. Cultural interaction between American and French blacks remains a living tradition in Paris. In 1975, for example, a Martinicuan actor named Benjamin Jules-Rosette founded the Theatre Noir in a working-class district on the east side of Paris. Following the tradition of negritude decades earlier, the theater emphasized the Caribbean experience, but also showcased music, dance, and drama by African and African American performers during the 1970s and 1980s. French blacks, especially the young, continue to demonstrate a vital interest in the African American experience. A certain Malcolm X cult prevails in the working-class neighborhoods and suburbs where black youth live. Many

trendy young blacks, and whites, in France have adopted the English language word *black* instead of *noir* in everyday slang, further emphasizing the
transatlantic parallels.

Both the increase in racism and the growth of large populations of color
have made Paris seem more like the United States than ever before to its black
American residents and visitors. Given the fact that levels of discrimination
against blacks (as opposed to Arabs) seem to be relatively low, this growing
similarity in some ways makes daily life easier, or at least more familiar, for the
African American in the French capital. However, it also poses with renewed
force questions about the symbolic importance of the expatriate option. If
from the point of view of race Paris no longer represents much difference from
America, does then the choice of hundreds of African Americans to live there
mean anything important to blacks or race relations in the United States? The
belief of most black expatriates that they, and blacks in general, are still treated
better in France than America provides one response.

But there is another, more fundamental way of considering this question.
For many African Americans, expatriate or not, the question of French color-
blindness has little to do with actual conditions for people of color in France,
and everything to do with American racism. The idea of Paris as a city that
receives blacks with dignity and respect should be considered not just a statement of objective reality (although much evidence supports it), but equally as
a conceptual strategy for criticizing continued discrimination in the United
States. Portraying Paris, a city whose name spells prestige among all Americans, as a haven of tolerance and success for black Americans serves to
undermine the racial status quo on the other side of the Atlantic by placing it
in an unfavorable international perspective. In the course of discussing this
book with both blacks and whites, I have often noticed that whereas black
Americans tend to agree with the idea of a relatively color-blind France, most
whites immediately raise the issue of French racism. It is a question of viewpoint, of whether the glass is half full or half empty, but the difference here
results from conditions in the United States, not the French capital. Color-
blind Paris is a city of the mind, a legendary place of refuge whose boundaries
correspond only in part to those of earthly urbanity. As long as racial hierar-
chies remain central to life in America, the importance of the black expatriate
experience as a symbolic escape from, and critique of, racism will endure.

THE WORLD OF THE ARTS

In February 1992, a major conference on "African-Americans and Europe"
took place in Paris at the Université de la Sorbonne Nouvelle. Organized by

professors Michel Fabre of the Sorbonne and Henry Louis Gates, Jr., of Harvard, the conference featured well over one hundred presentations on different aspects of the history of black expatriates by scholars throughout the world. The experience of blacks in Paris received particular consideration at the conference, which featured not only academic presentations on that history, but also the participation of many notable past and present African American residents of the French capital. Wendell Jean-Pierre, Paule Marshall, Vertamae Smart-Grosvenor, Ed Clark, Herbert Gentry, Sim Copans, Nathan Davis, Barbara Chase-Riboud, Samuel Allen, Ollie Harrington, and Bette Woody all took part, passing on reflections about their own lives in Paris to fascinated audiences. The conference ended with the dedication of a plaque from the French government in honor of Richard Wright. Hundreds of conferees and interested onlookers gathered on a wintry Sunday morning to witness the ceremony in the street before the Wrights' old home in the rue Monsieur-le-Prince, and to listen to speeches commemorating the great author by Ellen Wright, Julia Wright, Michel Fabre, and others. The plaque ensured that Richard Wright, and the expatriate black American community he represented, will occupy a permanent place on the Parisian landscape for many decades to come.

The 1992 conference was a milestone, representing by far the most important acknowledgment and exploration of the African American presence in twentieth-century Paris. It was particularly interesting in that it both acknowledged a rich historical heritage and also featured members of the current black American community in the French capital. Blacks living in Paris took part both as presenters and observers, and conferees were able to explore music clubs and art galleries showcasing African American talent. Writers penned poems and essays especially for the conference, which appeared in its program. Melvin Dixon contributed "Climbing Montmartre":

> Langston in the twenties and ole Locke too,
> Cullen from the Hotel St. Pierre
> Wright from rue Monsieur le Prince, even too,
> Martin came to climb Montmartre.

Even that veteran landmark, Haynes restaurant, joined in by organizing a lunch for participants. This dual consciousness of past and present serves as a useful way of considering the lives of American blacks in Paris today. Many are acutely aware of the legacy of Richard Wright and Josephine Baker, and of the French capital's long reputation for attracting the best and brightest of black America. At the same time, these are individuals whose lives do not necessarily fit any preconceived patterns; they came with their own dreams and their own destinies. Although African American Paris may be hallowed ground for some, it is no museum but rather a dynamic community continually involved in re-creating a living tradition.

African Americans engaged in the arts, especially music, literature, and visual art, still symbolize the black experience in Paris for many in both France and the United States. In spite of increased opportunities for black artists and intellectuals in America, the French capital has retained its ability to attract creative African Americans, offering physical beauty, cultural stimulation, and an enviable style of life. As in the past, some stay in Paris for a year or two before returning to the United States, whereas a smaller number elect to remain for both personal and artistic reasons. Many of the black American writers, musicians, and artists who live and work in Paris today are veterans of the French scene, having first arrived in the 1960s. This creative community includes many who are well respected in their chosen fields and have made solid contributions to the cultural life of both France and America. Their emphasis on both individual artistic freedom and the importance of black culture continues to make these artists central figures of a community whose members demand the right to be treated as blacks and simply as human beings at the same time.

James Emanuel is generally recognized as the dean of African American writers in contemporary Paris. A handsome, scholarly-looking man with a slender build, Emanuel grew up in Nebraska. There he demonstrated an early commitment to literary pursuits, writing several short stories as a teenager and a novel during his sophomore year of college. As a young man, he opted for an academic career, earning a doctorate from Columbia University in 1962, then obtaining a position as professor of literature at the City University of New York. It was this career that first brought him to France in the fall of 1968, as a Fulbright exchange professor at the University of Grenoble in the scenic French Alps. In part, James Emanuel ended up in France by chance, yet at the same time Countee Cullen's collection of sonnets *To France* had long inspired the young poet to discover that country. Emanuel and his wife settled into a house in the countryside near Grenoble, where he spent the next year teaching, writing poetry, and gradually becoming used to the charming lifestyle of provincial French universities. He returned to New York at the end of the academic year charmed by France and planning to return. In 1971, another Fulbright lectureship enabled him to come back to France as a professor, this time to the University of Toulouse. There James Emanuel stayed for several years, enjoying the peaceful ambience of one of France's most charming cities and writing prolifically. During that time, he wrote the poems that were collected as *Black Man Abroad: The Toulouse Poems*. Emanuel returned to the city frequently after the end of the Fulbright lectureship, finding there a space to pursue his literary craft undisturbed.

In 1984, however, James Emanuel left both Toulouse and the United States for good, choosing to move to Paris, where he still lives. The move represented a turning point in his life. He had divorced in 1974 and taken early retirement from the City University of New York. Emanuel therefore came to Paris as a man who had stripped his life of all personal and professional encumbrances, in order to devote himself single-mindedly to his writing. This intensely focused existence has enabled the writer to continue his prodigious literary output, which has included a major critical study of Langston Hughes, a history of black literature in America, and more than two hundred poems published since 1958. Emanuel's poetry represents a diverse body of work, in which the author transforms both personal reflections and political concerns into artistic statements. In Paris, James Emanuel has been able to find both inspiration and concentration, qualities fundamental to the pursuit of his life's work. As he commented in a 1991 interview,

> To me, although I accept no guidance from institutionalized religion, all experience is a spiritual journey; and I have always tried to understand and appreciate events and individuals in terms of their "spiritual" impact upon their environment. Living in Paris, knowing the material beauty so plentifully around me and believing that the "Liberté, Egalité, Fraternité" so lightly accessible upon the French tongue has not lost all of its original substance, I have found my creativity in Paris free to expand in whatever directions daily life might illuminate.

Today, James Emanuel lives on the boulevard du Montparnasse, a stone's throw from the heart of that storied and busy neighborhood. The contrast between his residence and the surrounding area reveals much about the attractions of Parisian exile. Outside all is animation: in one of the city's busiest intersections, honking taxicabs, cars, and buses vie for room in the street while huge crowds throng the cafés, restaurants, stores, and movie theaters. Once inside Emanuel's building, however, one discovers an oasis of calm and (amazingly) quiet, hard to imagine given the lively turmoil a few feet away. Emanuel's small apartment, complete with a view of Montmartre in the distance, mirrors this combination of turbulence and tranquility. Books and papers are everywhere, yet the seeming disorder in fact testifies to the writer's overwhelming dedication to his art, furnishing an atmosphere where everything is subordinate to its dictates. When I went to visit, James Emanuel received me graciously, responding to my questions about his life in Paris with consideration and interest. Yet he also made it clear that his literary work came first. As he noted in 1991, "We African American writers who leave our native land — Richard Wright, Chester Himes, and James Baldwin being my most notable predecessors — achieve some vital gain, whether or not we consciously deem ourselves 'expatriates' or acquire a new citizenship. I deem myself only a poet." Like many black American writers who crossed the ocean earlier in the century, Paris has provided Emanuel with the space to pursue his craft to the exclusion of all else.

In 1994 the African American community in Paris lost one of its most respected writers with the death of Hart LeRoy Bibbs at the age of sixty-four. A dark-skinned, quiet, and elegant individual, Bibbs came to Paris as a representative of the same avant-garde milieu that produced Ted Joans. In 1969, after several rejections by American publishers, Bibbs published his *Dietbook for Junkies* in Paris. Although the book, a Beat-inspired violent diatribe, won only modest praise from Parisian critics, it did establish him as a literary figure. Originally from Kansas City, Kansas, Bibbs lived in France for nearly thirty years before his death, and although never one to seek out the limelight, he became well known in many different Parisian circles, among black expatriates and French artists, musicians, writers, and others. His gentle personality as well as his artistic gifts won him the affection of people from many walks of life. Like the sculptor and writer Barbara Chase-Riboud, Bibbs made his mark in both literature and the visual arts. Bibbs had long been inspired by jazz, especially the free jazz movement of the 1960s. He explored the link between music, writing, and politics in his pamphlet "Polyrhythms to Freedom." Self-trained as a photographer, he specialized in color portraits of jazz performers, vibrant, surreal studies of musicians like Miles Davis and Max Roach which explored the romance of the night. In 1979, a Montmartre art gallery sponsored an exhibit of his work entitled "Paris Jazz Seen," consisting of studies of fifteen jazz musicians in the city. Bibbs's love of music also made itself felt in his poetry, which the French novelist Simon Njami called "a poetry made of notes rather than words, that one could sing." Hart LeRoy Bibbs's poems have been performed by musicians as well as published widely. In 1992, some of his last work appeared in *Double Trouble,* a collection coauthored with Ted Joans, and including a preface by James Emanuel. The slender volume brings together a range of poems by the two black expatriates, commenting both on life in Paris and the issues confronting blacks in the United States.

After thirty-five years of exile, during which he has used Paris as a home base for travels throughout the world, Ted Joans is going as strong as ever. In the preface to *Double Trouble*, James Emanuel succinctly summed up Joans's appeal: "Probably the most colorful poet in Paris, Ted Joans offers us a verbal armful of himself: his jazzy, earthy, knowledgeable reflections of his enriching friendships, worldwide experiences, and wise pondering over matters ranging through sex, art, myth-as-history, and ritualized bloodshed — all 'Teducation' rendered with humor and lively impact." A self-proclaimed surrealist, Joans has published several volumes of poetry, including *Afrodisia, Black Pow-Wow,* and *Flying Piranha* (with Joyce Mansour), and has even written a few poems in French. He has participated in conferences and poetry readings around the world. His verse combines discordant images to jolt the reader out of complacency. In my interview with him, Joans described the kind of poetry he likes to write: "a poem about me having a sex relation with seven species of mammals, and it's not a human mammal . . . then when I wake up this animal has turned into a gingko tree who is having a cup of tea. Inside the cup of tea, there is W.E.B. Du Bois arguing with Booker T. Washington." Joans remains determined to shock the bourgeoisie, the poet as cultural revolutionary.

Yet even more than his artistry, Ted Joans's public persona has brought him renown. Perhaps more than anyone else today, Joans symbolizes the African American expatriate in Paris. When the English-language magazine *Paris Passion* featured an article on blacks in Paris in 1986, his photograph graced the cover. A slight man with a bearded, expressive face, Joans remains very much a public figure, appearing at gathering places of the American community in Paris like the bookstore Shakespeare and Company and circulating wherever the expatriate action is. In the time-honored tradition of Parisian intellectuals, notably surrealists like André Breton and Louis Aragon, he continues a practice of appearing for a set time every week at the Café le Rouquet, on the boulevard Saint-Germain just up the street from the famous cafés of Saint-Germain-des-Prés. There Joans meets old and new friends of all descriptions, fellow black expatriates, young writers from America seeking his advice, and the curious interested in the phenomenon of the Black Writer in Paris. His sessions at the Café le Rouquet represent both a nod to history and the practical continuation of a tradition, providing Paris residents and visitors alike a glimpse of the creative sociability of the era of the Tournon and the Monaco. Ted Joans has created his life in Paris as a self-conscious work of art, and the Café le Rouquet represents the most important of the many galleries in which he has chosen to display it.

Barbara Chase-Riboud, who like Ted Joans has lived in Paris since the early

1960s, has remained as active as ever in her dual roles of writer and visual artist. Chase-Riboud is an artist of impressive achievements, second to none among the African American community in the French capital. Over the last ten years, she has published three books in America: a collection of poems entitled *Portrait of a Nude Woman as Cleopatra*, which won the Carl Sandburg poetry prize in 1988; a novel, *Echo of Lions*, taking as its themes African American slave revolts; and her most recent work, the historical novel *The President's Daughter*, concerning the legend of Sally Hemings, reputedly the black mistress of Thomas Jefferson. This last book, continuing the story set forth in Chase-Riboud's 1979 novel *Sally Hemings*, has encountered opposition from historians who reject the possibility of a Hemings-Jefferson liaison. The controversy demonstrates the continuing tension over the role of blacks in American history; as Chase-Riboud responds to her critics, "What they're saying is that Thomas Jefferson could never have done anything so ignoble as to fall in love with a black woman."

Julia Wright works as a free-lance journalist and is also completing a study of her father, entitled *Daughter of a Native Son*. And many who live elsewhere nonetheless make periodic trips to Paris, continuing the city's importance in the world of African American literature. Paule Marshall; Trey Ellis, the novelist and author of *Platitudes*; Melvin Dixon; John A. Williams; Ernest Gaines; John Edgar Wideman; Toni Morrison; Jayne Cortez; and others visit the French capital from time to time and maintain friendships there. While interviewing Ted Joans at the Café Le Rouquet, I met Jake Lamar, the author of the critically praised novel *Bourgeois Blues*, who was spending a year in Paris while working on his next book. Lamar is a friendly, engaging, and sharp-witted young writer whose first novel skillfully explores black middle-class life in America from a coming-of-age perspective. Richard Wright and James Baldwin may be no more, but the tradition of African American letters in Paris they did so much to create has lived on.

Black American music in Paris today also represents a living tradition. Jazz is certainly no longer the novelty it was in France during the 1920s or even the 1950s. Yet jazz remains a staple of Parisian nightlife, and continues to showcase black American musicians, both those who live in the city and those passing through on tour. Jazz clubs abound, from the smoky medieval *caves* of the gentrified Les Halles to venerable stalwarts like the Latin Quarter's Caveau de la Huchette or New Morning on the Right Bank. Moreover, jazz is still esteemed by both French intellectuals and French popular culture. In 1986, the French director Bertrand Tavernier released the film *'Round Midnight*, an artistic and accurate re-creation of Parisian jazz life in the 1960s, starring the veteran saxophonist Dexter Gordon as a self-destructive musician modeled on Bud Powell. As the *New York Times* commented in a review of the city's current jazz scene: "jazz has blended as easily with bourgeois society as it did with beat culture. In Paris, jazz is all over the city, and its audience isn't enveloped in a romantic Gauloise haze. . . . Jazz has become part of the city's consciousness in a way that challenges even New York." Just as the formerly existentialist haunt of Saint-Germain-des-Prés is now a favored site for upscale tourism, so has jazz in Paris migrated from the margins to the mainstream of cultural life. A 1987 review of Paris jazz clubs in the *Wall Street Journal* confirmed the position of jazz in France's musical establishment.

While the contemporary jazz clubs in Paris have not assumed the function of African American community center as did Bricktop's in the interwar years or the Living Room in the 1960s, they still offer a certain black American presence, both onstage and off. Black jazz artists continue to find both popularity and respect for their musical talents. As one musician commented, "Opportunities for me are better — for what I do there's less competition. . . . And, I enjoy the lifestyle here. If you're a musician in the States, you live in either Los Angeles or New York because those are the two basic centers and there's a lot of people there — doing what you do. I love New York, but here I feel a lot more relaxed and a lot more human . . . it's been a good experience for me — learning the language and learning a different lifestyle, different people."

African American women continue to make their mark as entertainers in Paris. The undisputed veteran is Nancy Holloway, who has been performing in Paris since the late 1950s. Originally from Cleveland, the young woman was working as a telephone switchboard operator in New York when she was discovered by a talent scout who launched her singing career. Soon she found herself performing at the Flamingo Club in the French capital. Holloway carved out a place in the Parisian entertainment scene during the 1960s by singing rock and roll, and learning to do so in French, which enabled her to perform with French music stars like Johnny Hallyday and Frank Alamo. Nancy Holloway has also made a practice of singing jazz and blues, starring in nightclubs and making several recordings, as well as working in French films and television. Holloway remains a fixture of Parisian nightlife today, performing widely in Paris and throughout Europe. She lives near Montmartre, in a neighborhood full of memories of the days when jazz was young in Paris. And like Bricktop before her, she is devoted to the city where she has built her career. Nancy Holloway often rejects offers to perform in America, recently declaring, "I love it here, and as long as there's work in Paris I'll stay."

Dee Dee Bridgewater has also achieved success and happiness as a performer in Paris. If Nancy Holloway's life in France at times reminds one of Bricktop, with her residence in Montmartre and long association with the French capital, Bridgewater's career has certain parallels with that of Josephine Baker. Bridgewater grew up in Flint, Michigan, where from an early age she longed to become an international singing star. Like Baker and many others, her path to Paris went through New York, where she first discovered the world of jazz musicians. She first came to the attention of the entertainment world as a singer in the black Broadway musical *The Wiz*, earning a Tony for her performance. Yet this success did not bring her acceptance on her own musical terms. After *The Wiz* closed, Bridgewater tried to work as a recording artist, wanting to sing the kind of experimental jazz she had learned in New York while working with Dizzy Gillespie. However, she soon found that her record company wanted her to adopt a more commercial style, singing the kind of soul and disco music that black women were "supposed" to sing. So, in contrast to the Soviet artists who fled Russia for America in search of artistic freedom, Dee Dee Bridgewater left America for Paris to find that elusive prize. "I left the States and I came to France, and for me . . . I couldn't have picked a better country to . . . go through my healing process because I have a liberty here that I've never, ever, ever felt in America . . . Paris has always been very important, I think, in the history of jazz music. . . . You have a freedom to experiment . . . and to grow, and you're not, like, put into a box where they say, 'This is all you do.'"

Since then Dee Dee Bridgewater has made a place for herself on the musical stage in the French capital. Her performance in *Lady Day*, a musical version of the life of Billie Holiday, was a big hit before audiences in both Paris and London, and she followed that up with a starring role in a jazz version of the Bizet opera *Carmen*. More recently, she has worked on the Parisian stage in a new version of *Cabaret*. Today, Bridgewater lives in Paris, happily married to her French road manager, Jean-Marie Durand, and records music with the great pianist and composer Horace Silver. Her latest album, *Keeping Tradition*, recently received a Grammy nomination. Her life has renewed the tradition of Josephine Baker, demonstrating that while the dream of acclaim in Paris may remain just that for most who seek it, luck, talent, and determination can turn it into a reality.

The continued vitality of the jazz club scene in Paris enables a number of African American musicians to work and live in the French capital today. The white saxophonist Steve Lacy, who works with a band composed of both black and white American musicians, has lived in France since 1970. He stays in Paris for many reasons, including the feeling that his black colleagues might not want to accompany him if he moved back to the United States. The

Golden Gate Quartet, four black men who sing gospel and other forms of traditional African American music, came to Paris in 1959 and has remained there ever since. A fixture of Parisian concert life, the quartet also travels widely and has recorded several albums in both America and France. Tenor sax player Hal Singer is another veteran of the world of Parisian jazz. Born in Tulsa, Oklahoma, in 1919, Singer has been working as a professional musician ever since he finished his studies at Virginia's Hampton Institute in the early 1940s. He first came to Paris in 1965 to perform at the Trois Mailletz nightclub, where he met Arlette, the young Frenchwoman to whom he is still married. Today, Hal Singer lives with his family in a comfortable house in suburban Nanterre. The very picture of the settled musician, he has lived in France for thirty years, raising two daughters in the process. At the same time, he remains active playing in Parisian nightclubs and touring throughout the world. As he ended his 1990 autobiography, *Jazz Roads*, "I have had the good fortune to enjoy a magnificent profession, and I think that I will always be ready for new encounters, with musicians and all kinds of audiences, in Moscow and Rome, Paris, Los Angeles, Strasbourg or Peking."

Yet jazz is not the only form of African American music to have established a presence in the French capital. From its origins in the ghettos of the South Bronx, hip-hop has grown to become a major expression of contemporary youth culture throughout the world, and France is no exception. The difference between the reception of the two black American musical forms in Paris reveals important shifts in twentieth-century French society. Whereas jazz in Paris has often been performed by African Americans, providing a way for many to live in the city, its audience there has always been overwhelmingly white. In sharp contrast, while few if any black rappers from the United States have spent time in France, the music has found listeners not only among the French population as a whole, but especially among French black and brown "second-generation immigrant" youth. In 1984, for example, Sydney Duteil, a young man from Guadeloupe, became the first black to have his own show on French television. This achievement was major, although the fact that it did not happen until 1984 confirmed the marginalization of French blacks in France. A dance program featuring music from America, Britain, Africa, and elsewhere, Duteil's show was entitled *Hip-Hop* and targeted black, Arab, and white youth from the working-class neighborhoods and suburbs of the Paris area. One of the most popular sounds in Paris today is rai music, symbol of the culture of North African youth in France. Originating in Algeria during the 1920s, rai has a history similar to that of the blues in America, reflecting the impact of migration and urbanization on a rural culture. Yet contemporary rai has adopted many of the musical and performing styles of African American rap, increasingly resembling its transatlantic cousin. Expressing the same racial and urban anger so key to hip-hop in the United States, the evolution of rai in France exemplifies a new form of African American musical influence in Paris. In a very different way from that of the plush jazz clubs of the Latin Quarter or the Right Bank, it demonstrates that black music from the United States continues to play an important role in French culture.

African American visual artists still flock to the City of Light. In January and February 1992, two art galleries in San Francisco, the Bomani Gallery and the Jernigan Wicker Fine Arts gallery, jointly hosted an international exhibition of the work of blacks who have worked in Paris. The "Paris Connections" exhibit featured pieces by seventeen artists, including Arthur Beatty, Sam Gilliam, Faith Ringgold, Barbara Chase-Riboud, and Robert Colescott. Curated by Raymond Saunders, the show represented one of the most important presentations on black American artists in Paris to date. Two years later, a similar gathering took place in Paris itself. Entitled "A Visual Arts Encounter: African-Americans and Europe," the conference lasted for three days and brought together exhibits of works by prominent black artists, as well as fostering spirited academic interchanges among art critics and many of the artists themselves. Some of the conference organizers expressed disappointment that more figures from the French art world did not attend. "Almost nobody came from the Paris galleries, despite my invitations," complained Marie-Françoise Sanconie, a French specialist in African American art and one of the prime movers behind the conference. To a much greater extent than the San Francisco events, the Paris meeting was an academic conference, rather than an artists' exhibition, which may explain why the art world gave it little notice. Yet some participants rated the meeting a success, arguing that the Parisian location enabled participants to voice opinions, such as those critical of "political correctness," usually not accepted in American academic and artistic discussions. In January 1996, Harlem's Studio Museum opened a major exhibit entitled "Explorations in the City of Light: African-American Artists in Paris, 1945–1965." On opening day, the lines for admission stretched around the block, and those present at the opening included Loïs Mailou Jones and other veterans of the Paris art world.

All of this activity reveals an ongoing fascination with African American artists in Paris, yet the experience of the 1994 Paris conference suggests that this fascination is shared more by other African Americans than by the artists' French hosts. In contrast to black American music and even literature, black American visual art seems to have made relatively little impact on the French art scene over the decades. From the days of Henry Ossawa Tanner to the present, some fortunate artists have found acclaim and success in the Parisian art world, but African Americans have developed no collective presence, no Paris school. Black artists in Paris may spend time together and learn from one another's work, but they do not speak with a single voice. As Raymond Saunders commented at the Paris conference, "I don't do black art . . . I'm just a black person who happens to be a painter." This emphasis on the individual muse has a long history among black Americans in Paris. Because African American visual artists, unlike musicians or even writers, came to Paris to learn by sitting at the feet of the French masters, they have been more likely to integrate into the city's art world rather than collectively creating a new addition to it. However, their assimilation certainly does not mean that black artists in France simply leave their blackness behind when they cross the Atlantic. As some noted at the Paris conference, they often view blackness as an aesthetic imperative to be embraced and explored. The quilter Faith Ringgold expressed this viewpoint clearly: "There is no art that comes out of nothing. Images have a color, and the most significant image is one's own. Mine is black. That's good and I love it."

One difference between the experience of African American artists in France today versus earlier in the century is a decline in the relative importance of the Parisian sojourn. In the past, especially during the years of the Harlem Renaissance, a stay in Paris constituted part of the necessary training of a black artist from the United States; those who went found upon their return open doors that would have otherwise remained shut. Blacks who had studied in France found it much easier to gain both critical recognition of their work, as well as jobs teaching art at American schools and colleges. Paris certainly remains a destination of choice for black American artists today, but the imperative is no longer as compelling.

Both the relative decline of Paris as the world's art center and increased opportunities for blacks in the art galleries and museums of the United States have made residence overseas less crucial than in the past. As a result, while black Americans still travel to France, the pattern is now more often one of brief stays than prolonged residencies. There are of course exceptions; Barbara Chase-Riboud still lives in Paris and remains productive as an artist as well as a writer. Her impressive multimedia sculptures have won critical acclaim and are displayed in prestigious locations like the Metropolitan Museum and the Museum of Modern Art in New York.

More common are the artists who spend time in Paris and remain firmly based in the United States. Ed Clark, a veteran of the expatriate art world in France, today spends summers painting in Paris, then returns each fall to his home in New York where he works for the rest of the year. Raymond Saunders, who curated the 1992 "Paris Connections" show, is also a surrealist-inspired creator of his own drawings. He had his first solo art exhibit in Paris almost ten years ago, and has since stated that he regards the city as a second home. Faith Ringgold, whose quilt series "The French Collection" commemorates her experiences in Paris, today divides her time between the San Diego suburb of La Jolla and her native Harlem. Paris continues to play a role in the lives and art of these and other African American artists, but they no longer need choose between France and the United States. Chase-Riboud recently rejected the idea of herself as an expatriate, arguing, "There's no such thing in the [late] 20th century . . . I can get on the Concorde and fly to New York in a few hours." For some African American artists, therefore, the traditional sojourn in Paris has given way to a more global approach to the art world.

The brief, brilliant career of Jean-Michel Basquiat further illustrates this change. Brooklyn-born to middle-class Caribbean immigrants in 1960, Basquiat demonstrated a talent for drawing by the time he turned four. He never received any formal artistic training, instead dropping out of high school at the age of seventeen and moving to Manhattan's East Village to pursue fame and fortune on the strength of his talents. Unlike most who undertake similar pilgrimages to the big city, Basquiat soon found both. He began working as a graffiti artist together with his friend Al Diaz, then moved on to creating bright, dramatic canvases blending written words and images from the African American experience. Drawing on traditions of abstract expressionism but lending them a fresh, consciously black voice, Basquiat burst into the international art world in the early 1980s. At age twenty-one, he became the youngest artist ever to participate in Germany's prestigious Documenta exhibition of contemporary art. His works soon featured prominently in SoHo art galleries, selling briskly for five-figure prices. By 1988, the mercurial young genius had produced roughly a thousand paintings and two thousand drawings, featured in nearly forty gallery exhibits in America, Europe, and Japan. Jean-Michel Basquiat died in August 1988 at the tragically young age of twenty-seven, as the result of a heroin overdose. Whether the root cause of his death lay in too much success too soon or in his lifelong struggle with emotional inner demons, the live fast–die young trajectory had claimed yet another victim.

Basquiat's relationship to the Paris art world differed dramatically from that of other African American artists. Unlike many of his peers and predecessors, Basquiat never studied or lived for an extended time in Paris, remaining from first to last a product of New York's downtown art world. The only times he traveled to France were to attend openings of his gallery exhibitions. Yet Jean-Michel Basquiat's work has had a profound impact upon art circles in Paris, probably greater than that of any artist since Henry Ossawa Tanner himself. Parisians first had a chance to view his work at the Galerie Marianne et Pierre Nahon in 1982. The success of that exhibition led to renewed presentations of Basquiat's compositions at Parisian showings in 1984, 1985, 1987, and 1988. During the 1994 conference on black artists, the Galerie SEITA sponsored an important exhibit on Basquiat. Lionized by French reviewers as, among other things, a black Picasso, Basquiat has remained popular in France since his untimely death. The French reception of his work provided the first major example of an African American artist who achieved success in Paris without ever living there. In contrast to most black Americans who came to Paris to study art at renowned French art schools, Basquiat encountered France as a fully formed product.

The world of black American artists in Paris remains a rich and complex aspect of its broader African American community. Black visual artists have found respect in the City of Light, although none has achieved the spectacular success of Josephine Baker. More important, African Americans there search for both recognition as individual creative spirits and acknowledgment of the value of the black aesthetic. On the one hand, some still see it as a place where blacks can reach out and touch the common humanity of all mankind; as Raymond Saunders has written, "Art projects itself beyond race and skin color, beyond America. It is universal." For them, the Parisian art world beckons as an embodiment of the age-old African American dream, a color-blind universe. On the other hand, Paris represents a place where white people still believe black is beautiful and meaningful. Even though Jean-Michel Basquiat worked largely outside of black art circles in New York, in Paris he was hailed as the latest important representative of transatlantic negritude. The only major biography of the African American artist so far was written in French, by Michel Enrici. The two themes can be and often are contradictory. However, together they have ensured that black artists still dream of crossing the ocean to work in a Parisian atelier. The city symbolizes a hope for a color-blind society in which blackness will not be avoided but celebrated.

BLACK PROFESSIONALS IN PARIS

In recent years, some have suggested that while black writers, musicians, and artists still come to Paris, their importance as symbols of the expatriate experience has declined relative to those who have come to the city for more pedestrian reasons. This line of thinking contends that the typical African American in France is no longer a writer living in a garret, but more likely a tourist staying in a nice hotel or a corporate executive whose company has transferred him. Tony Hall, a writer who came to Paris in the late 1960s with dreams of emulating the life of Ted Joans, was pleased to hear about my study of the *real* black expatriates in Paris, those who had made sacrifices to experience *la vie bohème*, as opposed to those who might as well be in Cleveland or California. This idea fits well into the end-of-Utopia approach to contemporary African American life in Paris, implying that the community has lost some of its distinctive character today.

The idea that the French capital is no longer as special as it once was certainly has merit; jet travel and the age of mass tourism have rendered Europe easily accessible for many Americans. However, the new role of black American business and professional people in Paris once more underscores the city's role as a refuge from the racism of the United States. Given the discontent of many black professionals in America, the French capital offers attractions that speak directly to their condition. African Americans in Paris have always been a diverse group, including people from all walks of life. By virtue of its history, its romantic legend, and its self-awareness, the black American community in Paris remains singular. There are many ways to be black, in Paris or in the United States, and all have a contribution to make.

If Tony Hall represents the black American in Paris as romantic expatriate, Reginald Lewis stands for the polar opposite, the black corporate executive. Lewis, who died in 1993 at the age of fifty, was one of America's wealthiest businessmen, and almost certainly its richest African American. A product of Baltimore's black working class, Reginald Lewis was a graduate of Virginia State University and Harvard Law School. After finishing his studies, he gravitated to Wall Street and the lucrative world of venture capital. During the 1970s and 1980s, he undertook a series of ever larger business deals, culminating with his $1 billion buyout of Beatrice Foods in 1987. In 1992, he gave $3 million to Harvard Law School, making him the largest individual donor in the school's history. By the time of his death, Lewis controlled TLC Beatrice International, the largest company in the United States run by an African American. He left a huge personal fortune estimated at $400 million. If ever a black person had achieved success in America on America's own terms, that person was surely Reginald Lewis.

Yet Lewis also found his way to Paris. As a young man, he literally became a Francophile at the knee of his grandfather, Sam Cooper, who told him stories about his exploits fighting in France during World War I. Reginald Lewis first traveled to the French capital as a law student, immediately falling in love with the city. In 1988, he moved there with his family to oversee Beatrice Foods's European operations. For the rest of his life, he led a transatlantic existence, shuttling among Paris, New York, and other locales. While in Paris, Lewis lived as a veritable captain of industry, in a manner befitting his position and immense wealth. Upon moving to France, Lewis leased an eighteenth century flat in one of the wealthiest parts of the Left Bank, a neighborhood where small apartments sell for hundreds of thousands of dollars. He also took advantage of his life there to gain an understanding of French culture, learning enough of the language to conduct business meetings in French, and collecting art by Matisse, Picasso, and other masters of the Paris school. Reginald Lewis and his family did not spend much time with the African American community in the French capital, having little in common with the artists and adventurers who dominated it, yet the Lewises enjoyed the city, taking advantage of its beauty and cultural opportunities. For Reginald Lewis, however, Paris meant business above all, and as a world corporate and financial capital the opportunities it offered enabled him to expand his global vision of success.

Reginald Lewis is an extreme example of the successful life some African American professionals have created for themselves in Paris. More typical of this group is Ben Davis, a lawyer for the International Chamber of Commerce. A personable man in his late thirties, Davis is firmly ensconced in the corporate world, representing respectability more than Bohemianism. The son of a foreign service diplomat, Davis was born in Liberia and spent much of his childhood in Africa and Europe before attending prep school in the United States. He was educated at Morehouse College and Harvard, where (like Reginald Lewis) he earned a law degree as well as a master of business administration. Ben Davis first came to Paris shortly after leaving Harvard, determined to establish a career in international business. Today, he lives with his wife, Christina, and two children in a comfortable Left Bank neighborhood.

For Ben Davis, Paris is a city of numerous attractions. It offers not only beauty and intellectual excitement, but also a vast panoply of different cultures and the feeling of being at the center of the world. When I interviewed Davis, he was learning Chinese in order to work for his firm in Asia. In particular, Paris has ties to Africa that help facilitate his interest in development work on that continent. Davis also appreciates the atmosphere of physical safety, in contrast to the increasing violence of urban life in the United

States. Perhaps most important, Paris has enabled Ben Davis and his family to escape some of the vicissitudes of black life in America. Commenting on life "back home," Davis noted, "There's a whole series of games that happen in the U.S.A. to black American professionals that really are very bizarre, because they're part of the way things are done there. I'm completely out of phase with all that stuff, and it's actually funny to me, it's almost like an alien culture." He is well aware of racism in France, especially as it affects North Africans, and he movingly described his own daughter's encounter with prejudice. Yet he notes that race has a different significance in the two countries.

> When you grow up in the States, you have instincts for racial issues, but when you come over here none of those instincts are valid anymore, because it's a different history, and so you feel sort of a breath of fresh air. . . . Then after you are here for a while you see that there's a whole different series of [problems] that come out. Some of them you've heard before in the States. For example, in my daughter's school, a French person says, "Gosh, she dances so well, it must be genetic." That kind of stuff. But it doesn't feel like it has the same edge . . . as it does in the States.

For Ben Davis, Paris represents more than an exciting place to live and work. He sees himself as part of a historic African American community abroad, one that supports his desire to be both black American and a citizen of the world. In 1992, in association with the Sorbonne conference, Davis took the lead in organizing the effort to place a commemorative plaque in front of Richard Wright's former residence on the rue Monsieur-le-Prince. Using connections with the French administration facilitated by common ties to Harvard's business school, he was able to cut through the red tape and ensure that the event went off without a hitch. In speaking of the plaque, he noted, "It was important to me, because I figured all the people who come here as tourists would see something for the first time. There's a whole history of black Americans coming through Paris at different stages. . . . The standard routine is with people in the arts and literature who have been here. In a certain sense, I felt like I'm part of a vanguard of people in the professions here in Paris. One of the things about Richard Wright that was great for me was that all this history of blacks here in Paris helped me know that I was not isolated, that I was just part of another wave." In Paris, therefore, Ben Davis has found both an ability to reach out to the world and a tradition of black community based on that cosmopolitan tradition.

The world of *haute couture* has provided another space where African

Americans have been able to enjoy a successful life in Paris. In few endeavors do art and business intersect so completely as in the world of fashion, and though Paris may no longer dominate international corporate affairs or the visual arts, her leadership of the fashion industry remains largely unquestioned. Although not everyone agrees, Parisian fashion enjoys a reputation for a willingness to employ blacks, especially black women models, reflecting both French tolerance toward blacks and French fascination with black bodies. Josephine Baker herself had modeled dresses by the great designer Paul Poiret during the 1920s. In recent years, a few African Americans have found a place for themselves as fashion designers in the French capital.

Perhaps the best known has been Patrick Kelly. A product of a classic black Southern background, Kelly grew up in Vicksburg, Mississippi, where as a child he became known for wearing baggy pants and T-shirts, anticipating what would become the uniform of the hip-hop generation. He got his start in the fashion industry when at the age of eighteen he moved to Atlanta and began working in the rag trade. While collecting old clothes for a charity group, he patched up some of his finds and resold them, soon opening a boutique to market his unique re-creations. From Atlanta, Kelly moved to New York, where he studied fashion at the Parsons School of Design. In 1981, he left New York for Paris, arriving penniless in the middle of the winter. Turning lemons into lemonade, the young designer began making winter coats by hand in his room in order to get by. These coats made his fortune, for one of his customers introduced him to Françoise Chassagnac, a buyer for a leading Parisian boutique. Chassagnac not only bought more coats, but also lent Kelly money to pay for his first ready-to-wear showing.

The show took place in 1985 and immediately catapulted Patrick Kelly to the heights of Paris fashion. Designers, buyers, and customers were captivated by his eclectic mix of styles, ranging from conservative tailored suits to low-cost T-shirt dresses, motorcycle helmet hats, and fabrics decorated with watermelons and plastic hearts. Mismatched buttons became a Kelly trademark, one the designer remembered from his childhood when his grandmother used to mend his clothes. Bergdorf Goodman bought the entire 1985 collection, and soon the orders began pouring in. By the end of the decade, Kelly's Parisian shop was thriving, making both relatively inexpensive street fashions and outfits costing thousands of dollars for clients like Grace Jones, Madonna, and the Princess of Wales. In 1988, Patrick Kelly became the first American designer ever admitted to the Chambre, the elite inner sanctum of Parisian fashion that included names like Yves Saint-Laurent, Chanel, and Christian Dior. Kelly's irreverent personality as well as his clothes brought him public attention and approval. As a reporter from the *Christian Science Monitor* noted that year: "He charms . . . *tout Paris* with his buoyant laughter, though his pidgin French, distorted by his deep Southern drawl, often left them baffled. He fixes them fried chicken and hominy grit dinners, and hands out hundreds of black doll pins every week, while riding his skateboard in the streets of Paris."

Like Jean-Michel Basquiat, Patrick Kelly brought a whiff of African American street culture to elite Parisians. His own persona and dress, wearing clothing like basketball shoes, baggy pants, and the obligatory baseball cap, gave him the look of a refugee from a rap concert who somehow found himself on a Parisian runway. The use of icons like black dolls and watermelons in his clothing flaunted and parodied black stereotypes in a way reminiscent of black youth styles in the United States. Kelly also reached out to similar cultures in France, incorporating their ideas into his designs. He used to peruse the city's flea markets in search of material, and loved to take American buyers on tours of the heavily immigrant Barbès neighborhood of Paris, an area that attracted him because of its youth street culture. Unfortunately, also like Basquiat, Patrick Kelly died young of AIDS, cut down in his prime on New Year's Day 1990 at the age of forty. With his passing, French fashion lost a seminal figure, one who knew how to bridge the worlds of *haute couture* and hip-hop culture.

The photographer Richard Allen is another African American man who has worked successfully in the French fashion industry. An intense, dynamic individual, Allen has worked in many different fields in his life, including economics, photojournalism, and musical performance. Originally from New York, he first came to Paris as a tourist in 1970, after finishing his undergraduate studies at Morehouse College. Like many others, he immediately took to the French capital. "I loved it, even though it rained almost every day . . . I went up the Eiffel Tower on the first of April. Looking down from the second floor, the only thing I could think of was 'April in Paris.' It was snowing so much, I couldn't see anything. I remember nice, cozy apartments, fireplaces and a certain charm about Paris." Allen returned home to start a graduate program in economics at Cornell University, only to be drafted into the army instead. He spent the next two years serving in uniform at the Pentagon and at NATO headquarters in Belgium. While with NATO, he began working in the military's photographic laboratories, refining a skill that had interested him since childhood.

After finishing his military service, Richard Allen moved to Paris, where friends introduced him to the American Center on the boulevard Raspail. There he resumed his work as a photographer and began to make a name for himself. In 1977, he began working with UNESCO as a photojournalist, completing assignments that took him throughout Africa and as far afield as Mongolia. The wealth of opportunities offered by the fashion industry proved an irresistible lure, however, so by the late 1970s Allen found himself working primarily in that genre. Fashion offered excitement, glamour, and money; when Allen bought his second Mercedes, he paid for it in cash. Yet ultimately Richard Allen found the world of *haute couture* unsatisfying.

> I think I was probably at a point where every photographer would love to be at in Paris. I worked with ten fashion houses, and I worked with Givenchy for nine and a half years. I was their fashion photographer. I worked with Christian Dior for three and a half years. But I just could not make it through the bullshit. I mean the French people first of all are very, very snobbish . . . the moment people get a little bit of authority they exaggerate it. I couldn't deal with that. But then I realized that from the model's point of view I was just as bad. A lot of models knew that I was a photographer, and there's very few black photographers over here. It was difficult [for them] to get tests because a lot of the French photographers didn't really want to work with the black models, and stuff like that. So a lot of models were, "Oh hi, how are you doing!" etc., etc. They're your best friends till they get the pictures. Once they get their pictures, they don't need to know you . . .
>
> The sisters from the States, they were semifaithful, as far as friendship was concerned. But nevertheless the percentage [of black models] was pretty low, overall. I mean they have a lot coming through, because the major thing that blacks are able to do over here is the runways. But, you see, to get print work, it was almost, no, it was no.

In 1986, Allen left the fashion industry to carve out a new career for himself as a singer. He persuaded friends who owned a nightclub to let him sing one evening, and got other friends and associates from the fashion world to pack the place for his opening. The success of that first night led Allen to branch out and begin singing in other venues. He now works with two other singers in a group called Faith, which gives gospel concerts throughout Paris. As he commented in our interview, "I've always had these fantasies about singing in a nightclub in Paris. Well, I just felt like I was in a position to exercise the fantasy." Richard Allen has succeeded handsomely in his new career, so much so that he earns just as much money as he did in fashion. At the same time, he continues to work as a photographer, especially for travel glossies and magazines like *Essence*. His ability to prosper in such diverse undertakings exemplifies both the variety of the African American experience in Paris, and the many ties that bind its members together.

COMMUNITY LIFE

As in the past, African Americans in Paris today are an extremely diverse constellation of individuals immersed in a large foreign city. Yet the delicate balance between individual freedom and collective solidarity that has for so long characterized their presence in the French capital still holds true. Although nothing forces black Americans in France to come together or have any involvement with one another, a sense of elective community, of interaction and shared interests, exists as an option for those living in Paris or merely passing through. One may or may not choose to avail oneself of the opportunities offered by this subculture, but its presence constitutes a resource and another attraction of the City of Light. Community networks can take many forms, ranging from informal friendship circles to imposing organizations, yet given the diversity and dispersion of black Americans throughout Paris, formal institutions play an important role. Restaurants, nightclubs, and cafés constitute spaces of African American culture open to all, and any newcomer need only go to one of these places to meet other African Americans and be quickly drawn into their networks.

Haynes restaurant is the preeminent black American institution in Paris today. Nearing its fiftieth year in continuous operation, the restaurant still sits where it has been since 1964, in a small space on the rue Clauzel in the heart of what black musicians used to call Montmartre in the 1920s and 1930s. Although Leroy Haynes has passed on, his restaurant continues to operate under the ownership and management of his widow, Maria, who employs a predominantly African American staff. To walk into Haynes is to walk into history. Vintage photographs of famous jazz musicians, movie stars, and all kinds of expatriates line its walls. The flamboyant interior makes it clear that this is no ordinary restaurant; as Paule Marshall described it recently, "Sinuous Turkish columns, which I'm convinced were stolen from some harem, support what looks like a 1920's tin ceiling, painted dark green; the walls are cream-colored suburban stucco, the floor tenement linoleum."

More remarkable is the restaurant's clientele. Haynes serves a cosmopolitan mixture of people, both French and American, black and white, and many others as well, but nowhere else in France does one encounter so many African Americans, tourists and residents of Paris, young and old, male and female. The place radiates a friendliness and warmth from both the best tradition of Paris cafés and the interest of expatriates in the visitor from back home. Even more than that, Haynes has an atmosphere of romance that immediately plugs one into the myth of the African American in Paris. There is no quicker way of learning about the black American community in Paris than by going to Haynes and striking up a conversation. I learned a great deal there, but my fondest memory of the restaurant is of Don and Naté, two employees, dancing slowly to the languid rhythms of soft jazz on a Saturday night.

When I last visited Haynes, in 1994, Liz Goodrum was the cook. She had originally come to Paris in 1979 to attend fashion school after a career in the industry along New York's Seventh Avenue. Like Richard Allen, she worked in Paris fashion for over a decade, collaborating closely with Patrick Kelly, before becoming disenchanted with the business. Cooks earn much less than fashion designers, but Goodrum noted that her restaurant job left her more time for a personal life, as well as a box seat in the center of the black American community in Paris. Commenting on Haynes restaurant today, she observed, "The clientele is mainly French. But there are people who are old clients that come through Paris that just come here for nostalgic reasons. The old people who know we are here, or some people who have read about us in *Let's Go: Europe*, looking for a soul food restaurant. They'll come in and they're very happy. . . . Five black boys came in here for Thanksgiving for the afternoon, and one of the wives said, 'Are you American?' And I said, 'Honey, aren't you eating black-eyed peas and fried chicken?'"

Until the end of 1994, Paris could claim not one but two African American restaurants. Tourists and Parisians roaming the Left Bank's Mouffetard neighborhood frequently came across Randy Garrett's Rib Joint, a classic soul food restaurant serving barbecued ribs, fried chicken, corn bread, and coleslaw. Garrett is an affable expatriate from Seattle who has lived in Paris for over twenty years, and the Rib Joint occupied a tiny space, large enough for a bar and a few tables, supplemented by sidewalk seating in good weather. The Rib Joint lacked the long history of Haynes and did not operate in one of the city's traditional centers of black American culture. Yet it was able to build and for a while sustain a loyal clientele, thanks to the quality of its food, its location in the midst of a thriving restaurant district, and the infectious warmth of its owner. Like Haynes, its customers included a mixture of African American tourists and residents, other Americans, Parisians, and foreigners. One often met the same people in both places, so that the two restaurants seemed to constitute a black archipelago in the French capital. The Rib Joint would frequently hold parties and advertised catering for private events; it even featured special "barbecruises" on the Seine. When I visited during the city's annual music festival in June, Garrett had hired a band to perform outside the restaurant, creating his own street party in the midst of the larger festivities.

Randy Garrett is himself a fascinating figure, whose life blends the model of the romantic expatriate with that of the small businessman. Garrett first came to France in the early 1970s, leaving his home in Seattle to spend over a decade traveling around Europe. He converted an old English bread truck into a camper van, driving it through Yugoslavia, Italy, and Austria. But he always came back to Paris when the lure of the open road faded, gradually developing ties to the French capital. After years of making soul food for friends, Garrett decided to try to earn a living at it, and so the Rib Joint was born. Garrett clearly loves his adopted city and has no desire to return to the United States. Nonetheless, he considers the free and easy lifestyle that initially attracted him to Europe to be very much a thing of the past. Moreover, he says the decline of idealism has affected the character of African American interaction in Paris.

> Paris is always a beautiful city to live in. And it was always such an international, cosmopolitan city. It was always such a crossroads for so many different people who came here . . . and there was a lot of interaction. There still is, but not like it used to be. The 1980s, things made a big change, you know, because they became a bit tighter economically. It became a lot more expensive and the attitude changed. People were more aware in the sixties and seventies, people were more into traveling and seeing the world. They would come over for maybe two or three months, whereas now it's two weeks, maybe a month at maximum, and then they're back . . . the eighties were a period where people were less into love and understanding, and more into let me make a dollar and forget anybody else.
>
> Nowadays . . . so many black Americans, the ones that are here often don't make a great point of frequenting black places like they used to do in the past. With their independence, they will go to a French restaurant before they'd come here. And there's not that many of us over here. Then you've got to take into consideration, lately, since the late sixties or seventies, you had that sort of milieu of black people that . . . came over in a professional capacity, you know, with major companies, and they've got the money to spend and they don't necessarily frequent this place.

These changes, and the vagaries of the restaurant trade in Paris, led Garrett to close the Rib Joint at the end of 1994. Garrett remains in the French capital, however, and if his past is any indication, will certainly find a way to continue his romantic life there.

Unlike the 1920s and 1930s, Paris today does not feature any music clubs owned or managed by African Americans. Jazz is now big business in France, and few black Americans have the capital or interest necessary to invest in it overseas. Modern-day finance perhaps explains why there is no contemporary equivalent of Bricktop's, no nightclub where all black Americans in Paris inevitably end their evenings. Nonetheless, jazz clubs still bring many together, serving as places to meet black Americans in Paris. In discussing her own social life in Paris, Jennifer Bullock observed, "The way I meet people, really, is through clubs and class . . . I've found when my friends all go out, we're all African Americans mostly, and we sort of have formed our own little clique." New Morning, a large ramshackle club in an out-of-the-way Right Bank neighborhood, is perhaps the best place in the French capital to see big-name jazz performers. More a concert hall than a nightclub, New Morning caters to a diverse group of fans, featuring musicians like Herbie Hancock and Gil-Scott Heron.

If there is a geographical center of Parisian jazz today, it exists in the gentrified medieval streets of the Les Halles district, near the Pompidou Centre and the former site of the city's central marketplace. The rue des Lombards in particular hosts a constantly changing cluster of nightclubs, often located in subterranean *caves* following the tradition of the 1940s existentialist wave. There one can find the Duc des Lombards, a dark, intimate room decorated with murals of John Coltrane and Duke Ellington, not to mention a statue of Louis Armstrong outside. The Duc showcases French and American jazz artists performing in a casual atmosphere. La Villa, in Saint-Germain-des-Prés, caters to a much more upscale crowd, wealthy Parisians and foreigners for the most part, who can afford the hefty drink prices. This small, very elegant club features leading American jazz artists booked for week-long runs. While not all American blacks in Paris frequent such places, many go there from time to time, forming a part of the vibrant community of jazz lovers in the French capital. As the sax player Johnny Griffin, who now lives in the French provinces, recently commented, "Sometimes I think French people reckon they invented jazz. They love Louis Armstrong, they love Sidney Bechet. And in Paris the people hanging out in clubs are like a family; they all know each other."

Small businesses like these restaurants and nightclubs constitute an important institutional network for African Americans in Paris. A number of informal associations, regular meetings, and other types of get-togethers reach out to blacks with shared interests. A group called Sisters, led by a journalist named Pamela Grant, organizes activities around issues of concern to black American women, and black Americans in general, in Paris. Jennifer Bullock attended once and met several other young African American women. She never returned, however, finding the group not quite right for her. "It seems as if it's more for older women who have money who want to socialize in Paris. . . . It's not like a Barnard organization of black women where we all get together and talk about experiences and sort of help each other out with problems and that sort of thing. I mean, it is a good organization, I'm sure, to have." In spite of Bullock's experience, however, Sisters has clearly played an important role in bringing together African American women in the French capital.

One member of Sisters who has been especially energetic in organizing African Americans in Paris is Patricia Laplante-Collins, a black woman from Atlanta who has lived in the French capital for over a decade. In addition to her involvement with Sisters, Ms. Laplante-Collins is a founding member of the Minority Caucus of Democrats Abroad, which sponsors a variety of cultural events aimed at the local African American community. She also recently founded a bilingual group called Peuple de Couleur/People of Color, to bring together Paris-based blacks from America, Africa, and the Caribbean around their common heritage and interests. A meeting of this group in January 1996 attracted 140 people. A month later, Laplante-Collins served as guest editor of the on-line expatriate newspaper *AngloFiles* for its special edition devoted to Black History Month.

In June 1994, Sisters organized the city's first celebration of Juneteenth, the traditional Texas holiday celebrating the end of slavery, at Haynes restaurant. The following December a group of blacks, including Dean Ferrier, Tannie Stovall, and Ted Joans scored another first by holding a Kwanzaa ceremony in Paris. One musician, Titus Williams, who has lived in Paris for many years, has organized a large gospel choir. Composed mostly of black singers living in the French capital, it provides a way for them to get to know one another as well as enjoy their common musical heritage. Ted Joans's weekly sessions at the Café le Rouquet help bring together those interested in literature. Devotees of that quintessential black male bonding ritual, basketball, frequently meet at Haynes, often brought there by Charles Beecham, a coach who works with teams in the city. All African Americans in Paris may not necessarily know each other, but they have many ways of participating in that community if they so desire.

The importance of community, of a multitude of connections between individuals, thus continues to characterize the African American experience in Paris. This type of community differs sharply from that among blacks in the United States. There is no black church, family connections are unimportant, and few if any black Americans in Paris have known one another since childhood. More generally, the African American community there is not restrictive; no one, American or French, black or white, puts pressure on black Americans in the French capital to exclude others. Many African Americans who live in or visit Paris have little or no contact with their fellow expatriates. And the black community itself embraces many who are not black, including the white clientele of soul food restaurants and jazz clubs and those whites who attended the Kwanzaa ceremony in December 1994, or meet Ted Joans at the Café le Rouquet. Above all, it includes nonblack spouses and romantic partners, French, American, or other. These mixed relationships contrast strikingly with the situation of blacks in the United States, so much so that many would question the relevance of the black community to Paris at all. Yet even those African Americans who have integrated themselves fully into French life can exercise the option of eating black food, listening to black music, or simply surrounding themselves with black compatriots whenever they choose. The presence of whites in a variety of roles does not alter the central place of black American culture and the black American experience to this group. This true multicultural integration represents the flowering of black life freed from the constraints of racism; as such, it has much to teach us in the United States.

Black Americans in Paris resist any easy characterization. Nonetheless, one can still speak of a black American community in Paris today. Its members may not all know each other, but connections exist, not to mention shared experiences and a common history. Many of the various individuals I interviewed either knew or had heard of one another, and time and time again I found my contacts suggesting other people for me to meet. All of them knew about Haynes and the Rib Joint, and most had spent time there or in other places where African Americans tended to congregate. Some went out of their way to meet other blacks from the United States, while others found such encounters virtually impossible to avoid. Yet in many different ways, most expressed some sense of interrelatedness with other African Americans in the city.

The continued presence of this community exemplifies several important themes in the history of African Americans in Paris. It testifies to the importance of tradition; many blacks in contemporary Paris were drawn there by historical connections between France and black America, and see themselves in one way or another as perpetuating past achievements. It constitutes a commentary on American racism, whose seemingly inexhaustible vitality still gives a political character to the decision of African Americans to live abroad. Finally, it shows the power of myth and legend, strong enough to overcome all sorts of Parisian inconveniences from tenement walk-ups to Jean-Marie Le Pen. Many years ago Countee Cullen observed that Paris was a good place for him to build his castles in Spain. For both the African Americans who live in the French capital now, and the many more in the United States who find themselves intrigued and inspired by their example, this remark still rings true.

ACKNOWLEDGMENTS

NOTES

SELECTED
BIBLIOGRAPHY

INDEX

ACKNOWLEDGMENTS

MANY FRIENDS AND COLLEAGUES have given generously of their time and advice to help me write this book. I would first of all like to thank my literary agent, Marie Brown, for her vision in making *Paris Noir* possible. She went far beyond the traditional duties of an agent, offering the full benefits of her experience in the publishing field. Her comments and encouragement were invaluable. Janet Silver and Wendy Holt, who edited this book for Houghton Mifflin, gave the manuscript a close and excellent reading. They were supportive yet unsparing in pointing out weaknesses in the text, and helped me tie the project together into a coherent and readable whole. Thanks to them, revising the initial version of the book, usually a nightmare for authors, became a pleasant learning experience. I also deeply appreciate their willingness to answer my many basic questions about the technical side of book publishing. Jayne Yaffe did a wonderful job of copyediting the manuscript, energetically correcting errors and rephrasing instances of wooden prose. My two research assistants, Shalon Parker and Robin Hardy-Jensen, made major contributions; their hard work, enthusiasm, and professionalism were a big help. Financial assistance for research and writing was provided by the Academic Senate of the University of California, Santa Cruz; the Center for German and European Studies, University of California, Berkeley; and the Humanities Research Institute, University of California, Irvine. At a time when funding for the humanities seems more threatened than ever, I am grateful for their investment in my work.

I, and all readers of *Paris Noir*, have benefited enormously from the willingness of several individuals to read and critique successive drafts. Michael Vann made detailed, excellent comments on the entire manuscript, pulling no punches in spite of my position as his dissertation adviser. I am also grateful to Santa Cruz colleagues Lisbeth Haas and David Anthony for taking time out from their busy schedules to read the book, as well as to Earl Lewis, Keletso Atkins, Tiffany Patterson, Laura Klein, Martha Hodes, Carolyn Thomason, and Michael Sibalis for their suggestions and support. The New York French History Group kindly invited me to present some of my research at one of their meetings. I thank members Herman Lebovics, Ann Alter, Bryant T. Ragan, Robert Frost, Rosemary Wakeman, Seth Schulman, Jeff Freedman, David Schalk, Jane Bond, Joanne Smith, Myriam Maayan, Vera Zolberg, Sheldon Silberstein, Emmanuelle Saada, Francine Goldenhar, Susan Rogers, Shanny Peer, Pam Sunderland, Valerie Mercer, and Louise Tilly for their warm welcome and incisive comments. Thanks also to the Center for African and African-American Studies at the University of Michigan, and the Society for French Historical Studies, for giving me opportunities to discuss African Americans in Paris. I appreciate the help and suggestions of all those who took the time to read parts of this book in manuscript form; any errors here remain, of course, the responsibility of the author.

I am especially grateful to those who allowed me to interview them. Not only did they speak at length about their own lives in Paris, but they also suggested other contacts, and in many cases opened their homes to me. The kindness and enthusiasm of my respondents helped make this project a labor of love, as well as concretely demonstrating the importance of community to the African American experience in the French capital. I would also like to express my appreciation to the many other individuals who showed interest in my book, suggesting people to talk to or books and articles to consult. At times it seemed that virtually every black person I talked to about this subject knew or knew of someone who had lived in France, confirming my own belief about the key role of the Paris sojourn in African American life. Regrettably, I was not able to pursue all leads, but I thank those who thought enough of my work to offer their own ideas.

More than anyone else, two strong, dynamic African American women deserve my eternal gratitude. My dear friend Brenda Wade not only put me in touch with Marie Brown and many other important individuals, but also read multiple drafts of *Paris Noir*. Without her vision and constant encouragement, it might very well never have seen the light of day. My wife, Denise Herd, gave generously of her own time to read my writing and listen to my ideas. During the entire long process of writing, she proved once again to be not only my best friend, but my best critic. Her insistence on the significance of the topic, as well as her remarkable ability to see what was most interesting and important about the black American experience in Paris, kept me going during even the most difficult moments of this project, and her love and support made it all worthwhile.

My fondest thanks to you all! May you learn as much from *Paris Noir* as I did, and may you enjoy reading it as much as I enjoyed writing it.

—TYLER STOVALL
Santa Cruz, California

NOTES

1. FREEDOM OVERSEAS

1 "What right have I to do": Henry Ossawa Tanner to Atherton Curtis, September 14, 1914, in Dewey F. Mosby, *Henry Ossawa Tanner*, 242.

3 "My father had told me": Eugene Bullard in P. J. Carisella and James W. Ryan, *The Black Swallow of Death*, 39.

4 "When I got off": Ibid., 68–69.

7 "The poorer class of backwoods negro": "Disposal of the Colored Drafted Men," May 16, 1918, in Arthur E. Barbeau and Florette Henri, *The Unknown Soldiers*, 191.

8 "They are the finest workers": George Freeman in Ibid., 102.
"While white American soldiers": Addie W. Hunton and Kathryn M. Johnson, *Two Colored Women with the American Expeditionary Forces*, 102.

9 "It is really marvelous": Ralph W. Tyler in Emmett J. Scott, *The American Negro in the World War*, 325.

10 "On the other hand": Charles Williams, *Sidelights on Negro Soldiers*, 149.
"No, sir, I am not going": Scott, 275.

12 "The regiment never lost": Ibid., 203–4.
"In the engagements around Verdun": Ibid., 233–34.

13 "failed in all their missions": Barbeau and Henri, 137–63.
"TO THE COLORED SOLDIERS": Scott, 139.

14 "Poor negroes": Robert Bullard, in Barbeau and Henri, 138.
"With a few exceptions": Scott, 431.

15 "Enlisted men of this organization": Hunton and Johnson, 186.
"Joe went cruising": John Dos Passos, 1919, 245–46.

17 "The Americans!": "The Colored Americans in France," *The Crisis*, February 1919, 167–168.

18 "the French soldiers": Scott, 204.
"These French people": W. Allison Sweeney, *History of the American Negro in the Great World War*, 195.
"Take back these soldiers": Michel Fabre, *La Rive Noire*, 49.
"Thank you for your friendship": Hunton and Johnson, 190.

19 "Bravo riflemen!": Charles John Balesi, *From Adversaries to Comrades in Arms*, 116.

20 "Blacks were highly esteemed": Balesi, 117.

20 "promiscuous peoples": Jean Vidalenc, "La main-d'oeuvre étrangère en France et la première guerre mondiale," *Francia*, vol. 2, 1974.
   "The first thing": Scott, 305.
21 "the whole audience began to sway": Scott, 308.
22 "the black soldier": W.E.B. Du Bois, "The Black Man in the Revolution of 1914–1918," *The Crisis*, March 1919, 218–23.
23 "But when the French": Hunton and Johnson, 242.

2. BRINGING THE JAZZ AGE TO PARIS

25 The American writer Samuel Putnam: Samuel Putnam, *Paris Was Our Mistress*, 5.
27 "every community in Mississippi": Barbeau and Henri, 177.
28 "We *return*": *The Crisis*, May 1919.
29 The racial pride that: On the Harlem Renaissance, see Jervis Anderson, *This Was Harlem*.
30 "If we must die": Claude McKay, "If We Must Die," Anderson, 196.
31 "the intelligence of modern man": Paul Guillaume in Phyllis Rose, *Jazz Cleopatra*, 43.
32 "Civilization, civilization": René Maran, *Batouala*, 9–10.
33 "to obtain authoritative": P. Olisanwuche Esedebe, *Pan-Africanism*, 80. On the 1919 Pan-African Congress, see Scott, 470, and W.E.B. Du Bois, "Opinions of W.E.B. Du Bois," *The Crisis*, May 1919, 7–9.
34 "to participate in the government": Esedebe, *Pan-Africanism*, 83.
35 "decided to remain": Rayford Logan, "Confessions of an Unwilling Nordic," *The World Tomorrow*, July 1927, 299.
   "The effectiveness of their blows": Ibid., 300.
36 "Well, you never saw or heard": Carisella and Ryan, 202. This and many other direct quotations in *The Black Swallow of Death* are taken directly from an unpublished journal left by Eugene Bullard.
38 "Two of the boys": Elliot Carpenter in Chris Goddard, *Jazz Away from Home*, 19–20.
   "At that time": Alain Romans in Ibid., 278.
39 "A rickety, open-air Paris taxi": Bricktop with James Haskins, *Bricktop*, 85.
40 "Two more shiploads of savages": Ralph Nevill, *Days and Nights in Montmartre and the Latin Quarter*, 35.
   "Those who in the years": Joseph Kessel, *Princes of the Night*, 125–28.
41 "The Negroes would go": Elliot Carpenter in Goddard, 302.
   "In 1919 it was impossible": Elisabeth de Gramont in Louis Chevalier, *Montmartre du plaisir et du crime*, 323.
   "This is disgusting!": Chevalier, 323.
42 "Her grace, charm and personality": *Chicago Defender*, May 11, 1933.
43 "Florence's in the Rue Blanche": Nevill, 43.
   "who shattered champagne glasses": Langston Hughes, *The Big Sea*, 156.
   "straight out of a": John Chilton, *Sidney Bechet*, 83–84.
45 "my greatest claim to fame": Bricktop with Haskins, 98.
   "After an hour": F. Scott Fitzgerald, "Babylon Revisited," *Babylon Revisited and Other Stories*, 214.

47 "where one may get sausages": J. A. Rogers, "The American Negro in Paris," *New York Amsterdam News*, September 21, 1927.

48 "the headquarters for many": Ivan Browning, "Across the Pond," *Chicago Defender*, August 6, 1927.

"Rue Pigalle in the early": Gwendolyn Bennett, "Wedding Day," 1926. Reprinted in Marcy Knopf, ed., *The Sleeper Wakes*, 50.

"The Boulevard de Clichy": J. A. Rogers, "The Paris Pepper Pot," *Pittsburgh Courier*, July 27, 1929.

49 "All are in a Negro village": Rogers, "The American Negro in Paris," *New York Amsterdam News*, September 14, 1927.

50 "I never forget my people": Josephine Baker in Bryan Hammond and Patrick O'Connor, *Josephine Baker*, 2.

51 "She was the little girl": *Dance Magazine*, September 1927, in Hammond and O'Connor, 9.

52 "she resembled some tall": Ibid., 12.

The Plantation Club: See Lewis Erenberg, *Steppin' Out*.

"France . . . I had dreamed": Baker and Bouillion, 42.

53 "She made her entry": Janet Flanner, *Paris Was Yesterday*, xx–xxi.

55 "Midnight. A sea of bare shoulders": Hammond and O'Connor, 47–48.

57 "'I recognized the Champs Elysées'": Hughes, *The Big Sea*, 144–45.

58 "'You must be crazy, boy'": Ibid., 146.

"The cream of the Negro musicians": Ibid., 162.

59 "I never thought there": Claude McKay, *A Long Way from Home*, 230. The striking ambivalence of this passage accurately reflects McKay's own divided opinions about the city, and about his role as a black expatriate in general.

61 "Paris is where I would love": Countee Cullen in Fabre, *La Rive noire*, 127.

"For two days now": Gwendolyn Bennett, diary entry of June 26, 1925, at the Schomburg Center for Black Culture, New York Public Library.

"There never was a more": Ibid., June 28, 1925.

62 "Thence to 'Le Royal'": Ibid., August 8, 1925.

65 "French artists and critics": "Beth Prophit [*sic*] Is Hailed in Paris as Real Artist," *Baltimore Afro-American*, August 3, 1929.

"During those years in Paris": Hale Woodruff in Catherine Bernard, *Afro-American Artists in Paris*, 24.

67 "not as a symbol of cold": Anna Julia Cooper in Louise Daniel Hutchinson, *Anna J. Cooper*, 142.

"In New York I had spent": Alfonso Brown in Eduardo Arroyo, *"Panama" Al Brown*, 39.

68 "all I need to live": Ibid., 85.

70 "everything we've ever read": Paul Achard in Rose, 8.

"crazed body": Hammond and O'Connor, 19.

"the most direct assault": Hammond and O'Connor, 35.

"She encountered in the heavy beat": Paul Morand, *Magie Noire*, 169.

71 "this young witch pulverised": Ibid.

"In the most famous": Review "Bonsoir," March 15, 1919, Paris, Archives de la Préfecture de Police, BA 861.

73 "I could never think": J. A. Rogers, "Paris Draws the Line," *New York Amsterdam News*, July 24, 1929.
    "Recently I have received": Gratien Candace in "Personal Glimpses," *The Literary Digest*, September 1, 1923.

74 "The Americans show themselves": Georges de la Fouchardière, Ibid.
    "when elephants live": *Chicago Defender*, April 6, 1929.
    "Everybody was sleeping around": Bricktop with Haskins, 131.

75 "One thing stupefied me": Morand, "Charleston," *Magie Noire*, 86.
    "My father-in-law gave us": Eugene Bullard in Carisella and Ryan, 209–10.

76 "Leon Crutcher": *Le Figaro*, February 27, 1926, 3.
    "Mud on his nice": Bennett, "Wedding Day," in Knopf, *The Sleeper Wakes*, 54.

77 "Hello, Maud, what": Cunard, *Black Man and White Ladyship*, 103.
    "she would not feel": Cunard, 105.

79 "Tall, coffee skin, ebony eyes": Ernest Hemingway in Hammond and O'Connor, 44.
    "Frankly to say, I never": McKay, *A Long Way from Home*, 243.

80 "On the *Rochambeau*": Putnam, 49.

3. DEPRESSION AND WAR: PARIS IN THE 1930S

85 "It takes more": Tony Allan, *Paris*, 163.
    "One may see Frisco": "European Writer Finds That White Americans Reserve Prejudice for Own Colored Compatriots," *Journal and Guide*, October 8, 1932, press clipping file, Schomburg Center for Black Culture, New York Public Library.

86 "the Negroes of Montmartre": Ibid.

88 "Paris was as wild": Bricktop with Haskins, 148.

89 "I love him to this very day": Bricktop with Haskins, 184–85.
    "Both Paul and the Duke": Ibid., 198.
    "Bricktop was very intelligent": Arthur Briggs in Goddard, 287.

91 "Negro wench": *Time*, February 10, 1930, 41.

92 "Josephine had a bad reputation": Bricktop with Haskins, 186. Bricktop blamed Baker's standoffishness on her manager Pepito, not on Baker herself.

93 "We were only in Paris": Ethel Sheppard in Jean-Claude Baker and Chris Chase, *Josephine*, 180.
    "It might seem that in Europe": *Philadelphia Tribune* in Ibid., 199.
    "Seeing Noble made me think": Baker and Bouillon, 88–89.

95 "from the point of view": Hugues Panassié in Marshall Stearns, *The Story of Jazz*, 139. By way of contrast, Panassié wrote in *Hot Jazz*, 29, that "white musicians, in adopting the Negro style, unconsciously brought to it certain purely musical qualities from their superior culture."
    "the sources of this swing music": Ibid., 294.

96 "the hottest thing": Bricktop with Haskins, 200.
    "The unity of the four": *New York Times*, July 7, 1985, H18.

97 "The orchestra is original": *Pittsburgh Courier*, August 17, 1929.

98 "do a mean bit": *Chicago Defender*, August 24, 1929.

99 "I don't like it": Countee Cullen in Michel Fabre, *From Harlem to Paris*, 81.

100 "Extravagantly wide sidewalks": Eslanda Goode Robeson, "Black Paris," *Challenge*, vol. 1, no. 4, January 1936, 12–13.
"In such a setting": Ibid., 13.
101 "For many years France": Mercer Cook, "The Race Problem in Paris and the French West Indies," *Journal of Negro Education*, vol. 8, no. 4, October 1939, 673.
102 "Heads of thought and reflection": Nancy Elizabeth Prophet in Jessie Carney Smith, ed., *Notable Black American Women*, 896.
103 "It was like being": Loïs Mailou Jones in the *Oakland Tribune*, January 13, 1992.
"When I took *Les Fétiches*": Loïs Mailou Jones in Bernard.
106 "The average French Negro": Eslanda Goode Robeson, "Black Paris," *Challenge*, vol. 1, no. 4, January 1936, 12–18.
107 "It was during the years": Léopold Senghor, letter of February 1960, in Lilyan Kesteloot, *Black Writers in French*, 63.
"To give to the intelligentsia": "Our Aim," *Revue du Monde Noir*, 1931.
108 "Negroes are essentially artists": Louis Achille, "L'Art et les Noirs," Ibid.
109 "It was a relief": McKay, *A Long Way from Home*, 277.
"Ray's thoughts were far and away": Claude McKay, *Banjo*, 319.
110 "'Beguin', 'jelly-roll'": Ibid., 105.
"What struck me in the book": Aimé Césaire in Kesteloot, 72.
111 "'To bring back'": David Diop, preface to *Coups de pilon* (1956) in Jean-Claude Blachère, *Le Modèle Nègre*, 203.
112 "slurring his own people": Aubrey Bowser, *Amsterdam News*, in Wayne F. Cooper, *Claude McKay*, 258.
"Demand that nightclub owners": National Archives of France, series F 7 13541, police report of November 24, 1931.
113 "The European unions of musicians": *The Afro-American*, August 26, 1933.
114 "Several of the old time": *Chicago Defender*, September 23, 1933.
"The Depression . . . brought": Bricktop with Haskins, 195–96.
115 "It is nearly three years": Edgar Wiggins, "Artists Live Queer in Paris Latin Quarter," *The Afro-American*, May 13, 1933.
116 "some of the most popular": U.S. Consul General in Paris to Monique Iversen, March 9, 1932, in *Correspondence*, vol. XLI, National Archives of the United States of America, Washington, D.C., 1932.
"By 1935 all the bad": Arthur Briggs in Goddard, 287.
117 "Between Boudon's and Lisieux's": Bill Coleman, *Trumpet Story*, 95–96.
118 "even after I knew": Bricktop with Haskins, 201.
120 "Nightclubs were almost deserted": Eugene Bullard in Carisella and Ryan, 231–32.
"It seemed the perfect way": Baker and Bouillon, 118.
121 "The last night I saw": Bricktop with Haskins, 205–6.
122 "Major Bader said I was": Eugene Bullard in Carisella and Ryan, 242.
123 "He told me it would": Ibid., 243.
"The orchestra became": *Chicago Defender*, September 23, 1944.
124 "So each morning": *Ebony*, vol. VIII, no. 12, October 1952, 69–70.
125 "Nothing was too good": Roy Porter, *Uncensored France*, 45.
126 "lived in daily dread": René Maran in Roi Ottley, *No Green Pastures*, 90.
127 "I left Paris": Baker and Bouillon, 119.

127 "Foxy . . . when are we": Josephine Baker in "Rémy," *J.A.: Episodes de la vie d'un agent du S.R. et du contre-espionnage français*, 37.
"It can fairly be said": Baker and Bouillon, 120.

4. LIFE ON THE LEFT BANK

134 "the expression of a rotting bourgeoisie": Antony Beevor and Artemis Cooper, *Paris after the Liberation*, 348.
"The Negress sings": Jean-Paul Sartre, *Nausea*, 177–78.
138 "Paris is still Paris": Edward Toles, *Chicago Defender*, September 30, 1944, 2.
139 "Its windows are boarded": Rudolph Dunbar, Ibid., 7.
"I saw my first black G.I.": "In Paris, Black G.I.s Have Come to Know and Love Freedom," Richard Wright, *Samedi-Soir*, May 25, 1946, 2.
140 "A French girl": Ottley, 74.
141 "So, I met old Harris": Oliver Harrington, *Why I Left America, and Other Essays*, 105.
143 "We were very free": Herbert Gentry in Myron Schwartzman, *Romare Bearden*, 162.
144 "It was the Americans": Ibid., 163.
145 "Now at last I'm": Romare Bearden to Carl Holty in Ibid., 168–69.
146 "freest of cities": Ed Clark in Marie-Françoise Sanconie, "Paris 1945–1991," in Asake Bomani and Belvie Rooks, eds., *Paris Connections*, 45.
"Those who approach": *Le Monde*, February 25–26, 1973, in Ibid.
147 "In 1956, in Paris": Ed Clark in Ibid.
"One of the all-time": Harrington, back cover.
"a wonderful place": Ibid., 105.
148 "Ollie became my": Chester Himes, *My Life of Absurdity*, 35.
"The art community": Ibid., 58–59.
149 "It was a special club": Herbert Gentry in Schwartzman, 163.
150 "a million people": Baker and Chase, 263.
151 "We're going to be so happy": Baker and Bouillon, 162.
152 "Montmartre looked like a wreck": Bricktop with Haskins, 237–38.
153 "average Americans": Ibid., 238.
"Thanks for the memories": Ibid., 243.
154 "We were fooling ourselves": Ibid., 246.
155 "More American Negro women": William Gardner Smith, *Pittsburgh Courier*, July 26, 1952.
156 "There is the great Katherine": Boris Vian, "Le Spectacle de K. Dunham," *Autre écrits sur le jazz*, vol. 2, 59.
"Opening night in Paris": Eartha Kitt, *Thursday's Child*, 145–46.
"I looked at myself": Ibid., 161–62.
157 "Being tall and digging the theater": Vertamae Smart-Grosvenor, *Vibration Cooking*, 59.
"Right by the Café Dupont": Ibid., 176–77.
159 "I was surprised how hip": Coleman, 165.
160 "Naturally a Paris boulevard": Harrington, 57–58.
161 "It's six years ago": *Pittsburgh Courier*, September 20, 1952.
162 "Lily [his wife]": Coleman, 179.

165 "Seen from the outside": Boris Vian in Noel Arnaud, *Les vies parallèles de Boris Vian*, 145.
167 "It is annoying": Boris Vian, "50–35, ou un demi-siècle de jazz," *Autres écrits sur le jazz*, February 1953, 215.
168 "Dizzy Gillespie and his orchestra": Vian, "Dizzy Gillespie a revelé le be-bop hier soir à Pleyel," *Autres écrits sur le jazz*, vol. 1, 242–33.
169 "It was fantastic": Kenny Clarke in Ursula Broschke Davis, *Paris without Regret*, 50.
171 "I felt when I settled": Sidney Bechet, *Treat It Gentle*, 194–95.
"Even after his triumphs": Chilton, *Sidney Bechet*, 233.
"As I sat sipping": Ibid., 242.
172 "Sidney could have become": Ibid., 277.
173 "Sidney never became big-headed": Charles Delaunay in Ibid., 251.
174 "The rhythm came from Africa": Sidney Bechet in Ibid., 284.
"Sidney's return to his native": Bill Russell in Ibid., 217–18.
175 "So I played": Bechet, 200.
"I was so happy": Coleman, 171.
176 "It was a beautiful": Ibid., 195.
"I wanted to go to France": Kenny Clarke in Ursula Broschke Davis, 39.
178 "The music has gotten into": Kenny Clarke in Arthur Taylor, *Notes and Tones*, 195.
"The French acted more wisely": Dizzy Gillespie in Ursula Broschke Davis, 50.
179 "My income was much greater": Kenny Clarke in Ibid., 55.
"I had never": Miles Davis with Quincy Troupe, *Miles*, 126.
180 "while I didn't": Ibid., 218.
181 "Wright pointed out": Harrington, 13.
"One must belong": Beauford Delaney in Judd Tully, "Beauford Delaney," *Art Magazine*, June 1979.

5. THE GOLDEN AGE OF AFRICAN AMERICAN
LITERATURE IN PARIS

183 "To live in Paris": Richard Wright, "I Choose Exile," unpublished essay, Department of Special Collections and Archives, Kent State University, 10.
"I wasn't really choosing France": James Baldwin in W. J. Weatherby, *James Baldwin*, 63.
"I received a deluge of letters": Chester Himes, *The Quality of Hurt*, 141.
184 "I live in voluntary exile": Wright, "I Choose Exile," 1.
186 "The sordid French hotel room": James Baldwin, *Notes of a Native Son*, 127.
187 "The moment I began living": Ibid., 139.
"At the outset of his sojourn": Richard Wright, "There's Always Another Café," *Kiosk*, no. 10, 1953, 81.
188 "The Monaco was a typical": Harrington, 59–60.
"a garish splash of green": William Gardner Smith, *The Stone Face*, 12.
"The evenings I went": Himes, *My Life of Absurdity*, 37.
192 "Whites can no longer": Richard Wright in Kenneth Kinnamon and Michel Fabre, *Conversations with Richard Wright*, 75.
194 "Wright also had a": Fabre, *The Unfinished Quest of Richard Wright*, 382–83.

195 "there is no Negro": Kinnamon and Fabre, 233.

198 "I'm of African descent": Richard Wright, *Black Power*, 137.
"I'd seen these same": Ibid., 56–57.

201 "In general, only the Negro entertainers": Baldwin, "Encounter on the Seine," *Notes of a Native Son*, 118. This essay was originally published under the title "The Negro in Paris."

202 "Below the surface of this novel": "Everybody's Protest Novel," Ibid., 23.

204 "My real fear was buried": James Baldwin, *Giovanni's Room*, 126.

205 "spent most of their time": James Baldwin in Ursula Broschke Davis, 21.

207 "hate runs through": *Atlantic Monthly* and *Commentary* in Himes, *The Quality of Hurt*, 100.

208 "Most of the brothers": Himes, *My Life of Absurdity*, 41–42.

209 "During her terrible grieving": Ibid., 323–24.
"All of the American blacks": Ibid., 34–35.

211 "I tried to think": Ibid., 56.
"'It's a trap'": Smith, *The Stone Face*, 176–77.

213 "I had started out to write": Ibid., 102.
"On the 22nd of January": Ibid., 112–13.

6. NEW PERSPECTIVES ON RACE

218 "He managed to be": Kurt Mohr in Chilton, *Sidney Bechet*, 285.
"His disappearance closes": Ibid., 287.

219 "Do you know why": Oliver Harrington, 23.
"From that time Wright": Ibid., 24.
"feverish with a desire": Chester Himes, *A Case of Rape*, 31.
"He was also hailed": Ibid., 32–33.

220 it remained unfinished: The manuscript *Island of Hallucinations* remains sealed to the public, according to the wishes of Richard Wright and his widow, Ellen Wright. My discussion of this book relies on that provided by Michel Fabre in his *The Unfinished Quest of Richard Wright*.
"The primary question explored": Fabre, *The Unfinished Quest of Richard Wright*, 480–81.

221 "I've never met a Black": Harrington, 109.

225 "In France he had become": Robert Lantz in Weatherby, 304.

226 "That was what we most disliked": Himes, *My Life of Absurdity*, 343.

227 "I had become a celebrity": Ibid., 249.
"I went back to Paris": Ibid., 270.
"Larry was one of the": Ibid., 310.

230 "a man of medium build": Ernest Dunbar, *The Black Expatriates*, 127.

231 "I know a cat from the States": Art Simmons in William Gardner Smith, *Return to Black America*, 61.

232 "There is a Paris": Dunbar, 148–49.

233 "They put up a good front": "France: Negroes in Paris," *Newsweek*, September 21, 1964, press clipping file, Schomburg Center for Black Culture, New York Public Library.

233 "The French tend to": Edward Barnett in *New York Times*, November 29, 1966.

234 "mother confessor to": "Negroes in Paris," [1963 or 1964], press clipping file, Schomburg Center for Black Culture, New York Public Library.

237 "Sam Middleton was": Ted Joans, "An Abbreviated Autobiography of Afro-American Artists Over Yonder" in Bomani and Rooks, 38.

240 "Yeah, I remember one time": Nathan Davis in Bill Moody, *The Jazz Exiles*, 128.
"The thing with European musicians": Donald Byrd in Ursula Broschke Davis, 108.

242 "It's no longer a novelty": Art Simmons in Dunbar, 130.

243 "There is no Negro 'community'": Dunbar, 131.

247 "We have all been saddened": S. Emery Delaney to Beauford Delaney, December 1963, Beauford Delaney papers, Schomburg Center for Black Culture, New York Public Library.
"The United States for me": William Gardner Smith, *National Guardian*, March 7, 1960.
"How many lynchings": Harold Flender, *Paris Blues*, 29.

248 "There isn't a place": *Paris Blues*, Pennebaker Productions/Diane Productions, 1961.
"things are much better": Ibid.

249 "I don't think any American": *New York Times*, 1969; Schomburg press clipping file, Schomburg Center for Black Culture, New York Public Library.

250 "I remember Klook": Donald Byrd in Ursula Broschke Davis, 110–11.

253 "I lived mainly among": James Baldwin in Weatherby, 68.
"The Algerian war was": Himes, *My Life of Absurdity*, 199.

254 "There was a lot of sympathy": Richard Gibson in James Campbell, *Exiled in Paris*, 203.
"And that night, dressed": William Gardner Smith, *Pittsburgh Courier*, August 9, 1952.

255 "Hey! How does it feel": Smith, *The Stone Face*, 55.
"We're the niggers here": Ibid., 56–57.
"I wouldn't rent": Ibid., 63.
"'Forget it, man'": Ibid., 105.

257 "Man, when I arrived": Smart-Grosvenor, 68.

258 "Jesse sipped his coffee": Smith, *Return to Black America*, 93–94.

259 "Moving along an Accra boulevard": Smith, *Return to Black America*, 97.

260 "The idea of American black": Ibid., 93–94.
"I am very sad": William Gardner Smith in Leroy Hodges, *Portrait of an Expatriate*, 84.

261 "In America I would": *New York Times*, 1969, Schomburg press clipping file, Schomburg Center for Black Culture, New York Public Library.

263 "While black American students": Ibid.

264 "The challenge for us": Telephone interview with Bette Woody, March 5, 1995.

266 "We want to serve notice": *New York Times*, August 18, 1963.
"We cannot physically": Ibid., August 19, 1963.
"It was a beautiful": Art Simmons in Dunbar, 131.

267 "There were a lot": Himes, *My Life of Absurdity*, 291.
"undesirable in France": Peter Goldman, *The Death and Life of Malcolm X*, 253.
"The day he was supposed": Bette Woody interview.

269 "This is no place": Kathleen Rout, *Eldridge Cleaver*, 169.
   "The heavy pedestrian traffic": Eldridge Cleaver, *Soul on Fire*, 187–88.
270 "I was getting sarcastic": Ibid., 208–9.
271 "You'll be Cock": Rout, 193.
272 "I've talked to many": *New York Times*, 1969, press clipping file, Schomburg Center
   for Black Culture, New York Public Library.
   "The black man who established": Smith, *Return to Black America*, 71.
274 "That was the beginning": Interview with Dean Ferrier, Cravant, France, June 23,
   1994.
275 "Renault workers were marching": Himes, *My Life of Absurdity*, 356–67.
   "It was a great time": Ferrier interview.
   "The other time somebody": Smart-Grosvenor, 127–28.
276 "This is a novel": Frank Yerby, "A Note to the Reader," *Speak Now*.
   "My people, *le Bon Dieu*": Ibid., 98.
278 "A lot of American": Dean Ferrier interview.
279 "May '68 killed it": Interview with Tannie Stovall, June 21, 1994.

7. AFRICAN AMERICANS IN PARIS TODAY

284 "She had been turned": Rose, 249.
286 "Josephine Baker, like the other": *Le Figaro*, April 14, 1975.
287 "Although many black Americans": *Los Angeles Times*, March 22, 1993.
   "Paris is the pleasure capital": Ibid.
288 "They say it's almost worse": Interview with Jennifer Bullock, Paris, June 25, 1994.
   "The fact that you have": Tannie Stovall interview.
289 "I can't handle the": Interview with Randy Garrett, Paris, June 20, 1994.
   "I remember the first": Interview with Jean Stovall, June 1994.
292 "I felt I had": Tannie Stovall interview.
293 "there is no place": Jean Stovall interview.
294 "Integration was easier": *Los Angeles Times*, March 31, 1992.
295 "For the past two": *Washington Post*, July 13, 1993.
296 "with father, three or four": Jacques Chirac in *New York Times*, March 18, 1992.
298 "As for black French people": Interview with Benjamin Davis, Paris, June 1994.
299 "The city boasts": *New York Times*, April 20, 1984.
   "I think that English": Jennifer Bullock interview.
301 "Langston in the twenties": Melvin Dixon, "Climbing Montmartre," *African Americans and Europe: Conference Booklet*, 34.
303 "To me, although I accept": James Emanuel in *Negative Capability*, vol. XI, no. 3,
   1991, 252.
304 "We African American writers": Ibid., 251.
   "a poetry made of": Simon Njami in Ted Joans and Hart LeRoy Bibbs, *Double
   Trouble*.
305 "Probably the most colorful": James Emanuel in "Preface," Ibid.
   "a poem about me": Interview with Ted Joans, Paris, June 1995.
306 "What they're saying": Barbara Chase-Riboud in *Los Angeles Times*, August 30, 1994.
   "jazz has blended": *New York Times*, January 15, 1995.

307 "Opportunities for me": Interview with Tansee Mayer, Paris, June 1994.
    "I love it here": Nancy Holloway in *Paris Connections* (program notes, Time Warner, 1992), 26.

308 "I left the States": Dee Dee Bridgewater, CBS News "Sunday Morning," February 26, 1995; Burrelle's Transcript, 20.

309 "I have had the": Hal Singer, *Jazz Roads*, 280.

310 "Almost nobody came": Marie-Françoise Sanconie in the *New York Times*, February 7, 1994.

311 "I don't do black art": Ibid.
    "There is no art": Ibid.

312 "There's no such thing": Barbara Chase-Riboud in the *Los Angeles Times*, August 30, 1994.

313 "Art projects itself": Raymond Saunders in Marie-Françoise Sanconie, "Paris 1945–1991," Bomani and Rooks, 48.

316 "There's a whole series": Benjamin Davis interview.
    "When you grow up": Ibid.
    "It was important to me": Ibid.

318 "He charms . . . *tout Paris*": *Christian Science Monitor*, August 25, 1988.
    "I loved it, even though": Interview with Richard Allen, Paris, June 1994.

319 "I think I was": Ibid.
    "I've always had": Ibid.

320 "Sinuous Turkish columns": Paule Marshall, *New York Times*, October 18, 1992.

321 "The clientele is mainly": Interview with Liz Goodrum, June 1994.

322 "Paris is always a beautiful": Randy Garrett interview.

323 "The way I meet people": Jennifer Bullock interview.
    "Sometimes I think French": Johnny Griffin in *Wall Street Journal*, September 14, 1987.
    "It seems as if it's": Jennifer Bullock interview.

SELECTED
BIBLIOGRAPHY

ARCHIVES

National Archives, Washington, D.C.
Schomburg Center for Black Culture, New York Public Library, New York
Bancroft Library, University of California, Berkeley, California
Archives nationales, Paris, France
Archives de la préfecture de police, Paris, France
Archives nationales — section outre-mer, Aix-en-Provence, France
Department of Special Collections and Archives, Kent State University, Kent, Ohio

MEMOIRS, AUTOBIOGRAPHIES, AND
OTHER PRIMARY SOURCES

Angelou, Maya, *Singin' and Swingin' and Gettin' Merry Like Christmas*. New York: Random House, 1976.
Aragon, Louis, *Aurelien*. New York: Duell, Sloan, and Pearce, 1947.
Baker, Josephine, and Jo Bouillon, *Josephine*. New York: Paragon House, 1988.
Baldwin, James, *Giovanni's Room*. New York: Dell, 1956.
———, *Notes of a Native Son*. Boston: Beacon Press, 1955.
Bechet, Sidney, *Treat It Gentle: An Autobiography*. New York: Hill and Wang, 1960.
Bennett, Gwendolyn, "Tokens," in Charles Johnson, ed., *Ebony and Topaz*. Freeport, N.Y.: 1971.
———, "Wedding Day," 1926. Reprinted in Marcy Knopf, ed., *The Sleeper Wakes: Harlem Renaissance Stories by Women*. New Brunswick, N.J.: Rutgers University Press, 1993.
Bricktop, with James Haskins, *Bricktop*. New York: Atheneum, 1983.
Cleaver, Eldridge, *Soul on Fire*. Waco, Tex.: Word Books, 1978.
Coleman, Bill, *Trumpet Story*. Boston: Northeastern University Press, 1989.
Cousturier, Lucie, *Des inconnus chez moi*. Paris: Editions de la Sirène, 1920.
Crowder, Henry, *As Wonderful as All That?* Navarro, Calif.: Wild Trees Press, 1987.
Cunard, Nancy, *Black Man and White Ladyship: An Anniversary*. London: Utopia Press, 1931.
———, *Negro: An Anthology*. New York: Negro Universities Press, 1969.
Davis, Miles, with Quincy Troupe, *Miles: The Autobiography*. New York: Simon and Schuster, 1989.
Dos Passos, John, *1919*. New York: New American Library, 1969.

Fitzgerald, F. Scott, "Babylon Revisited," *Babylon Revisited and Other Stories*. New York: Charles Scribner's Sons, 1960.

———, *Tender Is the Night*. New York: Charles Scribner's Sons, 1961.

Flanner, Janet, *Paris Was Yesterday: 1925–1939*. New York: Viking, 1972.

Flender, Harold, *Paris Blues*. New York: Ballantine Books, 1957.

E. Franklin Frazier, *Black Bourgeoisie*. Glencoe, Ill.: Free Press, 1957.

Harrington, Oliver, *Why I Left America, and Other Essays*. Jackson, Miss.: University Press of Mississippi, 1993.

Heath, Gordon, *Deep Are the Roots*. Amherst, Mass.: University of Massachusetts Press, 1992.

Himes, Chester, *The Autobiography of Chester Himes: Vol. 1, The Quality of Hurt; Vol. 2, My Life of Absurdity*. New York: Paragon House, 1971–72, 1976.

———, *A Case of Rape*. Washington, D.C.: Howard University Press, 1984.

Hughes, Langston, *The Big Sea*. New York: Hill and Wang, 1979.

———, "The Blues I'm Playing," *The Ways of White Folks*. New York: Vintage, 1990.

Hunton, Addie W., and Kathryn M. Johnson, *Two Colored Women with the American Expeditionary Forces*. Brooklyn, N.Y.: Brooklyn Eagle Press, 1920.

Joans, Ted, and Hart LeRoy Bibbs, *Double Trouble*. Paris: Editions Bleu Outremer, 1992.

Johnson, James Weldon, *Black Manhattan*. New York: Knopf, 1930.

Kessel, Joseph, *Princes of the Night*. New York: The Macauley Company, 1928.

Kitt, Eartha, *Thursday's Child*. New York: Duell, Sloan, and Pearce, 1956.

Malartic, Yves, *Au Pays du Bon Dieu*. Paris: Table Ronde, 1947.

Maran, Réné, *Batouala*. New York: Thomas Seltzer, 1922.

McGee, Alice, *Black America Abroad*. Boston: Meador, 1941.

McKay, Claude, *Banjo*. San Diego: Harvest/HBJ, 1957.

———, *A Long Way from Home*. New York: L. Furman, 1937.

Morand, Paul, *Magie Noire*. Paris: Ferenczi, 1936.

Nevill, Ralph, *Days and Nights in the Latin Quarter*. New York: George H. Doran, 1927.

Ottley, Roi, *No Green Pastures*. New York: Charles Scribner's Sons, 1951.

Panassié, Hugues, *Hot Jazz: The Guide to Swing Music*. New York: M. Witmark and Sons, 1934.

Paynter, John H., *Fifty Years After*. New York: Margent Press, 1940.

Proctor, Henry Hugh, *Between Black and White: Autobiographical Sketches*. Freeport, N.Y.: Books for Libraries Press, 1971.

Putnam, Samuel, *Paris Was Our Mistress*. Carbondale, Ill.: Southern Illinois University Press, 1947.

"Rémy," J.A.: *Episodes de la vie d'un agent du S.R. et du contre-espionnage français*. Paris: Editions Galic, 1961.

Sartre, Jean-Paul, *Nausea*. New York: New Directions, 1964.

Scott, Emmett, *The American Negro in the World War*. Chicago: Homewood Press, 1919.

Singer, Hal, *Jazz Roads*. Paris: Edition #1, 1990.

Smart-Grosvenor, Vertamae, *Vibration Cooking*. New York: Ballantine Books, 1992.

Smith, William Gardner, *Return to Black America*. Englewood Cliffs, N.J.: Prentice-Hall, 1970.

———, *The Stone Face*. New York: Farrar, Straus and Company, 1963.

Stewart, Ollie, *Paris Here I Come*. Baltimore: Afro-American Company, 1953.

Van Peebles, Melvin, *Le Chinois du XIVe*. Paris: Le Gadenet, 1966.

Vian, Boris, *Autres écrits sur le jazz*, 2 vols. Paris: Christian Bourgois, 1982.

———, *Manuel de Saint-Germain-des Prés*. Paris: Chene, 1974.

Williams, Charles, *Sidelights on Negro Soldiers*. Boston: B. J. Brimmer, 1923.

Wright, Richard, *Black Power*. New York: Harper, 1954.

———, "I Choose Exile," unpublished essay.

———, *The Outsider*. New York: Harper and Row, 1989.

Yerby, Frank, *Speak Now*. New York: Dial Press, 1969.

SECONDARY SOURCES

Allan, Tony, *Paris: The Glamour Years, 1919–1940*. New York: Gallery Books, 1977.

Anderson, Jervis, *This Was Harlem*. New York: Farrar, Straus, and Giroux, 1981.

Arnaud, Noel, *Les vies parallèles de Boris Vian*. Paris: C. Bourgois, 1981.

Arnold, James, *Modernism and Negritude*. Cambridge, Mass.: Harvard University Press, 1981.

Arroyo, Eduardo, *"Panama" Al Brown*. Paris: J. C. Lattès, 1982.

Autrement, Black. Special issue, no. 49, April 1983.

Baker, Jean-Claude, with Chris Chase, *Josephine: The Hungry Heart*. New York: Random House, 1993.

Balesi, Charles John, *From Adversaries to Comrades in Arms: West Africans and the French Military, 1885–1918*. Waltham, Mass.: Crossroads, 1979.

Barbeau, Arthur E., and Florette Henri, *The Unknown Soldiers: Black American Troops in World War I*. Philadelphia: Temple University Press, 1974.

Beevor, Antony, and Artemis Cooper, *Paris after the Liberation*. New York: Doubleday, 1994.

Benjamin, Tritobia Hayes, *The Life and Art of Loïs Mailou Jones*. San Francisco: Pomegranate Artbooks, 1994.

Benstock, Shari, *Women of the Left Bank*. Austin: University of Texas Press, 1986.

Bernard, Catherine, *Afro-American Artists in Paris: 1919–1939*. New York: The Hunter College Art Galleries, 1989.

Blachère, Jean-Claude, *Le Modèle nègre: Aspects littéraires du myth primitiviste au XXe siècle chez Apollinaire, Cendras, Tzara*. Dakar: Nouvelles Editions Africaines, 1981.

Bomani, Asake, and Belvie Rooks, eds., *Paris Connections: African American Artists in Paris*. San Francisco: Q.E.D. Press, 1992.

Campbell, James, *Exiled in Paris*. New York: Scribner, 1995.

———, *Talking at the Gates: A Life of James Baldwin*. London: Viking, 1991.

Carisella, P. J., and James W. Ryan, *The Black Swallow of Death*. Boston: Marlborough House, 1972.

Chevalier, Louis, *Montmartre du plaisir et du crime*. Paris: Robert Laffont, 1980.

Chilton, John, *Sidney Bechet: The Wizard of Jazz*. New York: Oxford University Press, 1987.

———, *The Song of the Hawk*. London: Quartet, 1990.

Collier, James Lincoln, *Louis Armstrong*. New York: Oxford University Press, 1983.

Cooper, Wayne F., *Claude McKay*. Baton Rouge: Louisiana State University Press, 1987.

Cose, Ellis, *The Rage of a Privileged Class*. New York: HarperCollins, 1993.

Davis, Lenwood, *Blacks in the American Armed Forces*. Westport, Conn.: Greenwood Press, 1985.

Davis, Ursula Broschke, *Paris without Regret*. Iowa City: University of Iowa Press, 1986.

Dewitte, Philippe, *Les mouvements nègres en France pendant les entre-deux-guerres*. Paris: Harmattan, 1985.

Dunbar, Ernest, *The Black Expatriates*. New York: E. P. Dutton, 1968.

Echenberg, Myron, *Colonial Conscripts: Tirailleurs Sénégalais in French West Africa, 1857–1960*. Portsmouth, N.H.: Heinemann Educational Books, 1992.

Esedebe, P. Olisanwuche, *Pan-Africanism*. Washington, D.C.: Howard University Press, 1982.

Fabre, Michel, *From Harlem to Paris*. Urbana, Ill.: University of Illinois Press, 1991.

———, *La Rive noire*. Paris: Lieu Commun, 1985.

———, *The Unfinished Quest of Richard Wright*. Urbana and Chicago: University of Illinois Press, 1993.

Fabre, Michel, and John A. Williams, *Guide to African Americans in Paris*. Paris: CEAA, 1994.

Fanoudh-Siefer, Léon, *Mythe du nègre et de l'Afrique noire dans la littérature française*. Paris: C. Klincksieck, 1968.

Feather, Leonard, *The Encyclopedia of Jazz in the Sixties*. New York: Horizon, 1966.

Fitch, Noel, *Sylvia Beach and the Lost Generation*. New York: W. W. Norton, 1983.

Gilroy, Paul, *The Black Atlantic*. Cambridge, Mass.: Harvard University Press, 1993.

Goddard, Chris, *Jazz Away from Home*. New York and London: Paddington Press, 1979.

Goldman, Peter, *The Death and Life of Malcolm X*. Urbana, Ill., and Chicago: University of Illinois Press, 1979.

Hacker, Andrew, *Two Nations: Black and White, Separate, Hostile, Unequal*. New York: Ballantine Books, 1992.

Hammond, Bryan, and Patrick O'Connor, *Josephine Baker*. Boston: Little, Brown, 1988.

Haney, Lynn, *Naked at the Feast: A Biography of Josephine Baker*. New York: Dodd and Mead, 1981.

Hasse, John Edward, *Duke Ellington*. New York: Simon and Schuster, 1993.

Henri, Florette, *Bitter Victory: A History of Black Soldiers in World War II*. Garden City, N.Y.: Doubleday, 1970.

Hennessey, Mike, *Klook: The Story of Kenny Clarke*. London: Quartet Books, 1990.

Hodges, Leroy, *Portrait of an Expatriate: William Gardner Smith, Writer*. Westport, Conn.: Greenwood Press, 1985.

Hoffman, Léon-François, *Le Nègre romantique: Personnage littéraire et obsession collective*. Paris: Payot, 1973.

Hutchinson, Louise Daniel, *Anna J. Cooper: A Voice from the South*. Washington D.C.: Smithsonian Institution Press, 1981.

Kaspi, Andre, *Le Temps des Américains: Le concours américain à la France en 1917–1918*. Paris: Publications de la Sorbonne, 1976.

Kesteloot, Lilyan, *Black Writers in French*. Washington, D.C.: Howard University Press, 1991.

Kinnamon, Kenneth, and Michel Fabre, eds., *Conversations with Richard Wright*. Jackson, Miss.: University of Mississippi, 1993.

Martinkus-Zemp, Ada, *Le Blanc et le Noir*. Paris: A-G. Nizet, 1975.

Miller, Michael, *Shanghai on the Metro*. Berkeley, Calif.: University of California Press, 1994.

Moody, Bill, *The Jazz Exiles*. Reno, Nev.: University of Nevada Press, 1993.

Mosby, Dewey, *Henry Ossawa Tanner*. Philadelphia: Philadelphia Museum of Art, 1991.

Porter, Roy, *Uncensored France*. New York: Dial Press, 1942.

Rose, Phyllis, *Jazz Cleopatra*. New York: Doubleday Press, 1989.

Rout, Kathleen, *Eldridge Cleaver*. Boston: Twayne Publishers, 1991.

Schwartzman, Myron, *Romare Bearden*. New York: H. N. Abrams, 1990.

Smith, Jessie Carney, ed., *Notable Black American Women*. Detroit: Gale, 1972.

Stearns, Marshall, *The Story of Jazz*. New York: Oxford University Press, 1958.

Sweeney, W. Allison, *History of the American Negro in the Great World War*. Chicago: Cuneo-Henneberry, 1919.

Taylor, Arthur, *Notes and Tones*. New York: Da Capo Press, 1993.

Todd, Emmanuel, *Le destin des immigrés*. Paris: Seuil, 1994.

Vaillant, Janet, *Black, French, and African: A life of Léopold Sedar Senghor*. Cambridge, Mass.: Harvard University Press, 1990.

Weatherby, W. J., *James Baldwin*. New York: Donald I. Fine, 1989.

Wynn, Neil, *The Afro-American and the Second World War*. London: Elek, 1976.

Zwerin, Michael, *La Tristesse de Saint Louis: Jazz under the Nazis*. New York: Beech Tree Books, 1985.

ARTICLES AND ESSAYS

Achille, Louis. "L'Art et les Noirs/The Negroes and Art," *Revue du Monde Noir* (1931).

"American Negroes Like Paris, Finding Prejudice at Minimum," *New York Times* (November 29, 1966).

"Beth Prophit Is Hailed in Paris as Real Artist," *Afro-American* (August 3, 1929).

"Civil Rights March Planned by 50 Americans in Paris," *New York Times* (August 18, 1963).

Cohen, Roger. "Once Welcomed, Black Artists Return to an Indifferent France," *New York Times* (February 7, 1994).

"Colored Frenchmen and American Meteques," *Literary Digest* (September 1, 1923), 41–44.

Cook, Mercer. "The Race Problem in Paris and the French West Indies," *Journal of Negro Education* (vol. 8, no. 4, October 1939), 673–80.

Dissly, Meggan. "An American in Paris Fashion," *Christian Science Monitor* (August 25, 1988).

Drummond, Tammerlin. "Adieu, Utopia," *Los Angeles Times* (March 22, 1993).

Du Bois, W.E.B. "Returning Soldiers," *Crisis* (no. 17, May 1919), 13–14.

Dunbar, Rudolph, "Trumpet Player Briggs Freed after Four Years in Nazi Camp Near Paris," *Chicago Defender* (September 23, 1944).

———. "Writer Returns to Paris and Spot American Musicians Made," *Chicago Defender* (September 30, 1944).

"European Writer Finds That White Americans Reserve Prejudice for Own Colored Compatriots," *Journal and Guide* (October 8, 1932).

"France: Negroes in Paris," *Newsweek* (September 21, 1964).

Grose, Peter. "Baldwin Speaks at Paris Church," *New York Times* (August 19, 1963).

Johnson, Thomas. "Paris: Negroes' Way Station," *New York Times* (1969).

Logan, Rayford. "Confessions of an Unwilling Nordic," *The World Tomorrow* (July 1927), 297–300.

Marshall, Paule. "Chez Tournon: A Homage," *New York Times* (October 18, 1992).

Robeson, Eslanda Goode. "Black Paris," *Challenge* I (vol. 1, no. 4: 12–18); II (vol. 1, no. 5, 9–12).

Rogers, Joel Augustus. "The American Negro in Paris," *New York Amsterdam News* (September 14 and 21, 1927).

———. "Paris Draws the Line," *New York Amsterdam News* (July 24, 1929).

———. "The Paris Pepper-Pot," *Pittsburgh Courier* (July 27, 1929).

Smith, William Gardner. "European Backdrop." *Pittsburgh Courier* (July 26, August 9, and September 20, 1952).

———. "The Oldest Negro in Paris," *Ebony* (vol. 8, no. 2, October 1952), 65–66, 68–72.

———. "Why some American Negroes Prefer Life Abroad," *National Guardian* (March 7, 1960).

Watrous, Peter. "In Paris, Le Jazz Hot," *New York Times* (January 15, 1995).

Wiggins, Edgar. "Artists Live Queer in Paris Latin Quarter," *Afro-American* (May 13, 1933).

———. "Many Artists Plan to Return to America," *Chicago Defender* (September 23, 1933).

———. "Race Actors Shine in Paris," *Chicago Defender* (May 11, 1933).

Wilson, John. "Black Jazzmen Made 30's Paris Jump," *New York Times* (July 7, 1985).

Wright, Richard. "A Paris, Les G.I. Noirs Ont Appris A Connaître Et A Aimer La Liberté," *Samedi-Soir* (May 25, 1946).

———. "American Negroes in France," *Crisis* (June–July 1951), 381–83.

———. "There's Always Another Café," *Kiosk* (no. 10, 1953), 79–85.

INTERVIEWS

Richard Allen, Paris, June 1994.

Jennifer Bullock, Paris, June 1994.

Benjamin Davis, Paris, June 1994.

Dean Ferrier, Cravent, France, June 1994.

Randy Garrett, Paris, June 1994.

Liz Goodrum, Paris, June 1994.

Ted Joans, Paris, June 1994.

Tansee Mayer and Valerie Mathis, June 1994.

Hal Singer, Nanterre, France, June 1994.

Tannie Stovall, Jean Stovall, and Frederic Stovall, Paris, June 1994.

Bette Woody, telephone interview, Cambridge, Mass., March 1995.

INDEX

Abadie, Claude, 166
Abatino, Giuseppe (Pepito), 54, 91, 92
Abbey, Leon, 49, 124
Abernathy, Ralph, 245
abstract expressionism, 142, 145
Abtey, Jacques, 120, 127, 128
Académie de la Grande Chaumière, 64, 143, 146, 147; WWII veterans at, 141, 143
Académie Julian, 64, 141
Achille, Louis, Jr., 103, 106, 107, 108
Achille, Louis, Sr., 106
"Adieu, Utopia" (*Los Angeles Times*), 286–87
Africa: French images of, 16; French identification of American blacks with, 70–71; rediscovered by African Americans in 1930s, 99–112; and negritude movement, 104–8; Richard Wright and, 197–99; W. G. Smith and, 228, 258, 259–60; 1960s appeal to black Americans, 257–62; 1960s politics in, 259–60; tribalism in, 260
African American culture: artists (*see* art and artists); musicians (*see* jazz); writers (*see* writers); influence on French blacks, 105–6, 107
African American interracial sex relations, 74–78, 208–12
African American middle class: black-owned businesses in 1920s Paris, 47; growth of, 289–91; in 1990s Paris, 291–93, 297, 300, 313–19
African Americans: in WWI, 6–16 (*see also* World War I); in 1920s Paris, 25–81; in 1930s Paris, 82–118; rediscovery of African culture in 1930s, 99–112; in 1940s Paris, 118–44; service in WWII, 136–38 (*see also* World War II); new post-WWII Parisian community, 136–41, 214–15; in 1950s Paris, 144–81; in 1960s and 1970s Paris, 216–81;

1960s community, 243–44; in 1980s and 1990s Paris, 282–326; 1990s community, 320–26
"African-Americans and Europe" conference (Paris, 1992), 300–301
African American women: in business (*see* business); singers and performers (*see* *individual performers*); writers in 1920s Paris, 61–62; scholars, 66–67; in post-WWII Paris, 154–58; marrying Frenchmen, 155; in the 1960s, 236–37; Sisters, 323–24
African art, 64, 99; American blacks influenced by, 101–4; French intellectuals and, 110–11
African (black) colonials, French. *See also* colonialism; colonials: service in WWI, 19–20
African (black) ex-colonials, French. *See also* immigrant workers: and negritude movement, 104–12 (*see also* negritude movement); compared with Arabs, 298; in 1990s France, 298, 299
Afrodisia (Joans), 305
Aga Khan, 45, 88
Agence France-Presse, 214, 222, 228, 249
Alabamians (band), 77
Alamo, Frank, 307
"Alas, Poor Richard" (Baldwin), 224
Aldridge, Ira, xiv, 3, 54
Alex, Joe, 53
Algeria, 261, 269; fundamentalists in, 295–96
Algerian war, 131, 217, 244, 251–55, 287, 295–96, 298; W. G. Smith's novel on, 254–56
Allen, Richard, 318–19, 321
Allen, Samuel, 301
All Shot Up (Himes), 226
Amazon (Savage), 101
Amen Corner, The (Baldwin), 225

348